LINGUISTICS:
AN INTRODUCTION
TO LANGUAGE AND
COMMUNICATION

LINGUISTICS: AN INTRODUCTION TO LANGUAGE AND COMMUNICATION

Adrian Akmajian
Richard A. Demers
Robert M. Harnish
University of Arizona

Second Edition

The MIT Press
Cambridge, Massachusetts
London, England

Sixth printing, 1988

This book was set in VIP Times Roman by Village Typographers, Inc. and printed and bound in the United States of America by Halliday Lithograph.

Library of Congress Cataloging in Publication Data

Akmajian, Adrian.
  Linguistics, an introduction to language and communication.

  Bibliography: p.
  Includes index.
  1. Linguistics.   2. Animal communication.
I. Demers, Richard A.   II. Harnish, Robert M.   III. Title.
P121.A4384   1984   410   83-25634
ISBN 0-262-01078-X (hardcover)
ISBN 0-262-51029-4 (paperback)

To Adrian Akmajian
1944–1983

CONTENTS

Contents viii

Contents

Contents

ACKNOWLEDGMENTS

For the evolution of this second edition we would like to thank the many students we have taught and from whom we have learned; our colleagues in the Department of Linguistics at the University of Arizona, especially Ann Farmer, Rich Janda, Eloise Jelinek, and Adrienne Lehrer; our artists Paul Akmajian and Linda Carey; our colleagues at the University of Arizona, Bill Christie, Richard Diebold, and Chris Tanz; our colleagues Elizabeth Bowman, Peter Culicover, Sue Foster, Ellen Kaisse, and Moira Yip; and, finally, all our colleagues and friends who took the time to fill out questionnaires assessing the first edition. We also want to thank Barbara Hollenbach for the glossary and Tom Larson for the index. To Teresa Huard-Lentz go special thanks for her superb job in typing numerous drafts as well as the final manuscript.

NOTE TO
THE TEACHER

This second edition of our text evolved from our continuing collaboration in teaching introductory linguistics at the University of Arizona. Classroom experience, as well as valuable feedback from students and colleagues around the country, revealed ways in which the material of the first edition could be expanded, reorganized, contracted, or otherwise improved. Among the new features of this edition are (1) a single, condensed, shortened chapter on animal communication systems, now organized around a model we term the *Message Model;* (2) a significantly revised chapter on pragmatics, organized around general themes deriving from our examination of the inadequacies of the Message Model in accounting for the subtleties and complexities of human communication; (3) an entirely new chapter on psychology of language, presenting students with material on the production and comprehension of speech; and (4) new subsections providing students with information on child language acquisition (chapter 11), discourse and conversations (chapter 9), ATN sentence-parsers (chapter 5), auxiliary verbs and tag questions (chapter 5), and traditional part-of-speech classifications (chapter 3). In addition, most chapters have been revised and reorganized to a greater or lesser extent to incorporate improvements of various sorts, which will be clear to those familiar with the first edition.

Despite the changes we have made, certain aspects of the text remain unchanged. In particular, we must emphasize once again our concern with imparting basic conceptual foundations of linguistics and the methods of argumentation, justification, and hypothesis testing within the field. In no way is this edition intended to be a complete survey of the facts or putative results that have occupied linguists in recent years. On the contrary, we have chosen a small set of linguistic concepts that we understand to be among the most fundamental within the field at this time, and in presenting these concepts we have attempted to show how to argue for linguistic hypotheses. By dealing with a relatively small number of topics in detail, students can get a feeling for how work in different areas of linguistics is done. If an introductory course can impart this feeling for the field, it will have largely succeeded.

Although we have added a small number of linguistic examples from other languages (such as Japanese in chapters 3 and 5), we have drawn the examples in this edition, as in the first, almost exclusively from English. Once again we should note that we recognize the great importance of studying language universals and the increasingly significant role that comparative studies will play in linguistic research. In presenting conceptual foundations of linguistics to students who have never been exposed to the subject before, however, we feel it is crucial that they should be able to draw upon their linguistic intuitions when required to make subtle judgments about language, both in following the text and in doing the exercises. This is not merely for convenience, to set up as few obstacles as possible in an introductory course; rather, we feel that it is essential that students be able to evaluate critically our factual claims at each step, for this encourages a healthy skepticism and an active approach toward the subject matter. Given that the majority of our readers will be native speakers of English, our focus on English examples provides benefits that we feel far outweigh the lack of data from other languages. Obviously, the general principles we discuss must be applicable to all languages, and some teachers may wish to emphasize universals and cross-language data in their lectures.

Lesson Plans

We have organized this edition to give teachers maximum flexibility in designing a linguistics course for their own (and their students' own) special needs. The book has been designed specifically so that teachers can skip over entire sections or chapters not relevant for their own pedagogical purposes; thus, it can be used in a modular fashion. We will take up some specific examples.

For teachers working in the quarter system, this edition can be used easily for a one-quarter course. For a course oriented toward more traditional topics in linguistics, the following is a possible schedule (with variations depending on the teacher):

Chapter 3: Morphology	2 weeks
Chapter 4: Phonology	2 weeks
Chapter 5: Syntax	2 weeks
Chapter 7: Language Variation	2 weeks
Chapter 8: Language Change	2 weeks

The chapters cited do not depend crucially on the ones that have been skipped over (chapters 1, 2, 6, and 9–12); thus, we have ensured that a traditional core exists within this edition.

For a one-quarter course with an emphasis on psycholinguistics, cognitive science, or human communication, the following is a possible format:

Chapter 2: Animal Communication	1 lecture, or 1 week
Chapter 3: Morphology	1 week
Chapter 4: Phonology	1 week
Chapter 5: Syntax	1 week
Chapter 6: Semantics	1 week
Chapter 9: Pragmatics	2 weeks
Chapter 10: Psychology of Language	2 or 3 weeks
Chapter 12: Language and the Brain	1 week (if included)

The individual chapters are designed with numerous subsections (some of which are labeled "optional" or "technical"), in such a way that core material is often presented first, with additional material following. In this way, teachers who can only spend a week on a certain chapter are able to choose various subsections, so that students are exposed to the material most relevant for that particular course.

Teachers working within the semester system (or teaching courses that run two quarters in the quarter system) will find that this edition can be used quite comfortably within a 14- or 15-week term. For example, for a one-semester linguistics course oriented toward more traditional topics, the following is a possible schedule:

Chapter 3: Morphology	2 weeks
Chapter 4: Phonology	3 weeks
Chapter 5: Syntax	2 weeks
Chapter 6: Semantics	1 week
Chapter 7: Language Variation	2 weeks
Chapter 8: Language Change	2 weeks
Chapter 9: Pragmatics	1 week

This sequence accounts for 13 weeks, leaving either one or two weeks (depending on the system) for other topics, or to allow for expansion of the topics listed (such as 4 weeks on phonology).

Obviously, teachers with other interests will pick a different set of modules for a course. For example, given a course with a psycholinguistic, cognitive science, or human communication orientation, the following seems to be a reasonable schedule:

Chapter 2: Animal Communication	1 week
Chapter 3: Morphology	1 week
Chapter 4: Phonology	2 weeks
Chapter 5: Syntax	2 weeks
Chapter 6: Semantics	1 week
Chapter 9: Pragmatics	2 weeks
Chapter 10: Psychology of Language	2 or 3 weeks
Chapter 11: Language Acquisition	1 week
Chapter 12: Language and the Brain	1 week

Again, one or two weeks have been left open to allow for variations on the part of individual teachers.

In short, by varying the selection of chapters and subsections, teachers from diverse backgrounds and in diverse academic departments will be able to design an introduction to linguistics that is custom-made for their purposes.

Part One
_____
BACKGROUND

Chapter One

WHAT IS LINGUISTICS?

Many people, even highly educated people, will tell you that they have heard of linguistics but have only a vague idea of what it is about. Some people will tell you that a linguist is a person who speaks many languages and may work as a language teacher or as an interpreter at the United Nations. Still others will tell you that a linguist is someone who can help you decide whether it is better to say "It is I" or "It is me." Yet it is quite possible to be a professional linguist (and an excellent one at that) without having taught a single language class, without having interpreted at the UN, and without speaking any more than one language. As you will discover, the field of linguistics—the scientific study of language—goes far beyond the popular conceptions we have just cited. Although linguistics is still largely unknown to the educated public (it is a subject not taught in high school and has only recently been introduced into the undergraduate college curriculum), it is nevertheless a growing and exciting field, with an increasingly important impact on other fields as diverse as education, anthropology, sociology, language teaching, cognitive psychology, philosophy, computer science and artificial intelligence, and others. Indeed, the last three fields cited, along with linguistics, are the key components of the newly emerging field of cognitive science (the study of the structure and functioning of human cognitive processes).

What is linguistics, then? Fundamentally, the field is concerned with the nature of language and communication. It is apparent that people have been fascinated with language and communication for thousands of years, yet in many ways we are only beginning to understand the complex nature of this aspect of human life. If we ask, What is the nature of language? or How does communication work? we quickly realize that these questions have no simple answers and are much too broad to be answered in any direct way. Similarly, questions such as What is energy? or What is matter? cannot be answered in a direct fashion, and indeed the entire field of physics is an attempt to answer them. Linguistics is no different: the field as a whole represents an attempt to break down the broad questions about the nature of language and communication into smaller, more manageable questions that we can hope to answer, and in so doing establish reasonable results that we can build on in moving closer to answers to the larger questions. Unless we limit our sights in this way and restrict ourselves to particular frameworks for examining different aspects of language and communication, we cannot hope to make progress in answering the broad questions that have fascinated people for so long. As we will see, the field covers a surprisingly broad range of topics related to language and communication.

Part one of this text considers background concepts in linguistics. This includes an examination of animal communication systems (chapter 2), a topic not traditionally considered part of linguistics. Its inclusion reflects our interest in communication in general, as well as a growing interest, in many disciplines, in comparing animal systems with human language. As we will see, animal communication systems can be described in terms of a model of communication we call the *Message Model*. In part three it will become apparent that the Message Model is much too simple to account for the complexities of human communication. Hence, our examination of animal communication systems will provide an excellent contrast with human communication, a contrast that helps us understand better the nature of human language and language use.

Part two, The Structure of Human Language, examines four traditional subfields that deal with the structural components of human language: morphology (the study of words and word-building), phonology (the study of the sounds of language and their patterning), syntax (the study of the structure of sentences and phrases), and semantics (the study of meaning and reference). We will see that human language, at every level of organization, is structured in a complex and highly systematic way. Moreover, in very general terms, we will see that the analysis of human language at each structural level is stated in terms of (1) a set of *discrete units* of some sort, and (2) *rules for combining* those units. Each chapter in this section will discuss the relevant discrete units and rules for combination that have played an important role in linguistic investigation.

We then discuss a number of subfields and topics within linguistics that provide us with a view of human language in broader contexts. In chapter 7 we examine language variation (how speakers, and groups of speakers, of a language differ from each other in terms of the various forms of language they use). In chapter 8 we examine language change (how language changes over time and how languages can be historically related). Finally, although our particular examples in this section will be drawn almost exclusively from English, we assume that the general principles of analysis and the general methods for representing language structure are valid for all languages.

Having examined certain structural properties of human language in part two, we turn to functional properties in part three, Communication and Cognitive Science. Here we find that the simple Message Model is inadequate to account for human communication. In chapter 9 we discover some of the problems involved in describing human communication, and we propose certain communication strategies that people use when they talk to each other. The remaining chapters examine psychology of language (how language is cognitively processed and perceived) (chapter 10), biological aspects of language (chapter 11), and language and the brain (how language is stored and represented in the brain) (chapter 12).

To turn now from the particular to the general, what are some of the background assumptions that linguists make when they study language? Perhaps the most important fundamental assumption is that human language at all levels is rule-governed. Every language that we know of has systematic rules governing pronunciation, word formation, and grammatical construction. Further, the way in which meanings are associated with phrases of a language is characterized by regular rules. Finally, the *use* of language to communicate is governed by important generalizations that we can express in rules. The ultimate aim of each chapter of parts two and three, therefore, is to formulate linguistic rules to describe and explain the phenomena under consideration. (Indeed, chapter 7 shows that even so-called casual speech is governed by systematic regularities expressible in rules.)

At this point we must add an important qualification to what we have just said. That is, we are using the terms *rule* and *rule-governed* in the special way that linguists use them. This usage is very different from the layman's understanding of the terms. In school most of us were taught so-called rules of grammar, which we were told to follow in order to speak and write "correctly"—rules such as "Do not end a sentence with a preposition," or "Don't say *'ain't',*" or "Never split an infinitive." Rules of this sort are called *prescriptive rules;* that is to say, they all prescribe, or dictate to the speaker, the way the language supposedly should be written or spoken in order for the speaker to appear correct and educated. Prescriptive rules are really rules of style rather than rules of grammar.

In sharp contrast, when linguists speak of rules, they are not referring to prescriptive rules from school grammar books. Rather, linguists try to formulate *descriptive rules* when they analyze language, rules that describe the actual language of some group of speakers (and not some hypothetical language that speakers "should" use). Descriptive rules actually express generalizations and regularities about various aspects of a language. Thus, when we say that language is rule-governed, we are really saying that the study of human language has revealed numerous generalizations about and regularities in the structure and function of language.

Another important background assumption that linguists make is that the various human languages constitute a *unified phenomenon:* linguists assume that it is possible to study human language in general and that the study of particular languages will reveal features of language that are universal. What do we mean by universal features of language?

So far we have used the terms *language* and *human language* without referring to any specific language, such as English or Chinese. Students are sometimes puzzled by this general use of the term *language;* it would seem that this use is rarely found outside of linguistics-related courses. Foreign language courses, after all, deal with specific languages such as French or Russian. Further, specific human languages appear on the surface to be so different from each other that it is often difficult to understand how linguists can speak of language as though it were a single thing.

Although it is obvious that specific languages differ from each other on the surface, if we look closer we find that human languages are surprisingly similar. For instance, all languages that we know of are at a similar level of complexity and detail—there is no such thing as a primitive human language. All languages provide a means for asking questions, making requests, giving orders, making assertions, and so on. And there is nothing that can be expressed in one language that cannot be expressed in any other. Obviously, one language may have terms not found in another language, but it is always possible to invent new terms to express what we mean: anything we can imagine or think, we can express in any human language.

Turning to more abstract properties, even the formal structures of language are similar: all languages have sentences made up of smaller phrasal units, these units in turn being made up of words, which are themselves made up of sequences of sounds. All of these features of human language may seem obvious, and that perhaps is the problem: these features are so obvious to us that we may fail to see how surprising it is that languages share them. When linguists use the term *language* (or *human language*), they are revealing their belief that at an abstract level, beneath the surface variation, languages are remarkably similar in form and function and conform to certain universal principles.

In relation to what we have just said about universal principles, we should observe once again that virtually all the illustrative examples in this book are drawn from the English language. This should not mislead you into supposing that what we say is relevant only to English. We will be introducing fundamental concepts of linguistics, and we believe that these have to be applicable to all languages. We have chosen English examples so that you can continually check our factual claims and decide whether our claims are empirically well founded. We encourage you to use your knowledge of English as actively as possible in evaluating our discussions.

Finally, we offer a brief observation about the general nature of linguistics. To many linguists the ultimate aim of linguistics is not simply to understand how language itself is structured and how it functions. We hope that as we come to understand more about human language, we will correspondingly understand more about the processes of human thought. In this view the study of language is ultimately the study of the human mind. This goal is perhaps expressed best by Noam Chomsky in his book *Reflections on Language* (1975, 3–4):

Why study language? There are many possible answers, and by focusing on some I do not, of course, mean to disparage others or question their legitimacy. One may, for example, simply be fascinated by the elements of language in themselves and want to discover their order and arrangement, their origin in history or in the individual, or the ways in which they are used in thought, in science or in art, or in normal social interchange. One reason for studying language—and for me personally the most compelling reason—is that it is tempting to regard language, in the traditional phrase, as "a mirror of mind." I do not mean by this simply that the concepts expressed and distinctions devel-

oped in normal language use give us insight into the patterns of thought
and the world of "common sense" constructed by the human mind.
More intriguing, to me at least, is the possibility that by studying language we may discover abstract principles that govern its structure and
use, principles that are universal by biological necessity and not mere
historical accident, that derive from mental characteristics of the species. A human language is a system of remarkable complexity. To come
to know a human language would be an extraordinary intellectual
achievement for a creature not specifically designed to accomplish this
task. A normal child acquires this knowledge on relatively slight exposure and without specific training. He can then quite effortlessly make
use of an intricate structure of specific rules and guiding principles to
convey his thoughts and feelings to others, arousing in them novel ideas
and subtle perceptions and judgments. For the conscious mind, not
specially designed for the purpose, it remains a distant goal to reconstruct and comprehend what the child has done intuitively and with
minimal effort. Thus language is a mirror of mind in a deep and significant sense. It is a product of human intelligence, created anew in each
individual by operations that lie far beyond the reach of will or
consciousness.

Bibliography

Chomsky, N. (1975) *Reflections on Language*, Pantheon Books, New York.

Chapter Two

ANIMAL
COMMUNICATION

Within the next decade or two the human species will establish communication with another species: nonhuman, alien, possibly extraterritorial, more probably marine; but definitely highly intelligent. (Lilly 1961)

2.1 GENERAL BACKGROUND

The human desire to communicate with other species can be detected in stories, songs, and myths throughout history. In one sense, humans have communicated for centuries with animals of other species: we talk to domesticated animals and pets as if they understand human language, and indeed the animals seem to respond in various ways when we talk to them. However, the desire to communicate with other species seems to go much beyond this: contemporary studies of animal communication and intelligence often contain allusions of various sorts to discovering an animal's "world view," as it were, through an appropriate study of its communication system.

It is important to note that with respect to animal communication systems, we are all "nonspeakers": we are faced with the task of recognizing the significant units of the system, given the sounds, movements, and postures that we can observe. The problem of studying an animal communication system is compounded by the fact that we do not learn animal communication systems in the same way that we learn a second human language. Even as adults we are able to acquire a second language with skills approaching fluency. In contrast, we can only know natural animal communication systems externally, as outside observers. Put another way, we do not arrive at the "messages" of the animal communication system in the same way that we can learn to encode and decode the messages of another human language.

If this is the case, then what can the study of animal communication systems contribute to the study of human language? The answer to this question is twofold. First, human language is in part the product of evolution, and humans are not the only animals that have a system of communication. A study of other communication systems found in nature may lead to a better understanding of the basic properties of human language and may even provide evidence bearing on the evolution of human language. Second, we have already noted that in studying animal communication we are forced to view these systems externally. This external view of communication contrasts sharply with our natural tendency to view human language from a participant's internal perspective. This problem in the study of human language has been observed by the noted linguist Noam Chomsky in his book *Language and Mind* (1972, 24–25):

Phenomena can be so familiar that we really do not see them at all, a matter that has been much discussed by literary theorists and philosophers. For example, Viktor Shklovskij in the early 1920's developed the idea that the function of poetic art is that of "making strange" the object depicted. "People living at the seashore grow so accustomed to the murmur of the waves that they never hear it. By the same token, we scarcely ever hear the words which we utter. . . . We look at each other, but we do not see each other any more. Our perception of the world has withered away; what has remained is mere recognition." Thus, the goal of the artist is to transfer what is depicted to the "sphere of new perception"; as an example, Shklovskij cites a story by Tolstoy in which social customs and institutions are "made strange" by the device of presenting them from the viewpoint of a narrator who happens to be a horse.

By accustoming ourselves to viewing communication systems externally and abstractly, we can attempt to view human language in the same way.

What is an appropriate external and abstract framework for a comparative study that will facilitate comparison among the various animal communication systems and human language? Perhaps the most general theory of communication is the *Message Model* developed by Shannon and Weaver (1949), depicted in figure 2.1.

In surveying the structures of the communication systems of various animals, we will examine both the structure of the signal and the structure of the messages that can be transmitted. Of course, it is not possible to determine exactly what the signal "means" to the communicating animal; rather, we will specify the relationship between the

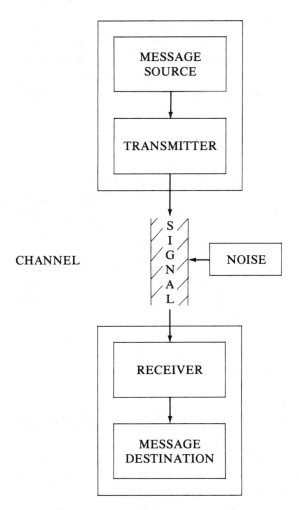

Figure 2.1
Diagram of the main components of the Message Model. The sender's message is sequentially encoded and transmitted as a signal. The signal reaches a receiver, where it is sequentially decoded into a message.

structure of the signal and the behavior of the animals, and then make the best prediction we can. In the sections that follow we will discuss the communication systems of honeybees, birds, dolphins and whales, and primates. First we will present the facts regarding these communication systems, and then in the final section we will show how these systems are instances of the Message Model.

2.2 BEE COMMUNICATION

One of the most remarkable communication systems found in the non-human world is that of the European honeybee. Imagine the evolutionary advantage for a honeybee if it is able to communicate the location of an especially rich food source to its hivemates when it returns to the hive. The honeybee is, in fact, able to do this.

Beekeepers had long suspected that bees communicated with each other before the properties of this communication system were scientifically established. For example, beekeepers noticed that if a single bee happens upon a particularly rich source of nectar or pollen, other bees from the hive will soon be found at the food source in significant numbers. It was also noted that large numbers of bees from a certain hive may all be gathering at the same type of food source, while large numbers of bees from an adjacent hive may be gathering food from an entirely different type of flower. This selective food gathering suggested a coordination of efforts on the part of the bees that could be the result of some method of communication.

These facts about bee behavior are now much better understood. We now know that honeybees do communicate, and the most important properties of their communication system have been identified through the research of Karl von Frisch and his colleagues (von Frisch 1967). They have established that when a foraging bee has discovered a rich food supply and returns to the hive, it is able to communicate a surprisingly complex message to its hivemates. The transmitted message is actually a recruitment device, indicating to the hivemates how far to fly, what direction to fly, and what type of food to seek. How is this accomplished?

The scout bee's message is communicated through patterns of movement, called *dancing,* on the vertical walls of the hive. There are two major types of dance depending on the location of the food source with respect to the hive: the round dance and the tail-wagging dance. If the source is within 10 meters of the hive, the bee performs only the round dance. For distances greater than 100 meters the bee performs only the tail-wagging dance. For intermediate distances (between 10 and 100 meters), bees may perform either of the two dances, although with distances approaching 100 meters honeybees tend to perform the tail-wagging dance more frequently (but see the discussion of dialects in the bee communication system).

The Round Dance

Structure
In performing the round dance, the bee traces a circular path in one direction and then turns around and retraces the same path in the opposite direction, a pattern that is repeated several times within a small area (see figure 2.2). The dancing bee will frequently stop and pass out samples of food to hivemates who have been alerted by the dancing activity.

Function
The primary function of the round dance is to recruit hivemates to gather nectar and pollen at a newly discovered food source. The round dance has the following major functional features:

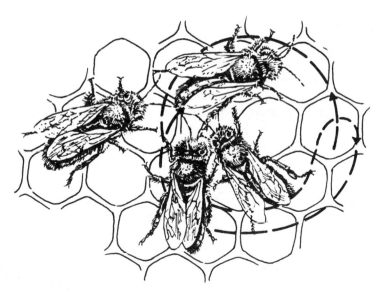

Figure 2.2
Pattern of the round dance. (Adapted from von Frisch 1967.)

1. It signals that the food source is within 10 meters of the hive.
2. The intensity of the dance (speed and duration) signals the richness of the food source.
3. The scent on the dancing bee signals to the new recruits the type of food source to seek.

Experimental Evidence

In order to test the honeybees' ability to alert their hivemates to a good food source, von Frisch and his colleagues (1967) conducted a wide variety of experiments. In one experiment, bees were first trained to collect food at a feeding station near the hive. They were fed a relatively weak sugar solution, and during the feeding they were marked with small dots of paint so that they could be identified. When the supply was interrupted, most of the bees of the original group stopped coming, although a few scout bees would occasionally recheck the feeding station. When an extra-rich supply of a scented sugar solution was later introduced at the feeding station, the scout bees flew back to the hive and performed a vigorous round dance. Out of 174 bees of the original collecting group that came in contact with the dancing scout bee, no fewer than 155 returned to the feeding station within five minutes.

Dancing bees are also able to recruit new bees to gather at a recently discovered food source. The newly recruited bees do not waste time searching for the wrong type of flower, since they have noted the specific fragrance on the dancing scout bee. Once the recruited bees have been alerted by the round dance, they fly randomly around the hive seeking the scent they had detected on the dancing bee. To aid recruited bees in finding their goal, a scout will often secrete a special scent over an especially rich food source.

Interestingly, a scout bee will not perform the round dance in an empty hive (nor in one that has been emptied for experimental purposes), which indicates that the dance is not merely an automatic response conditioned by the return to the hive with a rich supply of food. Other bees must be present to trigger the dance, thus underscoring its communicative nature.

The Tail-Wagging Dance

By far the most impressive aspect of the honeybees' communication system is the ability to indicate the location of food sources beyond 100 meters. As with the round dance, a returning scout bee performs a dance indicating that it has found a profitable gathering site. When the distance from the hive is great, however, it would not be efficient for the recruited bees to begin searching randomly for the source, as they do in response to the round dance. For example, for a source one kilometer away, the recruited bees would have to search an area of 3 million square meters. The European honeybee has in fact evolved a dance that not only indicates the direction the recruited bees must travel but also enables them to fly the proper distance. Both aspects of the dance have a remarkable degree of accuracy.

Structure
The tail-wagging dance consists of two roughly semicircular paths of movement with a straight-line portion in between, during which the bee waggles, as illustrated in figure 2.3.

Figure 2.3
Pattern of the tail-wagging dance. (Adapted from von Frisch 1967.)

Function
The tail-wagging dance serves the following functions:

1. The orientation of the straight-line portion of the dance communicates the direction that the bees must fly with respect to the position of the sun.
2. The length of time spent during the tail-wagging portion of the dance communicates the distance that must be flown.
3. Finally, the general level of excitation during the dance communicates the richness of the source.

The first two functions are discussed in more detail below.

Function: Communicating Direction of Source via the Structure of the Dance
Since the working surfaces inside the hive are vertical, the dancing bee is not able to point directly toward the location of the food source. Given this, how can it indicate the proper direction? For the purpose of indicating the direction of the food source, the bee uses the direction of the force of gravity. For example, there are three typical situations that the bee faces, as shown in figure 2.4. First, if the recruited bees are to fly along the ground in the direction of the sun, the straight-line portion of the tail-wagging dance points directly upward (dance A, figure 2.4). Second, if the recruited bees are to fly along the ground away from the sun, the dancing bee will orient the straight-line portion of the dance directly downward (dance C). Third, if the recruited bees are to fly, say, 80° to the left of the sun, the dance will be oriented 80° to the left of vertical (dance B). In other words, the gravity-oriented dance of the scout bee functions systematically as a compass or a map to direct the solar-oriented flight of the recruited bees.

Function: Communicating Distance of Source via the Structure of the Dance
There is increasing evidence that the length of time the dancing bee spends in the straight-line portion of the tail-wagging dance is the critical feature representing the distance to the food source. During this portion of the dance the bee also makes a special buzzing sound, and it has been proposed that it is the length of the buzzing that actually communicates the distance. The length of time that the bee spends in the straight-line portion of the tail-wagging dance is also related to the number of complete circuits the bee makes per unit of time. The fewer

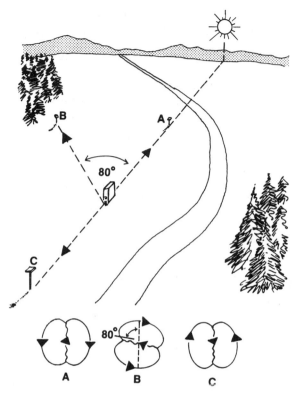

Figure 2.4
Relation of solar-oriented flight to force of gravity. Box at center of landscape
is the hive; three test feeding stations, A, B, and C, surround it. At bottom:
dances corresponding to the paths to the three feeding stations. (Adapted from
von Frisch 1967.)

circuits per unit time (or equivalently the longer the bee spends in the
tail-wagging portion of the dance), the farther the source is from the
hive. For example, if the bee makes nine or ten circuits within a 15-
second period, the distance to the food source is 100 meters; six circuits
per 15 seconds indicate a distance of 500 meters; and four circuits per
15 seconds indicate a distance of 1500 meters (almost a mile). Experiments have shown that bees can accurately communicate distances up
to 11 kilometers—almost 7 miles.

Experimental Evidence: Accuracy of Communicated Direction

The accuracy of the bees' ability to communicate direction is best illus-trated by another experiment performed by von Frisch. Several bees were first trained to feed on a meager food source at a station located 250 meters from the hive. The source was kept meager so that the bees would not become excited enough to start recruiting their hivemates. After a few bees had been induced to feed regularly at the station, a rich sugar solution scented with a fragrant oil was fed to them. The feeding station was then removed as soon as a few scout bees left it to return to the hive. At 200 meters from the hive, seven cards scented with the same oil used in the feeding solution were placed on an arc. The middle card was in a straight line from the hive to the feeding station and the other cards were 15° apart along the arc, as shown in figure 2.5a.

The recruited bees, flying from the hive looking for the food source, alighted upon the cards. The number of bees landing on the card in line with the original feeding station was substantially greater than the num-ber alighting on cards farther out along the arc, illustrating the accuracy of the message communicated by the dancing bees (see figure 2.5b).

One of the more remarkable aspects of the bee communication sys-tem is that the successful forager who returns to dance is able to indi-cate the direction to the source without having flown exactly that same direction itself. Once a scout bee has located a profitable food source, it

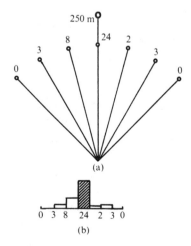

Figure 2.5
Number of bees alighting on scent cards placed 200 meters from hive. (Adapted from von Frisch 1967.)

returns directly to the hive, where it must communicate the reverse of its own return trip.

Experimental Evidence: Accuracy of Communicated Distance
The accuracy of the dancing bees' communication of distance is revealed by the results of a typical experiment in which a small number of bees were induced to fly out to a feeding station located 2000 meters from the hive, where they were fed a meager sugar solution. On the following morning the same meager feeding was continued, but for a period of two and a half hours an extremely rich sugar solution scented with a fragrant oil was substituted for the meager feeding. The feeding station was then removed, and scent cards were placed at intervals in a straight line from the hive out to and beyond the feeding station. Most of the recruited bees landed on the cards that were closest to the original feeding station (see figure 2.6). What is remarkable is that bees flew over and ignored scent cards closer to the hive than those near the feeding station—even at 1200 meters only one bee alighted on a closer card. Had the bees been seeking scent alone, more of them would have landed on the cards closest to the hive.

The clustering of the bees at the cards closest to the original feeding station offers an excellent indication of the quality of information that the bee has when flying to a target food source. There is even evidence that the recruited bee anticipates the distance before flying to a food source, inasmuch as it takes on fuel (honey) in proportion to the distance it must fly to the source (see table 2.1).

Dialects in the Communication System

Not all honeybees of the same or related species communicate in the same way; the bee system, like human language, has dialectal variation. The dancing patterns discussed in the previous sections are those

Table 2.1
Distance bee must travel related to amount of honey taken in before the trip. (Based on data from von Frisch 1967.)

Distance	Weight of Honey Taken In
5 meters	.782 mg.
500	1.6
1000	2.2
1500	4.13

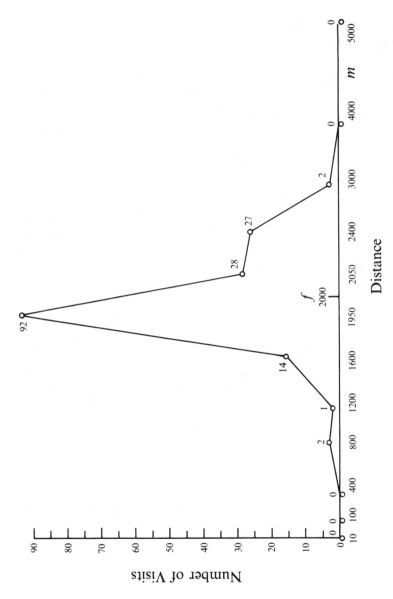

Figure 2.6
Number of bees visiting scent cards when feeding was at 2000 meters. (Adapted from von Frisch 1967.)

Food source

Figure 2.7
Sickle dance of Italian honeybee. (Adapted from von Frisch 1967.)

of the black Austrian honeybee. In contrast, the Italian honeybee, a member of the same species as the black Austrian honeybee, has a slightly different mode of dancing. For distances up to 10 meters the Italian bee, like the black Austrian honeybee, does the round dance. But for distances between 10 and 100 meters the Italian honeybee performs a dance called the sickle dance, which is not used by the black Austrian honeybee. The sickle dance is a flattened figure-eight pattern bent into a semicircle; the center of the semicircle points toward the food source (see figure 2.7).

For distances beyond 100 meters the Italian honeybee does the same type of tail-wagging dance as the black Austrian honeybee. The only difference is that the tempo (pace) of the Italian honeybee dance is somewhat slower than that of the Austrian honeybee dance. When these two types of honeybee are placed together in the same hive and the black Austrian honeybee is aroused by the dance of the Italian bee, it will search for food at a point beyond the location actually indicated in the framework of the Italian bee.

Acquisition of the Communication System

The bees' ability to dance and navigate is innate, but experience can play a role in increasing the accuracy of these activities. Von Frisch reports: "During their first outward flights, young bees have to acquire individual experience with the sun's course in order that their compass orientation shall function properly. But in this process, becoming acquainted with the sun's course over a few hours suffices for them to find the proper direction later, at another time of day" (1967, 525).

Outside of increasing the precision of its activities through experience, there is no evidence that the bee has to learn any of its behavior.

Individual bees raised in isolation from the hive function normally when they are introduced to the hive for the first time. Thus, it appears that the general communication system is innate but that the finer details of the system can be modified by learning. The same characteristic seems to hold for some species of birds and primates.

Additional support for the innateness of the bee communication system has come from studies of the dances of hybrid offspring of black Austrian and Italian honeybee parents. "Offspring that bear the Italian bee's yellow body markings often do the Sickle Dance. In one experiment sixteen hybrids strongly resembling their Italian parent used the Sickle Dance to represent intermediate distances 65 out of 66 times, whereas fifteen hybrids that resembled their Austrian parent used the Round Dance 47 out of 49 times" (von Frisch 1962, 80). In other words, the offspring inherit the dance patterns of the parents they resemble physically, just as they inherit other genetic traits.

In sum, the honeybee has a remarkably complex communication system, especially for an organism with a brain the size of a grass seed. Indeed, the system shows a degree of internal complexity that is unrivaled in the more advanced species we will take up next.

2.3 BIRD COMMUNICATION

From the human standpoint, bird songs can be a source of aesthetic enjoyment. However, it is not easy to discover the structure and function of such vocalizations, which range from a single note to intricate melodies. An important task in ornithology is to determine what communicative functions these vocalizations might serve. Complicating the matter is the fact that birds also use many visual devices to communicate. The mating dance of grebes, the bobbing dance before mating of the mockingbird, the brilliant display of the peacock, and even the bright colors of the males of most bird species are all prime examples of visual displays related to communication. Although these visual features belong in a complete account of bird communication, they have not been studied extensively. In contrast, bird vocalizations have long been studied in great detail, and with the advent of the sound spectrograph (a device that displays sounds visually), more careful qualitative and quantitative studies have been undertaken. In this section we will limit ourselves to the vocal aspects of bird communication.

Ornithologists distinguish two major classes of vocalizations: calls and songs. Although these two categories overlap somewhat in structure and function, the distinction is useful for purposes of discussion.

Bird Calls

Structurally, calls are sound patterns consisting of single notes or short note sequences associated with the following functional events and activities: flight, specialized alarm (for example, mobbing call, aerial predator call), pleasure, distress, territorial defense, feeding, nesting, flocking, aggression, and general alarm (Thorpe 1961). We will discuss here the first two types of calls.

Flight Calls

Tree sparrows live in colonies that may consist of as many as a hundred birds, and they have at their disposal three different calls relating to flight. One call is used just before takeoff, another during flight, and the third while looking for food and just before landing at nesting sites. The function of these calls seems to be to coordinate the activities of the numerous members of the colony. For instance, the in-flight call seems to be used to keep the flock together in flight, and the landing call seems to be used to announce an imminent landing.

Specialized Alarm: Mobbing Call

The mobbing call is a sharp note, which often sounds like the word "chink." When a predator is discovered nearby, such as an owl in a tree, the birds fly up to it and announce its presence with their mobbing calls. These calls attract other birds, who in turn make the same call. One effect of this activity is that the predator may be driven off. The primary effect, however, is that the calling greatly reduces the chance of a predator's capturing a bird with the element of surprise. It is easy for a small bird to evade a predator if the bird can keep the predator in sight. The function of the mobbing call, then, is to alert the birds in the area to the presence and location of a potential predator.

The mobbing call shows an interesting structure-function adaptation. Because the call has an abrupt onset and offset, it is easy for birds to establish the direction from which the sound comes. The sound arrives at slightly different times at the left and right ears of each bird, allowing the direction of the sound to be localized. Thus, because of the struc-

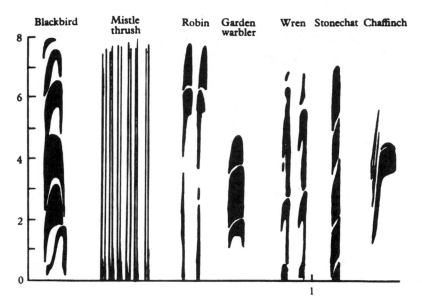

Figure 2.8
Mobbing calls of different bird species. Frequency (vertical axis) is in kilo-cycles per second. (From Thorpe 1961.)

ture of the sound, a bird giving the call attracts attention to itself and so helps other birds locate the predator.

The structure of this alarm call is shared by many birds, and an alarm sounded by one bird will cause a mobbing reaction among different species. The similarities in the structure of this call can be seen in figure 2.8, a collection of spectrograms of mobbing calls. Spectrograms are made by a device called a spectrograph, which analyzes acoustic signals (sounds) and displays them visually. Frequency is shown on the vertical axis and time is shown on the horizontal axis. The degree of darkness of the figure on the spectrogram correlates with the intensity of the sound. The call of the blackbird, for example, is shown with six concentrations of sound energy (called resonances), all of which rise and fall abruptly. The first (lower) resonance begins at 300 cycles per second (or 300 Hertz), and rises to almost 2000 Hertz before it falls again. As the figure shows, although the acoustic patterns of the mobbing calls of the various birds are different, they nevertheless share an important similarity, namely, the abruptness with which they begin and end. (Contrast the sharp beginnings and ends of the calls in figure 2.8 with the tapered beginnings and ends of the calls in figure 2.9.) Thus, the structure (abrupt onset and offset) is adapted to the function of the call (to alert other birds in the area to the presence and location of a potential predator).

Specialized Alarm: Aerial Predator Call

If a predatory bird is spotted flying overhead, many ground birds will emit a call whose structure is decidedly different from that of the mobbing call. Instead of beginning abruptly, the aerial predator call begins gradually and is at a much higher frequency. It is referred to as the "seet" call. When birds near the ground hear it, they may either become motionless or move rapidly for cover. These reactions are clear evidence that the function of the call is to minimize the birds' chances of being caught by surprise from above.

Again, the aerial predator call involves an interesting type of structure-function adaptation. In contrast to the mobbing call, the aerial predator call has an imperceptible onset and offset combined with a high-frequency "seet"; thus, locating the source of this call is very difficult. Using this call, a bird can announce the presence of an overhead predator while minimizing its own danger of being located and captured. The "seet" call too is shared by birds of many different species; when it is given by one bird, members of other species will take evasive action. Figure 2.9 shows a striking similarity in the structure of the "seet" calls of different species, given when a hawk flies overhead. Each of the spectrograms in figure 2.9 begins with a slow taper on the left, remains fairly uniform, and then tapers off to a point on the right.

In sum, these representative bird calls demonstrate that this aspect of the bird communication system consists mainly of a small collection of discrete sounds, each with a fixed range of functions. This system is surprisingly similar to those of totally unrelated species to be examined later, namely, the primates and the whales and dolphins.

Bird Songs

It is instructive to compare these typical bird calls with some bird songs, which are more complex than the calls and are used chiefly by male birds to establish territories and attract mates during the breeding season.

In experiments carried out by Falls (1969), recordings of several white-throated sparrow songs were played in areas where particular male white-throated sparrows had established their territory. Songs were played both of neighboring birds and of strangers who had never before been heard in the established male's territory. When confronted with a song of another male in his territory, the established male flew up to the source (in this case a loudspeaker) and performed his song. When the songs of strangers were played, the established male re-

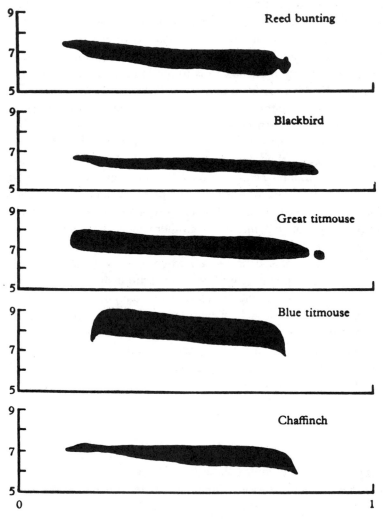

Figure 2.9
Aerial predator calls of five species, given when a hawk flies overhead. Frequency (vertical axis) is in kilocycles per second. (From Thorpe 1961.)

sponded much more aggressively and sang more frequently than he did when the songs of neighbors were played. Moreover, when the song of a neighbor was played from a direction that did not correspond to the location of the neighbor's territory, the established male responded to the song as if it were the song of a stranger. Thus, the white-throated sparrow is able to recognize the individual songs of its neighbors.

One function of the song is to allow males to delimit their territory and to minimize overlap with other males. Singing, then, is a highly efficient device for maintaining territory, since less energy is expended than would be the case if the bird had to patrol and actually battle to defend his territory. Once the male bird has established his territory, the song then functions to attract females, which is shown by the fact that unpaired chaffinch males sing more than those who have found a mate (Thorpe 1961). Since the song serves two major functions, it is not surprising that some species have two distinct songs, one for each function. The Pekin robin, for example, has one song for establishing and holding territory and another that is used to keep in contact with its mate.

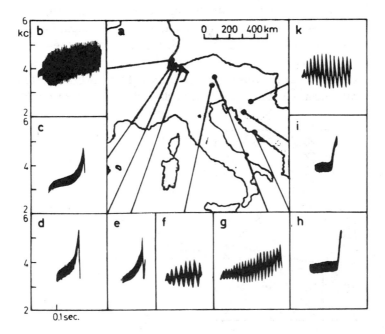

Figure 2.10
Spectrograms of rain calls of the chaffinch. (From Thielcke 1976.)

Dialects in Calls and Songs

One of the best-known examples of dialect variation in bird calls is found in the chaffinch rain call (so named because many believe that the bird uses this call before it rains), which will vary depending on the geographic location of the birds. Figure 2.10 displays the wide variety of acoustic signals corresponding to the rain call. The functions of these different rain calls have not been established.

Dialects are much more common in bird songs than in bird calls. Two questions immediately present themselves: Are the different dialects learned or part of the birds' genetic inheritance? And what functions do dialects serve? In the case of the chaffinch, the answer to the first question is known, but the answer to the second has not been established.

It has been shown (Thorpe 1961) that the young male chaffinch learns the dialect of the area in which he sings during its first breeding season. The basic structure of the song is learned during the first four months after hatching, but the dialects appear to be the result of more careful learning during the following spring when the one-year-old bird is acquiring his final song. Banding experiments (in which birds are identified by leg bands) have shown that birds will return to the general area where they were raised. Suppose we have a number of adjacent dialect areas, like those shown in figure 2.11. If a brood is raised at the intersection of dialect areas a, b, and c, it is equally probable that the offspring will settle in any of the three adjacent areas. Thus, brothers from the same original nest will acquire different dialects, each learning the

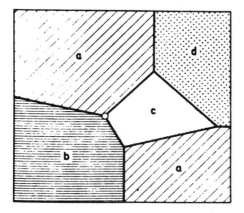

Figure 2.11
Mosaiclike spread of dialects. (From Thielcke 1976.)

dialect of the area where he ends up breeding: a, b, or c. This is excellent evidence that the dialects of the chaffinch are learned, and not innate.

Acquisition of Calls and Songs

Bird calls are largely innate; nevertheless, there are species in which the learning of calls has survival value. In one of these species the function of a certain call is to allow prompt reuniting of parent and offspring whenever they become separated. Common murre families brood on rock ledges in very close proximity to each other. Disturbances cause the parents to abandon their ledges and fly into the air, while the chicks scurry for cover under the nearby rocks. When the danger is past, the parents return, each giving a distinctive call. Parents and chicks are thus immediately reunited, and the chicks' exposure to cold and hunger is minimized, increasing their chances for survival.

How do the common murre chicks learn to recognize the distinctive calls of their parents? There is good evidence that they learn this in the two and a half to four and a half days before hatching (Thielcke 1976). They respond to the call of their own parents immediately after hatching, and calls from neighboring murres do not attract them.

During the first part of the brooding, the two parents alternate incubating the eggs in sixteen- to twenty-four-hour shifts; they are usually quiet during this period. Shortly before the eggs begin to hatch, the chicks inside begin to make a peeping sound, which activates a new set of behavior in the parents. They begin to bring food to the nest, and they also begin to emit their distinctive training call, which will eventually be used to summon the chicks. The actual hatching takes three days and fourteen hours, during which the chick saws its way out of the egg with its egg tooth. It is during this cutting period that it hears and learns the training call of its parents.

In controlled experiments a particular training call was played by means of a tape recorder to hatching chicks. Immediately after hatching, the chicks would run only to the loudspeaker that played the training call they had been exposed to when hatching, ignoring other loudspeakers playing calls they had not heard before.

Songs may be either innate, or entirely or partially learned. The European cuckoo's song is completely innate. Birds reared in isolation, deafened, or exposed to all songs but their own still sing the typical song of their species. In contrast, the song of the male bullfinch is al-

Table 2.2
Stages in the development of the song of the chaffinch. (Based on data from Thorpe 1961.)

	Spring, First Year		Summer
Developmental stages of typical song	(hatching) First subsong 2–3 seconds		Chirps and rattles
Point at which experiments were performed	↑ A	↑ B	

most completely learned. Investigators reared a young bullfinch in a cage with a canary (Nicolai 1959). In the spring during the breeding season, the bullfinch sang the song of the canary. Moreover, when the offspring of this particular bullfinch matured, they sang the canary song they learned from their father. One of these offspring raised yet another brood in a different cage and passed the canary song on to one of its offspring, who became a third generation canary singer. An interesting feature of the acquisition of the canary song is that the second generation offspring were also raised with normal bullfinches and heard the normal bullfinch song. In spite of this, they acquired the canary song of their father.

One of the most interesting features of bird song acquisition has been revealed by the work of Thorpe (1961) on the chaffinch song, which clearly exhibits a complex interplay of innate and learned characteristics. The song of a hand-reared, totally isolated chaffinch is a song of normal length (two and one-half seconds) but without any typical chaffinch structure. This rudimentary song prototype is apparently the biologically innate chaffinch song. In contrast, under normal conditions a chaffinch at around four months of age learns the structure of the chaffinch song (three phrases and flourish), although it does not produce this sequence until the following spring. At that time the young chaffinch produces this imprinted pattern and refines the song by countersinging with other chaffinches in its community. The usual development of the chaffinch song thus takes place in several critical stages.

Table 2.2 shows the normal developmental stages, matched with the seasons of the year. It also indicates points (A–F) at which experiments were performed. We will discuss the experiments and their significance in succession. At point A, hand-reared birds that are isolated

Fall	Winter	Early Spring	Spring, Second Year
Sustained series of chirped notes of varying pitch	Relatively quiet	Subsong	Full song development
↑		↑ ↑	↑
C		D E	F

from other chaffinches do not sing the normal chaffinch song; instead they develop a song that is the proper length but is not divided into phrases. If a chaffinch is deafened at three months (point B), the following spring its song will be similar to the food-begging call it performed as a three-month-old chick. Birds captured in September (point C) and kept in isolation during the following spring develop a song with the typical three initial phrases and flourish, but otherwise the song is not like that of normal chaffinches. September-captured birds that are allowed to countersing with each other develop more complex songs than isolated birds. During the breeding season (point D) females injected with the male hormone testosterone perform the song of the male. This experiment shows that though females do not normally perform the song, they nevertheless learn it, which they need to do in order to be attracted to males. During the early spring of the second year (point E), the young chaffinches develop an ever closer approximation to the final song of their species. Countersinging apparently accelerates, and is crucial to, final song development. Isolating a chaffinch at any of the various stages between D and F will result in an imperfect approximation to the final song. At thirteen months (point F), the ability to acquire the song ends. A chaffinch kept in isolation from others of its species up to this point will never acquire the chaffinch song, regardless of the learning conditions.

Having examined various properties of bird calls and songs in this section, we will end on a speculative note. In spite of the vast differences between the communication systems of birds and humans, there are nevertheless some interesting similarities. For instance, we have seen that many birds develop dialects in their songs (and the chaffinch has dialectal variation in one of its calls). Dialect variation is also a characteristic of human language (see chapter 7). Furthermore, the human language faculty is dominated by one hemisphere of the brain (see chapter 12). Surprisingly, there is evidence that hemispheric dominance in the brain plays a role in the control of bird song (Nottebohm 1970, 952). For instance, the chaffinch song is controlled by the left hypoglossus nerve; cutting that nerve causes the song to be destroyed or impaired. In contrast, if the right hypoglossus is cut, either the song is not altered or only a few of the simpler elements of the song are missing. Interestingly, if either of the nerves (but not both) is cut when the bird is young enough (before maturation), the song develops normally, under control of the other hemisphere. As we will see in chapter 12, in humans, as well, one hemisphere of the brain can control the language ability if the other hemisphere is impaired.

Finally, we have noted the complex interplay between innate and learned aspects in the chaffinch song: the general characteristics appear to be fixed biologically, whereas the details of the system appear to be learned. One of the more exciting proposals for human language acquisition, advanced by Noam Chomsky (1965), is that the general structure of human language is fixed biologically and the human language learner acquires those aspects of a language that differentiate it from other languages (see chapter 11). Interesting though these similarities are, however, do not be misled into thinking that bird communication and human language are even remotely analogous systems. As we will see in chapters 3–9, human language structure and language use are vastly more complex than any known animal communication system.

2.4 DOLPHIN AND WHALE COMMUNICATION

The behavior of dolphins and whales has attracted a great deal of attention, both in the popular media and in scientific research, and significant attempts have been made to discover the nature of their communication system(s). To begin with, it is striking to note the prevalence of the belief that these animals are highly intelligent. In the popular media, for example, dolphins are often portrayed as animals on a par with humans, with insight and subtle reasoning abilities that would be astonishing enough in most humans. Even the scientific literature is replete with anecdotal accounts of dolphin intelligence. A striking example is reported by Lilly (in McIntyre 1974, 69). During experiments, dolphins were fed fish as a reward for successful behavior. When the dolphins became satiated, they would continue taking fish, but would pile them on the bottom of the experiment tank, instead of eating them. When the dolphins wanted the experiments to stop, they would take a fish from the pile and give it back to the experimenters.

It would be natural to assume that the degree of intelligence of an animal species would correlate with a corresponding complexity in its communication system. For example, on the assumption that dolphins are more intelligent than birds, we might expect their communication system to be correspondingly more sophisticated and complex. Surprisingly, however, we find a remarkable similarity between the communication systems of dolphins and birds (and, as we shall see, a similarity between these and the primate system). As it turns out, the greater intelligence of the dolphin does not seem to be reflected in its communication system, which, as far as we can determine, is surprisingly rudimentary for an animal so widely believed to possess a "special" capacity of mind.

Dolphin Communication

The most studied of all cetaceans (the scientific name for the family that includes dolphins, whales, and porpoises) is the bottle-nosed dolphin (*Tursiops truncatus*); over half of all published material on cetacean communication concerns this species alone. We summarize below the results of some of the relevant research.

Structure

Dolphin vocalizations may be classified into two major types: pure tones and pulsed sounds (Caldwell and Caldwell 1977). The pure tones are further divided into whistles and squeals. The pulsed sounds are also divided into two types: trains of regular clicks and another class consisting of barks, yelps, moans, etc. These vocalization types are displayed in table 2.3.

There is still controversy regarding the production of these vocalizations. The leading hypothesis (Caldwell and Caldwell 1977) is that both types of sounds are produced in a group of air sacs in the dolphin's head just beneath the blowhole.

Function

It is generally thought that the trains of clicks are used primarily for echolocation. The dolphin generates the trains of clicks, which bounce off objects in its environment; it then interprets the reflected sounds, as if using a "sonar" system. The other pulsed sounds (barks, yelps, moans) are thought to express internal emotional states, such as distress.

As for dolphin whistles, it is still generally thought that dolphins are capable of producing a number of distinct whistles that carry different messages. Caldwell and Caldwell (1977) have proposed, however, that individual dolphins modulate their own whistles to convey different messages. Each dolphin possesses its own distinctive whistle (its signature whistle), and one-half second of any part of the whistle contains enough information for other dolphins to identify the companion who sent it. Various experiments have been carried out to determine the message(s) inherent in the whistle signals. For example, in one experiment (Dreher 1966) six different whistles were played by means of underwater loudspeakers to captive dolphins in a tank. The calls were those of other dolphins recorded in the wild. Each of the calls (played several minutes apart) had some immediate effect on the dolphins' behavior. One call (the fourth one played), known as a "double-humped" whistle, had the following effect on the captive dolphins:

At any rate, the effect was immediate and electrifying upon the animals. After a single-humped response, there was a furious burst of echolocation, a downward distress whistle, and much thrashing about in the water. As if to imitate, or to tease out a repetition of the sound from the loudspeaker, the dolphins immediately produced two five-humped calls, a six-humped call, and a four-humped variation, and then wild echolocation, squawks, and upward calls. . . . One dolphin was seen to go to the bottom of the tank, rub its head on the floor, and peer into the open drain. In addition to some chasing and leaping at various times there was further evidence that some of the animals were curious about the drain. The call density had soared from 3.5 to almost 5 per animal per minute. (Dreher 1966, 538)

Table 2.3
Types of vocalizations found in bottle-nosed dolphin. All types are hypothesized to play some role in the dolphin communication system. For example, the train of clicks, used mainly for echolocation, is thought to be used by dolphins to scan another dolphin's body to "read" its internal emotional state.

Tones	Pulsed Sounds
Whistles	Barks, yelps, moans, etc.
Squeals	Trains of clicks

The complexity of the dolphins' reactions, both physically and vocally, indicates the difficulty in determining the content of a message by studying the effect on the animals who hear it.

Structure-Function Adaptation

The literature on dolphin communication contains references to a distress call that dolphins make (Prince 1975). The structure of this call is a repeated double whistle. The first part of the whistle increases in loudness; the second part of the signal falls off in loudness. When other dolphins hear this signal, they immediately swim to the troubled animal, and if the animal is sick or injured, they raise it to the surface so that it can breathe. The distress call is similar in structure to the "seet" call of birds, in that it has a gradual onset and offset; thus, it is difficult for predators (such as sharks) to locate where the distress call is coming from. Because of the echolocation ability of dolphins (which sharks lack), the distressed dolphin can be easily found by other dolphins in the area. So we see, once again, that the structure of the calls has been adapted to its function.

Acquisition

Little is known about how dolphins acquire the ability to vocalize and communicate. Caldwell and Caldwell (1977) cite evidence that dolphins begin making their own distinctive whistles as early as the day they are born. There is also evidence that dolphins give off echolocation clicks soon after being born. Thus, part of the communication system would appear to be innate; but how dolphins come to use their communication system is still a subject of research.

Whale Communication

Much of the existing research on whale communication has involved underwater recording in the ocean. The most widely known vocalizations are those of the hump-backed whale, and some recordings are even available on phonographic discs. Perhaps the most striking fact about the vocalization of whales is that they engage in song sessions. The sessions, which may last for hours, consist of repeated units (songs), unique to each individual, that may last for half an hour. These songs are similar in structure to certain bird songs, in that they consist of repeated subunits. The function of the songs is unknown, but scientists have hypothesized that they not only identify individuals, but also may function to keep a herd of migrating whales together (Payne and McVay 1971). It is not known whether the subparts of the whale song carry distinct messages, but at present there is no evidence that they do. Ironically, the whale song, the vocalization of one of the world's largest creatures, appears to be similar in function to the flight calls of birds, one of the world's smallest creatures.

In sum, we can say that our understanding of the communication systems of dolphins and whales is limited at present. There is no solid evidence that cetaceans possess a system anywhere near as complex as human language. There is some evidence, however, that these animals, especially dolphins, possess a degree of intelligence, but this degree of intelligence (compared to that of birds, for example) does not seem to be associated with a more highly developed communication system. In fact, the communication system of cetaceans seems to be remarkably similar to that of birds, in that it appears to involve a small number of discrete vocalizations that have the function of referring to external conditions or internal states.

2.5 PRIMATE COMMUNICATION

People have been fascinated with primate communication for centuries. The fascination sometimes takes the form of wondering why, if primates are so smart, they don't talk. Probably the most ingenious answer to this question is the one reported by the seventeenth-century scholar, Antoine Le Grand (Chomsky 1972, 102). He noted that certain people of the East Indies believe that apes and baboons do not talk because they know that if they did, humans would put them to work.

Our interest in cracking the communicative code of another species is further motivated in this case by our close relationship to these creatures by evolution. Since we humans are primates too, we might discover in primate communication systems some clue as to the origin of human language. At present, however, the results in this area of investigation are disappointing. There seems to be nothing in the way of a linguistic system in use among primates, and the gap between primate communication systems and human linguistic communication is huge. As the noted primatologist Thelma Rowell (1972, 84) remarks, "Communication by monkeys is not qualitatively different from that of other animals, and the same principles apply to them. There is a complete break between people and other primates in this area, with the development of a verbal language capable of communicating . . . ideas, rather than objects or events in the immediate surroundings." In fact, one anthropologist (Lancaster 1975, 56) goes so far as to contend that "the interest in human evolution and in the origin of human language has distorted the study of the communication systems of the nonhuman primate. These systems are not steps toward language."

What motivates us, then, to study primate communication systems in this text? In brief, it is for contrast. By looking at primates, we complete a spectrum of different animal communication systems, all of which have striking similarities. We will then be in a better position to contrast natural animal systems both with human natural language and with some recent attempts to teach primates systems of communication that are artificial to them (see chapter 11). In this way, normal human linguistic achievements will be thrown into dramatic relief.

Communication Context

According to Lancaster (1975, 56–57), communication between complete strangers is very rare among primates. For the most part, communication takes place within a social group composed of members of both sexes and of disparate ages, who have spent most, if not all, of their lives together. "The context, then, of any communicative act includes a network of social relations that have a considerable history behind them, all of which is relevant to the message and how it is received and responded to." For example, primates form a variety of social relationships, one of which is dominance, wherein one primate has "priority of access to desirable goods" over another—the dominance usually being enforced by superior strength. Since dominance tends to organize groups into a hierarchy, "a juvenile would ignore, or even respond with teasing to a threat from a female of lower rank than his mother, but would flee screaming from the same gesture from a female of higher rank" (Rowell 1972, 96). In short, primate signals tend to be (a) context-bound, in that the message sent is heavily dependent on the salient features of the context, and (b) multimodal, in that a variety of sensory channels may be operating and contributing simultaneously (vision, hearing, and smell being the commonest).

Although most primate signals are multimodal and the visual element is generally the most important, we will concentrate on the vocal mode. This is necessary, given our interest in comparing natural primate communication with human spoken language. We will consider the communicative system of the vervet (*Cercopithecus aethiops*), since it is

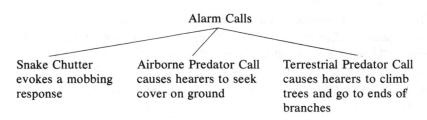

Figure 2.12
Vervet alarm calls

one of the most intensively studied primates from the point of view of vocal communication.

The vervet is a rather elegant looking semiterrestrial Old World monkey, found mainly in the grassy forests of southeast Africa—especially at the Amboseli Reserve in Kenya.

One estimate of the vervet's vocal repertoire puts the number of physically distinct sounds at about 36, evoked by 21 different situations and carrying roughly 22 different messages (Struhsaker 1967, 313).

Three of the more interesting vocalizations of the vervet are the alarm calls listed in figure 2.12. These are of particular interest because they are apparently used to convey information about the vervet's environment and so "are rare and represent important specializations of the few species that use them" (Lancaster 1975, 64).

The snake chutter call is emitted almost exclusively by juveniles and adult females. It is of low amplitude and is produced with teeth exposed in a sort of grimace. The monkeys cluster together about five feet from the snake; while emitting the call, they stare at the snake and follow it through the brush. The survival value of isolating a dangerous predator in this manner is obvious.

The airborne predator call is also emitted almost exclusively by juveniles and adult females. It is used to signal the presence of such airborne predators as the (monkey-eating) martial eagle and the crowned hawk eagle. It is a call of low frequency and high amplitude, making it a sort of "chirp," and is audible to ¼ mile. Upon hearing this call, vervets tend to drop out of the trees into the high grass or bushes for cover.

Although the terrestrial predator calls resemble the airborne predator call (to the human ear), their function is just the opposite—to get other monkeys to climb nearby trees and go out to the ends of the branches.

Seyfarth, Cheney, and Marler (1980) recorded the three types of alarm calls, then played them back to the vervets, under various conditions, in their habitat at Amboseli Reserve, Kenya. They hypothesized that it was the distinctive qualities of the alarm calls themselves, and not their length or loudness, that the monkeys were responding to. The results were interesting in that they confirmed earlier observations. First, vervets of all ages and both sexes looked toward the broadcast speaker through which the taped calls were being played back. They then scanned the surroundings as if looking for something. Second, the vervets' behavior was usually appropriate to the kind of call being broadcast. For instance, when the monkeys were on the ground, the terrestrial predator calls caused them to run to the trees; the airborne predator call made them look up and sometimes run into cover; and so on. On the other hand, the snake chutter was more likely to cause them to look down.

Unlike the bee dance, but like bird calls, the vocal repertoire of the vervet seems to consist simply of a small vocabulary of distinct calls, which are not combined with each other in any systematic fashion.

Processing and Acquisition

Not much is known about the neurological and psychological mechanisms underlying primate communication. Nor is much known about the details of its development and acquisition, especially in the wild. What seems to be emerging from preliminary work in the field of primate learning is that the general structure of the communication system is biologically fixed and that learning fills in the more detailed structure of the system. A comparison of the communicative repertoires of laboratory rhesus monkeys with repertoires of free-ranging ones illustrates this point (Mason 1960, 1961a,b). Although the two groups used the same basic repertoire of postures, gestures, and vocalizations, the communicative system of the free-ranging group showed more detail and subtlety.

There is also evidence that an infant monkey raised with monkeys of another species will apparently come to comprehend signals of the other species but will produce only those signals characteristic of its own species (Altmann 1973). These features are reminiscent, not of human language, but of human emotional displays such as laughing, crying, smiling, frowning, screaming, gasping, and so on. That is, these human expressions are, for the most part, biologically determined in form and function, even though the details may be modified or filled out by imitation and innovation. Like many, if not most, forms of behavior, communication systems in primates are probably complicated mixtures of genetic disposition, circumstances, and learning. For instance, Seyfarth, Cheney, and Marler (1980) report that infant vervets tend to give the terrestrial predator call in response to anything terrestrial, airborne predator calls in response to any bird, and snake chutters in response to any snake or long thin object. We will see in chapter 11 that this sort of "overgeneralization" is also quite common in human communicative development, as when a child calls any animal "dog" or any adult male "Daddy."

2.6 ANIMAL COMMUNICATION AND THE MESSAGE MODEL

The theory of communication depicted in figure 2.1 can be applied directly to the animal communication systems we have discussed in this chapter. In each case we will suppose that animals of the same species are the message sender and message receiver. The message sender encodes the message into a public signal and the message receiver decodes the public signal. The signals sent by various animals are shown in table 2.4.

Since we cannot ask the animal about its message, we must rely on more indirect evidence to suggest what the right message is. In particular, we must rely heavily on the contextual conditions of the sender and receiver, as well as on the subsequent behavior of the receiver. In characterizing these messages, we will therefore take our cue from the vocabulary of the scientists who have observed and recorded these relationships. However, it should be kept in mind that the exact nature of the broadcast message has yet to be determined.

Applying the Message Model to bee communication, we will assume that the message is a set of instructions, which we can paraphrase as: "Fly distance X, using a Y-orientation with respect to the sun." This message is then encoded in the appropriate dance, which acts as the signal. The dance signal is then decoded by the attending bees, who, following the message, fly distance X, using a Y-degree orientation with respect to the sun. Although many details are omitted (notably, how the message is encoded into the particular dance), the model seems to be a fair representation of communication among honeybees.

Bird communication can also be represented by the Message Model. If an individual bird spots an overhead predator, it will send the mes-

Table 2.4
The Message Model applied to different animal communication systems

Animal (Sender)	Signal	Decoding	"Message" (in Paraphrased English)	Subsequent Behavior of Receiver
Vervet	Snake chutter	→	Warning: snake nearby	Surround snake ("mobbing")
	Aerial predator call	→	Warning: eagle overhead	Seek cover on ground
	Terrestrial predator call	→	Warning: leopard nearby	Climb trees, go to ends of branches
Bird	Aerial predator call ("seet")	→	Warning: predator overhead	Take cover in bushes and remain motionless
	Mobbing call ("chink")	→	Warning: stationary predator nearby	Surround predator ("mobbing")
	Territorial song	→	Warning: other males keep away	Other males keep out of territory of message sender
			Invitation: females come here	Uncommitted females are attracted to sender
Bee	Round dance	→	Instruction: seek food source within 10 meters of hive	Search randomly within designated area
	Sickle dance (found in Italian honeybees)	→	Instruction: seek food source between 10 and 100 meters of hive	Fly in the direction of the bisector of the pattern of the dance (cf. fig. 2.7)
	Tail-wagging dance	→	Instruction: seek food source of distance X, flying at Y degrees with respect to the sun	Search for food at location indicated by the dance
Bottle-nosed dolphin	Distress whistle	→	Request: help!	Dolphins in the area come to distressed animal and raise it to the surface
Hump-backed whale	Song	→	?	?

sage announcing this fact. We can imagine that the message, "There's a predator overhead," is encoded into the "seet" call and then broadcast in the bird's general area. Upon hearing this signal, other birds instantly decode it and, arriving at the message, take the appropriate evasive action.

The Message Model is also applicable to the communication systems of whales, dolphins, and primates. All in all, the animal communication systems we have studied in this chapter can be easily analyzed as instances of this particular model. However, as we shall see in chapter 9, this Message Model is much too simple to account for human communication; a more complex model is needed to describe human language use.

Key Words

Message Model
encoding and decoding
structure-function adaptation
bee dances
bird calls
bird songs
primate calls
innate vs. learned
dialects

Study Questions

1. What is the structure of the honeybee's communication system?

2. What is the function of the communication system? How do aspects of the message correlate with aspects of the structure?

3. Why does the black Austrian honeybee search beyond the food source when aroused by the dance of the Italian honeybee?

4. What is the role of learning in the honeybee's communication system?

5. In discussing communication systems, the terms *icon* and *symbol* are sometimes used. An *icon* is a sign that bears some type of physical resemblance to its referent. For example, statues, road maps, and photographs are all icons. A *symbol* is an arbitrary sign; it bears no necessary physical relation to its referent. For example, the word *dog* does not resemble a dog. Is the communication system of the honeybee iconic or symbolic?

6. Does bee communication share any features with human communication?

7. What are the structural and functional differences between the mobbing call and the aerial predator call in birds?

8. Compare and contrast the bee communication system with some particular bird song in terms of structure and function.

9. The European cuckoo lays its eggs in the nests of over 120 different bird species, who raise the young cuckoos as their own. Would you expect the cuckoo song to be learned or innate, and why? Compare and contrast the song acquisition of the cuckoo with that of the chaffinch.

10. Bird calls are usually much shorter than songs. In terms of the functions calls and songs serve, why might this difference in relative length and complexity exist?

11. Compare and contrast the communication system of the bottle-nosed dolphin with the vocalization of birds.

12. Compare and contrast the "seet" call of birds with the distress call of the bottle-nosed dolphin in terms of structure and function.

13. Compare and contrast the mobbing calls of birds with the alarm calls of the vervet monkey.

14. To what aspect of human vocalizations do primate calls seem to correspond most closely?

Bibliography

Altmann, S. (1967). "The structure of primate social communication," in S. Altmann, ed., *Social Communication among Primates,* University of Chicago Press, Chicago.

Altmann, S. (1968). "Primates," in T. Sebeok, ed., *Animal Communication,* University of Illinois Press, Urbana.

Altmann, S. (1973). "Primate communication," in G. Miller, ed., *Communication, Language, and Meaning,* Basic Books, New York.

Andrew, R. (1972). "The information potentially available in mammal displays," in R. Hinde, ed., *Non-Verbal Communication,* Cambridge University Press, Cambridge.

Armstrong, E. A. (1963). *A Study of Bird Song,* Dover Press, New York.

Caldwell, D. K., and M. C. Caldwell (1977). "Cetaceans," in T. Sebeok, ed., *How Animals Communicate,* Indiana University Press, Bloomington and London.

Chomsky, N. (1965). *Aspects of the Theory of Syntax,* MIT Press, Cambridge, Mass.

Chomsky, N. (1972). *Language and Mind,* enlarged ed., Harcourt Brace Jovanovich, New York.

Dreher, J. (1966). "Cetacean communication: Small-group experiment," in K. Norris, ed., *Whales, Dolphins, and Porpoises,* University of California Press, Berkeley and Los Angeles.

Esch, H. (1967). "The evolution of bee language," *Scientific American* 216(4), 96–104.

Falls, J. (1969). "Functions of the territorial song in the White-Throated Sparrow," in R. Hinde, ed. (1969).

Hinde, R., ed. (1969). *Bird Vocalizations,* Cambridge University Press, Cambridge.

Jolly, A. (1972). *The Evolution of Primate Behavior,* Macmillan, New York.

Lancaster, J. (1975). *Primate Behavior and the Emergence of Human Culture,* Macmillan, New York.

Lilly, J. (1961). *Man and Dolphin,* Doubleday, Garden City, N.Y.

McIntyre, J. (1974). *Mind in the Waters,* Charles Scribner's Sons, New York, Sierra Club Books, San Francisco.

Marler, P. (1965). "Communication in monkeys and apes," in I. DeVore, ed., *Primate Behavior,* Holt, Rinehart and Winston, New York.

Marler, P., and W. J. Hamilton (1966). *Mechanisms of Animal Behavior,* Wiley, New York.

Mason, W. (1960). "The effects of social restriction on the behavior of Rhesus monkeys, I. Free serial behavior," *Journal of Comparative and Physiological Psychology* 53, 582–589.

Mason, W. (1961a). "II. Tests of gregariousness," *Journal of Comparative and Physiological Psychology* 54, 287–290.

Mason, W. (1961b). "III. Dominance tests," *Journal of Comparative and Physiological Psychology* 54, 694–699.

Nicolai, J. (1959). "Familientradition in der Gesangentwicklung des Gimpels (Pyrrhula pyrrhula L.)," *Journal of Ornithology* 100, 39–46.

Nottebohm, F. (1970). "Ontogeny of bird song," *Science* 169, 950–956.

Payne, R. S., and S. McVay (1971). "Songs of Humpback Whales," *Science* 173, 585–597.

Prince, J. H. (1975). *Languages and the Animal World,* Thomas Nelson, Nashville and New York.

Rosen, S. (1974). *Introduction to the Primates,* Prentice-Hall, Englewood Cliffs, N.J.

Rowell, T. (1962). "Agonistic noises of the Rhesus monkey," *Symposia of the Zoological Society of London* 8, 91–96.

Rowell, T. (1972). *Social Behavior of Monkeys,* Penguin Books, Baltimore, Md.

Rowell, T., and R. Hinde (1962). "Vocal communication by the Rhesus monkey," *Symposia of the Zoological Society of London* 8, 279–294.

Seyfarth, R., D. Cheney, and P. Marler (1980). "Monkey responses to three different alarm calls: Evidence of predator classification and semantic communication," *Science* 210, 801–803.

Shannon, C., and W. Weaver (1949). *The Mathematical Theory of Communication,* University of Illinois Press, Urbana.

Struhsaker, T. (1967). "Auditory communication among Vervet monkeys," in S. Altmann, ed. (1967).

Thielcke, G. (1976). *Bird Sounds,* The University of Michigan Press, Ann Arbor.

Thorpe, W. (1956). "The language of birds," *Scientific American* 195(4), 129–138.

Thorpe, W. (1961). *Bird-Song,* Cambridge University Press, Cambridge.

Thorpe, W. (1974). *Animal Nature and Human Nature,* Anchor Press/Doubleday, Garden City, N.Y.

von Frisch, K. (1962). "Dialects in the language of bees," *Scientific American* 207(2), 78–87.

von Frisch, K. (1967). *The Dance Language and Orientation of Bees,* translated by C. E. Chadwick, Harvard University Press, Cambridge, Mass.

Wenner, A. (1964). "Sound communication of honeybees," *Scientific American* 210(4), 116–124,

Part Two

THE STRUCTURE OF HUMAN LANGUAGE

Introduction

In part one we briefly examined certain background concepts in linguistics, as well as some of the properties of animal communication systems. In this section we turn our attention to the structure of human language, and in doing so we will discover a system of surprising complexity and sophistication. Beginning students of linguistics are often surprised to find that linguists spend considerable time trying to formulate theories to represent and explain the structure (as well as the functioning) of human language. What is there, after all, to explain? Speaking one's native language is a natural and effortless task, carried out with great speed and ease, and even four-year-old children can do it with little conscious effort. From this, it is commonly concluded that aside from a few rules of grammar and pronunciation there is nothing else to explain about human language.

But it turns out that there is a great deal to explain, if (following the suggestion of chapter 2) we "step outside" language and look at it as an object to be consciously studied and described and not merely used. Once we manage to "make strange" something as familiar as human language, we discover a new and exciting sphere of human knowledge previously hidden to us.

In beginning the study of the structural properties of human language, it is useful to note a common theme that runs throughout part two: the structural analysis of human language can be stated in terms of (1) discrete units of various sorts, and (2) rules and principles that govern the way those discrete units can be combined and ordered. In the sections on morphology (chapter 3), phonology (chapter 4), syntax (chapter 5), and semantics (chapter 6), we will be discussing the significant discrete units that linguists have postulated in the study of these subareas of human language. In addition to isolating discrete units such as morphemes, phonemes (and distinctive features), syntactic phrases, and semantic components, we will be discussing the rules and principles by which words are formed, sounds are combined, and syntactic units are structured and ordered into larger phrases and sentences.

In addition to discussing the core areas of morphology, phonology, syntax, and semantics, we will discuss two subfields of linguistics that draw heavily on those core areas, namely, language variation (chapter 7) and language change (chapter 8). In these sections, we discuss the ways in which language varies over time and space, that is, how language varies across individual speakers and dialect groups (regionally, socially, and ethnically) and how languages vary and relate to each other historically. Thus, having isolated important structural units and rules for combination in chapters 3–6, we then examine how such units and rules can vary along a number of dimensions.

The subfields represented in chapters 3–6 form the core of what has classically been known as *structural linguistics* (as practiced in the United States during the 1930s, 40s, and 50s), and they continue to form a central part of *transformational/generative linguistics,* the theoretical perspective we adopt here. (The latter dates from the publication of Noam Chomsky's 1957 work *Syntactic Structures,* and has been the dominant school of linguistics in the United States since that time; more recently, it has come to be a dominant school in Western Europe and Japan as well.)

The language data used in the following chapters are drawn almost exclusively from English. Assuming that the majority of our readers will be native speakers of English, we encourage you to use your native linguistic judgments in evaluating our arguments and proposals. It should be stressed, however, that the general aspects of the linguistic framework we develop here are supposed to hold for all languages, or at least for a large subset of languages, and we encourage you to think about other languages you may know as you study the English examples.

In using examples drawn from our readers' native language, there is a potential drawback: phenomena we discuss from English may seem commonplace and, in a real sense, obvious. As we have noted, it is quite important to distance oneself from the subject matter in order to get a feeling for structural analysis of language in the abstract, momentarily divorced from the facts of any particular language. In abstracting away from the particular facts of English, one is able to

How an extraterrestrial linguist might see universal properties of human language structure

Theory 1 (Order)	□	□	□	□	□	□
Theory 2 (Category)	$\triangle$	★	$\oplus$	$\diamond$	×	$\odot$
Theory 3 (Grouping)	$\triangle$	★	$\oplus$	$\diamond$	×	$\odot$
Theory 4 (Function)	$\triangle$	★ F_1	$\oplus$	$\diamond$ F_2	× F_3	$\odot$
Theory 5 (Dependency)	$\triangle$	★ F_1	$\oplus$	$\diamond$ F_2	× F_3	$\odot$

undertake the study of language structure in general. For the fundamental aim of this book is to impart a feeling for how general linguistic theory is formulated. A simple game can help in making this point.

Imagine that you are an extraterrestrial linguist from a nearby galaxy, sent to Earth in order to report on the nature of human language. To you as an alien creature, nothing about human language (or customs or culture) is obvious or plain. Every detail of human language structure is new to you, and all of language appears strange. After careful study of this marvelous mechanism of humans, you might see the structure of human language in the way it is depicted in the chart.

How might you arrive at this "strange" view of the structure of human language? By the time you have finished part two of this book, the answer will be clear. But it might be useful to see how you, as the alien linguist, might arrive at the picture we have drawn. After arriving on Earth, you notice humans emitting continuous streams of sound, which apparently have some sort of effect on other humans. As surprising as it may seem, it would not be at all obvious to an extraterrestrial creature that these streams of sound can be analyzed into discrete units, for example, words. In reality, the sentences we utter are physically continuous and not broken down into convenient separate chunks. It is therefore a major breakthrough for you as an alien linguist to propose theory 1, based on your discovery that human language is best analyzed as made up of *discrete units* in some sequential order (see theory 1 on chart). The discrete units all seem to be alike to you—they all appear to have the same status at first, as though they were identical boxes in a row. This is very much the way linguists describe the abstract properties of most bird songs (see chapter 2).

After more study, however, you quickly discover that the discrete units of human language are not all identical, but instead come in different categories. This leads you to theory 2: human language is structurally analyzable as discrete units of *different categories* (for example, the traditional parts of speech, as outlined in chapter 3), strung out in a sequential order. Now the units no longer resemble the identical boxes of theory 1 but take on distinctive shapes, just as the words in the following English sentence are all of distinct categories:

the	old	man	left	didn't	he
↕	↕	↕	↕	↕	↕
△	★	⊕	◇	×	⊙

Every human language has this property, and in fact some researchers have claimed that certain artificial languages taught to chimpanzees have discrete units of different categories (see chapter 11).

Your continuing exploration of human language begins to reveal an even more interesting structural property, formulated as theory 3: human language is analyzable as a sequential order of discrete (and distinctly categorized) units that are *grouped together* in various ways to form larger units, or phrases. Our particular English example is grouped in the following way:

the old man	left	didn't he
↕ ↕ ↕	↕	↕ ↕
△ ★ ⊕	◇	× ⊙

This is a significant discovery: to an alien linguist it is not obvious that words should go together to form phrases. Yet every human language has the property of grouping, and we know of no animal communication system with this property; from here on we seem to be in an exclusively human domain (see chapter 5).

Another important property of all human languages is revealed when you discover facts that lead to theory 4: the structural groupings of the discrete units have specific and distinct *functions*. Thus, the first grouping might have F_1, or function 1: the second grouping F_2, or function 2; and so on. In our English example, the first grouping has traditionally been called the subject, the second grouping the predicate, and the third grouping the tag question (chapter 5):

the old man   left   didn't he
$\updownarrow$ $\updownarrow$ $\updownarrow$ $\updownarrow$ $\updownarrow$ $\updownarrow$
$\triangle$ $\star$ $\oplus$ $\diamond$ $\times$ $\odot$

F_1: subject F_2: predicate F_3: tag question

Even though you as an alien linguist have already discovered that human language structure is a very sophisticated system, the story is not yet finished. Your further investigations show you that theory 5 must be postulated: in all human languages there are dependencies between words in completely different locations in a sentence. In our concrete example from English the dependency is this: the pronoun in the tag question *(he)* must agree in person, number, and gender with the subject of the sentence:

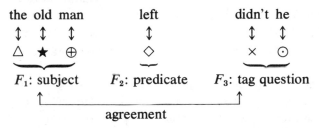

Thus, the symbols $\oplus$ and $\odot$ *(man, he)* are distinct but related units, bound together by a dependency relation traditionally called agreement (see chapter 5).

The properties represented by theory 5 do not exhaust the known abstract properties of human language, but they are certainly among the most important. As you begin the study of morphology, phonology, syntax, and semantics, keep in mind that abstract structural units of human language may seem obvious to you (once you have learned them!); this is to be expected, given that you are a user of a human language. As a linguist, however, you should keep trying to "step outside" language in order to get a glimpse of its remarkable structural properties.

Chapter Three

MORPHOLOGY: THE
STRUCTURE OF WORDS

3.1 WORDS: SOME BACKGROUND CONCEPTS

We begin our study of human language by examining one of the most
fundamental units of linguistic structure: the word. In the early stages
of learning our native language as children, we utter single words
("No!" "More!" "Mommy!"), and we must learn thousands more in
order to become fluent native speakers. Indeed, anyone who has mastered a language has mastered an astonishingly long list of facts encoded in the form of words. The total list of words for any language is
referred to as its *lexicon*.

When we think about our native language, the existence of words
seems obvious. After all, when we hear others speaking our native language, we hear them uttering words. In reading a printed passage, we
see words on the page, neatly separated by spaces. But now imagine
yourself in a situation where everyone around you is speaking a foreign
language that you have been studying for only a year. Suddenly the
existence of words no longer seems obvious. Listening to a native
speaker of Portuguese or Navajo or Swahili, as you strain to keep up
with what seems like an impossibly fast rate of speech, you hear a continuous blur of sound. If only the native speaker would slow down a
little (the eternal complaint of the foreigner!), you would be able to
divide that blur of sound into the individual words. The ability to
analyze a continuous stream of sound (spoken language) into discrete
units (for example, individual words) is far from trivial, and it constitutes a central part of language comprehension. When you have learned
your native language fluently, you have learned to recognize individual
words without effort, as well as many other things.

This brings us to the following question: what do we know when we know a word? To put it another way, what kinds of information have we learned when we learn a word? It turns out that the information encoded in a word is fairly complex, and we will see that a word is associated with different kinds of information. In discussing these types of information, we will in fact be referring to each of the subfields of linguistics that will be dealt with in this book:

A. *Phonological information:* For every word we know, we have learned a pronunciation. Part of knowing the word *tree* is knowing a certain sound—more precisely, a certain sequence of sounds. *Phonology* is the subfield of linguistics that studies the structure and systematic patterning of sounds in human language (see chapter 4).

B. *Morphological information:* For every word we have learned, we intuitively know something about its internal structure. For example, our intuitions tell us that the word *tree* cannot be broken down into any meaningful parts. In contrast, the word *trees* seems to be made up of two parts: the word *tree* plus an additional element, *-s* (known as the "plural" ending). *Morphology* is the subfield of linguistics that studies the internal structure of words and the interrelationships among words.

C. *Syntactic information:* For every word we learn, we learn how it fits into the overall structure of sentences in which it can be used. For example, we know that the word *reads* can be used in a sentence like *Mary reads the book,* and the word *readable* (related to the word *read*) can be used in a sentence like *The book is readable.* We may not know that *reads* is called a verb or that *readable* is called an adjective; but we intuitively know, as native speakers, how to use those words in different kinds of sentences. *Syntax* is the subfield of linguistics that studies the internal structure of sentences and the interrelationships among the internal parts (see chapter 5).

D. *Semantic information:* For virtually every word we know, we have learned a certain meaning. For example, to know the word *brother* is to know that it has a certain meaning (the equivalent of "male sibling"). In addition, we may or may not know certain extended meanings of the word, as in *John is so friendly and helpful, he's a regular brother to me.* *Semantics* is the subfield of linguistics that studies the nature of the meaning of individual words, and the meaning of words grouped into phrases and sentences (see chapter 6).

E. *Pragmatic information:* For every word we learn, we not only know its meaning or meanings, but we also know how to use it in the context of discourse or conversation. For instance, the word *brother* can be used not only to refer to a male sibling but also as a conversational exclamation, as in "Oh, *brother!* What a mess!" In some cases, words seem to have a use but no meaning as such. For example, the word *hello* is used to greet, but it seems to have no meaning beyond that particular use. *Pragmatics* is the subfield of linguistics that studies the use of words (and phrases and sentences) in the actual context of discourse (see chapter 9).

In addition to the types of information outlined here—information that we assume any native speaker must have learned about a word in order to know it—there are additional aspects of words that linguists study, which may or may not be known to native speakers. For example, words and their uses are subject to variation across groups of speakers. In American English the word *bonnet* can be used to refer to a type of hat; in British English it can be used to refer to the hood of a car.

Words and their uses are also subject to variation over time. For example, the English word *deer* at one time was the general word meaning "animal," but now it is used to refer only to a particular species of animal. These facts about word variation and historical changes may not be known to most native speakers—even for highly educated speakers, the history and dialectal variation of most words remain obscure—but such facts form the subject matter of other important subfields of linguistics (see chapters 7 and 8).

We have seen that words are associated with a wide range of information and that each type of information forms an important area of study for a subfield of linguistics. In this chapter we will be concerned with the subfield known as morphology, to which we now turn.

Some Basic Concepts of Morphology

Within the field of morphology, it is possible to pose many questions about the nature of words, but among the more persistent questions have been the following:

What are words and how are they formed?

How are more complex words built up from simpler parts?

What are the basic building blocks in the formation of complex words?

How is the meaning of a complex word related to the meaning of its parts?

How are individual words of a language related to other words of the language?

These are all difficult questions, and linguists studying morphology have not yet arrived at completely satisfactory answers to any of them. Once we begin to construct answers, we quickly discover that interesting and subtle problems arise.

To begin with, we can say that a word is an *arbitrary pairing of sound and meaning*. For example, the word *brother* is a sound (that is, a complex pattern of sounds) associated with a certain meaning ("male sibling"). There is no necessary reason why the particular combination of sounds represented by the word *brother* should mean what it does—nothing in the sound dictates what the meaning ought to be—and hence we say that the pairing of sound and meaning is *arbitrary*. It is true that every language contains *onomatopoeic* words—that is, words whose sounds imitate or mimic sounds in the world about us: *meow, bow-wow, splash, bang, hoot, crash,* and so on. But such words form a very limited subset of the words of any given language; for the vast majority of words the sound-meaning pairing is arbitrary.

Morphemes and Complex Words

It has long been recognized that words must be classed into at least two categories: *simple* and *complex*. A simple word such as *tree* seems to be a minimal unit; there seems to be no way to analyze it, or break it down further, into meaningful parts. On the other hand, the word *trees* is made up of two parts: the noun *tree* and the plural ending, spelled -*s* in this case. The following lists of English words reveal that the plural -*s* (or -*es*) can be attached to nouns quite generally:

(1)

Noun	Plural Form (+*s*)
boy	boys
rake	rakes
lip	lips
dog	dogs
bush	bushes
brother	brothers

Not every noun in English forms its plural in this fashion; for example, the plural of *child* is *children,* not *childs.* However, for nouns such as those in (1), and others of this large class, we can say that complex plural forms (such as *trees*) are made up of simple nouns (such as *tree*) followed by the plural ending -*s.* The basic parts of a complex word— that is, the different building blocks that make it up—are called *morphemes.* Each of the plural nouns listed in (1) is made up of two morphemes: (a) a *base morpheme* such as *boy, rake,* and so on, and (b) a *plural morpheme,* -*s,* which is attached to the base morpheme. The meaning of the plural forms listed in (1) is a combination, in some intuitive sense, of the meaning of the base morphemes and the meaning of the plural morpheme -*s.* In short, we will say that morphemes are the *minimal units of word-building* in a language: they cannot be broken down any further into recognizable or meaningful parts.

Morphemes are further categorized into two classes: *free* morphemes and *bound* morphemes. A free morpheme can stand alone as an independent word, such as the word *tree.* A bound morpheme cannot stand alone but must be *attached* to another morpheme—as, for example, the plural morpheme -*s,* which can only occur attached to nouns. Certain bound morphemes are known as *affixes* (reflecting the fact that they must be attached, or "affixed," to other morphemes). Affixes are referred to as *prefixes* when they are attached to the beginning of another morpheme (like the prefix *re-* in words such as *redo, rewrite, rethink*) and as *suffixes* when they are attached to the end of another morpheme (like the suffix -*ize* in words such as *modernize, equalize, centralize*). The morpheme to which an affix is attached is the *base* (or *stem*) morpheme. A basic classification of morphemes is summarized in figure 3.1.

Certain languages (but not English) also have affixes known as *infixes,* which are attached *within* another morpheme. For example, in

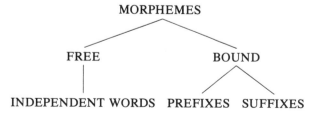

Figure 3.1
A basic classification of morphemes

Bontoc Igorot, a language of the Philippines, the infix *-in-* is used to indicate the product of a completed action (Sapir 1921). Taking the word *kayu,* meaning "wood," one can insert the infix *-in-* immediately after the first consonant *k* to form the word *kinayu,* meaning "gathered wood." In this way, the infix *-in-* fits into the base morpheme *kayu* in the internal "slot" *k- -ayu* (hence, *kinayu*). In addition, the infix *-um-* is used in certain verb forms to indicate future tense; for example, *-um-* can be added within a morpheme such as *tengao,* meaning "to celebrate a holiday," to create a verb form such as *tumengao-ak,* meaning "I will have a holiday" (the suffix *-ak* indicates the first person "I"). Here, the infix *-um-* fits into the base morpheme *tengao* in the internal "slot" immediately following the first consonant *(t- -engao).* Infixation is common in languages of Southeast Asia and the Philippines, and it is also found in some Native American languages.

It must be noted, in regard to figure 3.1, that not all bound morphemes are affixes. For example, in English certain words have *con-tracted* ("shortened") forms. The word *will* can occur either as *will,* in sentences such as *They will go,* or in a contracted form, spelled *'ll,* in sentences such as *They'll go.* The form *'ll* is a bound morpheme in that it cannot occur as an independent word and must be attached to the preceding word or phrase (as in *they'll*). Other contractions in English include *'s* (the contracted form of *is,* as in *The old car's not running anymore*); *'ve* (the contracted form of *have,* as in *They've gone jogging*); *'d* (the contracted form of *would,* as in *I'd like to be rich*); and several other contracted forms of auxiliary verbs. These contracted forms are all bound morphemes in the same sense as *'ll.*

Still another type of bound morpheme is illustrated by the morpheme *cran-,* which occurs in words such as *cranberry, cranapple,* and *cran-prune.* The form *cran-* cannot stand alone as a free morpheme, but must occur within words such as those just cited. For this reason, we say that *cran-* is a bound morpheme or *bound base.*

To sum up, then, we have seen that words fall into two general classes: simple and complex. Simple words are single free morphemes that cannot be broken down further into recognizable or meaningful parts. Complex words consist of two or more morphemes in combination.

Parts of Speech

Consider the following four words: *dog, pebble, resembles,* and *ex-plodes.* It turns out that the first two words share a certain property not shared by the last two words. That is, both *dog* and *pebble* can be preceded by a word such as *my* to form phrases such as *my dog* or *my pebble,* whereas the words *resembles* and *explodes* cannot (that is, there are no expressions such as *my resembles* or *my explodes*). This is just one small example of a general phenomenon found in all languages: namely, certain words of a language share significant properties with other words of the language. In order to account for this fact, we classify words into special subgroups, or categories, so that all words belonging to a given category share certain specific features. Traditionally, these categories have been known as *parts of speech,* such as *noun, verb, adjective, adverb,* and *preposition.* The parts of speech are difficult to define precisely, and we will attempt no definitions here. Instead, we will adopt certain traditional intuitive notions as forming the basis for the classification of the major parts of speech, as follows:

Intuitive Notions

Nouns. Proper names, as well as words for humans, animals and other living things, physical objects, and certain abstract ideas. Examples: *Mary, Edward, Fido, woman, man, dog, tree, chair, pebble, injustice, peace.*

Verbs. Words for actions, events, and relations. Examples: *kiss, explode, resemble.*

Adjectives. Words used to modify nouns. Examples: *tall, short, fat, skinny, pleasant, obvious, untrue* (as in *tall person, short book, obvious idea, untrue story*). When a word "modifies" another word, it provides additional relevant information. For example, in using the sentence *Short trees grow in deserts,* we are not merely talking about trees in general, but rather about short trees. In this sense, we can say that the adjective *short* modifies the noun *trees.*

Adverbs. Words used to modify verbs, adjectives, or other adverbs (often ending in -*ly* in English). Examples: *quickly, easily, exceptionally, ferociously* (as in *reads quickly, ferociously hungry, exceptionally quickly*).

Prepositions. Words for locations, directions, and instrumental relations. Examples: *in, under, to, toward, from, with, by,* (as in *in (the room), under (the table), to (the station), toward (the mountain), from (Boston), with (the knife), (death) by (fire)*).

The characteristics cited for each part of speech are in no way definitive. They merely serve as handy rules of thumb for distinguishing the traditional terms.

It is important to note that in any given language, words belonging to the same part-of-speech class share significant *grammatical properties*. For example, in English, the following are among the grammatical properties associated with each part of speech listed:

Grammatical Properties (in English)
Nouns
   a. Nouns can combine with *demonstratives*, such as *this, that, these, those,* to form phrases known as *noun phrases: this book, that woman, these ideas,* and so on. In addition, nouns can combine with *articles,* such as the *definite article, the,* or the *indefinite article, a,* to form noun phrases such as *the book* or *a book,* and with *possessive pronouns* (*my, your, her, his, its, our, their*) to form noun phrases such as *my book, your child, their idea, its wheels.* In chapter 5 we will discuss the structure of noun phrases in more detail; at this point we wish only to show that nouns can be distinguished from other parts of speech in terms of the words they combine with to form larger phrases.

   b. With a few exceptions, nouns can take the plural suffix *-s* (as in *book—books, brother—brothers, idea—ideas*). Exceptions: *woman— women, child—children, ox—oxen,* and so on.

Verbs
   a. Verbs take the suffix *-s* (as in *bake—bakes, walk—walks, hit— hits*) in the present tense. This is known as the "third person singular" form, because this is the form of the verb that occurs when the subject of the sentence is third person singular. The following present tense verb forms illustrate this:

	Singular	Plural
1st Person	I walk.	We walk.
2nd Person	You walk.	You walk.
3rd Person	She *walks*.	They walk.
	He *walks*.	
	It *walks*.	

Notice that the verb form remains the same in all cases, except when the subject is third person singular.

   b. Verbs can take the suffix *-ing,* as in *bake—baking, walk—walking, hit—hitting, sing—singing,* illustrated in sentences such as *They are baking, She is singing.*

c. Most verbs have a special form used in the past tense. Many verbs in English take the suffix *-ed* to form the past tense (for example, *wait — waited, walk — walked, play — played*), but English also has numerous "irregular" verbs that form the past tense in other ways (for example, *sing — sang, give — gave, bring — brought, fly — flew*), as well as a few verbs, such as *hit,* that have the same form in both present and past tense.

Adjectives

a. Adjectives can be modified by a class of words known as *intensifiers,* including the words *very, so, quite,* and *rather* (as in *very tall, so true, quite beautiful, rather obvious*).

b. As already noted, adjectives can modify nouns *(tall man, true story, beautiful flowers; The man is tall, The story is true, The flowers are beautiful).*

c. Adjectives can usually take the suffixes *-er* and *-est* (as in *big — bigger — biggest, red — redder — reddest, wise — wiser — wisest*). Some adjectives occur not with *-er* or *-est,* but instead with the comparative words *more* and *most (beautiful — more beautiful — most beautiful).* All adjectives occur with the comparative words *less* and *least* (as in *sweet — less sweet — least sweet*). All these forms are known as *comparative* forms of adjectives.

Adverbs

a. Adverbs share many of the properties of adjectives, and are often formed from adjectives by the addition of the suffix *-ly.* For example, the adjective *quick* can be converted into an adverb by adding *-ly,* to form *quickly* (and similarly for pairs such as *easy — easily, ferocious — ferociously, obvious — obviously*). (But note that adverbs are not the only class of words in English than can end in *-ly.* Adjectives can too: witness *lonely man, loneliest man.*)

b. As already noted, adverbs can modify adjectives (as in *obviously false, enormously tall*).

c. Like adjectives, adverbs can be modified by intensifiers (as in *very quickly, rather easily, so ferociously*).

d. Like adjectives, adverbs can occur with the comparative words *more, most, less, least* (as in *more quickly, less easily, least easily*).

Prepositions. Prepositions can be modified by the word *right;* that is, they can immediately follow *right* (as in *right into (the room), right under (the table), right up (the flagpole)).* (In some forms of American English, *right* can also modify adjectives, as in *That's right nice.*)

For each part-of-speech class, then, we have listed certain grammatical properties, in terms of either affixes that can be *attached to* or other words that can *combine with* words of the given class to form a larger phrase. Thus, when we examine the grammatical properties of words belonging to a particular part-of-speech class, we are examining in part how the words *function grammatically* within the language.

Let us illustrate how we can classify a given word, by using the intuitive notions and grammatical properties cited. For example, to what part-of-speech class would we assign the English word *father?* We know that this word denotes certain humans (and possibly certain animals); thus, from the point of view of the intuitive notions, *father* would count as a noun. This classification is confirmed when we observe that this word can combine with possessive pronouns to form phrases such as *my father;* it can also take the plural suffix *-s*, as in *their fathers*. But notice that the word *father* can also be used as a verb in English, as in the sentence *He fathered three children.* Here, *father* takes the past tense ending *-ed*, which is a grammatical property of verbs in English. Hence, English has both a noun *father* and a verb *father*. We can recognize which category the word belongs to by the way it is used.

To take another example, to what part of speech does the word *singing* belong? We have noted that the suffix *-ing* is attached to verbs (in this case, the verb *sing*), and indeed the word *singing* can be used as a verb (for instance, in *They are singing*). However, even though *sing* is a verb, if we attach *-ing* to it, the resulting word *singing* can also be used as a noun. Consider, for example, the sentences *Her singing is very beautiful* and *The loud singing bothers me.* Here the word *singing* combines with a possessive pronoun in the first sentence (*her singing*) and with the definite article and a modifying adjective in the second sentence (*the loud singing*). Hence, the word *singing* can be classified either as a verb or as a noun, depending on the grammatical properties it has in its various uses. (Indeed, words like *singing* also seem to function as adjectives; see exercise 20.)

These examples show that words of a language can belong to more than one part of speech class and that we can determine which part(s) of speech a word belongs to by examining how the word functions in phrases and sentences of the language.

The question now arises: are the part-of-speech classes we have discussed found in all languages, or just in English? The answer is by no means simple. However, linguists generally assume that certain "major" part-of-speech classes—in particular, nouns and verbs—exist in many, if not all, languages. The intuitive notions we have used to characterize nouns and verbs presumably hold for a wide range of languages: nouns typically are words for humans, animals, physical objects, etc., and verbs typically are words for actions, events, and relations. In addition, it may be that certain grammatical properties of a given part-of-speech class are found in a wide range of languages. For example, it may be that nouns in every language combine with demonstratives such as *this* or *that* to form noun phrases.

By and large, however, the grammatical properties of a given part-of-speech class are quite specific to a given language or small group of languages. For example, the property of English nouns of taking a plural suffix (*-s*) obviously cannot be used as a general defining property for nouns across languages. Although some other languages have a plural suffix for nouns (note, for example, German *Frau* "woman" versus *Frauen* "women"), other languages have no special affix for indicating a plural form for nouns. For example, in Japanese a noun like *hon* "book, books" can be used with either singular or plural meaning. In other languages the plural form for nouns (and in some cases, verbs as well; see exercise 12) is formed by a process known as *reduplication,* in which a specific part of the singular form is *reduplicated* (repeated) to construct the plural form. For example, in Papago, a Native American language of southern Arizona and northern Mexico, we find pairs such as *daikuḍ* "chair"—*dadaikuḍ* "chairs," *kawyu* "horse"—*kakawyu* "horses," *gogs* "dog"—*gogogs* "dogs," in which the first consonant + vowel sequence of the singular form is repeated at the beginning of the word to construct the plural form. Hence, there is no single affix to indicate plurality in these cases. We see, then, that in some languages there is no morphological indication of a plural form for nouns; in other languages the plural is morphologically indicated by an affix or by reduplication (among other ways). In short, in terms of our intuitive notions, we can probably say that nouns exist in many (if not all) languages; but it must be kept in mind that the specific grammatical properties associated with nouns can vary across languages.

While it may be true that most, if not all, languages share the categories noun and verb (and possibly a few others), it is also clear that other categories are found in some languages but not in others. For example, Japanese has a class of bound morphemes known as *particles,* which are attached to noun phrases to indicate grammatical function. In a Japanese sentence such as *John-ga hon-o yonda* "John read the book," the particle *-ga* indicates that *John* functions as the subject of the sentence (the "doer" of the action), and the particle *-o* indicates that *hon* "book, books" functions as the object (that which "undergoes" the action) of the verb *yonda* "read." English has no such particles to indicate subject or object; instead, such grammatical functions are indicated most often by word order. The subject of an English sentence typically precedes the verb and the object typically follows it, as in *John read the book*.

Conversely, English has grammatical categories not found in Japanese. For example, English has a class of words known as *articles,* including *the* (the so-called definite article) and *a* (the so-called indefinite article), as in *the book* or *a book*. Articles are not found in Japanese, as the example sentence *John-ga hon-o yonda* illustrates. The noun *hon* is followed by the particle *-o* (indicating its object function), but it is accompanied by no morphemes equivalent to the English articles. This is not to say that Japanese speakers cannot express the difference in meaning between *the book* (definite and specific) and *a book* (indefinite and nonspecific). Instead, this difference is determined by the context (both linguistic and nonlinguistic) of the sentence. For example, if a certain book has been mentioned in previous discourse, speakers of Japanese interpret *John ga hon-o yonda* as meaning *John read the book* rather than *John read a book*.

To sum up, whether or not all languages share certain part-of-speech categories, we nevertheless expect to find groups of words within any given language that share significant grammatical properties. To account for these similarities, we hypothesize that words sharing significant properties all belong to the same category. Such categories are traditionally labeled *noun, verb,* and so on, but we must remain open to the possibility that a given language may have a grammatical category not found in others. The existence of part-of-speech categories shows that the lexicon of a language (the total list of words for the language) is not simply a long, random list. Rather, it is structured into special subgroups of words (the various grammatical categories).

Content Words (Open Classes) and Function Words (Closed Classes)

In discussions about words, a distinction is sometimes made between *content words* and *function words*. Examples of content words include the English words *brother, run, tall, quickly,* and many more nouns, verbs, adjectives, and adverbs that can be said to have meaning as independent words. In contrast, function words cannot be easily defined as isolated words, but rather serve to indicate some grammatical function in a phrase or sentence. Examples of function words in English include conjunctions (*and, or*), articles and demonstratives (*the, a, this, that,* etc.), and prepositions (*to, from, at, with,* etc.). To take one specific case, consider the word *and.* It seems rather difficult to define this word as having a "meaning" as an isolated word, in the same sense that a word such as *brother* has a meaning ("male sibling"). Rather, the essential feature of the word *and* is that it functions grammatically to *conjoin* noun phrases (for instance, *the woman and the man*). Hence, we talk about the grammatical *use* of function words like *and,* rather than their "meaning."

One familiar variety of language in which the distinction between content words and function words is important is known as *telegraphic speech* (or *telegraphic language*). The term *telegraphic* derives from the kind of language used in telegrams, where considerations of space (and finances) force one to be as terse as possible: HAVING WONDER-FUL TIME; HOTEL GREAT; RETURNING FLIGHT 256; SEND MONEY; STOP. Generally speaking, in telegraphic forms of language the content words are retained, while function words are omitted wher-ever possible. Telegraphic forms of language are not limited to tele-grams and postcards, but can also be observed in early stages of child language (early multiword stages; see chapter 11); in the speech of peo-ple with certain brain disorders known as aphasic brain syndromes (see Bradley, Garrett, and Zurif 1980, as well as chapter 12); in hurried lec-ture notes taken by college students (Janda (forthcoming)); in classified advertising; in certain styles of poetry; and generally in any use of lan-guage where messages must be reduced to the absolute essentials.

Closely related to the terms *content word* and *function word* are the terms *open class* and *closed class*. The open-class words (correspond-ing to what we have termed content words) are those belonging to the major part-of-speech classes (nouns, verbs, adjectives, and adverbs), which in any language tend to be quite large and "open-ended." That is, many new words can be created and added to these classes in rela-tively short periods of time; indeed, English is augmented by many new open-class words each year. In contrast, the closed-class words (corre-sponding to what we have termed function words) are those belonging to grammatical, or function, classes (such as articles, demonstratives, conjunctions, and prepositions), which in any language tend to be small and "closed." That is, a closed class consists of a relatively small num-ber of fixed elements (for example, the class of articles consists of *a* and *the,* the class of demonstratives consists of *this, that, these, those,* and so on), and any change in membership of such a class happens only very slowly (over centuries) and in small increments. Thus, a speaker of English may well encounter dozens of new nouns and verbs during the coming year; but it is extremely unlikely that the English language will acquire a new definite article (or lose the current one) in the coming year (or even during a given speaker's lifetime).

The morpheme classifications discussed in this section are summarized in figure 3.2. (We will discuss a further distinction among affixes under the heading "Inflectional versus Derivational Morphology.") Note, incidentally, that affixes (and not just function words) could also be classified as belonging to "closed classes." For example, the classes of prefixes and suffixes also consist of a small number of fixed elements, augmented or changed only very slowly over time. It has been customary to use the term "closed class" to refer to function words (rather than to bound affixes), however, and we adopt that usage in figure 3.2.

It is important to note the similarities and differences between function words and bound morphemes (such as the affixes *re-* or *-ize* in English). On the one hand, function words, as opposed to affixes, are in fact free morphemes; that is, they are independent words of the language. This distinction is reflected in everyday spoken language, in that the sounds we make in hesitating or pausing, such as *umm* or *uh,* can occur between content words and function words (both free morphemes) but do not normally occur between a content word (free morpheme) and an affix attached to that word (bound morpheme). For example, in actual speech we might hear the phrase *Kim and Pat* pronounced *Kim—umm—and—uh—Pat,* but we would not expect to hear a word such as *modernize* (free morpheme *modern* followed by suffix *-ize*) pronounced in this way, as in *We will modern—umm—ize the house.* In other words, hesitation sounds such as *umm* and *uh* normally occur between free morphemes, not between a free morpheme and a bound morpheme. This fact allows us to establish that function words are free morphemes and thus distinct from affixes.

On the other hand, function words and affixes are similar in that they both serve to indicate grammatical function. We can illustrate this with the comparative form of adjectives. The function word *more* (see figure 3.2) serves to indicate a comparison in phrases such as *more gigantic (than).* However, the comparative form of adjectives can also be marked by the suffix *-er,* as in the phrase *bigger (than).* Hence, the grammatical function of comparison in adjectives can be indicated either by a function word (*more*) or by an affix (*-er*). For this reason,

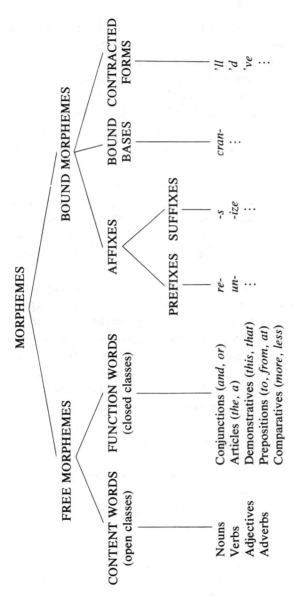

Figure 3.2
Summary of the classification of morphemes

function words and affixes are sometimes grouped together as *grammatical morphemes*.

3.2 HOW ARE NEW WORDS CREATED?

One of the more interesting ways to approach the questions and problems of morphology is to explore the question, How are new words created? By examining the processes involved in the creation of new words, we may be able to discover basic and general principles of word formation.

Coining of New Words

First of all, entirely new, previously nonexistent words can and do enter a language. This often happens when speakers invent (or *coin*) new words to name previously nonexistent objects that result from technological change. For example, coined words such as *radar, laser, kleenex,* and *xerox* are very recent additions to the English language.

The words *radar* and *laser* are *acronyms:* each of the letters that spell the word is the first letter (or letters) of some other complete word. For example, *radar* derives from *radio detecting and ranging,* and *laser* derives from *light amplification (by) stimulated emission (of) radiation.* It is important to note that even though such words are originally created as acronyms, speakers quickly forget such origins and the acronyms become new independent words.

The process of forming acronyms is just one of the processes of abbreviation, or shortening, that is becoming increasingly more powerful in American society (and perhaps internationally) as a means of word formation. For many Americans, one-time abbreviations such as *TV* have come to replace longer words, such as *television,* in most styles of casual speech—a new, previously nonexistent word has come into use. Various forms of identity cards are now simply called *ID;* venereal disease is widely referred to as *VD;* and although it was once a joke to use *OJ* to refer to orange juice, the word is beginning to come into wider use. Abbreviations such as *prof* for *professor, math* for *mathematics, gas* for *gasoline,* and so on, are in common use now (such shortenings are sometimes referred to as *clippings,* since the words have been "clipped" short).

No account of coined words would be complete, of course, without reference to possibly the most famous word in the English language,

Table 3.1
Some types of compounds in English

Noun + Noun	Adjective + Noun	Preposition + Noun	Verb + Noun
landlord	lowrider	overdose	hit-man
bathroom	high chair	outrigger	swearword
movie star	blackboard	onlooker	pickpocket
ape-man	sickroom	underdog	scarecrow

one that has become an international vocabulary item: *OK*. Dozens of theories have been advanced to explain the origin of this word. According to one theory, *OK* stands for *Old Kinderhook,* the name of a Democratic party organization, abbreviated as the O. K. Club, which supported President Van Buren for reelection in 1840 (Kinderhook being Van Buren's birthplace in New York State). According to another theory, OK stands for *oll korrect,* a parody spelling of *all correct.* The word *OK* is attested in American English as early as the 1830s, and there is some speculation that it may have been connected with another abbreviation, *D.K.,* for *don't know.* In any event, all of the theories seem equally dubious. The important point is that words such as *OK* and *TV* are felt to be complete words and not merely abbreviations, as evidenced by the fact that in casual styles of writing we now see spellings like *okay* and *teevee.*

The words *kleenex* and *xerox* represent another technique of coining previously nonexistent words, namely, using specific brand names of products as names for the products in general. Hence, *kleenex,* a brand name for facial tissue, has come to denote facial tissue in general. *Xerox* is the name of the corporation that produces a well-known photocopying machine, and much to the dismay of the company, the term *xerox* has lost its specific brand-name connotation and has come to be used to describe the process of photocopying in general. Hence, in casual speech we can commit the grave sin of talking about buying an IBM *xerox* machine.

New words can also be formed from existing ones by various *blending* processes, for example creating blends such as *motel* (from *motor hotel*), selectric (from *select* and *electric*), and *brunch* (from *breakfast* and *lunch*).

Adjective + Adjective	Noun + Adjective	Preposition + Adjective	Preposition + Verb
red-hot	nationwide	overripe	outrun
widespread	earthbound	underprivileged	overdo
blue-green	heartbroken	ingrown	uproot
bittersweet	skin-deep	above-mentioned	underfeed

Compounds and Compounding

In English (as in many other languages) new words can be formed from already existing words by a process known as *compounding,* in which individual words can be "joined together" to form a *compound* word, as illustrated in table 3.1. For example, the noun *ape* can be joined with the noun *man* to form the compound noun *ape-man;* the adjective *sick* can be joined with the noun *room* to form the compound noun *sickroom;* the adjective *red* can be joined with the adjective *hot* to form the compound adjective *red-hot;* and so on, for other examples shown in table 3.1, which lists some major types of compounds found in English (following Selkirk 1982).

Generally speaking, the part of speech of the whole compound is the same as the part of speech of the *rightmost* member of the compound, which is termed the *head* of the compound (Selkirk 1982). For example, the rightmost member (the "head") of the compound *high chair* is a noun (the noun *chair*); hence, the whole compound *high chair* is also a noun. The rightmost member of the compound *overdo* is a verb (the verb *do*); hence, the whole compound is also a verb.

Compounds are not limited to two words, as shown by examples such as *bathroom towel-rack* and *mother-in-law*. Indeed, the process of compounding seems unlimited in English: starting with a word like *sailboat,* we can easily construct *sailboat rigging, sailboat rigging design, sailboat rigging design training, sailboat rigging design training institute,* and so on.

Notice that in written English, compounds can be spelled as a single word (*bathroom*), as a hyphenated word (*ape-man*), or as two separate words (*high jump*). There is no general rule for how a compound should be spelled; one must simply be aware that the English spelling system does not reflect the difference between simple words and compound words in any systematic way.

Certain compounds have a characteristic stress pattern (accent pattern). For example, in compound nouns consisting of two words the main stress (position of heaviest accent) comes on the *leftmost* member of the compound. The compound noun *movie star* is pronounced *MOVIE star* (where capital letters indicate the location of the heaviest accent), not *movie STAR;* the compound noun *bathroom* is pronounced *BATHroom,* not *bathROOM.* The stress pattern can sometimes be a clue to whether a sequence of two words is a compound noun or not. For example, the sequence *high* and *chair* can be pronounced either *HIGH chair,* in which case it is a compound noun denoting a special kind of chair that babies sit in; or it can be pronounced *high CHAIR,* in which case it is simply the noun *chair* modified by the adjective *high,* denoting some chair that happens to be high (not necessarily a baby's high chair).

Although the meaning of a complex word such as *trees* is a combination of the meaning of its parts, the meaning of compounds cannot always be predicted in this way. For example, consider the contrast between the compounds *alligator shoes* and *horseshoes:* alligator shoes are shoes made from alligator hide; yet horseshoes are not shoes made from horsehide, but rather are iron "shoes" for horses' hooves. Similarly, a *salt pile* is a pile made up of salt, but a *saltshaker* is not a shaker made of salt. The compound *Bigfoot* refers to a mythical creature with large feet; but the compound *bigwig* does not refer to a large wig. Nevertheless, certain generalizations can be made about the meaning of compounds. For example, an *apron string* is a kind of string, whereas a *string apron* is a kind of apron; in other words, the meaning of the head of the compound seems to be central in the meaning of the whole compound, at least for certain kinds of compounds (Selkirk 1982).

Compounding is a rich source of new words in English, and many compounds are numbered among recent additions to the language, such as *spaceman, moon-walk, hot tub, pothead,* and many others.

Word Formation Rules

A very important means of word formation involves building up complex words from base morphemes and affixes. As an illustration, consider what are called *agentive nouns,* formed by adding the suffix *-er* to verbs:

(2)

Verb	Agentive Noun (V + *er*)
(to) write	writer
(to) kill	killer
(to) play	player
(to) win	winner
(to) run	runner
(to) farm	farmer
(to) open	opener
(to) scrape	scraper
(to) roll	roller
(to) level	leveler

The derived noun form means roughly "one who does *X*," or "an instrument that does *X*," where *X* is the meaning of the verb. Suppose that a new verb enters the English language, such as the verb *to xerox*. Native speakers of English automatically know that this verb can be converted into an agentive noun, *xeroxer*. This word would be perfectly natural in a sentence such as *If you want to get that copied, you'll have to see John, because he's our xeroxer around here*. Hence, the process of agentive noun formation (using the suffix *-er*) establishes a relationship between verbs and nouns. The study of how affixes combine with stems to *derive* new words is known as *derivational morphology,* and affixes such as the *-er* agentive suffix are known as *derivational affixes*.

There is evidence from many languages of the world that word formation follows systematic morphological principles. That is, there are rules by which complex words are built up from simpler words and morphemes and, conversely, rules by which complex words can be analyzed into simpler ones. We will examine the general process of word formation by examining in detail one such process in English, namely, the word formation rule for the derivational suffix *-able*. Consider the following sets of words:

(3)

(to) read	readable
(to) wash	washable
(to) break	breakable
(to) drink	drinkable
(to) pay	payable
(to) move	movable
(to) excuse	excusable

In the left-hand column is a set of verbs; in the right-hand column those same verbs have the derivational suffix *-able* attached to them. There is an obvious systematic relation between the words in the two columns. To native speakers of English who know the words listed in the left-hand column, many features of the words in the right-hand column are completely predictable. That is, the relation between *read* and *readable* is not arbitrary—rather, the suffix *-able* is a morpheme that is used in a highly systematic way. What are the various effects of the *-able* suffix? In what basic ways are the verbs changed when *-able* is added?

Obviously, there is a phonological change, which in this case is quite straightforward: when the *-able* suffix is added, the pronunciation of the verb must be augmented by a certain sequence of sounds that we can transcribe with the symbols *-əbl* (where the phonetic symbol *ə* stands for the vowel sound, spelled as *a,* in the suffix *-able*). With other derivational suffixes the phonological change is not so trivial. For example, when *-ion* is added to verbs, it triggers sound-changes in the verb stem itself:

(4)
deci*d*e   deci*s*ion
rela*t*e   rela*t*ion (*ti* pronounced as *sh*)

The suffix *-able* introduces another obvious change when it is added to a word. Note that when *-able* attaches to verbs, the resulting words are adjectives (and hence can modify nouns):

(5)
a. This book is readable.   (Compare: This book is blue.)
b. a readable book   (Compare: a blue book)

The suffix *-able* introduces a new element of meaning, roughly "able to be X'd," where X is the meaning of the verb. For example, *breakable* means roughly "able to be broken," *movable* means "able to be moved," and so on. Thus, at least three changes are associated with this suffix:

(6)
a. a phonological change (sound change)
b. a category change (part-of-speech change)
c. a semantic change (meaning change)

Other facts reveal that there are certain restrictions on the use of *-able*. For example, if we wish to express the idea that man is mortal, we cannot say *Man is dieable*. If a car is able to go, we nevertheless cannot say that it is *goable;* if John and Mary are able to cry, they are still not *cryable*. It is all too tempting to suppose that these cases are somehow exceptions or that no rule governs the data in question. But if we compare the columns in (7), a generalization emerges:

(7)

Verbs taking *-able*	Verbs not taking *-able*
read	die
break	go
wash	cry
ply	sleep
mend	rest
debate	weep
use	sit
drive	run
spray	stand

The verbs on the left are *transitive*—they occur with object noun phrases—whereas the verbs on the right are *intransitive*—they do not occur with objects. For example:

(8)
a. Pat <u>read</u> <u>the book</u>.   (*read + the book = transitive*
      | | *verb + object*)
   verb   object

b. Terry <u>broke</u> <u>the dish</u>.
         | |
       verb   object

c. John <u>washed</u> <u>his clothes</u>.
         | |
       verb   object

(9)
a. Pat died.   (*died = intransitive verb* with no following object)
b. Terry went.
c. John cried.

It seems to be the case that *-able* attaches only to transitive verbs, not to intransitive verbs.

An interesting relation emerges between sentences with transitive verbs and sentences with corresponding -*able* words. A comparison of the following examples will reveal what is going on:

(10)
a. We can read <u>these books</u>.   (*these books* = object of the verb *read*)

b. <u>These books</u> are readable.   (*these books* = subject of *are readable*)

(11)
a. We can wash <u>these clothes</u>.

b. <u>These clothes</u> are washable.

(12)
a. We can drive <u>this car</u>.

b. <u>This car</u> is drivable.

The relation that emerges is this: the subject of each (b) sentence corresponds to the object in the corresponding (a) sentence. In other words, the subject of V + *able* is always understood as the object (that which "undergoes" the action) of V. For this reason, if (at a tennis match) we say *Kim isn't beatable,* we mean that no other player can beat Kim (*Kim* is understood as the object of *beat*); we do not mean that Kim is unable to beat other players.

We can now state the -*able* word formation rule as follows:

(13)
a. *Phonological change:* When -*able* is attached to a base, the pronunciation of the base is augmented by the phonetic sequence -*əbl*.
b. *Category change:* -*able* is attached to transitive verbs and converts them into adjectives.
c. *Semantic change:* If *X* is the meaning of the verb, then -*able* adds the meaning "able to be *X*'d."

In general, then, whenever we postulate a systematic morphological relation between sets of words, we will describe (a) the systematic phonological changes, if any, (b) the category changes, (c) the semantic changes, if any, that characterize the relationship.

Not all affixes cause the sorts of changes we have observed with the *-able* suffix. For example, English has a so-called diminutive suffix, usually spelled *-y* (or *-ie*), which is added to nouns such as those in the following pairs: *dad—daddy, mom—mommy, dog—doggy, horse—horsie*. The suffix *-y* causes no phonological changes in the base word to which it is attached; it does not change the part of speech of the base (both *dad* and *daddy* are nouns); and finally, it causes no obvious semantic change (in the sense that both *dad* and *daddy* denote the same persons, except that the form *daddy* is used in baby-talk or intimate family contexts). In other words, although affixes *may* cause the types of changes we have discussed in connection with *-able*, it is not generally the case that affixes *must* cause such changes, and indeed affixes vary in the types of changes they cause in the stem to which they are attached.

Given these remarks, we can observe that word formation rules state *predictable* information about complex words. We can see this very clearly from a different point of view. Suppose someone invents a nonsense word, such as *glark*. Even though we know nothing about the meaning of this word, if we are told that *-able* can be added to *glark* to form *glarkable*, we in fact do know some very predictable things about this second word. First, we would say that *glarkable* includes the meaning "be able"; that is, it means "able to be glarked." Second, word formation rule (13) tells us that *-able* attaches to transitive verbs and converts them into adjectives. Hence, we can deduce that *glark* is a transitive verb and that *glarkable* is an adjective. Third, even though it was not mentioned in rule (13), all regular *-able* words can take the suffix *-ity* to form a corresponding abstract noun, as in the pair *readable—readability*. Hence, we can predict that *glarkability* is possible if *glarkable* is possible.

Problematic Aspects of Morphological Analysis

Productivity and Isolating the Base

Now we must face one of the hard facts of life in doing morphological analysis, namely, the exceptions or apparent exceptions to many aspects of a given analysis. For example, we have claimed that the suffix *-able* is attached only to transitive verbs. Yet English does have a small set of *nouns* that seem to occur with the same suffix *-able:*

(14)

peaceable	companionable
marriageable	impressionable
knowledgeable	actionable
saleable	reasonable
fashionable	

Does this mean that word formation rule (13) is wrong? The answer seems to be no. The nouns listed in (14) form a small, closed set, and as far as anyone can tell, few words, if any, are entering English in which -*able* is attached to a noun. Using more technical terminology, we say that the attachment of -*able* to transitive verbs is *productive*—that is, it happens quite freely—but attachment to nouns is not productive. New V + *able* forms continually enter the language, but the nouns in (14) are now fixed, or dead, expressions that are learned by rote, not formed by a productive rule.

Another general problem we must be sensitive to is the possibility of *false analysis*. Consider the following words:

(15)
hospitable
sizeable

Even though these words end in the phonetic sequence ∂bl, it is unlikely that we would want to analyze this sequence as the suffix -*able*. For one thing, *able* in these words does not seem to have the meaning "to be able," which is certainly a feature of regular (productive) -*able* words. For another thing, recall that the -*able* suffix can itself regularly take the suffix -*ity* to form a noun:

(16)

readable	readability
provable	provability
breakable	breakability

But this is not possible with the words listed in (15): *hospitability* and *sizeability* are not possible English words. We do not speak of the hospitability of our host or the sizeability of the crowd. In two respects, then, *able* in the words of (15) is significantly different from the productive suffix -*able;* hence, it would seem to be a false analysis to claim that the words of (15) contain the productive suffix -*able*. These words simply happen to end in a sequence spelled *able,* and they bear only an accidental resemblance to words with the real suffix -*able*.

Returning to the words in (14), we might try to make the case that these words end accidentally in the phonetic sequence əbl and that it would be a false analysis to claim that it is the -able suffix. Against this idea we note that some of the words do seem to include the meaning "be able" (for example, *marriageable* "eligible to marry"), and the -*ity* noun form *marriageability* does seem possible (although some speakers of English might well reject it). Other words of (14), however, are not so regular. In any event, in carrying out a morphological analysis we must always be careful to determine whether the processes in question are productive and whether a certain analysis might be a false analysis.

Closely related to these issues is another classic problem of morphology, namely, the case of a complex word with a recognizable suffix or prefix, attached to a base that is not an existing word of the language. For example, among the -*able* words are words such as *malleable* and *feasible*. In both cases the suffix -*able* (spelled *ible* in the second case because of a different historical origin for the suffix) has the regular meaning "be able," and in both cases the -*ity* form is possible, as in *malleability* and *feasibility*. We have no reason to suspect that *able/ible* here is not the real suffix -*able*. Yet if it is, then *malleable* must be broken down as *malle + able* and *feasible* as *feas + ible;* but there are no existing words (free morphemes) in English such as *malle* or *feas,* or even *malley* or *fease.* We thus have to allow for the existence of a complex word whose base exists only in that complex word (recall the earlier discussion of the bound base *cran-,* which occurs only in *cranberry* and a few other words).

The problems discussed so far are problems in isolating the *base* of a complex word: (a) sometimes the base (the form to which the affix is attached) comes from a closed set of forms no longer productive as the base for the word formation rule; (b) sometimes one must be alert to the possibility of a completely false analysis of the base; and (c) sometimes the base may not be an existing word. All of these problems have to do with correctly analyzing how the complex word is structured.

The Meaning of Complex Words

Another difficulty in morphological analysis is how to analyze the meaning of complex words and how to determine the relation between the meaning of an entire complex word and the meanings of its parts.

First, consider some complex words that appear to have a predictable meaning. For example, *fixable* seems to mean nothing more than "able to be fixed," *mendable* means "able to be mended," and *inflatable* means "able to be inflated." The meaning of each of these -*able* words seems to be a regular combination of the meaning of the verb stem and the simplest meaning of the *-able* suffix.

However, in other cases certain complications arise. Take, for example, the words *readable, payable, questionable,* and *washable*. The word *readable* does not mean simply "able to be read." When we say that a book is readable, we usually mean that it is well written, has a good style, and in general is a good example of some type of literature. A banker who says that a bill is payable on October 1 does not mean simply that the bill "can be paid" on that date—normally, we would understand *payable* as meaning "should be paid." If a theory or an explanation is *questionable,* it is not merely the case that it can be questioned. After all, any statement can be questioned, even very well established theories. Rather, a questionable theory or explanation is one that is, in fact, dubious and suspect. Finally, the word *washable* does not mean merely "able to be washed"; we in fact use the word in a very specialized way, to refer to certain types of objects, notably fabrics. Hence, though we can talk about washing a car, it would be somewhat odd to say that the car is washable (even if this is, strictly speaking, true). It is perfectly natural, however, to say that a shirt is washable or that the plastic parts of a table are washable (whereas the wooden parts are not).

These facts illustrate in a particularly clear way that the meanings of many complex words are not merely composites of the meanings of their parts. The word *washable* is more than a composite of *wash* and *-able;* rather, it has its own additional elements of meaning. When a word accrues some additional feature of meaning independent from its morphological origin, as *washable* has, we say that the word has undergone *semantic drift*. At least for the cases given here, the additional meaning, over and above the basic meaning of the complex word, involves a narrowing or restricting of the more general meaning of the complex word.

Inflectional versus Derivational Morphology

In the study of word formation, a distinction has often been drawn between *inflectional* and *derivational* morphology. The basis for the distinction has never been made entirely precise, but we can begin by listing the affixes of English that are referred to as *inflectional affixes* or *inflectional endings* (classified according to the part of speech each affix occurs with):

(17)
Noun inflectional suffixes
a. Plural marker *-s:* girl—girl*s* (*The girls are here*)
b. Possessive marker *'s:* Mary—Mary'*s* (*Mary's book*)
Verb inflectional suffixes
c. Third person present singular marker *-s:* bake—bake*s* (*He bakes well*)
d. Past tense marker *-ed:* wait—wait*ed* (*They waited*)
e. Progressive marker *-ing:* sing—sing*ing* (*They are singing*)
f. Past participle markers *-en* or *-ed:* beat—beat*en* (*She has beaten me*); bake—bake*d* (*He has baked a cake*)
Adjective inflectional suffixes
g. Comparative marker *-er:* fast—fast*er* (*She is faster than you*)
h. Superlative marker *-est:* fast—fast*est* (*She is fastest*)

English has only the inflectional affixes listed above, and all inflectional affixes in English are suffixes (none are prefixes, unlike the situation with derivational affixes, which include both suffixes and prefixes).

The distinction between inflectional and derivational affixes in English is based on a number of factors.

First, inflectional affixes never change the part of speech of the base morpheme to which they are attached. For example, both *eat* and *eats* are verbs; both *girl* and *girls* are nouns. In contrast, derivational affixes often change the part of speech of the base morpheme. Thus, *read* is a verb, but *readable* is an adjective. (As noted earlier though, some derivational affixes do not change part of speech: for example, derivational prefixes in English generally do not change the part of speech of the base morpheme to which they are attached, so that both *charge* and *recharge*, for instance, are verbs.) In short, an inflectional affix never changes the part of speech of its base morpheme, while a derivational affix may.

Second, inflectional and derivational suffixes occur in a certain relative order within words: namely, inflectional suffixes *follow* derivational suffixes. Thus, in *modernize—modernizes* the inflectional *-s* follows derivational *-ize*. If an inflectional suffix is added to a verb, as with *modernizes*, then no further derivational suffixes can be added. English has no form *modernizesable*, with inflectional *-s* followed by derivational *-able*. For these reasons it is often noted that inflectional affixes mark the "outer" layer of words, while derivational affixes mark the "inner" layer. These properties of derivational and inflectional affixes are summarized in table 3.2, which provides a morphological analysis of sample words containing selected English suffixes. (In the table we have ignored certain features of spelling; for example, *read* + *able* + *ity* is spelled *readability*.)

Intuitively, the function of certain derivational affixes is to create new base forms (new *stems*) that other derivational or inflectional affixes can attach to. Thus, the suffix *-ize* creates verbs from adjectives, and such *-ize* verbs, like other verbs, can have the inflectional ending *-s* attached to them. In this sense, then, certain derivational affixes create new members for a given part-of-speech class, whereas inflectional affixes always attach to already existing members of a given part-of-speech class. This intuitive distinction is reflected in the scheme shown in table 3.2.

Finally, inflectional and derivational affixes can be distinguished in terms of semantic relations. In the case of inflectional affixes, the relation between the meaning of the stem morpheme and the meaning of the stem + affix is quite regular. Hence, the meaning difference between *tree* and *trees* (singular versus plural) is paralleled quite regularly in other similar pairs of nouns and noun + plural affix combinations. In contrast, in the case of derivational affixes the relation between the

Table 3.2
Relative order of derivational and inflectional suffixes, with morphological analysis of sample words

Sample Word	Base ("Stem")	Derivational Suffixes ("Inner Layer")	Inflectional Suffixes ("Outer Layer")
modern	modern		
modernize	modern	ize	
modernizes	modern	ize	s (3rd person)
modernizers	modern	ize + er	s (plural)
write	write		
writer	write	er	
writer's	write	er	's (possessive)
readability	read	able + ity	
reading	read		ing (progressive)
big	big		
bigger	big		er (comparative)
biggest	big		est (superlative)
friend	friend		
friendly	friend	ly	
friendlier	friend	ly	er (comparative)

meaning of the base morpheme and the meaning of the base + affix is sometimes unpredictable, as we have seen. For example, the pair *fix* and *fixable* shows a simple meaning relation ("*X*" and "able to be *X*'d"); but recall pairs such as *read—readable* or *wash—washable*, where the *-able* form has undergone semantic drift and has accrued new elements of meaning beyond the simple combination of the meaning of the base and the meaning of *-able*. Such semantic drift is generally not found in cases of a base + inflectional affix, so that a word such as *trees* is simply the plural of *tree* and has not accrued any additional meaning.

Note that derivational and inflectional affixes can sometimes be identical in form. For example, *-ing* is an inflectional suffix that is attached to verbs. Thus, *-ing* can be attached to the verb *write* to form the verb *writing*, as in the sentence *I am writing*. However, there is also a derivational suffix *-ing*, which is attached to verbs to form a corresponding noun. For example, the verb *write* can be changed into a noun, *writing*, as in the sentence *Her writings are brilliant*. Notice that in this case the suffix *-ing* changes a verb into a noun, and this part-of-speech change leads us to classify *-ing* as a derivational suffix.

To sum up, then, inflectional affixes indicate certain grammatical functions of words (such as plurality or tense); they occur in a certain order relative to derivational affixes; and they are not associated with certain changes that are associated with derivational affixes (such as part-of-speech changes or unpredictable meaning changes). Inflectional affixes are often discussed in terms of word sets called *paradigms*. For example, the various forms that verbs can take (*bake—bakes—baking*) form a set of words known as a *verb paradigm*. Verb paradigms in English are rather simple compared to such paradigms in, say, the Romance languages (Italian, French, Spanish, Portuguese, and others) or Latin (in which, for example, a verb such as *amāre* "to love" is said to have at least 100 inflectional forms, including *amō* "I love," *amās* "thou lovest," *amat* "he loves," *amāmus* "we love," *amem* "I may love," *amāverint* "they will have loved," *amābāmur* "we were being loved," and so on).

Backformation

As we have seen, given a newly created verb such as *to xerox*, we can create another new word, *xeroxable*, based on the word formation rule for *-able*. In this way, word formation rules are not merely artificial creations of linguists; they correspond to processes used by speakers to create new words.

A particularly interesting case illustrating the "psychological reality" of morphological rules is a phenomenon known as *backformation*, in which word formation processes are reversed. We can illustrate backformation with the following examples, taken from Williams 1975. It is a historical fact about English that the nouns *pedlar, beggar, hawker, stoker, scavenger, swindler, editor, burglar, sculptor,* and *aggressor* all existed in the language before the corresponding verbs *to peddle, to beg, to hawk, to stoke, to scavenge, to swindle, to edit, to burgle, to sculpt,* and *to aggress.* Each of these nouns denoted a general profession or activity, and speakers simply assumed that the ending on the nouns was the agentive suffix *-er.* Having made this assumption, speakers could then subtract the final *-er* and arrive at a new verb—just as we can subtract the *-er* affix on *writer* and arrive at the verb *write.* This process of using a word formation rule to analyze a word as if it were a complex word in order to arrive at a simpler form is called *backformation.*

An interesting contemporary example of backformation with the agentive suffix involves the word *laser.* Recall that this word is an acronym; it ends in *er* only because *e* stands for *emission* and *r* stands for *radiation* (*l*ight *a*mplification (by) *s*timulated *e*mission (of) *r*adiation). Speakers quickly forget such origins, though, and before long physicists had invented the verb *to lase,* used in sentences such as *This dye, under the appropriate laboratory conditions, will lase,* where *to lase* refers to emitting radiation of a certain sort. The *er* on *laser* accidentally resembles the agentive suffix *-er,* and the word itself denotes an instrument; hence, physicists took this *er* sequence to be the agentive suffix and subtracted it to form a new verb.

Other examples cited in Williams 1975 are as follows:

(18)

Existed earlier	Formed later by backformation
resurrection	to resurrect
preemption	to preempt
vivisection	to vivisect
electrocution	to electrocute
television	to televise
emotion	to emote
donation	to donate

It is ironic that even the word *backformation* is undergoing backforma-tion. The technical linguistic term *backformation* existed in English first, and now one hears fellow linguists saying things such as *Speakers backformed word X from word Y,* creating a new verb in English, *to backform.* What is happening in all these cases is that speakers recog-nize that the ending *-ion* is used to create abstract nouns from verbs (for example, *to instruct—instruction*). Hence, they can take nouns ending in *-ion,* factor out the ending, and arrive back at a verb, which has a simpler morphological shape (that is, it lacks the ending).

Finally, a slightly different sort of backformation has applied to the word *cranberry.* Until very recently in American English, the *cran-* of *cranberry* existed in that word alone. In fact, linguists coined the term *cranberry morph* for bound bases, such as *cran-,* that occur in only one word of a language. Currently, however, even though the morpheme *cran-* is not yet an independent word, speakers of English have begun using it in other words besides *cranberry.* In particular, the fruit juice section of any supermarket will now reveal new linguistic blends such as *cranapple, cranicot,* and *cranprune,* all referring to juice mixtures. By subtracting the recognizable morpheme *berry* from *cranberry,* speakers have extended the use of the morpheme *cran-* by backforma-tion, using it in various new blends.

In sum, these cases show that morphological rules and analyses are not simply abstract aspects of morphological theory. In actuality, speakers produce (and hearers understand) new words using proce-dures corresponding to these rules and analyses.

Meaning Extensions: Metaphorical Extension, Broadening, and Narrowing

In this chapter we have discussed various ways in which new words can be created and added to a language. Thus far, we have focused our attention on morphological processes by which new words can be cre-ated. In closing the chapter, we will examine a set of processes that do not involve morphological mechanisms (such as affixation), but instead involve modification (or extension) of the meaning of already existing words, thereby creating new uses for old words.

When a language does not seem to have just the right expression for certain purposes, speakers often take an existing one and extend its meaning in a recognizable way. The language does not gain a new word as such, but since a word is being used in a new way, the language has been augmented, as though a new word has been added. Let us consider an example. Even though space exploration is a relatively recent phenomenon in human history, it is interesting to note that speakers of English have adopted many existing terms from the realm of ocean navigation to use in speaking of space exploration. For example, we use the word *ship* to refer to space vehicles as well as to ocean-going vessels; we speak of a spaceship *docking* with another in a way related to the way an ocean-going ship docks; we speak of *navigation* in both types of transportation; we could certainly speak of a spaceship *sailing* through space, even though no sails or wind are involved; we speak of certain objects as *floating* in space and of ships as floating on water; we speak of a *captain* and a *crew* for both kinds of ships; and we have carried over the names of ship parts, such as *hull, cabin, hatch,* and (at least on television shows) *deck.* It is striking that terms that basically derive from the historical epoch of wind-powered ocean navigation have with great ease been *extended* into the realm of space navigation. The technology in the two realms is radically different, yet we apparently perceive enough similarities to use already existing terms, in new ways, to describe the new phenomena. This is an important fact, for it shows that technological changes in a society will not necessarily result in the addition of previously nonexistent words to its language. Indeed, speakers of all human languages show great creativity and imaginative power in extending the existent language into new realms of experience.

The example just given is a case of *metaphorical extension,* in which certain objects, ideas, or events from one realm are described with words from a different realm of objects, ideas, and events. The metaphorical extension, if successful, becomes part of the conventional linguistic meaning of the word(s) in question. Another interesting case is the metaphorical extension of words from the physical realm of food and digestion into the mental realm of ideas and interpersonal exchange of ideas. For example, consider the following sentences:

(19)
a. Let me *chew on* these ideas for a while.
b. They just wouldn't *swallow* that idea.
c. She'll give us time to *digest* that idea.
d. On the exam, please don't merely *regurgitate* what I've told you.
e. He *bit off* more than he could chew. (Speaking of someone's research project.)

f.   Let's make them the offer and see if they *nibble* at it; after all, it is pretty good *bait*. (From the realm of fishing as well as food.)

g.   Will you stop *feeding* me that old line!

h.   You'd better *cook up* a good story this time!

i.   He's such a hypocrite—I don't see how he can say those pious things without *gagging* on his words.

j.   Her proposal left a *bad taste* in my mouth.

k.   Let's start examining the really *meaty* ideas—something we can *sink our teeth* into.

l.   She's really *hungry* for knowledge.

m.   I think that *spicy* ideas are better than *bland* thoughts.

n.   Let's *chew the fat*.

o.   My lecture was pure nonsense, but they really *ate it up*.

p.   What she says is *food for thought,* but it gives us only a *taste* of what she means.

q.   Where were you last night? Come on, *spit it out!*

r.   I wish they would stop *spoon-feeding* us these *predigested, half-baked* ideas.

In these examples, one realm (roughly, a realm involving ideas) is described in terms of words from another realm (food and digestion). A feature of this particular case is that words from a physical realm are being extended into a mental realm, perhaps because the physical vocabulary provides a familiar and public frame of reference for discussing our private mental life.

Metaphorical extension is not the only mechanism by which already existing words can be put to new uses. Sometimes the use of existing words can become *broader*. For example, the slang word *cool* was originally part of the professional jargon of jazz musicians and referred to a specific artistic style of jazz (a use that was itself an extension). With the passage of time, the word has come to be applied to almost anything conceivable, not just music; and it no longer refers just to a certain genre or style, but is a general term indicating approval of the thing in question.

Conversely, the use of a word can *narrow* as well. A typical example is the word *meat*. At one time in English it meant any solid consumable food (a meaning that persists in the word *nutmeat*), but now it is used to refer only to the edible solid flesh of animals.

Finally, *reversals* of meanings can occur. In certain varieties of American slang the word *bad* has come to have positive connotations, with roughly the meaning "emphatically good." Hollywood movies of the '30s and '40s reveal that the words *square* and *straight* had positive connotations, meaning "honest" and "upright," meanings that survive in the phrases *square deal* and *play it straight*. During the late '50s and into the '60s, the word *square* came to have a negative connotation, referring to anyone or anything hopelessly conventional and uncomprehending of "in" things. By the late '60s this use of *square* had itself come to be regarded as old-fashioned and the word dropped out of favor (which, incidentally, illustrates the rapid rate at which so-called slang terms enter and leave a language). In the same period the word *straight* came to be used in a wide range of areas, always with the general meaning of adhering to conventional norms: for example, a straight person is one who doesn't take drugs; who is heterosexual rather than homosexual; who is generally "out of it," and so on.

We have discussed various kinds of extensions and modifications of meaning as a way to create new uses for already existing words. Although this is one of the most interesting areas of word meaning, we unfortunately have very little understanding of the exact mechanisms of meaning change and extension. For one thing, we have very little idea *what* the meaning of a word is: Is the meaning an abstract idea, a concept? Is it an image? When we describe the meaning of the word, are we describing the thing that the word denotes? Or is meaning best described neither as an idea nor as a referent, but rather as the *use* of a word in some context? We discuss these possibilities in more detail in chapter 6, which deals with semantics. Suffice it to say here that because we do not know precisely *what* the meaning of a word is and because theories of the psychology of human thought are still at a rudimentary level, we can currently say very little about the exact nature of metaphorical extension or other meaning shifts. However, this area, especially the study of so-called slang, will be extremely important for future research because it provides fundamental evidence about speakers' linguistic creativity.

Key Words

lexicon
simple word
complex word
morpheme
bound morpheme

free morpheme
affix
base
parts of speech
content word
function word
open class
closed class
coined words
compound
word formation rule
derivational morphology
inflectional morphology
backformation
meaning extensions

Exercises

1. In this chapter we noted that *radar* and *laser* are acronyms. List three other recent English words that are acronyms and state their origin.

2. List three additional recent words that, like *TV* or *ID*, are abbreviations of longer words, and state their origin.

3. For the purposes of this exercise, use only the words in the following list:
sidewalk
daughter
laugh
cactus
alligator
A. Using these words, invent five new compounds of English, and state the meaning of each one.
B. What would you guess is a possible meaning of the compound *sidewalk-alligator laugh?*
C. What is the "head" of the compound listed in question B? State the reason(s) for your answer.

4. State the part(s) of speech that each of the following words belongs to:

a. massive   g. fortunately
b. friend   h. modify
c. friendly   i. wealthy
d. friendliness   j. smoking
e. over   k. killed
f. pilot   l. beside

In each case, list some grammatical properties of the word as justification for your answer. Follow the format of the example below. (Review section 3.1.)

Example

Word	Part of Speech	Justification
readable	Adjective	a. Can be modified by *very,* as in *very readable*. b. Can modify a noun, as in *readable book*.

5. In the well-known poem "Jabberwocky," Lewis Carroll coined a number of new words, as we can observe from the first stanza of the poem:

'Twas brillig, and the slithy toves
Did gyre and gimble in the wabe;
All mimsy were the borogoves,
And the mome raths outgrabe.

Answer the following questions concerning this stanza:

A. To what part of speech would you assign the following coined words? Present evidence to justify your answer in each case, in the manner of exercise 4:

a. toves
b. outgrabe
c. slithy
d. mimsy

B. Review the intuitive notions given for each part-of-speech class in section 3.1. Based on these intuitive notions, what part-of-speech class would you guess that the words *gyre* and *gimble* belong to?

C. Are the coined words in the poem content words or function words? Why did the poet choose to coin the one type rather than the other type?

6. English has a suffix *-en* whose use is illustrated in the following lists:

List A	List B
red	redden
black	blacken
mad	madden
soft	soften
hard	harden
sweet	sweeten
short	shorten
wide	widen
sharp	sharpen

In regard to these data, answer the following questions:

A. What part of speech does the suffix *-en* attach to? That is, what is the part of speech of the words in list A? Give some specific grammatical properties of one of those words, to justify your answer. Follow the format of exercise 4.

B. When the suffix *-en* is attached to a word, what part of speech is the resulting word? That is, what part of speech do the words in list B belong to? As with question A, give some specific grammatical properties of one of the words in list B, in order to justify your answer.

C. In what way does the suffix *-en* change the meaning of the word it is attached to?

7. English also has a prefix *un-*, whose use is illustrated in the following lists:

List A	List B
true	untrue
likely	unlikely
acceptable	unacceptable
wise	unwise
real	unreal
common	uncommon
natural	unnatural
graceful	ungraceful
refined	unrefined
tamed	untamed

A. What part of speech are the words that the prefix *un-* attaches to? That is, what part of speech are the words in list A?

B. When *un-* is prefixed to a word, what part of speech is the resultant new word? That is, what part of speech are the words in list B?

C. In what way does the prefix *un-* change the meaning of the word it attaches to?

D. Very recently, new words such as *Uncola* (a type of soft drink) and *Uncar* (used in a bus company advertisement to refer to a bus) have been added to the English language. Given the pattern established above in lists A and B, why are words such as *Uncola* and *Uncar* "irregular"?

8. Exercise 7 involved examples of a prefix *un-* in English. Now consider a new set of data, involving another prefix *un-:*

List A	List B
tie	untie
wrap	unwrap
cover	uncover
wind	unwind
dress	undress
fold	unfold
buckle	unbuckle
lock	unlock
fasten	unfasten
stick	unstick

How does the prefix *un-* illustrated here differ from the prefix *un-* illustrated in exercise 7? To answer this, answer the following specific questions:

A. What is the part of speech of the words that this second prefix *un-* attaches to? That is, what part of speech are the words in list A? Where a given word could be classified as belonging to more than one part of speech, what is the part of speech that *un-* attaches to?

B. When this prefix *un-* is attached to a word, what part of speech does the resultant new word belong to? That is, what part of speech are the words in list B?

C. In what way does this prefix *un-* change the meaning of the word that it is attached to? Describe this meaning change as carefully as you can.

D. How is the meaning change associated with this prefix *un-* different from the meaning change associated with the prefix *un-* illustrated in exercise 7?

9. Analyze the following English words, in the manner shown in table 3.2.

a. friendliness
b. tranquilizers
c. widening
d. Mary's
e. legalizability
f. person
g. personal
h. loudest
i. electrocution
j. lasers
k. employ
l. employer
m. employee
n. writings

Use the following format:

	Base	Derivational Suffixes	Inflectional Suffixes
friend	friend		
friends	friend		s
friendly	friend	ly	
friendlier	friend	ly	er

10. For this exercise, consider the following data from Turkish:

el "the hand"
eller "hands"
elim "my hand"
ev "the house"
eve "to the house"
ellerimiz "our hands"
ellerimde "in my hands"
evlerde "in the houses"
evden "from the house"
ellerim "my hands"
ellerinize "to your (pl.) hands"
evlerim "my houses"
elin "your (sing.) hand"

evimiz "our house"
evde "in the house"
elimde "in my hand"
evlerimiz "our houses"
evlerimden "from my houses"
evleriniz "your (pl.) houses"
evim "my house"
ellerimden "from my hands"
evler "houses"
eline "to your (sing.) hand"
ellerin "your (sing.) hands"
elimden "from my hand"
evine "to your (sing.) house"

In the English translations, we have listed *your* as singular (sing.) when it refers to one person, and as plural (pl.) when it refers to more than one person.

Using the data given above, answer the following questions:

A. Fill in each blank below with the appropriate Turkish morpheme:

(the) hand: _____   your (sing.): _____
(the) house: _____   your (pl.): _____
plural: _____   to: _____
my: _____   in: _____
our: _____   from: _____

B. Given the Turkish data, what is the order of the morphemes (indicating possession, person, and so forth) of the suffixes in a word?

C. Based on your answers to parts A and B, how would you translate the following English forms into Turkish?

from your (pl.) house: _____

to our houses: _____

in my house: _____

11. Consider the following data from Papago, a Native American language of southern Arizona and northern Mexico. Study the following lists carefully (from Zepeda 1983), and try to determine the relationship between the words in list A and the words in list B. What are the different morphemes that make up those words?

List A	List B
je'e "mother"	ñje'e "my mother"
'o:gĭ "father"	m'o:gĭ "your father"
kakkio "legs"	hakakkio "their legs"
no:nowĭ "hands"	'emno:nowĭ "your (pl.) hands"
'o'ohana "books"	t'o'ohana "our books"
kotoñ "shirt"	kotoñij "his/her shirt"
wopnam "hats"	twopnam "our hats"
mamgina "cars"	'emmamgina "your (pl.) cars"
papla "shovels"	hapapla "their shovels"
hoa "basket"	ñhoa "my basket"
taḍ "foot"	taḍij "his/her foot"
ki: "house"	mki: "your house"
na:nk "ears"	'emna:nk "your (pl.) ears"
to:ton "knees"	hato:ton "their knees"
we:nag "sibling"	we:nagij "his/her sibling"
si:l "saddle"	ñsi:l "my saddle"
taḍ "foot"	mtaḍ "your foot"
mo:mĭ "heads"	tmo:mĭ "our heads"
na:nk "ears"	na:nkij "his/her ears"
kakkio "legs"	'emkakkio "your (pl.) legs"
wuhi "eye"	ñwuhi "my eye"
mamgina "cars"	tmamgina "our cars"
da:k "nose"	ñda:k "my nose"
da:k "nose"	da:kij "his/her nose"

The symbol ' stands for a consonant known as a glottal stop (a sound heard between the two oh's in the English expression oh oh). The symbol : indicates that a vowel is long (hence, o: is a long o). The symbol ñ is pronounced like the Spanish ñ or the English sequence ny in the word canyon. The symbol ˘ indicates that a vowel is short (hence, ĭ is short). Finally, a dot under a consonant indicates a special pronunciation with the tongue slightly curled back.

Now answer the following questions:

A. For each of the following possessive morphemes of English, list the corresponding possessive morpheme in Papago:

my	_____
your	_____
his/her	_____
our	_____
your (pl.)	_____
their	_____

B. The Papago possessives are bound morphemes; are they prefixes or suffixes? What is special about the third person singular possessive morpheme (meaning "his/her") in Papago? (How is it *unlike* the other possessive morphemes?)

12. Consider the following verb forms from Papago:

Singular	Plural (used with a plural subject)
ñeok "speaks"	ñeñeok "we/you/they speak"
him "walks"	hihim "we/you/they walk"
dagkon "wipes"	dadagkon "we/you/they wipe"
helwuin "is sliding"	hehelwuin "we/you/they are sliding"
'ul "sticks out"	'u'ul "we/you/they stick out"

(The special symbols used in writing these Papago forms are explained in exercise 11.)

Now answer the following questions:

A. What is the name of the morphological process illustrated in the data? (Review discussion of parts of speech.)

B. Describe, as precisely as you can, how the plural verbs are formed from the singular verbs. (What must be done to a singular form in order to convert it into a plural form?)

13. Use the following two lists for this exercise:

List A

redo	regain	rebuild	resharpen
rewrite	reimport	restate	reshape
rework	reinterrogate	recalculate	rethink
reexamine	rerelease	redraw	reuse
recook	rerefine	reset	re-create
rebroadcast	retake	retool	rearrange
reorganize	repaint	relight	rediscover
reenter	refinish	refreeze	redecorate
re-form			

List B (impossible forms)

*rego	*resit
*recry	*revanish
*resleep	*rechange

State the word formation rule for the prefix *re-*. Follow the format given for the *-able* rule in this chapter. In particular, answer the following questions:

A. What phonological changes, if any, does the prefix *re-* cause in the word or stem to which it is attached?

B. What part(s) of speech does the prefix *re-* attach to? Note the contrast between list A and list B. What is the difference between these sets of words?
C. When *re-* is attached to a word or stem, what is the part of speech of the resulting word or stem?
D. In general, what meaning change(s) are caused by the addition of the prefix *re-?* In the ideal case, what is the meaning that the prefix *re-* adds to the word or stem to which it is attached?
E. Can you find any words with *re-* that have erratic or unexpected meanings? (Are there any *re-* words that systematically mean more than you would expect from the simple meaning of *re-* and the simple meaning of the base?)
F. Why are the following *re-* words problematic? Discuss three of them: *reduce, reflect, refine, refuse, repeat, relax, release, renew, replicate, revive, remember*.

14. Use the following word lists for this exercise:

List A

equalize	Italianize	Christianize
mobilize	actualize	animalize
personalize	familiarize	immortalize
legalize	fertilize	modernize
generalize	humanize	
centralize	constitutionalize	
naturalize		
federalize		
Americanize		

List B	List C
symbolize	dramatize
alphabetize	democratize
atomize	hypnotize
scandalize	colonize
revolutionize	energize
magnetize	harmonize
alcoholize	
fossilize	
crystallize	

State the word formation rule for the suffix *-ize*, using the format of exercise 13. In particular, answer the following questions:
A. What phonological change(s), if any, does the suffix *-ize* cause in the word or stem to which it is attached? Compare lists A, B, and C in order to answer this question.
B. What part(s) of speech does the suffix *-ize* attach to? Again, compare the lists to answer this.
C. When *-ize* is attached to a word or stem, what is the part of speech of the resulting word or stem?
D. In general, what is the meaning change caused by the suffix *-ize?* That is, in the ideal case, what element(s) of meaning will be contributed by the *-ize* suffix?

E. Are any of the *-ize* words listed above problematic for question D? (Are there any *-ize* words with erratic or unexpected meanings?)

F. Why are the following *-ize* words problematic? Discuss two of them: *galvanize, moralize. organize, scrutinize, winterize, weatherize*.

15. For this exercise, consider the following word lists:

List A	List B
repress	repressive
oppress	oppressive
impress	impressive
select	selective
express	expressive
progress	progressive
regress	regressive
prevent	preventive
elude	elusive
recede	recessive
permit	permissive
submit	submissive
deceive	deceptive
produce	productive

State the word formation rule for the suffix *-ive,* using the format of exercises 13 and 14. Pay careful attention to the phonological changes that *-ive* causes in the stem to which it is attached.

16. Discuss the meaning of the words *unthinkable* and *unbreakable.* The meaning of these complex words is more than the simple sum of the meaning of their parts. State why this is so, and discuss the relation, if any, between these words and the words of a similar nature discussed in the chapter (*readable, questionable, payable, washable*).

17. Words referring to spending and finances (such as *cost, spend, invest, buy, sell*) also have abstract metaphorical uses, as in *That mistake will cost you a lot, He invested a lot of time in the project, He paid dearly for his ways, You're only buying trouble if you do that.* List three additional examples of the metaphorical use of words from the realm of finance and discuss how the metaphorical uses are related to the concrete (financial) meanings.

18. Suppose a speaker of English invents the following italicized English words, as a joke: "They're always causing a commotion. I tell them not to *commote,* but they insist on being big *commoters.*" What process of word creation does this example illustrate, and why? What do the new words mean?

19. For open discussion. There is no single answer that is necessarily correct; however, try to provide specific evidence for your answer.

A. A classified advertisement for a racing car states that the car is customized for racing, but that it is also *streetable.* What would you guess is the meaning of *streetable* in this context? Why is the word *streetable* an apparent exception to the word formation rule for *-able* stated in the text? Is there any way to analyze *streetable* so that it would not be an exception to the *-able* rule?

B. The examples discussed in this chapter showed that affixes are attached to single words or single stems. In light of this, what can we say about the following forms, heard in informal speech?

a. move aroundable
b. pay backable
c. look upable

In these cases, it seems that *-able* is being attached to a two-word expression (*move around, pay back, look up*). In effect, the two-word expressions are behaving like single "words" in taking the suffix *-able*. Can you think of any further evidence that such two-word expressions should be analyzed as single "units" of some sort? (Consider, among other things, what part-of-speech class these "units" would belong to.)

20. For open discussion. We have already observed that a word such as *singing* can be classified either as a verb or as a noun, depending on the grammatical properties it has in its various uses. Now notice that the word *singing* (as well as many other *-ing* words of the type cited below) can be used in phrases such as:

a. the *singing* bird
b. a *flying* plane
c. a *crying* baby
d. the *limping* horse

Since the italicized *-ing* words all modify nouns, we would be led, as a first guess, to classify them as adjectives in the above examples. Note, however, that in traditional grammars, *-ing* words such as these, which can function both as verbs and as adjectives, are referred to as *participles*. In this way, traditional grammars distinguish between adjectives and *-ing* participles, despite the fact that the participles are used like adjectives in examples such as (a)–(d). Is there any justification for distinguishing participles and adjectives? That is, should these be distinct grammatical categories? (Hint: Can you think of any tests that would show that participles are distinct from adjectives?)

Bibliography

Adams, V. (1973). *An Introduction to Modern English Word Formation,* Longman, London.

Aronoff, M. (1976). *Word Formation in Generative Grammar,* MIT Press, Cambridge, Mass.

Bloomfield, L. (1933). *Language,* Holt, Rinehart and Winston, New York. (See chaps. 13 and 14.)

Bradley, D. C., M. F. Garrett, and E. B. Zurif (1980). "Syntactic deficits in Broca's aphasia," in D. Caplan, ed. (1980).

Caplan, D., ed. (1980). *Biological Studies of Mental Processes,* MIT Press, Cambridge, Mass.

Jackendoff, R. S. (1975). "Morphological and semantic regularities in the lexicon," *Language* 51, 639–671.

Janda, R. (Forthcoming). "The note-taking variety of English as a simplified register," *Discourse Processes*.

Jespersen, O. (1911). *A Modern English Grammar,* Allen and Unwin, London. (See vol. VI.)

Marchand, H. (1969). *The Categories and Types of Present-Day English Word-Formation,* 2nd ed., Beck, Munich.

Matthews, P. H. (1972). *Inflectional Morphology,* Cambridge University Press, Cambridge.

Matthews, P. H. (1974). *Morphology: An Introduction to the Theory of Word Structure,* Cambridge University Press, Cambridge.

Sapir, E. (1921). *Language,* Harcourt, Brace & World, New York. (See chap. 4.)

Selkirk, E. O. (1982). *The Syntax of Words,* MIT Press, Cambridge, Mass.

Williams, J. M. (1975). *Origins of the English Language,* Free Press, New York.

Zepeda, O. (1983). *Papago Grammar,* University of Arizona Press, Tucson.

Chapter Four

PHONOLOGY: THE
STRUCTURE AND
PATTERNING OF THE
SOUNDS OF
LANGUAGE

4.1 SOME BACKGROUND CONCEPTS

Phonology is the subfield of linguistics that studies the structure and systematic patterning of sounds in human language. Part of phonology involves an investigation of how speech sounds are produced (*articulated*) in the vocal tract (an area known as *articulatory phonetics*), as well as the study of the physical properties of the speech sound-waves generated by the vocal tract (an area known as *acoustic phonetics*). Whereas the term *phonetics* usually refers to the study of the articulatory and acoustic properties of sounds, the term *phonology* is often used to refer to the abstract rules and principles that govern the distribution of sounds in a language. In this chapter we will first focus our attention on articulatory phonetics and the ways in which speech sounds are produced in the vocal tract. We will then discuss some of the systematic ways in which sounds pattern in human language. The focus of this chapter will be on articulation rather than the acoustic properties of speech sounds; for further information on acoustic phonetics, see Ladefoged 1982.

How does one begin the study of phonology? What properties of sounds and sound patterns are we looking for? Perhaps the best way to begin answering such questions is to take a sample problem in phonology in order to see what phonological units and principles of combination we must postulate in order to solve it. That is, to account for the structure of words we found that we needed to isolate certain discrete units (morphemes) and certain principles for combining those units (word formation rules). In phonology we will find the same general analytical approach to be useful, just as we will later in the study of syntax and semantics.

In chapter 3 we discussed the English plural morpheme -*s,* as if that suffix had a single form for all the nouns that it is attached to. But it turns out that the plural morpheme does not always have the same pronunciation when affixed to nouns. In fact, a clue for this is the fact that the plural suffix is represented in two different ways by the English writing system: either as *s* (as in *cats*) or *es* (as in *bushes*), a spelling difference that—in this case—reflects an actual difference in pronunciation. The plural morpheme in *cats* is an "*s*-sound," whereas in *bushes* it consists of a *vowel* plus a "*z*-sound." That is, the last sound in *bushes* is more like the initial consonant in *zing* than the initial consonant in *sing,* even though the written form of the plural has the letter *s.* Moreover, the plural morpheme is pronounced as a single *z*-sound (that is, without a preceding vowel) in words such as *dogs.* The plural morpheme can therefore have three different pronunciations: an *s*-sound, used with words such as *cats;* a *z*-sound, used with words such as *dogs;* and *vowel* + *z,* used with words such as *bushes,* as summarized in table 4.1.

The question now arises: what governs the variation in pronunciation shown in table 4.1? What principles, if any, can we use to *predict* what form of the plural morpheme a given noun will take? Such questions are typical of phonological problems. Given certain *alternations* in pronunciation (such as those exemplified by the plural morpheme), are there any principles that can account for these alternations? As a major focus of this chapter, we will attempt to answer such questions for the English plural alternation, concentrating on two aspects of phonology, one more specific and one more general. On the one hand, phonology deals with that part of the grammar of a *specific* language describing the sounds of that language and the rules governing the distribution of those sounds. On the other hand, phonology also deals with that part of the general theory of human language concerning itself with universal properties of sound systems (that is, properties reflected in many, if not all, human languages). Thus, in this chapter we will describe a specific portion of the phonology of English, but we will also discuss aspects of

Table 4.1
Different pronunciations of the English plural morpheme

Example Word	cats	dogs	bushes
Pronunciation of Plural Morpheme	*s*-sound	*z*-sound	vowel + *z*

the more general universal theory of phonology into which the sound pattern of English fits. In addition, we will survey some of the phonological rules that are found in most dialects of American English.

As a general strategy, we will take the alternation in pronunciation of the English plural morpheme as an organizing theme for several topics in this chapter. For example, in regard to the plural morpheme, we can ask the following questions:

What is the proper description of the three different *sounds* of the English plural morpheme shown in table 4.1?

What are the *conditions on the alternation* that will predict where the three different phonological forms of the English plural morpheme occur?

These two questions lead naturally into the more general topics of this chapter:

What is the proper description of the various sounds that are found generally in human language?

What is the proper general framework for describing the sound patterns of human language?

How Speech Sounds Are Produced

How can we describe the different pronunciations of the plural morpheme? When suffixed to, say, the morpheme *cat,* it is pronounced as a short "hissing" *s*-sound. This sound is produced by air flowing from the lungs and passing through a narrow passage between the tongue tip and the roof of the mouth. The same hissing sound characterizes the *"z"* variant of the plural morpheme (as in *dogs*), but in this case the sound is perceived as having more of a buzz.

There is, in fact, an additional noise source in the throat that accompanies the production of the *z.* Generally speaking, then, there are three aspects to the production of these sounds: (1) a flow of air from the lungs; (2) a constriction of the airflow in the mouth; (3) an additional noise source in the throat. But expressions such as "noise source in the throat" are not very precise, and in order to understand the nature of speech sounds, we need a more detailed examination of the anatomical structures involved in speech.

Physiology of Speech Production

One commonsense view is that learning to speak a language consists of learning to control (by imitation of other speakers) a few muscles that move the lips, jaw, and tongue. These anatomical structures are the most easily observed, in any case. In reality the situation is much more complex, for over 100 muscles exercise direct and continuous control during the production of the sound-waves that carry speech (Lenneberg 1967). These sound-waves are produced by a complex interaction of (1) an outward flow of air from the lungs; (2) modifications of the airflow at the larynx (the "Adam's apple" or "voice box" in the throat; see figure 4.2); and (3) additional modifications of the airflow by position and movement of the tongue and other anatomical structures of the vocal tract. We discuss each of these components in turn.

Airflow from the Lungs during Speech

The flow of air from the lungs during speech differs in several important respects from the airflow during quiet breathing. First, during speech, three to four times as much air is exhaled than during quiet breathing. Second, in speech, the normal breathing rhythm is changed radically: inhalation is more rapid and exhalation is much more drawn out. Third, the number of breaths per unit time decreases during speech. Fourth, the flow of air is unimpeded during quiet breathing, whereas in speech the airflow encounters resistance from the obstructions and closures that occur in the throat and mouth. While these alternations in the normal breathing pattern are occurring during speech, the function of breathing (exchange of oxygen and carbon dioxide) continues with no discomfort to the speaker.

One of the primary mechanisms for expanding the lungs during both quiet breathing and speech is the contraction of the diaphragm (see figure 4.1), a sheet of muscular tissue that separates the chest cavity from the abdominal region. This contraction causes the diaphragm to lower and flatten out, leading to an increase in the size of the chest cavity. The other primary mechanism for the expansion of the chest cavity is the set of muscles between the ribs in the rib cage. Since the lungs are attached to the walls of the chest cavity, when the chest cavity expands, the lungs, being elastic, also expand. As the lungs expand, the air flows in, up to the point when inhalation is completed. In quiet breathing, the diaphragm relaxes at this point, and the stretched lungs begin to shrink, allowing air to flow out quite rapidly (as with air es-

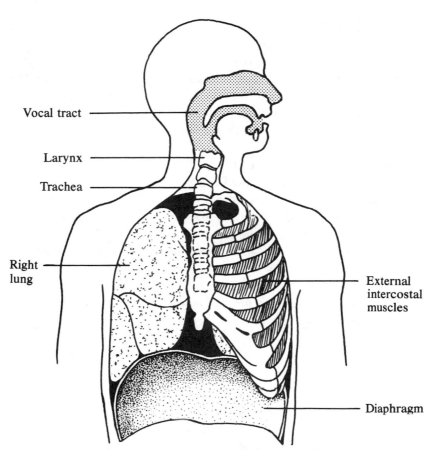

Figure 4.1
Major anatomical structures involved in the production of speech. Air driven
from the lungs through the trachea and the larynx into the vocal tract is the
primary source of the acoustic energy in speech. The lungs are attached to the
chest wall and diaphragm, and when the diaphragm lowers, the size of the chest
cavity is increased, the elastic lungs expand, and air flows inward. Similarly, air
also flows inward when the muscles between the ribs (the *external intercostals*)
contract and the rib cage expands outward, thus increasing the size of the chest
cavity. The muscles of the diaphragm and rib cage remain active during speech,
acting as a check on the outward flow of air.

caping from a filled balloon). During speech, however, the muscles of the diaphragm and rib cage (see figure 4.1) continue to be active, restraining the lungs from emptying too rapidly. Without this checking force, speech would be loud at first and then become quieter as the lungs emptied. Thus, humans have developed a special adaptation for breathing during speech: speech is not merely "added" to the breathing cycle; rather, the breathing cycle is adapted to the needs of speech.

The Role of the Larynx in Speech

The first point where the airflow from the lungs encounters a controllable resistance is at the *larynx,* a structure of muscle and cartilage located at the upper end of the *trachea* (or windpipe) (see figure 4.1). The controlled resistance to the airflow is due to the different positions of the vocal cords (or *vocal folds*), two muscular bands of tissue that stretch from front to back within the larynx (see figure 4.2). During quiet breathing the cords are relaxed and spread apart to allow the free flow of air to and from the lungs. During swallowing, however, the cords are drawn together to keep foreign material from entering the

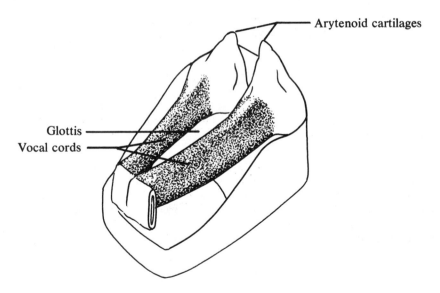

Figure 4.2
The larynx: display of the vocal cords. The periodic vibration of vocal cords during speech is called *voicing*. The space between the cords is called the *glottis*.

lungs. For speech, the most important feature of the vocal cords is that they can be made to vibrate if the airflow across them is sufficiently rapid and if they have the proper tension and proximity. This vibration is called *voicing*. The *frequency* of vibration determines the perceived *pitch*. The frequency of vibration of the vocal cords in adult males is relatively lower than the rate of vibration in females and children. The pitch of males' voices is thus perceived as lower than that of females and children.

Voicing is the "extra noise," the "buzz" that accompanies the production of the z-sound version of the plural morpheme. We say that the z-sound is *voiced,* whereas the s-sound is *voiceless* (that is, the vocal cords are tensed and spread apart and do not vibrate during the production of s). The only noise source for s is that of the turbulence, or friction, of the airflow in the narrow passage between the tongue tip and the roof of the mouth.

Finally, the space between the vocal cords is called the *glottis* (see figure 4.2), and linguists frequently refer to sounds that involve a constriction or closure of the vocal cords as *glottal sounds*.

The Vocal Tract
The vocal tract, the region above the vocal cords that includes the (oral) pharynx, the oral cavity, and the nasal cavity, is the space within which most of the speech sounds of human language are produced (see figure 4.5). We discuss the anatomical features of the vocal tract in relation to the vowels and consonants of English, to which we now turn.

4.2 THE REPRESENTATION OF SPEECH SOUNDS

English Orthography versus Systematic Transcription

In discussing the sounds of English, and the sounds of human language in general, we will need a set of symbols to *represent* those sounds. What sort of representation system will be most useful? If we try using the conventional English *orthography* (spelling system) to represent speech sounds, we face problems of two major types: first, a single letter of the alphabet often represents more than one sound; and conversely, a single speech sound can be represented by several different letters (see figure 4.3).

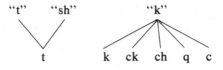

Speech Sound

Letters of the Current
English Alphabet

Figure 4.3
Types of inconsistencies in current English orthography. A single letter can
stand for more than one sound, and vice versa—several letters or groups of
letters can stand for the same sound. On the left, the letter *t* represents both the
t-sound in *tin* and the *sh*-sound in *nation*. On the right, the *k*-sound is represented by the letters *k* and *ck* as in the word *kick*, *ch* as in *choir*, *q* as in *quick*,
and *c* as in *cow*.

   As for problems of the first type, we have already seen that the letter
s in the words *dogs* and *cats* represents a *z*-sound and an *s*-sound, respectively. To take another case, the letter *t* can represent a *t*-sound as
in the word *tin;* but it can also represent a *sh*-like sound as in *nation*.
   Conversely, consider the *k*-sound in the word *kick*. This sound is
orthographically represented in two different ways: the letter *k* at the
beginning of the word and the letters *ck* at the end of the word. The
word *cow*, in turn, also begins with a *k*-sound, but here the letter *c* is
used to represent the sound. Similar problems arise with the initial
j-sound in *jug*. This initial sound is represented by the letter *j*, but it is
sometimes called "soft *g*" (and is spelled *g*) in words such as *giraffe*.
Even the sequence of letters *dge* represents the *j*-sound, in words such
as *ridge* and *edge*.
   In sum, English orthography is inconsistent as a representation of the
current speech sounds of American English. This lack of consistency in
representing sounds is due in part to the fact that the English writing
system became fixed several hundred years ago, although the pronunciation of the words has continuously changed since that period.
Clearly, we cannot use English orthography as a general system to represent speech sounds, given that we need a system that is consistent
and unambiguous. But what system of symbols should we use to represent the speech sounds of English? More importantly, what should
the symbols represent? The writing system we will now introduce uses
symbols that represent the particular configurations of the human vocal
tract that produce the various speech sounds of human language. This
system of writing is one that linguists refer to as a *transcription system*.
The crucial property of this system is that it represents each speech

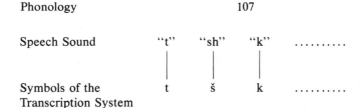

Figure 4.4
Systematic transcription system. Ideally, the transcription system represents each sound-unit with a single symbol, and each symbol represents only one sound.

sound of a language with one and only one symbol (see figure 4.4); thus, it will allow us to transcribe the sounds of English (or any other language) in a systematic and consistent way. Hence, we will be writing words using a *systematic transcription*. Moreover, the transcription system will enable us to discuss the different forms of the English Plural Rule in a precise manner.

The Consonants of American English

Table 4.2 displays the consonant symbols of English. A *consonant* is a speech sound produced when the speaker either stops or obstructs the airflow in the vocal tract. In addition to being classified as *voiceless* (like the *s*-sound in *cats*) or *voiced* (like the *z*-sound in *dogs*), consonants are described in terms of (a) the *place* and (b) the *manner* of their articulation. The *places* of articulation (see the top of table 4.2) are labeled in terms of anatomical structures, which include the lips and regions of the roof of the mouth. In the production of consonants, the lower lip or some part of the tongue approaches or touches the designated place of articulation.

The *manners* of articulation (see left-hand side of table 4.2) refer for the most part to how the articulators (lips or tongue) achieve contact or proximity with the places of articulation. We will now describe the consonants of English in terms of the scheme given in table 4.2, referring to the anatomical positions shown in figure 4.5.

The symbols we will use here are ones generally used by American linguists. There are other symbol systems, however, among them the commonly used International Phonetic Alphabet (IPA). Where the IPA symbols differ from our transcription, we will include them in parentheses after the symbols used in this text.

Table 4.2
The consonants of English

	PLACE OF ARTICULATION						
MANNER OF ARTICULATION	Bilabial	Labiodental	(Inter)dental	Alveolar	(Alveo)palatal or Palatal	Velar	Glottal
Stops voiceless	p			t		k	
voiced	b			d		g	
Fricatives voiceless		f	θ	s	š		h
voiced		v	ð	z	ž		
Affricates voiceless					č		
voiced					ǰ		
Nasals voiced	m			n		ŋ	
Liquids lateral ⎫ voiced nonlateral ⎭				l			
				r			
Glides voiced					y	w (ʍ)	

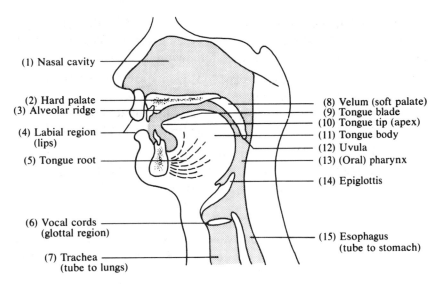

Figure 4.5
Cross section of the human vocal tract.

Stops
Stops are sounds produced when the airflow in the oral cavity is completely blocked off.

/p/ A voiceless bilabial stop. The speech sound symbolized by /p/ does not have accompanying vocal cord vibration and is therefore voiceless. The airflow is stopped by the complete closure of the two lips, which gives rise to the term *bilabial* (see 4, figure 4.5). The symbol /p/ represents the first sound in the word *pin*.

/b/ A voiced bilabial stop. The sound represented by /b/ has the same articulation as /p/, but it is accompanied by voicing. The symbol /b/ represents the first and last sounds in the name *Bob*.

/t/ A voiceless alveolar stop. The *alveolar* consonants of English are produced when the tongue tip (or *apex;* see 10, figure 4.5) approaches or—in the case of /t/ and /d/—touches the roof of the mouth at or near the alveolar ridge behind the upper teeth (see 3, figure 4.5). The English sound represented by the symbol /t/ thus differs from the *t*'s of many European languages in which the tongue tip touches the upper teeth. (A Spanish /t/, for example, is a voiceless dental stop.) The symbol /t/ represents the initial sound in the English word *tin*.

/d/   A voiced alveolar stop. The sound represented by the symbol /d/ has the same articulation as /t/, with /d/ being voiced. The symbol /d/ represents the first and last sounds in the word *Dad*.

/k/   A voiceless velar stop. Velar consonants are formed when the body of the tongue approaches or—in the case of /k/ and /g/—touches the roof of the mouth on the *soft palate* (usually called the *velum;* see 8, figure 4.5). The symbol /k/ represents the first sound in the word *kite*.

/g/   A voiced velar stop. The sound represented by the symbol /g/ has the same articulation as /k/, with /g/ being voiced. The symbol /g/ represents the first and last sounds in the word *gag*.

Fricatives

Fricatives are sounds produced when the airflow is forced through a narrow opening in the vocal tract so that noise produced by *friction* is created.

/f/   A voiceless labiodental fricative. The term *labiodental* indicates that the point of contact involves the (lower) lip and the (upper) teeth. The symbol /f/ represents the first sound in the word *fish*.

/v/   A voiced labiodental fricative. The sounds represented by the symbols /f/ and /v/ differ only in voicing, /v/ being voiced. The symbol /v/ represents the initial sound of the word *vine*.

/θ/   A voiceless (inter)dental fricative. The sound symbolized as θ, as well as its voiced counterpart /ð/, are spelled with *th* in the current English writing system. The (inter)dental sounds are produced when the tongue tip is placed against the upper teeth, friction being created by air forced between the upper teeth and the tongue. For most English speakers, the tongue tip is projected slightly between the upper and lower teeth. The symbol for this sound is the Greek letter *theta,* and in fact the first sound in the words *theta* and *thin* is represented by the symbol /θ/.

/ð/   A voiced (inter)dental fricative. The symbol /ð/ is called "eth" (or crossed *d*). You can hear the difference between the sounds symbolized by /ð/ and /θ/ if you say *then* and *thin* very slowly. You will hear (and feel) the voicing that accompanies /ð/ at the beginning of *then,* and you will note that the initial consonant of *thin* is not voiced. The symbol /ð/ also represents the initial sound of the words *this* and *that*.

/s/   A voiceless alveolar fricative. Note that the fricative sound represented by the symbol /s/ is much harsher than the fricative sound represented by the symbol /θ/. The turbulence is created by air passing between the front of the tongue (including the tip) and the alveolar ridge. The symbol /s/ represents the initial sound of the word *sit*.

/z/   A voiced alveolar fricative. The sounds represented by the symbols /s/ and /z/ differ only in voicing, /z/ being voiced. The symbol /z/ represents the first sound in the name *Zeke*.

/š/ (ʃ)   A voiceless (alveo)palatal fricative. The symbol /š/ (usually spelled *sh* in English orthography) represents a fricative similar to /s/, but the region of turbulent airflow lies just behind the alveolar ridge on the hard palate (see 2 and 3, figure 4.5). During the articulation of /š/ the tongue tip can be positioned either near the alveolar ridge itself (with the tongue blade arched) or just behind the alveolar ridge (in which case the tongue blade does not need to be arched). The symbol /š/ represents the initial consonant in the word *ship*.

/ž/ (ʒ)   A voiced (alveo)palatal fricative. Unlike /š/, the voiced counterpart /ž/ is rare (for some speakers, nonexistent) in word-initial position. The symbol /ž/ represents the first sound in foreign names such as *Zsa-Zsa* or *Jacques*. More commonly, /ž/ occurs in the middle of English words. For example, the letter *s* in *decision* and *measure* is pronounced as the sound represented by /ž/.

/h/   A "glottal" fricative. The /h/ sound is often called a *glottal* fricative because the vocal cords are positioned in such a way as to partially obstruct the airflow from the lungs. However, the primary noise source for this speech sound is turbulence created at different points along the vocal tract where the tongue body (or blade) approaches the roof of the mouth. The point where the friction is created is determined by the vowel that follows the /h/. In the articulation of the English word *heap*, for example, the tongue body is positioned high and forward, and the fricative noise is produced in the palatal region. The symbol *h* represents the first sound in the words *how* and *here*.

Affricates
An *affricate* is a single sound, beginning as a stop but releasing secondarily into a fricative.

/č/ (tʃ)   A voiceless (alveo)palatal affricate. The symbol /č/ represents the first sound in the word *chip* (/č/ is usually spelled as *ch*). In articulating this sound, the tongue makes contact at the same point on the roof of the mouth as in the articulation of the sound represented by /š/. Unlike /š/, though, /č/ begins with a complete blockage of the vocal tract (a stop), but then is immediately released into a fricative sound like /š/.

/ǰ/ (dž) A voiced (alveo)palatal affricate. The sounds represented by the symbols /č/ and /ǰ/ differ in voicing, /ǰ/ being voiced. The symbol /ǰ/ represents the first and last sounds of the word *judge* (/ǰ/ being spelled as both *j* and *dge,* in this case).

Nasals

In English, *nasals* are stops similar to voiced stops in that they are voiced and are produced with a complete obstruction in the oral cavity. However, with nasals the airflow is channeled into the nasal passages (see 1, figure 4.5), due to the lowering of the velum (see 8, figure 4.5).

/m/ A bilabial nasal. The sounds represented by the symbols /m/ and /b/ are articulated in the same manner, except that for /m/ the velum is lowered to allow airflow into the nasal passage. The symbol /m/ represents the first sound in the word *mice*.

/n/ An alveolar nasal. The sound represented by the symbol /n/ is articulated in the same position as /d/, with the velum lowered. The symbol /n/ represents the initial sound in *nice*.

/ŋ/ A velar nasal. The symbol /ŋ/ is called *eng* (or even *engma* or *engwa*) and represents the final sound in the word *sing*. The normal English spelling for this sound is *ng*. In order to hear the sound—and to hear that it *is* only one sound—compare the words *singer* and *finger*. For most speakers of American English the middle consonants of the word *finger* consist of a sequence of the velar nasal /ŋ/ followed by the velar stop /g/. In *singer,* however, only the velar nasal /ŋ/ occurs as the middle consonant, with no following /g/. Similarly, for most speakers of American English the word *long* in the name *Long Island* ends in /ŋ/ with no following velar stop /g/; but for certain speakers from New York City the stop /g/ is in fact pronounced (Long Island = Long *G*island).

The "*g*-like" quality of /ŋ/ is due to its being articulated in the same way as /g/, except that the velum is lowered. Thus, just as /m/ and /n/ are the nasal counterparts of /b/ and /d/, so /ŋ/ is the nasal counterpart of /g/. The sound represented by the symbol /ŋ/ does not occur in initial position in English words, but only in medial and final positions, as our examples show.

Finally, despite the fact that English orthography uses a *digraph* (a sequence of two letters) to represent /ŋ/ (namely, the letters *ng*), it should be stressed once again that the velar nasal is a *single* speech sound. Similarly, recall that other consonant sounds of English are represented by two-letter sequences in the spelling system: *th* for /θ/ and /ð/, *sh* for /š/, and *ch* for /č/. Yet each of these consonants—/ŋ/, /θ/, /ð/, /š/, and /č/—is a *single* speech sound. Note that the transcription system we use here has no two-letter symbols; thus, any sequence of two (or more) symbols in the transcription indicates a sequence of two (or more) speech sounds.

Liquids

Liquid sounds are found in the majority of the world's languages. English has two: /l/ and /r/. The term *liquid* is an impressionistic expression indicating that the sound is "smooth" and "flows easily." Liquids share properties of both consonants and vowels: as in the articulation of certain stop consonants, the tongue blade is raised toward the alveolar ridge; as in the articulation of vowels, air is allowed to flow freely from the mouth without great friction.

/l/   A lateral alveolar liquid. In the articulation of English /l/, the tongue blade is raised and the apex usually makes contact with the alveolar ridge. The sides of the tongue are lowered, permitting the air to flow outward. The symbol /l/ represents the initial sound in the word *life*.

/r/   A (nonlateral) alveolar liquid. American English /r/ is produced with the tongue blade raised toward the alveolar ridge, and many speakers curl the apex into a *retroflexed position* (curled upward and backward). In addition, this sound is produced with some lip rounding, and there is pharyngeal (throat) constriction due to a retraction of the tongue root (see 5, figure 4.5). The symbol /r/ represents the first sound in the word *red*.

Glides

Glides are vowel-like articulations that precede and follow true vowels. The term *glide* is based on the observation that the sequence of a glide and a vowel is a smooth, continuous gesture. Because the tongue position in articulating the glides *y* and *w* is similar to the tongue position of the vowels in *beet* and *boot,* respectively, these glides are sometimes referred to as *semivowels*.

/y/   A palatal glide. The sound represented by the symbol /y/ is formed with the body of the tongue arched in a high, front position, toward the hard palate. The symbol /y/ represents the first sound in the word *yes*.

/w/   A (labialized) velar glide. The sound represented by the symbol /w/ is formed with the body of the tongue arched in a high, back position toward the soft palate (velum). Lip rounding also accompanies the production of this sound. The symbol /w/ represents the initial sound in *wood*.

/ʍ/   A (labialized) velar glide (with a voiceless beginning). Some speakers of English have different initial sounds in the words *which* and *witch*. For these speakers the initial sound in *which* begins as a voiceless sound, followed immediately by the glide *w*. Some linguists write this initial sound as the digraph *hw*.

The Vowels of American English

Whereas consonants are formed by obstructions—either partial or total—of the vocal tract, vowels are produced with a relatively open vocal tract, which in effect serves as a resonating chamber. The different vowels are formed by the different shapes of the open resonating vocal tract, and the variety of shapes is determined by several articulatory factors: the position of the tongue, the relative opening of the lips, the relative opening of the oral pharynx (see 13, figure 4.5) and the position of the jaw (see figure 4.6). Although these articulators are, to some extent, anatomically connected, they can be independently controlled to produce the different vowels.

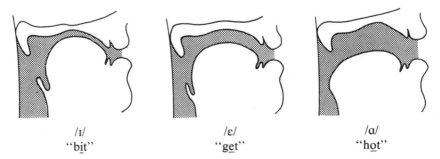

| /ɪ/ | /ɛ/ | /ɑ/ |
| "bit" | "get" | "hot" |

Figure 4.6
Vocal tract shapes for given English vowels

	Front	Central	Back
High	ɪ	(ɨ)	ʊ
Mid	ɛ	(ə)	ɔ
Low	æ	ʌ	ɑ

Figure 4.7
Short (lax) vowels and reduced vowels of American English

There are three major types of vowels in American English: *short* (or *lax*), *reduced,* and *long* (or *tense*). As the labels *short* and *long* suggest, short vowels are relatively shorter in duration than long vowels. Some linguists prefer the terms *lax* for short and *tense* for long. The term *lax* refers to the relatively lesser amount of muscular tension used in producing lax vowels as opposed to their tenser counterparts.

Short (Lax) Vowels
The symbols for the English short vowels are displayed in figure 4.7. If we imagine this figure superimposed on a cross section of the vocal tract (such as that depicted in figure 4.5), then the positions of the vowels in the chart represent the relative positions of the tongue in articulating them (assume the mouth opening to be on the left, as in figure 4.5). We can simplify our description of the articulation of vowels by limiting our discussion to the relative position of the tongue during vowel production.

/ɪ/   A short high front vowel. The terms *high* and *front* describe the position of the tongue in the mouth (see figure 4.6). The symbol /ɪ/ represents the vowel sound in the words *bit* /bɪt/ and *wish* /wɪš/.

/ɛ/   A short mid front vowel. The tongue position is relatively forward, as in the production of /ɪ/, but it is slightly lower (see figure 4.6). The symbol /ɛ/ represents the vowel sound in words such as *get* /gɛt/ and *mess* /mɛs/.

/æ/   A short low front vowel. This vowel (and the symbol for it) is called "ash" by many linguists, and the symbol /æ/ represents the vowel sound in the word *bat* /bæt/. It is produced with the tongue in a forward position, but with the tongue blade (see 9, figure 4.5) near the floor of the mouth.

/ʊ/   A short high back vowel. The vowel sound represented by the symbol /ʊ/ is found in words such as *put* /pʊt/ and *foot* /fʊt/. As you start to pronounce the vowel /ʊ/, you can feel your tongue move back and upward toward the velum. You will also very likely feel your lips become rounded (brought closer together) during the production of this vowel; hence, it can be called a *rounded vowel*.

/ʌ/ A short central low vowel. The vowel sound represented by the symbol /ʌ/, sometimes called "wedge," occurs in words such as *putt* /pʌt/ and *luck* /lʌk/. Note that the words *put* and *putt,* which differ in the number of final *t*'s in the English spelling system, actually differ in their vowels, /ʊ/ vs. /ʌ/, respectively.

/ɑ/ A short low back vowel. The position of the tongue is low and retracted in the articulation of the vowel /ɑ/ (see figure 4.6). There are several varieties of ɑ-like vowels in English; these vowels constitute one of the most difficult aspects of the study of English sounds. The difficulty is due in part to the fact that there is considerable dialectal variation in the pronunciation of these vowels. We leave it to your instructor to help you assign the appropriate symbols to represent the vowels of your own speech or of the English spoken in your area. The vowel sound represented by the symbol /ɑ/ (script-*a*) is the low back vowel shared by most speakers of American English. It is typically found in words such as *hot* /hɑt/ and *pot* /pɑt/.

/a/ A central low vowel. The vowel sound represented by the symbol /a/ (printed-*a*) is found—among other places—in the speech of New England, especially in Maine and eastern Massachusetts. One characteristic expression of the Boston area, "Park the car," contains two instances of the vowel represented by the symbol /a/. The /a/ vowel is actually *tense* and therefore does not appear in figure 4.7.

/ɔ/ A short mid back vowel. If you pronounce the words *cot* and *caught* differently, you probably have the vowel /ɔ/ in your pronunciation of *caught*. There is minor lip rounding in the articulation of this vowel.

For many (if not most) speakers of American English the pronunciation of the vowels in the words *father, froth,* and *fraught* will be the same. However, you may speak a dialect (for example, if you are a speaker of British English) in which each of the vowels in the three words is different. If you speak New York City English, we leave it to your instructor to assist you in assigning the appropriate symbols for the centralized vowels found in your speech.

Reduced Vowels

There are two so-called *reduced* vowels in English, shown in parentheses in figure 4.7. The most common reduced vowel is called *schwa,* a *mid central vowel* whose symbol is an upside down and reversed *e* /ə/. It is the last vowel sound in the word *sofa,* and sounds very much like the lax vowel represented by the symbol /ʌ/ (some linguists, in fact, use the same symbol for both of these sounds). Schwa /ə/ is called a *reduced* vowel because it is frequently an unstressed variant of a stressed (accented) vowel. Note how the accented vowel /έ/ in the word *democrat* /démɔkræt/ "reduces" to the unaccented vowel /ə/ in the word *democracy* /dɔmákrɔsiy/.

The other reduced vowel of English is a *high central vowel* represented by the symbol /ɨ/; it is referred to as *barred-i.* It is typically the vowel sound in the second syllable of *chicken* /čɪkɨn/. The vowel /ɨ/ also occurs only in unstressed (unaccented) syllables in a word. Some speakers make a distinction between /ɨ/ in the second vowel of *roses* versus /ə/ in the second vowel of *Rosa's.* There is, however, considerable variation in the pronunciation of these two vowels.

Long (Tense) Vowels and Diphthongs

In addition to its inventory of short and reduced vowels, English has a set of *long* (or tense) vowels, given in figure 4.8.

The long vowels differ from the short vowels not only in terms of length, but also in other respects. Comparing the vowel sounds of *bead* and *bid,* we note that the tense vowel in *bead* not only is longer than the lax /ɪ/ of *bid* but also sounds "higher." In addition, the long vowels of English can be analyzed as *diphthongs;* that is, they can be divided into two parts: an initial louder vowel and a transition into a less loud vowel-like sound. We will transcribe the English long vowels as a combination of two symbols: an initial vowel symbol followed by one of the symbols *y* or *w* representing the second half of the diphthong.

	Front	Back
High	iy	uw
Mid	ey	ow, oy
Low	(æw)	aw, ay

Figure 4.8
Long (tense) vowels of American English

/iy/ (i)   A long high front vowel. For this vowel, the *y* off-glide is difficult to hear since it is articulated at the same position as the initial vowel. The transcription /iy/ represents the vowel sound in words such as *bead* /biyd/ and *three* /θriy/.

/ey/ (e)   A long mid front vowel (with an accompanying *y* off-glide). This transcription represents the vowel sound in words such as *clay* /kley/ and *weigh* /wey/.

/uw/ (u)   A long high back rounded vowel. For this vowel, the *w* off-glide is difficult to hear since it is articulated at the same position as the initial vowel. This transcription represents the vowel sound in words such as *crude* /kruwd/ and *shoe* /šuw/. Note that the lips are rounded in articulating /uw/.

/ow/ (o)   A long mid back rounded vowel (with an accompanying *w* off-glide). This transcription represents the vowel sound in the words *boat* /bowt/ and *toe* /tow/. Again, note the lip rounding.

/oy/   A long mid back rounded vowel (with an accompanying *y* off-glide). The vowel sound represented by this transcription is found in words such as *boy* /boy/ and *Floyd* /floyd/.

/aw/   A long low back vowel (with an accompanying *w* off-glide). This transcription represents the vowel sound in the words *cow* /kaw/ and *blouse* /blaws/. In some dialects of American English this diphthong begins with a low front vowel and should be transcribed as /æw/.

/ay/   A long low back vowel (with an accompanying *y* off-glide). This transcription represents the vowel sound in words such as *my* /may/ and *thigh* /θay/.

One of the reasons that speakers of American English have some difficulty in pronouncing the vowels of languages such as Spanish and Italian is that the long vowels of English are diphthongs, whereas the corresponding vowels in Spanish and Italian are not. For example, an American learning Italian is likely to pronounce the word *solo* "alone" with two long *o*'s, as in the English word *solo* /sowlow/. For this reason, teachers of foreign languages such as Spanish and Italian often tell American students to try to use "pure" vowels, rather than the long vowels of American English.

Finally, in the articulation of /iy/ and /uw/ it is difficult to hear the off-glides. This is because the off-glides are articulated in the same place as the initial vowel. For this reason, in certain transcription systems such as the IPA, the vowels /iy/ and /uw/ are transcribed with the single symbols /i/ and /u/. Furthermore, in the IPA transcription system the vowels /ey/ and /ow/ are transcribed with the single symbols /e/ and /ǫ/. For the exercises at the end of this chapter, please use the transcription system that your instructor feels is the most appropriate.

The Form of the English Plural Rule: Three Hypotheses

Given that we now have a set of symbols to transcribe the consonant and vowel sounds of English in a precise way, we can reformulate table 4.1 more accurately, as table 4.3. Here the plural morpheme takes the shape /s/, /z/, or /ɨz/.

Even though we can now represent the different pronunciations of the plural morpheme, we are still left with the problem of accounting for the *distribution* (pattern of occurrence) of the different plural forms. What factors govern, or predict, this distribution? We will pursue this problem by formulating several hypotheses, which we will then test and revise in light of new data.

Nouns can take only one of the three different forms of the plural. Thus, for example, the plural /-ɨz/ that is added to *bush* to make *bushes* /bušɨz/ cannot be added to *cat* or *dog*. The result of doing so (/kætɨz/, /dɑgɨz/) sounds "foreign" to a native speaker of English. Thus, there must be *some* rule governing the pronunciation of the English plural morpheme. Now, the least interesting account of the plural distribution would be to say that the form of the plural morpheme to be used with any given noun is unpredictable, and that we must simply *list*, for each individual noun of the language, which plural form it takes. This would amount to saying that speakers of English have simply memorized the phonological form for the plural for each individual noun. The distribution of the forms of the plural would then be given by sets of statements such as the following:

Table 4.3
Systematic transcription of different forms of the English plural morpheme

Word in Traditional Orthography	cats	dogs	bushes
Word in Transcription	/kæts/	/dɑgz/	/bušɨz/
Isolated Plural Morpheme	-s	-z	-ɨz

(1)
English Plural Rule, Hypothesis 1 (Listing of words)
The forms of the plural morpheme are distributed according to the following *word lists:*
a. Use the plural form /-s/ with the words *cat, map, back,* and so forth.
b. Use the plural form /-z/ with the words *dog, can, tab,* and so forth.
c. Use the plural form /-ɨz/ with the words *bush, fish, ridge,* and so forth.

Hypothesis 1 is consistent with the fact that there are nouns such as *child, ox, sheep,* and *man,* which clearly require the speaker to memorize special plural forms: *children, oxen, sheep, men.* However, hypothesis 1 implies that for any new word (not already found in our lists) we will not be able to predict which of the three forms of the plural morpheme it will take. But this is clearly false. Speakers of English can spontaneously form the plural for nouns they have never heard before and therefore could not have memorized. We may never have heard the noun *glark* before (since it is a nonsense word), yet we can indeed predict that the form of the plural would be /-s/ and not /-z/ or /-ɨz/; in fact, it seems that *every* noun that ends in /k/ takes the plural form /-s/, whether it is a nonsense word or not. Similarly, *every* noun that ends in, say, /g/, such as *dog,* takes the plural form /-z/; and *every* noun that ends in /š/, such as *bush,* takes the plural form /-ɨz/. It is, in fact, possible to *group* the nouns that take only /-s/, or only /-z/, or only /-ɨz/ in terms of their *last sound.* This leads us to a second hypothesis about the distribution of the different forms of the plural morpheme:

(2)
English Plural Rule, Hypothesis 2 (Listing of final sounds)
The forms of the plural morpheme are distributed according to the following *speech sound lists:*
a. The plural morpheme takes the form /-s/ if the noun ends in /p, t, k, f, or θ/.
b. The plural morpheme takes the form /-z/ if the noun ends in /b, m, d, n, g, ŋ, v, ð, l, r, w, y/, or any vowel.
c. The plural morpheme takes the form /-ɨz/ if the noun ends in /s, z, š, ž, č, or ǰ/.

Notice that hypothesis 2 will now automatically *predict* the plural form for any new word the speaker of English encounters. Accordingly, the task faced by the language learner in learning the distribution of the forms of the plural is different under hypothesis 2 than under hypothesis 1. That is, language learners do not memorize the particular plural form for every noun; rather, it appears that they acquire a *rule* to determine what plural form is associated with a particular noun (in terms of its final sound). Of course, there still are nouns whose plural form has to be memorized, as with the "exceptional" nouns *children, oxen, sheep, men,* and so forth. However, it is a telling fact that when children are learning English they make "errors" that conform to hypothesis 2, such as saying *childs* /čayldz/, *oxes* /ɑksɨz/, *sheeps* /šiyps/, and *mans* /mænz/ (or even *mens* /mɛnz/), indicating that they are learning *rules* for the distribution of the plural; they are not memorizing individual words (for further discussion of this point, see chapter 11).

In the case of the Plural Rule we may now ask the further question: Is there any principle that will account for the groupings of consonants and vowels given in hypothesis 2? That is, what special features allow us to distinguish, in a more general fashion, the lists given in (a), (b), and (c) of hypothesis 2? If we compare words that end in, say, f (which take the plural form /-s/) and words that end in v (which take the plural form /-z/), we can observe that /f/ and /v/ represent similar sounds that differ only in a single feature—namely, /f/ is *voiceless,* whereas /v/ is *voiced.* Further, words with, say, the final consonant /k/ (which is voiceless) take the plural /-s/, whereas words with a final /g/ (which is voiced) take the plural /-z/. If we set aside the nouns that take /-ɨz/ for a moment, we can make the following observation: if a noun ends with a voiceless sound, then it will take the voiceless plural form /-s/; but if it ends with a voiced sound then it will take the voiced plural form /-z/. Notice that we now have an account for why hypothesis 2 groups nouns ending in *vowels* with nouns ending in *voiced consonants* such as *b, d,* and *m* (see hypothesis 2, part (b): those final sounds are all voiced, and so it follows automatically that all nouns ending in those sounds will take the plural form /-z/.

Let us now turn to the nouns that take the plural form /-ɨz/. We note that the final consonants of these nouns (/s, z, š, ž, č, ǰ/) all have a common phonetic property: a fricative "hissing" or "hushing" sound. (Recall that the affricates, /č/ and /ǰ/, release secondarily into a fricative made at the same point of articulation as the initial stop.) Thus, it appears that words whose final sound has a "hissing" or "hushing" component take the plural form /-ɨz/.

We can now introduce slightly more technical vocabulary: we will use the term *sibilant* to characterize the "hissing" or "hushing" property of the sounds represented by /s, z, š, ž, č, and ǰ/. Since no English sounds other than these are sibilant, we can say that the /-ɨz/ plural is added only to nouns that end in *sibilant consonants*. We can now postulate hypothesis 3 of the Plural Rule:

(3)
English Plural Rule, Hypothesis 3 (Use of phonetic features to state generalizations)
The forms of the plural morpheme are distributed according to the following conditions:
a. The plural morpheme takes the form /-ɨz/ if the last sound in a noun is a *sibilant consonant*.
Otherwise:
b. The plural morpheme takes the voiced form /-z/ if the last sound in a noun is *voiced*.
c. The plural morpheme takes the voiceless form /-s/ if the last sound in the noun is *voiceless*.

Hypothesis 3 illustrates an important property of phonological rules: they are not stated in terms of lists of speech sounds, but rather in terms of smaller component parts of these sounds: *the features of articulation of which they are made up*. These articulatory features (such as voicing) define whole subclasses of sounds that *pattern together* in phonological rules; hence, the features provide a way to express general properties of sound patterning in human language. Instead of merely listing individual sounds in stating a rule (as in hypothesis 2), we can now refer to general classes of sounds that share significant features, such as the class of *voiced* or *voiceless* sounds. Classes of sounds that can be characterized by a smaller number of shared features are often referred to as *natural classes*. We will discuss phonetic features and natural classes further in section 4.3.

Additional factual evidence supports hypothesis 3 over hypothesis 2. This evidence is found in the pronunciation of foreign words that contain speech sounds not found in English. Some people, especially announcers on radio stations that play classical music, pronounce the name of the German composer Bach as it is in German, with a final voiceless velar fricative. This sound, symbolized as /x/, is not found in English. If the name *Bach* (/bɑx/) is used in the plural, as when someone refers to two generations of *Bachs,* the name obeys part (c) of hypothesis 3 and an *s* is added (*Bachs* = /bɑxs/). Notice, then, that hypothesis 3 in which rules are stated in terms of their phonetic features, accounts for the English speaker's use of the voiceless plural form /-s/, whereas hypothesis 2 fails to predict any plural form whatever for *Bach* since the sound *x* does not appear in the list of word-final sounds.

Let us consider once again the relationship between the plural forms /-s/ and /-z/. As we have seen, aside from subcase (a) of hypothesis 3 (involving sibilants), the voiceless form of the plural morpheme /-s/ is used when the final consonant of the noun is voiceless, whereas the voiced form of the plural morpheme /-z/ is used when the final sound of the noun is voiced. Thus, the presence or absence of voicing of the final sound "continues" into the plural morpheme. Linguists use the term *assimilation* to describe phenomena in which phonetic features of one sound are transferred to another nearby sound. In the present example involving the Plural Rule, the assimilation is said to be *progressive,* since the feature of voicing in the final sound of the noun is carried over progressively into the following sound of the plural morpheme.

We have now discussed three versions of the Plural Rule (given as hypotheses 1–3), and in doing so we have provided answers to two of the questions that we posed at the beginning of this chapter:

What is the proper description of the three different *sounds* of the English plural morpheme shown in table 4.1?

What are the *conditions on the alternation* that will predict where the three different phonological forms of the English plural morpheme occur?

As we have seen, we can describe the different pronunciations of the plural morpheme in terms of a set of symbols defined on the basis of a set of articulatory features that combine to make up individual sounds. Further, the same articulatory features (such as voicing) can be used to state the phonological generalizations governing where the different forms of the plural morpheme will occur. Recall that we also posed two more general questions at the beginning of the chapter:

What is the proper description of the various sounds that are found generally in human language?

What is the proper general framework for describing the sound patterns of human language?

We have begun to provide answers to these questions, but in order to develop such answers appropriately we must investigate in more detail some further properties of the phonology of English, as well as of languages in general. In the rest of section 4.2, and in section 4.3, we will briefly survey additional aspects of phonology that will aid in placing our more general questions into a broader perspective.

Phonetic Variations on a Phonemic Theme

So far we have assumed that the sounds represented by the transcription symbols of English are articulated in more or less the same way each time they are produced. In one sense this is true, but in another sense this view ignores an important aspect of the pronunciation of speech sounds. We discuss below several variations in the pronunciation of certain American English consonants, illustrating how these variations in pronunciation are rule-governed.

Types of /t/ in English

Aspirated t. When the sound /t/ occurs at the beginning of a syllable, its pronunciation is accompanied by a puff of air called *aspiration*. You can observe the presence of aspiration if you hold a thin, flexible piece of paper close to the front of your mouth when you say the word *ton* /tʌn/. The paper will flutter immediately after the *t* is pronounced. In contrast, the pronunciation of the /t/ in the word *stun* /stʌn/ is unaspirated; it will not cause the piece of paper to flutter. In order to represent more detailed aspects of pronunciation (such as aspiration), linguists use a system called *(close) phonetic transcription.* By convention, phonetic symbols are enclosed in square brackets [ ], as opposed to the more general transcription we have been using that enclosed the symbols in slant lines / /. This more general transcription system, when it satisfies conditions to be discussed below, is called a *phonemic transcription.* We will discuss the differences between *phonetic* and *phonemic transcriptions* after we have discussed some of the finer phonetic details of American speech. A phonetic symbolization for pronunciation of the words *ton* and *stun* would be [tʰʌn] and [stʌn], respectively. A superscripted *h,* as in [tʰ], indicates that a sound is aspirated, whereas its absence indicates that the sound, in this case [t], is unaspirated. We will discuss the relationship between phonetic and phonemic symbols later in this section, but note for the present that phonetic symbols in square brackets represent more detailed articulatory features or pronunciation than phonemic symbols do.

Unreleased t. The pronunciation of final *t* in words such as *kit* is frequently *unreleased* in the speech of many Americans: the tongue
touches the alveolar ridge but does not immediately drop to "release"
the sound. (In contrast, in most American dialects the pronunciation of
the final stop /t/ in words such as *fast* is in fact released.) For most
speakers of American English, in the pronunciation of the word *kit* /kɪt/
the voicing ends and the airflow stops *before* the tongue reaches the
alveolar ridge in articulating the final /t/. Where and how is the airflow
stopped in this case? It turns out that before the /t/ in the word *kit* is
articulated, the airflow is stopped by a closure at the vocal cords. Thus,
the primary stop articulation in the pronunciation of final /t/ in words
such as *kit* occurs in the larynx, rather than in the region of the alveolar
ridge (even though the tongue tip does indeed make contact with the
alveolar ridge immediately *after* the closure of the vocal cords). Recall
that the *glottis* is the space between the vocal cords, and a stop created
by closure at the glottis is called a *glottal stop,* represented as the symbol [ʔ]. (A glottal stop occurs between the two *oh*'s of the expression *oh
oh!,* which we can phonetically transcribe as [ʔʌʔow] or [ʔowʔow].) An
unreleased /t/ that is produced with a glottal stop immediately preceding the alveolar (or dental) articulation is symbolized as [ʔt] (such
sounds are sometimes referred to as *preglottalized*). Thus, the characteristic pronunciation of the word *kit* for most American dialects is represented phonetically as [kɪʔt].

Glottal stop replacement of t. In certain words the tendency to have
a glottal closure with the articulation of /t/ in certain environments
reaches such an extreme that the glottal stop actually replaces /t/. In
many speakers' pronunciation of words such as *button* and *kitten,* the
stop articulation is actually carried out at the glottis, and the tongue
does not, in fact, move toward the alveolar ridge until the /n/ of the final
syllable is articulated. It turns out that /t/ is generally replaced by the
glottal stop if the following syllable is a *syllabic* /n/. The term *syllabic*
here refers to the fact that nasal consonants (such as /n/) can function as
syllables by themselves, without any accompanying vowel. In the word
button, for example, the only sound in the second syllable is the nasal
[n]—there is no true vowel at all in that syllable. A syllabic *n* is indicated by placing a straight apostrophe (or tick mark) under the symbol:
[n̩]. The phonetic transcription of *kitten* would thus be [kɪʔn̩]. (We discuss syllabic consonants further, later in this section.)

Flapped t. In words such as *pitted,* /t/ is regularly pronounced as a voiced "*d*-like" sound by most speakers of American (but not British) English. This sound is articulated by making a quick "tap" with the tongue tip on the alveolar ridge. Because of the rapidity of the articulation of this sound, it is referred to as a *flap* (or a *tap*), transcribed phonetically with the symbol [D] (or in the IPA with the symbol [ɾ]). Thus, a word such as *pitted* is phonetically transcribed as [pʰɪDɨd]. The flap [D] is always voiced, and occurs primarily *intervocalically* (between vowels).

To sum up, there are a number of phonetic variations of the phoneme /t/ in American English. These variations and their conditioning environments are shown in table 4.4.

The phonetic variations of the phoneme /t/ given in table 4.4 represent an important aspect of the pronunciation of American English, but the fact that native speakers of American English hear all of the above variations as the same sound—as some type of *t*—is a clue to the nature of the relationship between phonetic and phonemic representations (which we will discuss shortly).

The Aspiration Rule. Recall from our discussion of the Plural Rule that phonemes often pattern together in natural classes that can be specified by a small number of shared features. Phonological regularities are stated in terms of such features, rather than in terms of lists of phonemes. With this in mind, let us now note that the phoneme /t/ is not the only consonant of American English that is aspirated in syllable-initial position. The phonemes /p/ and /k/ are also aspirated in the same environment: for example, the initial consonants in *pin* [pʰɪn] and

Table 4.4
Phonetic variants of the phoneme /t/ in American English

Articulatory Description	Phonetic Symbol	Conditioning Environments	Example Words
Released, aspirated	[tʰ]	when syllable-initial	ton [tʰʌn]
Unreleased, preglottalized	[ʔt]	word-final, after a vowel	kit [kʰɪʔt]
Glottal stop	[ʔ]	before a syllabic *n*	kitten [kʰɪʔn̩]
Flap	[D]	between vowels, when the first vowel is stressed (approximate environment)	pitted [pʰɪDɨd]
Released, unaspirated	[t]	when the above conditions are not met first	stun [stʌn]

kin [kʰɪn] are aspirated, while /p/ in *spin* [spɪn] and /k/ in *skin* [skɪn] are not aspirated. Thus, /p/, /t/, and /k/ all pattern together with respect to the environment for aspiration. The question immediately arises: How can we characterize this set of phonemes in terms of a small set of shared features? Note that /b/, /d/, and /g/—that is, the *voiced* counterparts of /p/, /t/, and /k/—are not aspirated (for example, the word *bid* is never pronounced [bʰɪd]). It turns out that we can state the phonological generalization concerning aspiration in American English quite simply: all *voiceless stops* are aspirated in syllable-initial position. Once again, we see that we can state a generalization by referring to the inherent phonetic features of phonemes that allow us to pick out natural classes of sounds.

The Relationship between Phonetic and Phonemic Representations

We have seen that the phoneme /t/ in American English has a number of phonetic variants depending on its *position* in a syllable or morpheme. Keeping this in mind, we can see that the phonemic symbol /t/ is actually a *cover symbol* for a range of different sounds (or *phones*). We can refer to all the sounds/phones for which /t/ is a cover symbol as its *allophones* (sometimes also called *positional variants,* since they occur in specific positions in a syllable or morpheme). In this sense, the positional variants that we transcribe as [t], [tʰ], [ʔt], [ʔ], and [D] are all instances of the same phoneme: those particular allophones of the English "*t*-sound" are all represented by the same phonemic symbol /t/. It is important to stress that every *phone* (symbol used in phonetic writing, such as [tʰ]) is an *(allo)phone* of some phoneme. Thus, we can refer to the allophones [kʰ], [tʰ], or [ʔt], but we must keep in mind that [kʰ] is an allophone of the phoneme /k/, whereas [tʰ] and [ʔt] are allophones of the phoneme /t/. Criteria for determining whether two or more phones are members of the same phoneme or different phonemes are discussed below.

It is clear, then, that we are using two distinct systems of representation for the sounds of English (and of human language in general) and that different information is encoded in the two different systems. For example, the phonetic representation system explicitly represents information concerning aspiration, preglottalization, and flapping, using notational devices such as superscripted *h* and other special symbols summarized in table 4.4. In contrast, the phonemic representation system is more abstract in nature; it ignores such features as aspiration, preglottalization, and flapping. Thus, the symbol /t/ represents a basic voiceless alveolar stop. Since we are using two representation systems for sounds, the question immediately arises, Why should this be so? How can we justify two systems for encoding phonological information? Why should one representation system ignore (or leave unrepresented) articulatory information encoded by the other system? Why shouldn't we simplify our phonological theory and use only *one* representation system for sounds?

There are some fairly intuitive ways to answer these questions, and so we must stress that we will be providing informal answers here (rather than precise definitions). Furthermore, we must also point out that part of our discussion will assume certain traditional (or "classical") views on the distinction between phonemic and phonetic representations, in which, for the sake of exposition, we will gloss over a number of problems that have arisen in recent work.

The basic idea behind the distinction between phonetic and phonemic representation systems can be best illustrated by considering pairs of words that linguists refer to as *minimal pairs:* pairs of words that have the same number of phonemes, but differ in meaning from each other and also differ in only a single phoneme in a corresponding position in the two words. For example, the words *sip* and *zip* differ in meaning, but phonologically they differ only in the *contrast* between initial /s/ and initial /z/. Thus, *sip* and *zip* constitute a minimal pair.

Now let us consider two possible pronunciations of the word *kit:* [kʰɪt] versus [kʰɪʔt]. For some speakers of English, the final consonant of *kit* is sometimes released (= [t]) and sometimes unreleased (= [ʔt]). The important point is that no meaning difference is associated with the different pronunciations [kʰɪt] and [kʰɪʔt]: both are perceived by native speakers of American English as instances of the *same* word *kit*. Thus, the distinction between the allophones [t] and [ʔt] in word-final position is not contrastive, and we can say that, for some speakers, these allophones of /t/ are in *free variation* (or of optional occurrence) in that position.

The allophones of a phoneme can also occur in what is called *complementary distribution;* that is, one allophone can occur in a position where the other allophone(s) can never appear, and vice versa. The term complementary distribution is used because the distribution of one allophone is the complement of the distribution of the other. For example, in the position following /s/, the phoneme /t/ has the positional variant [t], but the allophones [tʰ] and [ʔt] never occur in this position. Allophones of a single phoneme, then, are always either in free variation or in complementary distribution, but in either case they are not contrastive with one another. The phones [kʰ] and [tʰ] are *contrastive*, however, since they function to distinguish words—for example, *kin* [kʰɪn] from *tin* [tʰɪn] or *cap* [kʰæp] from *tap* [tʰæp]. Therefore, the phones [kʰ] and [tʰ] are members of different phonemes. In sum, when phones function contrastively, they are members of *different phonemes;* when phones are either in complementary distribution or in free variation, they are members of the *same phoneme*.

The phoneme is actually more than just a cover symbol for a collection of sounds (phones)—it has a psychological aspect as well. The phoneme can be viewed as the speaker's internalized representation of a single speech sound, which, however, can have different phonetic shapes depending on the environment in which it appears. To speakers of American English, for example, the phones [tʰ], [t], [ʔt], and so forth, are all heard as a single *t*-sound. This "single *t*-sound" is the phoneme /t/.

Some linguists understand the phoneme somewhat more concretely and view it as a representation of an ideal articulatory target. Because of the effects of the environment in which the phoneme occurs, however, it may be produced in different allophonic shapes. In any case, phonemic writing represents the *basic, contrasting* sound units of a language.

The aspiration of syllable-initial voiceless stops is, nevertheless, a regularly observable feature of English pronunciation, and we want to represent this phonetic regularity in some way. To fail to do so would be to fail to give a proper characterization of American English pronunciation. For this reason we require a phonetic representation system as well as a phonemic representation system in order to characterize the sounds of English (and of human language in general).

Note that the crucial information to be encoded by phonological representation systems is in the form of individual phonological (phonetic) features that serve as the basis for defining phonological symbols such as /t/, /d/, and so on (as in the cross-classifying features in table 4.2). That is, unitary phonemic symbols actually abbreviate *groups* (or bundles) of phonetic features. Recall the minimal pair *sip* and *zip*. In this pair of words, the contrast actually reduces to a difference in a single articulatory feature: voicing. That is, /s/ and /z/ are articulated in the same way, except that /s/ is voiceless and /z/ is voiced. Given that the words *sip* and *zip* differ in meaning, we see that in English the *feature* of *voicing* can function to *distinguish* words. If we voice the first consonant in *sip,* we will change that word into the semantically distinct word *zip*. We say that features are minimally *distinctive* (or *contrastive*) when they function alone to distinguish meanings in this way.

Serving as the minimal contrasting units in phonemes is not the only way that phonetic features manifest themselves. Indeed, in any fully adequate phonological theory, phonological generalizations will be stated not in terms of phoneme symbols (such as /p/, /t/, /k/), but directly in terms of phonetic features (such as voicing). We noted earlier that the class of phonemes that are aspirated in syllable-initial position is uniquely defined as the *voiceless stops*. For present purposes, however, we can continue to use phonemic and phonetic symbols (which indirectly encode phonetic features, given the way in which we define the symbols). See section 4.3 on distinctive feature theory for more discussion of this point.

In many cases the distinction between phonemic and phonetic representations will not be crucial for our purposes in this chapter. For example, the phonemic representation /ɪ/ and the phonetic form [ɪ] will not differ in any significant way, and thus it will not matter whether we cite the vowel as /ɪ/ or [ɪ]. Generally speaking, we will use phonetic representations, using [ ], when discussing specific details of the pronunciation of a word or syllable, and phonemic representations, using / /, when discussing individual consonants and vowels at a more abstract level, as part of a phonological system.

So far we have taken care to specify that our phonemic and phonetic generalizations are based on American English. It is important to note, however, that languages can differ with respect to what features function distinctively. For example, in Hindi, a language of India, the feature of aspiration does in fact function distinctively in voiceless stops. For speakers of Hindi, the consonants /kʰ/ (aspirated) and /k/ (unaspirated) are perceived as two completely different consonant sounds, and indeed we can find minimal pairs in Hindi showing the contrast between the two. For example, /kʰiil/ means "parched grain," whereas /kiil/ means "nail." Speakers of English tend to hear Hindi /kʰ/ and /k/ as free variants of one another, or else they perceive Hindi unaspirated /k/ as English /g/, given that voiced stops in English are unaspirated. But Hindi /kʰ/ and /k/ also contrast with Hindi /g/. This example brings up an important point: whether or not a feature is contrastive (phonemic) is a language-particular phenomenon. That is, a phonetic distinction that functions phonemically in one language may or may not function phonemically in another language. Aspiration functions phonemically in Hindi, but it has no such function in English.

In certain languages of East Asia, such as Japanese and Korean, no phonemic contrast exists between the consonants *r* and *l*. Japanese has both [r] and [l], but as free variants of one phoneme usually labeled /r/. Korean also has both [r] and [l], but in complementary distribution as allophones of a single phoneme usually labeled /l/. Speakers of American English are baffled by the fact that to a Japanese speaker the English words *led* and *red* sound like the same word. How can sounds that seem so different be heard as the same sound? Again, the answer is that phonemic distinctions in one language are not necessarily phonemic distinctions in another language. Speakers of Japanese perceive English /r/ and /l/ analogously to the way that speakers of English perceive Hindi /k/ and /kʰ/: as phonetic variants of the same consonant phoneme.

More Phonetics: Contractions in Casual Spoken English

In discussing the phonetic properties of English, we have so far focused our attention on phonetic details within single words. Now we must note that in casual spoken forms of American English there are a number of phonological contraction processes in which a sequence of words is contracted, or reduced, to a shorter sequence. For example, consider the various phonological contractions of forms of the verb *to be*, illustrated in tables 4.5 and 4.6. Taking table 4.5 first, notice that a sequence of words from formal written language such as *she is* will be pronounced in careful, or formal, speech as a sequence of two separate words [šiy] [ɪz], whereas in more casual, rapid speech they are "merged" into a single bisyllabic (two-syllable) form [šíyɨz], with stress

Table 4.5
Phonetic form of contractions of the verb *to be* with personal pronouns in American English: Bisyllabic forms

Formal Written	Formal Spoken	Casual Spoken Bisyllabic Forms
I am	[ay æm]	[áyəm]
you are	[yuw ɑr]	[yúwr̩]
she is	[šiy ɪz]	[šíyɨz]
he is	[hiy ɪz]	[híyɨz]
it is	[ɪt ɪz]	[ɪ́Dɨz]
we are	[wiy ɑr]	[wíyr̩]
they are	[ðey ɑr]	[ðéyr̩]

Table 4.6
Phonetic form of contractions of the verb *to be* with personal pronouns in American English: Monosyllabic forms

Casual Written	Casual Spoken Monosyllabic Forms
I'm	[aym] or [ɑm]
you're	[yʊr] or [yər]
	[yr̩]
she's	[šiyz]
he's	[hiyz]
it's	[ɪts]
we're	[wɪr]
they're	[ðɛr]

on the first syllable (indicated by the accent mark, ´ , above the first vowel). Notice further that in the bisyllabic form [šíyɨz], the vowel [ɪ] of [ɪz] has become reduced to [ɨ], a reduction phenomenon that also takes place when the two-word sequence *I am* becomes a single bisyllabic form [áyəm], where [æ] has been reduced to [ə] in the unstressed syllable. Recall that the reduced vowels [ɨ] and [ə] occur only in unstressed syllables of a word (as in, for example, *sofa* [sowfə] and *chicken* [číkɨn]). In other words, the bisyllabic forms [šíyɨz] and [áyəm] reflect phonetic patterns characteristic of single words, and indeed we can consider such bisyllabic contractions as single phonological words.

The same point can be illustrated by considering the pronunciation of the sequence *it is* in both careful and casual speech styles. In a more formal speech style, *it is* is pronounced as a sequence of two words [ít] [íz]; in the casual, rapid speech style, the two words have become "merged" into the single bisyllabic form [íDɨz]. Notice that the [t] of [ɪt] has become a flap [D] in the casual bisyllabic form, which is just what we expect. Recall that /t/ is realized as the allophone [D] when it occurs intervocalically (between vowels) and the immediately preceding vowel is accented. In single words we can see this phenomenon in contrasting pairs such as *atom* [ǽDəm] and *atomic* [əthámɨk]: in *átom* the vowel preceding /t/ is stressed (and /t/ is phonetically realized as [D]), whereas in *atómic* the stress is shifted to the vowel following /t/, and /t/ is not realized as [D] (but rather as [tʰ]). Thus, the bisyllabic contraction [íDɨz] reflects a phonetic property found in single words (in that /t/ is realized as [D]), and it is in this sense that [íDɨz] can be considered a single phonological word.

To take a final example from table 4.5, consider the sequences with the form *are: you are, we are, they are*. Notice that in the bisyllabic contracted forms of casual speech, *are* [ɑr] has been reduced to [r] alone (the vowel [ɑ] having been lost), and in fact this [r] functions as the second (unstressed) syllable. Syllabic [r], like the syllabic nasal [n̩], is represented by placing a straight apostrophe beneath the symbol, [r̩], indicating that it can function as a syllable by itself, without an accompanying vowel. In the forms [yúwr̩], [wíyr̩], and [ðéyr̩], notice that the long vowels [uw], [iy], and [ey] are in the first (stressed) syllable, and [r̩] forms the following syllable. It turns out that this sequencing reflects a syllabic pattern found quite generally in single words of American English: /r/ is never part of the same syllable with a preceding long vowel. Even though one-syllable words such as *beer* are often perceived by speakers of American English as containing a vowel like the tense diphthong [iy] followed by [r], in actuality the vowel in the word *beer* is the lax vowel [ɪ], and the word should be phonemically transcribed (for most speakers) as /bɪr/. The reason that [ɪ] is heard as being more like [iy] involves a *coarticulation effect:* for many speakers, American English /r/ is articulated with a raised tongue blade, and in articulating a sequence such as [ɪr], the tongue begins to raise during the articulation of the vowel in anticipation of the raised position it will have to assume in order to articulate [r]. This coarticulation, or *anticipatory,* phenomenon has the effect of raising the vowel [ɪ] somewhat, creating the auditory impression of [iy]. Since it is a phonological property of American English that the two members of the sequence *long vowel* + /r/ must be in different syllables, then, this syllabic pattern is just what we find in the bisyllabic contractions [yúwr̩], [wíyr̩], and [ðéyr̩]. As we will see, however, short vowels and /r/ can appear in the same syllable.

The English writing system reflects phonological contractions with the orthographic (spelling) device of the apostrophe ', as illustrated in table 4.6. Notice that in the casual speech pronunciations of the contractions in table 4.6, the bisyllabic (two-syllable) forms of table 4.5 have become monosyllabic (one-syllable). (It should be noted, in passing, that some speakers of American English also have a bisyllabic pronunciation of some of the casual written contractions of table 4.6, but that is irrelevant to the present discussion.) In these examples, we see that *am, are,* and *is* have lost their vowels entirely, and have become reduced to [m], [r], and [z], respectively. Thus, *I'm* is pronounced as a monosyllabic [aym] or [ɑm], having lost the schwa [ə] of the bisyllabic [ayəm]. In the forms *you're* ([yur] or [yṛ]), *we're* ([wɪr]), and *they're* ([ðɛr]), notice that [r] is in the same syllable as the preceding vowel; however, the vowel is now a *short vowel* ([ur], [ṛ], [ɪr], and [ɛr]) and thus [r] can occur with it as part of the same syllable. In fact, [ṛ] can even be the only vowel-like sound in a contraction such as *you're* [yṛ]. That the phoneme /r/ "acts like" a vowel is a rather striking property of American English, though for expository reasons we did not introduce this fact earlier. Consider words such as *packer* [pʰækṛ] or even *bird* [bṛd] and *fur* [fṛ]. In these words there is no accompanying "pure" vowel preceding the *r* in the syllable containing the *r*. (We discuss below additional examples of consonants that can function in a vowel-like way in English.) Once again, we see how contracted forms reflect phonological (in this case syllabic) properties of single words.

Finally, let us consider the contraction of the verb form *is* in combinations such as *she's* [šiyz], *he's* [hiyz], and *it's* [ɪts]. In the first two cases, *is* has become reduced to [z], as noted above. But the form *it's* [ɪts] has an interesting feature: *is* is reduced to the voiceless [s], rather than the voiced [z] of the other forms. It appears that an *assimilation* process is working here: the forms *she* and *he* end in a voiced sound (the vowel [iy]), whereas *it* ends in a voiceless consonant [t], suggesting that the reduced verb [z] (from *is*) becomes voiceless when attached to a form that ends in a voiceless consonant.

This assimilation process is the same one seen in the Plural Rule (recall hypothesis 3, part (c), stating that the plural morpheme takes the form [s] when attached to a noun that ends in a voiceless consonant), and in fact we can observe the same assimilation process in another set of data involving contractions with question words such as *who, what, where,* and *when.* To see this, consider the following sets of data, illustrating casual speech contractions:

(4)
a. What's it look like? (= What *does* it look like?)
b. What's he doing now? (= What *is* he doing now?)
c. What's he been up to? (= What *has* he been up to?)

(5)
a. How's he like his new job? (= How *does* he like his new job?)
b. How's it going? (= How *is* it going?)
c. How's she been, lately? (= How *has* she been, lately?)

These examples show that the auxiliary verbs *does, is,* and *has* all reduce to a single consonant when contracted onto question words such as *what* or *how.* This consonant is represented as *'s* in the English writing system, but notice that it has two phonetic forms in these examples: it is realized as voiceless [s] in *what's* [wʌts] (or [wats]), but as voiced [z] in *how's* [hawz]. Once again, notice that the form *what* [wʌt] (or [wat]) ends in a voiceless consonant, [t], whereas *how* [haw] ends in a voiced sound, the diphthong [aw]; and the reduced auxiliary [z] assimilates in voicing to the voiceless [t], becoming voiceless [s]. We find in fact that for all question words other than *what,* the contraction *'s* is pronounced [z], and it turns out that all those question words end in voiced sounds. In sum, the voicing assimilation phenomenon found in single plural words such as *cats* [kʰæts] and *dogs* [dɔgz] is reflected in casual speech contractions. The behavior of contractions is excellent evidence for the validity of the phonological rules discussed earlier. Our survey of contractions also underscores the fact that two basic elements determine the pronunciation of language: sounds and rules. Whenever combinations of speech sounds are uttered, regardless of whether they are the result of contraction, or perhaps the result of different styles of rapid speech, these combinations are subject to the overall phonological rules of the language. Thus, our speech is shaped by the rules of our own language, and when we speak another human language, our "foreign accent" is a direct result of our own language's phonological system, of which we have little conscious awareness.

Possible Words and Possible Syllable Structures

As words "merge" in the contraction processes of casual speech, it appears that the final phonological contraction must itself be a "possible word" of English; that is, it must conform to certain systematic phonological patterns characteristic of individual words. For example, the sequence of phonemes /tz/ cannot end a word in English (despite the fact that names such as *Katz* are spelled with the letters *tz,* that final sequence is actually pronounced [ts]). We have noted that this constraint on sequencing is reflected in plural forms such as *cats* [kæts] and in contracted forms such as *what's* [wʌts] (or [wats]), where voicing assimilation has taken place, thereby avoiding the sequence [tz].

It turns out that every language has certain conditions, or constraints, that govern the *possible sequences of phonemes* in its words (sometimes referred to as *phonotactic constraints*), and these various conditions in effect add up to a kind of phonological "template" (or pattern) that all words and syllables of the language must conform to. For example, in English there are constraints on the possible sequences of three word-initial consonants. That is, in words beginning with three consonants, the first consonant must be /s/. The second consonant can only be one of the voiceless stops /p/, /t/, or /k/. If /p/ is the second consonant, then /r/, /l/, or /y/ can be the third (as in *spread* /sprɛd/, *spleen* /spliyn/, and *spew* /spyuw/). If the consonant following /s/ is /t/, then in most dialects only /r/ can follow as the third consonant (as in *stream* /striym/). However, there are some dialects of English that also allow /y/ to follow an /st/ sequence, if the following vowel is the diphthong /uw/ (hence, one can also hear the pronunciation [styuw] for *stew* instead of the more common [stuw]). Finally, if the consonant following /s/ is /k/, then /r/, /l/, /w/, or /y/ can be the third consonant (as in *scream* /skriym/, *sclerosis* /sklərówsɪs/, *square* /skwɛr/, and *skew* /skyuw/). These, then, are the only sequences of three consonants found in word-initial position in English.

But notice now that the constraints on possible three-consonant sequences characterize not only English word structure, but also English *syllable* structure. For example, the sequence /str-/ can appear not only in word-initial position (as in *strain* /streyn/), but also in syllable-initial position (as in the second syllable of the word *constrain* /kən - streyn/). In other words, when we talk about the phonological structure of possible words in a language, we are also necessarily saying something about the phonological structure of possible syllables of the language.

Although native speakers of English can learn to recognize how many syllables a word has (*cat* has one syllable /kæt/, *catfish* two syllables /kæt - fɪš/, *catalogue* three syllables /kæ - tə - lɑg/, and *catatonic* four syllables /kæ - tə - tɑ - nɪk/), it is no easy task to define what, precisely, a syllable is. Across a wide range of languages, the most common type of syllable has the structure CV(C), that is, a single consonant (C) followed by a vowel (V), possibly followed in turn by a single consonant. Vowels usually form the "center" (or "core") of a syllable, and hence are often called the *nucleus* of the syllable; consonants usually form the beginning (the *onset*) and the end (the *coda*) of the syllable, as shown in figure 4.9, part A. A word such as *napkin* would have the syllable structure shown in figure 4.9, part C.

We will not elaborate further on a definition of the notion *syllable* (there are numerous complications that would take us far afield from the purposes of this chapter), but we can at least point to certain in-

A.

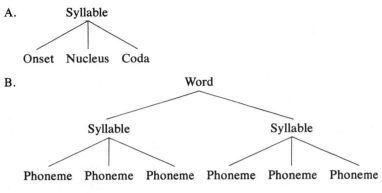

B.

C.

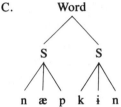

Figure 4.9
Typical syllable structure (A), hierarchical organization of phonological units (B), syllable analysis of sample word (C)

teresting problems that exist in the study of syllable structure. First, recall from our previous discussion of syllabic /ɹ̩/ and /n̩/ that these consonants can function as syllables by themselves. In fact, /m/ and /l/ have syllabic variants too, and thus we can find words such as *bottom* [bádm̩] and *apple* [ǽpl̩] in addition to words such as *butter* [bʌ́Dɹ̩] and *bútton* [bʌ́ʔn̩]. In each case the second syllable (/m̩/, /l̩/, /ɹ̩/, and /n̩/, respectively) consists solely of a consonant. Hence, we must allow for syllables that contain no vowel nucleus.

Second, we must allow for *ambisyllabic* consonants, that is, consonants that function simultaneously as the coda of one syllable and the onset of the immediately following syllable (*ambi-* in the term *ambisyllabic* is a prefix of Greek origin meaning "both"). For example, in slow, careful speech, for instance in calling out a name to fetch someone for dinner, one might divide a name like *Emma* /ɛmə/ into the syllables /ɛ - mə/ or /ɛm - ə/. However, in normal conversational speech, /m/ is actually part of both syllables, functioning both to "close" the first syllable and to initiate the second.

Finally, we must formulate certain principles of syllabification that will allow us to choose a single correct syllable structure when more than one is available. For example, consider the word *contrast* /kántræst/. The intuitively most natural syllable division would be *con - trast* /kán - træst/. But hypothetically, we could have divided the word in other ways: *cónt - rast, có - ntrast,* or even *cóntr - ast.* What allows us to make the judgment that the first syllable analysis is the most "natural"? It seems that there exists a syllabification principle of the following sort: sequences of word-internal consonants are divided up so that the number of consonants beginning the second syllable is in fact the maximum number of consonants that can begin a syllable. A good way to determine how many consonants can begin a syllable is to check on how many consonants can begin a word, since the beginning of a word pronounced in isolation is always the beginning of a syllable. English words can begin with the sequence *tr* (as in *train* /treyn/) or the consonant *r* (as in *rain* /reyn/), but no English word begins with the sequence *ntr.* Thus, of the three sequences *ntr, tr,* and *r,* the sequence *tr* is the maximum possible sequence that can begin the second syllable of the word *contrast.*

These considerations show that our theory of syllable structure will have to account for certain complications; that is, simple diagrams such as figure 4.9, part A, will by no means tell the whole story. However, the point we wish to stress here is that the syllable forms a *unit of phonological structure:* individual phonemes occur in sequences that make up syllables, and syllables in turn occur in sequences that make up words (see figure 4.9, part B). Although syllables in all languages generally follow the abstract pattern CV(C) (that is, the onset-nucleus-coda structure depicted in figure 4.9, part A), the detailed principles of syllabification of words nevertheless vary across languages.

In closing, we should emphasize that speakers of a language really do implicitly come to know the principles of syllable structure for their native language, and can easily recognize when hypothetical words violate these principles. Thus, invented brand and company names such as *Biz* and *Exxon* conform to the syllable structure of English, and native speakers judge that such words "sound like" English words. However, if zealous advertising executives were to invent a brand name such as *Ntra,* they would have violated the constraints on English syllable structure: among other things, the constraint that if three consonants begin a word, then the first one must be /s/. Native speakers will immediately recognize such a word as being "strange" or "foreign," based on the principles of syllable structure they have internalized as part of learning their native language.

In sum, syllable structure rules are best expressed as principles that externally organize strings of phonemes, more or less as represented in figure 4.9. We have already seen that strings of phonemes are organized into structural units such as morphemes and words, and thus syllables represent an intermediate structure between phonemes and the word. Phonemes themselves also have internal structure; as we will see, they are to be viewed as complexes of phonetic (or distinctive) features.

4.3 ORGANIZATIONAL PRINCIPLES OF PHONOLOGY

Distinctive Features

Some Background Arguments
As we have seen, phonological rules and generalizations are stated in terms of phonetic features (the smaller units that combine to make up phonemes), rather than in terms of phonemes themselves. Returning to the English Plural Rule, let us recall that we must use the feature of voicing to state an important generalization about the form of the plural morpheme: aside from cases where a noun ends in a sibilant consonant, the phonological form of the plural morpheme is determined by a general assimilation process, whereby the plural form is voiceless if the final phoneme of the noun is voiceless, but is voiced if the final phoneme of the noun is voiced. The feature of voicing, then, allows us to state a generalization that we miss by merely listing phonemes (compare, again, the discussion of hypotheses 2 and 3 of the Plural Rule).

It turns out that the Plural Rule exemplifies an important point about determining which phonetic features of a language are in fact the significant ones for a theory of phonology. Notice that in English the phonetic feature of voicing plays an important *dual role:* (a) it is distinctive, in that it serves to distinguish phonemes such as /s/ and /z/ in minimal pairs such as /sɪp/ and /zɪp/; and (b) it plays a crucial role in the statement of phonological regularities (in the Plural Rule). In general, then, the significant phonetic features of a language will be those that distinguish phonemes from one another and/or play a crucial role in the statement of phonological rules.

In table 4.2 we listed a number of place- and manner-of-articulation features that in fact serve to cross-classify consonants of English in important ways. Using such features, we can pick out *natural classes* of sounds; for example, given the features listed in table 4.2, we can pick out the class of *voiceless stops* in English, /p/ - /t/ - /k/. It is not just for convenience that we wish to refer to a class of voiceless stops—as we have seen, important phonological generalizations are crucially stated in terms of this class (recall the Aspiration Rule for English, whereby all voiceless stops become aspirated in syllable-initial position). Thus, the organization of table 4.2 (in particular the manner- and place-of-articulation features that are encoded in it) plays an important role in allowing us to state phonological rules of English: the table picks out the very classes that are referred to in phonological generalizations.

But now we must point out that the system embodied in table 4.2 is not quite right for a general theory of phonology. This is because the table is stated entirely in terms of English phonology; that is, the articulatory descriptions in table 4.2 are based entirely on the way consonants are articulated in English. For example, the stops /t/ and /d/ are listed as *alveolar,* given that in English those stops are articulated with the tongue tip making contact with the alveolar ridge. But this is not how *t* and *d* are articulated in all languages. For example, in certain continental European languages (such as Spanish), as well as in Japanese, *t* and *d* are *dental* stops: that is, the tongue tip makes contact on the teeth, rather than on the alveolar ridge (immediately behind the teeth). Thus, the feature system that forms the basis for table 4.2 would actually not be accurate for Spanish and Japanese (at least not with respect to the phonemes /t/ and /d/).

This leaves us in an unsatisfactory position: after all, there is an intuitively natural sense in which we want to say that Spanish, Japanese, and English all have the stop consonants *t* and *d,* and whether one type is basically dental (tongue tip touching teeth) and the other type is basically alveolar seems irrelevant. Furthermore, even in diverse languages quite similar phonological processes apply to stops such as *t.* For example, in many languages *t* becomes *palatalized* (that is, it is articulated in the palatal region and partly fricativized, thus becoming /č/) under certain circumstances (usually preceding a high front vowel or the glide /y/). Thus, in English the casual speech contraction of *don't* + *you* as *dontcha* [downčə] shows that the final /t/ of *don't* becomes [č] when combined with the glide /y/ of *you.* In Japanese, the phoneme /t/ has the positional variant [č] when followed by the high vowel /i/, a palatalization process also found in Brazilian Portuguese (which, like Spanish, has an apicodental *t*). These examples are simply meant to illustrate that despite the differences in the articulation of *t* that exist across languages, that stop undergoes very similar palatalization processes (among others) in the various languages. Therefore, we want to be able to talk about stops such as *t* and *d* across a number of languages, in a general way that will overlook irrelevant details in articulation.

A good deal of research in phonology has been aimed at defining a set of phonetic features that will, in fact, allow us to abstract away from English (and other specific languages), in such a way that we can refer to consonants and vowels in a general fashion, with cross-linguistic validity. For example, instead of using the phonetic feature *alveolar* to describe /t/ and /d/, phonologists have postulated a feature *coronal* to describe *all* articulations in which the tongue blade raises to approach or contact the teeth, the alveolar ridge, or the prepalatal region of the roof of the mouth. The feature *coronal* is clearly a more general feature than the feature *alveolar,* in that it includes a wider range of possible articulations. Thus, regardless of the fact that Spanish and Japanese have dental *t,* whereas English has alveolar *t,* we can say that these languages all have *(voiceless) coronal stops.*

Let us take another example. Following tradition, we stated earlier in this chapter that the phoneme /k/ in English is a voiceless velar stop. But in fact it is not always the case that /k/ is completely velar—under certain circumstances /k/ is articulated with the body of the tongue making contact with the roof of the mouth at the point where the hard palate joins the velum (that is, as prevelar or postpalatal /k/). For example, whenever /k/ is followed by the tense vowel diphthong /iy/ or the glide /y/, it has a prevelar/postpalatal articulation. In words such as *key* /kiy/ or *cute* /kyuwt/, /k/ is postpalatal, because of a coarticulation effect: in articulating /iy/ or /y/, the tongue body is raised into a high position near the hard palate, and in articulating /k/ before these phonemes, we *anticipate* the articulation of /iy/ or /y/ and shift the tongue forward from the velum toward the palatal region. In contrast, when /k/ is followed by a back vowel, as in words like *cool* /kuwl/, it is indeed a velar consonant. However, there is an important feature that *all* instances of /k/ share: all /k/'s of English are articulated with a *high* tongue body, and differ only in how far *front* or *back* the high tongue body makes contact with the roof of the mouth. Thus, phonologists have proposed that the phonetic features *high* and *back*—the same features used in the description of certain vowels—should characterize /k/, rather than a feature *velar*. The /k/ that precedes front vowels, such as /iy/, will be characterized as *high* but *nonback;* the /k/ that precedes back vowels, such as /uw/, will be characterized as both *high* and *back*. In other words, /k/ is in both cases *high,* but its specification for *backness* will reflect that of the following vowel. Incidentally, in some languages, such as Rumanian, palatal *k* (high and nonback) versus velar /k/ (high and back) are contrasting phonemes and can thus serve to differentiate minimal pairs. Thus, by replacing a feature such as *velar* with the features *high* and *back,* we can now properly distinguish the types of /k/ in English from those in other languages, at the same time capturing what all the different types of /k/ have in common. In addition, we will see that using the same tongue-body features (such as *high* and *back*) to describe consonants as well as vowels permits insightful descriptions of phonological regularities.

As we examine a range of languages, it becomes clear that we will ultimately need to devise a feature system that will have universal validity, one that will be valid for characterizing the phonetic possibilities in all languages, and not just English (or a small subset of languages). To get a somewhat wider perspective, consider now the consonants listed in table 4.7, drawn from four unrelated, geographically separated languages. This consonant pattern is quite common in the world's languages. Notice that all four languages form their stops at the same general points along the vocal tract. The Navajo system of stops, though lacking a phoneme /p/, is otherwise quite similar to the English system. Ganda (a member of the Bantu family of languages spoken in Africa) has a system similar to that of English and Navajo, except that its pal-

Table 4.7
Stop and affricate consonants in four unrelated and geographically separated languages

	Labial	Dental/alveolar	Palatal	Velar
English (Europe, Australia,	p	t	č	k
North America)	b	d	ǰ	g
Navajo (North America)	(missing)	t	č	k
	b	d	ǰ	g
Ganda (Africa)	p	t	c (stop)	k
	b	d	j (stop)	g
Japanese (Asia)	p	t	č	k
	b	d	ǰ	g

atal stops are not affricates (that is, the Ganda phoneme /c/ is pronounced something like [ky], and /j/ something like [gy]). Finally, the Japanese system is like those of the other languages, except that /t/ and /d/ are apicodental, rather than apicoalveolar (the pattern for the other three languages).

It is striking that, despite various minor differences in articulation, the consonant systems of these diverse languages (and indeed those in the majority of the world's languages) cluster around the labial, dental/alveolar, palatal, and velar regions. There is intriguing evidence that these particular points of articulation are regions of *acoustic stability* (Stevens 1972). For example, the sound produced by tongue-tip contact throughout the dental and alveolar region is acoustically stable, in that the sound is relatively constant regardless of minor shifts in the position of the tongue within this region. In contrast, the points of articulation between the commonly occurring points of articulation—for example, the area on the border between the dental/alveolar region and the palatal region—are regions of acoustic instability, where even a small shift in the position of the tongue can lead to radical changes in the acoustic properties of the sound. Thus, it is apparently only for articulations made in the vocal tract's regions of acoustic stability that there is considerable "leeway" for tongue position. It is probably not an accident, therefore, that the majority of the world's languages have consonantal systems with places of articulation similar to those shown in table 4.7.

For these reasons, then, it is clear that the manner- and place-of-articulation features listed in table 4.2 are not necessarily the optimum set of phonetic features for the world's languages; rather, they reflect specific details of articulation in English that may be irrelevant from a wider, cross-linguistic perspective. A number of linguists have proposed alternative universal phonetic feature systems, and we will now examine one of these in some detail.

An *SPE*-based System
In tables 4.8 and 4.9 we have listed the consonants and vowels of English as they are classified in the distinctive feature system based on the one proposed by Morris Halle and Noam Chomsky in their 1968 work, *The Sound Pattern of English* (*SPE*). Their proposals in turn build on the pioneering work in distinctive feature theory done by Roman Jakobson (Jakobson and Halle 1956). In the *SPE* system, the articulatory features are viewed as basically *binary*, that is, as having one of two values: either a *plus* value (+), which indicates the presence of the

Table 4.8
Distinctive feature composition of English consonants

	p	b	m	t	d	n	k	g	ŋ	f	v
Syllabic	−	−	−	−	−	−	−	−	−	−	−
			(+)			(+)					
Consonant	+	+	+	+	+	+	+	+	+	+	+
Sonorant	−	−	+	−	−	+	−	−	+	−	−
Voiced	−	+	+	−	+	+	−	+	+	−	+
Continuant	−	−	−	−	−	−	−	−	−	+	+
Nasal	−	−	+	−	−	+	−	−	+	−	−
Strident	−	−	−	−	−	−	−	−	−	+	+
Lateral	−	−	−	−	−	−	−	−	−	−	−
Distributed	−	−	−	−	−	−	−	−	−	−	−
Affricate	−	−	−	−	−	−	−	−	−	−	−
Labial	+	+	+	−	−	−	−	−	−	+	+
Coronal	−	−	−	+	+	+	−	−	−	−	−
Anterior	+	+	+	+	+	+	−	−	−	+	+
High	−	−	−	−	−	−	+	+	+	−	−
Back	−	−	−	−	−	−	+	+	+	−	−
Low	−	−	−	−	−	−	−	−	−	−	−

feature, or a *minus* value (−), which indicates the absence of the feature. Each phonetic feature represents an individually controllable aspect of articulation. For example, the feature *nasal* is related to the raising or lowering of the velum (nasal sounds are produced with a lowered velum, which allows air to enter the nasal passages; nonnasal sounds are produced with a raised velum, which blocks off the nasal passages from the oral cavity). The phoneme /m/ thus has the feature [+nasal], whereas the phoneme /b/ has the feature [−nasal]; this indicates that in the articulation of /m/ the velum is lowered, and in the articulation of /b/ the velum is raised. (Distinctive features, by convention, are enclosed in square brackets [   ].) In a similar fashion, all phonemes in the *SPE* system are regarded as *bundles of features,* that is, as groups of binary features with pluses and minuses, as can be seen in table 4.8. Notice that the features allow us to distinguish all the conso-

	s	z	θ	ð	š	ž	č	ǰ	l	r	w	y	h
Syllabic	−	−	−	−	−	−	−	−	−	−	−	−	−
									(+)	(+)			
Consonant	+	+	+	+	+	+	+	+	+	+	−	−	−
Sonorant	−	−	−	−	−	−	−	−	+	+	+	+	+
Voiced	−	+	−	+	−	+	−	+	+	+	+	+	−
Continuant	+	+	+	+	+	+	−	−	+	+	+	+	+
Nasal	−	−	−	−	−	−	−	−	−	−	−	−	−
Strident	+	+	−	−	+	+	+	+	−	−	−	−	−
Lateral	−	−	−	−	−	−	−	−	+	−	−	−	−
Distributed	−	−	−	−	+	+	+	+	−	−	−	−	−
Affricate	−	−	−	−	−	−	+	+	−	−	−	−	−
Labial	−	−	−	−	−	−	−	−	−	−	+	−	−
Coronal	+	+	+	+	+	+	+	+	+	+	−	−	−
Anterior	+	+	+	+	−	−	−	−	+	+	−	−	−
High	−	−	−	−	+	+	+	+	−	−	+	+	−
Back	−	−	−	−	−	−	−	−	−	−	+	−	−
Low	−	−	−	−	−	−	−	−	−	+	−	−	(+)

nant phonemes from one another and at the same time to refer to natural classes of sounds (for instance, /p/, /t/, and /k/ form a class that we wish to refer to in a general fashion as voiceless stops, all sharing the features [−voiced] and [−continuant]). The features of our *SPE* system, which we will now briefly describe individually, are intended as universal features, and not merely as features peculiar to English.

Syllabic. The feature [+syllabic] is assigned to phonemes that occur in the nucleus position of syllables (see figure 4.9). The vowels of English are, of course, syllabic, and the phonemes /r/, /l/, /m/, and /n/ can also be syllabic in unstressed syllables.

Consonant. Phonemes with the feature [+consonantal] are formed in the vocal tract with an obstruction that is at least as narrow as that of a fricative. Note that the glides are therefore not true consonants—nor, as we will see, are they true vowels.

Sonorant. "Sonorant sounds are produced with a vocal tract cavity in which spontaneous voicing is possible" (*SPE,* 302). In other words, the vocal tract is not constricted to the extent that airflow across the glottis is inhibited. Vowels, glides, liquids, and nasals are all sonorants. Nonsonorant consonants are frequently referred to as *obstruents.*

Voiced. Phonemes are voiced when their articulation is accompanied by a periodic vibration of the vocal cords. All of the phonemes in the word /bɪd/ are [+voiced], whereas the phonemes /p/, /t/, /k/ are [−voiced].

Continuant. Noncontinuant sounds are made with a complete blockage of the oral tract. Continuant sounds are made without such a blockage. By this definition nasals are oral noncontinuant stops, although air is shunted through the nasal cavity.

Nasal. Phonemes have the feature [+nasal] when the velum is lowered during speech, thus permitting the airflow to activate resonances in the nasal cavity.

Strident. Strident sounds are characterized by the high-frequency turbulent noise that accompanies the production of some fricatives and affricates. The phoneme /s/ is [+strident], whereas the phoneme /θ/ is [−strident].

Lateral. If the tip of the tongue is partially blocking the airstream, but the air is allowed to pass along one or both sides of the tongue, the resulting sound is lateral. The phoneme /l/ is the only [+lateral] sound in English.

Distributed. The term *distributed* refers to the relative length of contact that the tongue makes along (not across) the roof of the mouth. The tongue has a relatively longer region of approximation to the roof of the mouth in articulating /š/ as opposed to /s/; thus, /š/ is [+distributed] but /s/ is [−distributed]. The terms *apical* ([−distributed]) and *laminal* ([+distributed]) are more traditional terms for this articulatory difference.

Affricate. Recall that affricates are produced by articulatory gestures during which the airstream is temporarily stopped, but the stoppage is secondarily released into a fricative. This sequence of a stop plus a fricative functions in English as a single phoneme, as in /č/ and /ǰ/.

Labial. A labial articulation involves an approaching or closing of the lips. The phonemes /f/, /b/, /m/ are all [+labial].

Coronal. The blade of the tongue is raised toward or touches the teeth or the alveolar ridge. Dental, alveolar, and alveopalatal consonants are coronal phonemes.

Anterior. Anterior sounds are made with the primary constriction in front of the alveopalatal position. Labials, dentals, interdentals, and alveolar articulations are anterior.

High. The body of the tongue (not the blade) is raised toward or touches the roof of the mouth. The phonemes /k/, /ŋ/, /č/ are all [+high].

Back. Back phonemes are made with the tongue body slightly retracted from the rest (quiet breathing) position. Nonback phonemes (also called *front*) are made with the tongue body in a relatively forward position. The phoneme /č/ in *chuck* is [−back], whereas the /k/ in that word is [+back].

Low. Phonemes with this feature are made with the tongue body lowered and retracted. American English /r/ is [+low] because of its associated pharyngeal constriction.

We now turn to the phonetic features of the vowels given in table 4.9. The features *high, low,* and *back* are the same tongue body features used for characterizing consonants. The gestures associated with these features in vowels are not as extreme, however, as they are for consonants.

The feature *round* refers to the pursing (or rounding) of the lips that is a feature of English nonlow back vowels such as /uw/, /ʊ/, /ow/, and /ɔ/. The feature *labial* discussed earlier is not the same as *round.* The phoneme /f/, for example, is [+labial], but not [+round]. The term *long* is

Table 4.9
Distinctive feature composition of English vowels

	i (iy)	ɪ	e (ey)	ɛ	æ	u (uw)	ʊ	ʌ	o (ow)	ɔ	ɑ
Syllabic	+	+	+	+	+	+	+	+	+	+	+
High	+	+	−	−	−	+	+	−	−	−	−
Back	−	−	−	−	−	+	+	+	+	+	+
Low	−	−	−	−	+	−	−	−	−	−	+
Round	−	−	−	−	−	+	+	−	+	+	−
Long (tense)	+	−	+	−	−	+	−	−	+	−	−

used to distinguish /ɛ/ and /ey/, although we have already noted that there is more than a difference in length and muscle tension between these vowels: /ey/ begins in a higher position in the mouth than /ɛ/, and /ey/ also has a high off-glide. We have therefore listed the long vowels /iy/, /ey/, /uw/, /ow/ in terms of the features of their first segment. The remaining diphthongs /ay/, /aw/, /oy/ are not listed in table 4.9; they are to be analyzed as clusters of two phonemes: for example, /ay/ = /a/ + /y/.

Phonemes as Groups of Distinctive Features

As we have seen, the phonemes of all languages may be described in terms of differing subsets of the universally available set of distinctive features, some of which were discussed in the description of English phonemes. Although all languages draw from the same universal set of features, individual languages differ in the groups of features that make up their phonemes. The features *coronal, lateral, affricate,* and *distributed* are all found in English, but they never occur together in a single phoneme. In contrast, in Navajo (as well as in many other Native American languages of north America), these features do occur together in a single consonant, called a *lateral affricate;* the Navajo word *tłah* "ointment" begins with this phoneme, which is represented by the two letters *tł* in the Navajo writing system. Different groupings of features also occur in vowels. English, for example, does not have the feature of rounding in front vowels, but many European languages do, including French, German, Hungarian, and Finnish, among others. Thus, the widely differing sounds occurring in the world's languages are actually based on various combinations of a relatively small, restricted set of features such as those given in tables 4.8 and 4.9.

We do not wish to underestimate the fact that there are important differences between languages. For example, in the African language Xhosa, certain "click" phonemes are an integral part of the consonant system. Such click sounds do not exist in English (and most other languages), although English speakers utilize clicks in nonlinguistic communication (for example, in the United States a very common sound used to control horses is technically classified as a click sound). In the production of clicks, the tongue makes contact with the roof of the mouth not just at one point but at two points (both at the velum and at one other point). Further, between the stoppages at the two points of articulation, a partial vacuum is created by the dropping of the tongue at the velum, and when the front stoppage is finally released and air rushes into the vacuum, a click sound results. Very few languages in fact make use of the "suction features" that are necessary to characterize clicks; thus, we see that the set of universal phonetic features is one that is *available* for the description of various languages, though not necessarily actually fully utilized by all languages.

The Role of Distinctive Features in the Expression of Phonological Rules

We have been arguing that the fundamental contrasting units of a language are features of phonemes such as voicing. (Recall that voicing is the basic feature that distinguishes /z/ from /s/, for example.) Additional support for analyzing phonemes into their constituent features comes from the insightful way that phonological regularities can be stated in terms of the features that make up the phonemes.

Let us return one final time to the English Plural Rule and reformulate it in terms of the phonetic features presented in the previous section. The only difference will be the replacement of the term *alveolar* with the term *coronal*, and the term *sibilant* with *strident*.

(6)

English Plural Rule (final version)

a. The plural morpheme takes the form [ɨz] if the last phoneme of the noun contains the features [+strident, +coronal].

Otherwise:

b. The form is the voiced variant [z] if the last phoneme of the noun is [+voiced].

Or:

c. The form is the voiceless variant [s] if the last phoneme of the noun is [−voiced].

The patterning of regularities seen in the English Plural Rule offers additional justification for the analysis of phonemes into feature clusters. The phoneme classes that participate in the formulation of rules can usually be defined in terms of a relatively small number of phonetic features. As we have noted, each of these small lists of phonetic features is the basis for isolating a natural class of phonemes (see also Halle 1962), which we can roughly define as follows:

(7)

Natural Class (informal definition)

A natural class is a grouping of phonemes uniquely defined by a small number of distinctive features such that that grouping plays a significant role in expressing the phonological regularities found in languages.

For example, in Plural Rule (6) the groupings of phonemes used to state the rule are natural classes: the class of phonemes that take the [ɨz] ending is the class of *strident coronal* consonants; the class of phonemes that take the [z] ending is the class of *voiced* phonemes; and finally, the class of phonemes that take the [-s] plural is defined by its lack of voicing.

The statement of phonological regularities in terms of distinctive features has advantages in addition to expressing explicitly the patterning of phonemes in a language. In order to see these advantages, let us consider the salient distinctive features of the different plural shapes juxtaposed with the natural class descriptions of the noun-final phonemes, as shown in (8).

(8)

Natural class description of noun-final phonemes		Partial phonetic feature specification of plural morpheme shapes

a. $\begin{bmatrix} +\text{coronal} \\ +\text{strident} \end{bmatrix}$ + $\text{ɨ} \begin{bmatrix} +\text{coronal} \\ +\text{strident} \\ \vdots \end{bmatrix}$ (z)

b. $\begin{bmatrix} +\text{voice} \\ \vdots \end{bmatrix}$ + $\begin{bmatrix} +\text{voice} \\ \vdots \end{bmatrix}$ (z)

c. $\begin{bmatrix} -\text{voice} \\ \vdots \end{bmatrix}$ + $\begin{bmatrix} -\text{voice} \\ \vdots \end{bmatrix}$ (s)

Although the plural morpheme always contains a sibilant, there are nonetheless two major structural differences in the form of the morpheme: (1) the presence versus absence of *i*, and (2) the presence versus absence of voicing in the sibilant when *i* is absent. The *i* is present in (8a) to separate the final *z* (which is [+strident, +coronal]) from the (natural) class of phonemes that are also [+strident, +coronal]. That this intervening *i* facilitates the perception the plural morpheme can be easily observed by trying to produce the plural of a word such as *hiss,* using a plural shape without the intervening *i*. Thus, an additional advantage to the statement of the distribution of the plural morpheme in terms of distinctive features is that it explicitly reveals a (likely) explanation for why a particular class of phonemes takes the intervening *i* as part of the plural marker.

Yet another advantage to the distinctive feature notation was noted earlier: namely, the presence versus absence of voicing in the plural marker without the intervening *i*. The feature of voicing is carried over (progressively assimilated) from the noun-final phoneme to the plural morpheme sibilant. We noted that it is just the class of voiced (or voiceless) phonemes ((8b) or (8c), respectively) that has the voiced or voiceless form of the plural morpheme. The English Plural Rule, then, demonstrates the extent to which the phonological regularities are best stated in terms of phonological rules based on distinctive features.

Next we present two additional examples of phonological regularities from distinct languages that exhibit further evidence that (1) phonemes pattern in terms of natural classes, and (2) the nature of the phonological regularity is explicitly revealed by the rule expressed in distinctive features. Moreover, these two examples exhibit two additional types of phonological regularities found in natural language.

Mongolian

Mongolian has two sets of stops made in the velar region, a front set /g'/, /k'/, which are pronounced in a more forward position in the vocal tract, and a back set /G/, /q/, which are pronounced farther back in the vocal tract. (Additional phonetic qualities of these stops are not important for this example and will not be discussed here, although interested readers can find more details in Grønbech and Krueger (1955).) Some examples are listed in (9).

(9)

(Front) velar	(Back) velar
nig'en "one"	qoyar "two"
deg'ü "younger brother"	g'udurGa "tail strap"
köbeg'ün "son, boy"	Gajar "land, country, place"
k'er "how"	Gobi "barren steppe, desert, Gobi"

The more forward consonants /g'/, /k'/ occur before the vowels /e/, /ö/, /ü/, and the back consonants /G/, /q/ occur before /a/, /o/, /u/. The vowels /ö/ and /ü/ are the front vowels /e/ and /i/ pronounced with lip rounding (like the vowels found in French and German, for example). The distribution of the front consonants /g'/, /k'/ versus the back set /G/, /q/ is predictable, in that the former set appears before front vowels, the latter before back vowels, as shown in (10).

(10)

a. The ([−back]) consonants /g'/, /k'/ occur before [−back] (front) vowels.

b. The ([+back]) consonants /G/, /q/ occur before [+back] vowels.

Once again, if we stated the facts in terms of two lists of phonemes, /e/, /ö/, /ü/ versus /a/, /o/, /u/, we would fail to express the relevant generalizations that are captured by the distinctive feature formulation in (10). This notation reveals that the groups of phonemes /e/, /ö/, /ü/ and /a/, /o/, /u/ pattern as the two natural classes of front ([−back]) and back vowels, respectively.

This example also reveals that the use of the same tongue-body features (*high, low,* and *back*) to describe vowels as well as consonants leads to a natural explanatory account of the distribution of the two different types of consonants. The [−back] variants of the velar consonants occur before the [−back] vowels, and the [+back] variants occur before the [+back] vowels. As was the case in the statement of the English Plural Rule, the exact nature of the assimilation process between two adjacent phonological segments is explicitly expressed.

Note, however, that the assimilation differs in two major ways from the assimilation occurring in the English plural morpheme. First, the assimilation is between a consonant and a vowel (in the case of the English Plural Rule, the voicing assimilation is between two consonants). Second, the assimilation "goes in the other direction." When features of one phoneme are transferred to a (temporally) earlier phoneme, this process is called *regressive assimilation*. Psychologists (and some linguists) use the terms *perseverative coarticulation* (progressive assimilation) and *anticipatory coarticulation* (regressive assimilation), terms that reflect more accurately the nature of the assimilation phenomenon. (Coarticulation phenomena are discussed in more detail in chapter 10.) In any case, assimilation rules are very common in the world's languages, and they are clearly best stated in rules based on phonetic features.

Navajo

Most speakers of Navajo have a phonological alternation in the pronunciation of the forms of the prefix meaning "my." This alternation is demonstrated in (11).

(11)
"shi-forms"	*"si*-forms"
/šɪ-ma/ "my mother"	/sɪ-k'ɪs/ "my friend"
/šɪ-beež/ "my knife"	/sɪ-tsɛ'/ "my rock"
/šɪ-taa'/ "my father"	/sɪ-dziid/ "my strength"

The sequences of letters *ts* and *dz* actually represent a single sound, an affricate; one is the voiceless and the other the voiced *apical* alveolar affricate (similar to the final sequence of sounds in the English words *cats* and *lads*.

Navajo speakers automatically use either the prefix /šɪ-/ (represented in the Navajo alphabet by *shi*) or /sɪ-/ (represented in the Navajo alphabet by *si*), depending on the phonemes in the noun the prefix is attached to. Whenever a following noun contains one of the phonemes /s/, /z/, /ts/, or /dz/, the /sɪ-/ prefix is used. What these four phonemes have in common is that they are the natural class of [+strident], [−high], [−distributed], [+anterior] consonants. The distribution of the two prefixes is thus expressed informally in (12):

(12)
a. Use the prefix /sɪ-/ whenever the following noun contains a consonant with the features

$$\begin{bmatrix} +\text{strident} \\ -\text{high} \\ -\text{distributed} \\ +\text{anterior} \end{bmatrix}$$

b. Otherwise, use the prefix /šɪ-/.

This example illustrates two new points. First, it illustrates that phonological regularities may involve nonadjacent segments. In the word *si-k'is* "my friend," for example, it is the word-final *s* that is the conditioning factor for the occurrence of the *si-* prefix. Second, it illustrates an even deeper point. Note that the features [+high], [−distributed], [+anterior] of the conditioning phonemes are exactly those features that distinguish *s* from *š*. It would appear that the /sɪ-/ form is the result of a rule of regressive assimilation, similar to the type of examples discussed earlier. But what is /sɪ-/ assimilated from? The answer is obviously /šɪ-/, since this is the form that appears in all the other cases. In other words, we do not really need the (12b) case as part of the actual rule. We can state that the first person singular possessive prefix in Navajo is /šɪ-/, and unless the conditions in (12a) are met, the prefix will appear in its unassimilated form.

One task currently being carried out by phonologists, then, is to establish the basic forms and the phonological rules of the world's languages. Interested readers can consult the readings given in the bibliography at the end of this chapter for further discussion of the issues involved.

Conclusion

At the beginning of this chapter we posed the following questions:

What is the proper description of the various sounds that are found generally in human language?

What is the proper general framework for describing the sound patterns of human language?

We are now in a position to provide answers for these questions:

The speech sounds of human language at either the phonemic or the phonetic level of representation are best viewed as complexes of phonetic (distinctive) features, from which the sounds are composed.

Phonological regularities are best expressed in terms of the phonetic (distinctive) features of phonemes. The statements (rules) typically refer to small classes of features that identify natural classes of phonemes.

Key Words

orthography
transcription system
vocal tract
allophones
phonemes
phonological rules
distinctive features
natural class

Exercises

1. George Bernard Shaw, in ridiculing the English spelling system, claimed that a possible spelling for *fish* could be *ghoti*. Why did he claim this? (Hint: The *o* in *women* /wɪmɪn/ is pronounced as an /ɪ/.)

2. Give the English speech sound symbol that corresponds to the following articulatory descriptions:

a. voiceless bilabial stop
b. voiced alveolar stop
c. high front short vowel
d. voiceless alveolar fricative
e. lateral

f. voiced interdental fricative
g. voiceless (alveo)palatal affricate
h. high back long vowel
i. low front short vowel
j. voiceless velar stop

3. Describe each of the following speech sound symbols using articulatory features:

a. /ŋ/   f. /a/
b. /u/   g. /ɛ/
c. /š/   h. /h/
d. /z/   i. /g/
e. /m/   j. /ʌ/

4. Write the speech sound symbol for the *first* sound in each of the following words. Examples: *fish* /f/, *chagrin* /š/.

a. psychology   f. though
b. use   g. pneumonia
c. thought   h. cybernetics
d. cow   i. physics
e. knowledge   j. memory

5. Write the speech sound symbol for the *last* sound in each of the following words. Examples: *bleach* /č/, *sigh* /ay/.

a. cats   f. judge
b. dogs   g. rough
c. bushes   h. tongue
d. sighed   i. garage
e. bleached j. climb

6. Write the speech sound symbol for the *vowel* in each of the following words. Examples: *fish* /ɪ/, *table* /ey/.

a. mood   f. five
b. caught   g. bait
c. cot   h. toy
d. and   i. said
e. tree   j. soot

7. Note the following pairs of words:

a. /bæd/ *bad* and /bæg/ *bag*
b. /sɪn/ *sin* and /sɪŋ/ *sing*
c. /bɛd/ *bed* and /bɛg/ *beg*

You may speak a dialect of American English in which the vowels in the words on the right differ from those on the left. Describe the differences and try to determine why the vowels are different. (Hint: Consider tongue movement.)

8. Write the following words in the transcription system given in this chapter:

a. 1. through   6. though
   2. rough   7. blink
   3. gouge   8. hinge
   4. Knox   9. hang
   5. draft   10. try

b. 1. miss   6. three
   2. his   7. paste
   3. shoe   8. trash
   4. edge   9. blunt
   5. foot   10. thigh

c. 1. bow (bend at waist)   6. lose
   2. bow (for shooting arrows) 7. which
   3. hand   8. witch
   4. hands   9. tasks
   5. loose   10. chat

d. 1. strengths   6. yeast
   2. halve   7. gym
   3. salve   8. mend
   4. cloths   9. sixths
   5. clothes   10. boil

9. Write the names of the letters of the English alphabet using the symbols given in this chapter. For example, *a* = /ey/, *b* = /biy/, *c* = /siy/, and so forth. Can you find any "rhyme or reason" to the vowels that appear with the alphabetic consonants?

10. Write the following words using the *phonetic* symbols discussed in this chapter.

a. water   f. splat
b. lit   g. tin
c. eaten   h. beading
d. pull   i. beating
e. craft   j. beatin' (casual speech)

11. In some of the following words (for example, *play*) the *l*'s and *r*'s are voiceless. Identify these words and try to establish the conditions under which *l* and *r* lose their voicing.

a. Alpo   f. try
b. archive   g. splat
c. black   h. spread
d. play   i. leap
e. dream   j. read

12. Transcribe the following words exhibiting vowels before *r*. (Dialectal variations will abound in these words.)

a. boor   f. dear
b. bore   g. fir
c. poor   h. mire
d. care   i. sewer
e. car   j. mirror

13. Write the following combinations as contractions (monosyllables, if possible), using the phonetic symbols given in this chapter. For example, *she will* = [šɪl].

a. I will   g. I would
b. you will   h. you would
c. she will   i. she would
d. it will   j. it would
e. we will   k. we would
f. they will   l. they would

Bonus: Write a contracted form (there is more than one version for each of these expressions) for the following sequences, as though they were pronounced in the frame "____ want?" For example, in *What do I want?*, *what do I* = [wʌDəway].

a. what do I
b. what do you
c. what does she
d. what does it
e. what do we
f. what do they

14. Transcribe the following words that contain the reduced vowels (ə or ɨ). For example, *sofa* = /sowfə/.

a. attitude   f. torrent
b. predator   g. Arab
c. about   h. Arabian
d. demonstrate   i. police
e. compensate   j. potato (Is the sound symbolized by the first *o* voiced?)

15. (Extra Credit) Describe the action of the tip (apex) and blade of your tongue when pronouncing the last two alveolar sounds in words such as *bottle* and *little*. Describe the tongue movement and invent a symbol (or symbols) to describe this articulatory sequence.

16. The problems given here are drawn from some of the world's languages, and serve to illustrate the role of natural classes of phonemes in the phonological regularities of these languages. In each of the problem sets a small number of phonetic features will serve to describe the class of segments that condition the change described in each problem. Assume that the data are representative of the phonological system of the particular language in question and that the phonemic symbols have the same phonetic feature specifications as the symbols in tables 4.8 and 4.9; refer to the tables in solving these problems. A sample problem and solution are given first, in order to acquaint you with some strategies to follow in solving these problems.

Sample Problem: In English, the /ɪ/ vowel becomes long (and is thus written [ɪ:], where the colon (:) indicates length), under certain conditions. Consider the examples listed below, then (1) list the phonemes that condition the change of /ɪ/ to [ɪ:], and (2) state what feature(s) uniquely specify this class of phonemes.

a. [hɪs]   h. [hɪ:d]
b. [wɪš]   i. [mɪθ]
c. [pɪ:g]   j. [rɪ:b]
d. [pɪt]   k. [lɪ:z]
e. [lɪ:m]   l. [snɪp]
f. [trɪk]   m. [rɪ:ǰ]
g. [bɪ:l]   n. [kɪ:ŋ]

Start with the fact that [ɪ] is basic—that short [ɪ] becomes long [ɪ:]. The change from short [ɪ] to long [ɪ:] is phonologically determined; that is, the lengthening takes place in the presence of certain phonemes. A good strategy is first to list the phonemes to the right of long [ɪ:], then to list those to the left. Since [h] is on the left in both item (a) and item (h), it is not possible that the lengthening in question is caused by a phoneme to the left. As an answer to part (1), then, you would propose that /ɪ/ becomes [ɪ:] whenever the phonemes to the right (/d, m, l, b, z, ǰ, ŋ/) occur immediately after that vowel. This hypothesis looks promising because, in fact, the short variant [ɪ] never occurs before these segments. The next question is: what is it about the phonemes on the right that unifies them as a class? If you look at their feature specifications in table 4.8, you will find that these phonemes are all voiced ([+voiced]), and, in fact, the short /ɪ/ never lengthens before voiceless segments. Thus, the answer to part (2) of the problem is that the vowel [ɪ] is lengthened before (the natural class of) voiced consonants.

Problem A: English. A particular dialect of English exhibits a predictable variant /ʌy/ of the diphthong /ay/. Answer the two questions: (1) What phonetic segments condition this change? (2) What feature(s) uniquely describe the class of conditioning segments?

a. /bʌyt/ bite   i. /fʌyt/ fight
b. /tay/ tie   j. /bay/ buy
c. /rayd/ ride   k. /rʌys/ rice
d. /fayl/ file   l. /tʌyp/ type
e. /lʌyf/ life   m. /naynθ/ ninth
f. /taym/ time   n. /fayr/ fire
g. /rayz/ rise   o. /bʌyk/ bike
h. /rʌyt/ write

Problem B: Papago. In Papago, a Native American language of the southwestern United States, the phone [č] is a variant of /t/. Answer the following three questions: (1) Find and list the set of phonemes that condition this change. (2) What feature(s) characterize this class? (3) How would a Papago speaker pronounce the word [tuksan] "Black Base (of a mountain)" with a Papago accent? This pronunciation is found in Sells, Arizona, and is the source of the city name *Tucson*. A colon after a vowel symbol indicates that the vowel is long; /ṣ/ is a voiceless fricative similar to English /š/; and /ɨ/ is a high back unrounded vowel. Other unfamiliar phonemic symbols as well as the translations are not important for the solution to this problem.

a. ta:t   i. ču?i
b. to:n   j. toha
c. ton   k. čɨhok
d. čin   l. toha
e. čɨm   m. tokit
f. čuk   n. tatk
g. čikpan   o. ta:ñ
h. čɨ:kor   p. taṣ

Problem C: Luganda. In the following words from Luganda, a Bantu language spoken in East Africa, the phone [ř] (a flapped "r" sound) is a predictable variant of [l]. Answer the two questions: (1) What are the phonemes that condition the change of [l] to [ř]? (2) What feature(s) characterize the class of conditioning segments? A rising accent mark indicates high pitch, the absence of an accent mark indicates low pitch. Double vowels represent long vowels. Data from Cole 1967.

a. mukířa "tail"   g. kutúulá "to sit down"
b. lumóóndé "sweet potato"   h. okútábáála "to attach"
c. kulímá "to cultivate"   i. eříñá "name"
d. éfířímbí "whistle"   j. oolwééyó "a broom"
e. kuwóólá "to scoop or hollow out" k. kwaanířízá "to welcome, invite"
f. kuwólá "to lend money"   l. kuujjúkířá "to remember"

Problem D: English. For the following English words, state the conditions under which the different forms of the past tense appear. What determines whether /t/, /d/, or /ɨd/ is used? Data: Write the past tense marker phonemically in order to discover whether the ending for a given verb is pronounced /t/, /d/, or /ɨd/. For example, *crushed* has final /t/, but *pitted* has final /ɨd/. What phonetic features define each conditioning environment?

a. crushed   k. turned
b. heaped   l. hissed
c. kicked   m. plowed
d. pitted   n. climbed
e. deeded   o. singed
f. bagged   p. hanged
g. killed   q. cinched
h. nabbed   r. played
i. thrived   s. hated
j. breathed   t. branded

   Problem E: English. The possessive morpheme is indicated in the current orthography either by adding apostrophe + *s* (as in *Bill's book*) or simply by writing an apostrophe after words already ending in *s* (*Chris' book*). Determine (1) whether or not there is any variation in the pronunciation of the possessive morpheme; and (2) if there is variation, what the phonetic variations are, and what principles will allow you to predict the occurrence of the different forms.

Bibliography

Anderson, S. (1974). *The Organization of Phonology,* Seminar Press, New York.

Chomsky, N., and M. Halle (1968). *The Sound Pattern of English,* Harper and Row, New York.

Cole, D. (1967). *Some Features of Ganda Linguistic Structure,* Witwatersrand University Press, Johannesburg.

Denes, P., and E. David, Jr. (1972). *Human Communications: A Unified View,* McGraw-Hill, New York.

Fodor, J., and J. Katz, eds. (1964). *The Structure of Language: Readings in the Philosophy of Language,* Prentice-Hall, Englewood Cliffs, N.J.

Grønbech, K., and J. Krueger (1955). *An Introduction to Classical (Literary) Mongolian,* Harrassowitz, Wiesbaden.

Halle, M. (1962). "Phonology in a generative grammar," *Word* 18, 54–72. Reprinted in J. Fodor and J. Katz, eds. (1964).

Halle, M., and G. N. Clements (1982). *Problem Book in Phonology: A Workbook for Introductory Courses in Linguistics and in Modern Phonology,* MIT Press, Cambridge, Mass.

Hyman, L. (1975). *Phonology: Theory and Analysis,* Holt, Rinehart and Winston, New York.

Jakobson, R., and M. Halle (1956). *Fundamentals of Language,* Mouton, The Hague.

Kahn, D. (1976). *Syllable-Based Generalizations in English Phonology*, Doctoral dissertation, MIT, Cambridge, Mass.

Kenstowicz, M., and C. Kisseberth (1979). *Generative Phonology: Description and Theory*, Academic Press, New York.

Ladefoged, P. (1982). *A Course in Phonetics*, 2nd ed., Harcourt Brace Jovanovich, New York.

Lenneberg, E. (1967). *Biological Foundations of Language*, Wiley, New York.

Smalley, W. (1963). *A Manual of Articulatory Phonetics*, rev. ed., William Carey Library, South Pasadena, Calif.

Sommerstein, A. (1977). *Modern Phonology*, University Park Press, Baltimore, Md.

Stevens, K. (1972). "The quantal nature of speech: Evidence from articulatory-acoustic data," in P. B. Denes and E. E. David, Jr., eds. (1972).

Chapter Five _____

SYNTAX: THE STUDY
OF SENTENCE
STRUCTURE

5.1 SOME BACKGROUND CONCEPTS

So far in our study of language, we have focused on morphology and phonology, and thus we have been focusing on the level of the *word*. Now we turn our attention to the analysis of larger structural units of a language: *phrases* and *sentences*. In focusing on these larger structural units, we will discover some rather striking properties of the syntax of human language.

Let us begin by considering a sentence that you have never heard before:

(1)
A man being boiled alive in a pot of stew is in no position to finance a leftist revolution.

Probably this sentence has never before been written or uttered. Yet, as a native speaker of English, you are able to comprehend the sentence (as long as you know the meaning of the individual words). In other words, even if you have not encountered a particular sentence in your previous linguistic experience, you are nevertheless able to understand it because you recognize familiar units (words that you know) combined in a novel but appropriate way.

All of us, as native speakers of a language, are able to produce and comprehend an infinite number of phrases and sentences of that language, many of which we have never heard or produced before. How is it possible that speakers of a language can carry out such an impressive task? One thing is clear: we know that speakers cannot simply have memorized all the phrases and sentences of a language. This is suggested by example (1): if you had simply memorized all the sentences of

English, how could you understand a sentence you had never been exposed to before? And in fact we can show that it is impossible, in principle, for a speaker to memorize all the sentences of his or her native language.

A simple set of examples will show this. Consider first a simple sentence of English: *Kim is brilliant*. Notice that we can create a longer sentence of English using this first sentence, by *embedding* it within a larger sentence: *Mary thinks that Kim is brilliant*. This sentence in turn can be embedded in an even larger sentence: *Pat said that Mary thinks that Kim is brilliant*. Indeed, there is, in principle, no limit on this embedding process: *Darby told me that the newspapers reported that quite a few professors were of the opinion that it was most likely that Sid was spreading rumors that Pat had said that Mary thinks that Kim is brilliant*. (In section 5.3 we will return to a more formal discussion of embedding.) Of course, such a long and unwieldy sentence might not ever be uttered in actual speech—it has become long enough to put a strain on our memory—but as native speakers of English we can make an intuitive judgment that all of the examples we have discussed so far are well-formed: they conform to regular patterns of English syntax that we encounter in many other sentences and phrases. We will return to a discussion of such intuitive judgments, which form a crucial part of each speaker's linguistic knowledge. But at this point, note that no matter how long we make a certain sentence, we can always embed that sentence in a slightly longer one. This means that the number of sentences in English (or any other language) is *infinite:* we could never exhaustively list all the sentences of a language, because no matter how many sentences we had on the list, there would always be other sentences that were longer that we had not put on the list. Of course, any individual sentence itself is finite in length. But the total *set* of sentences in any language is infinite. An infinite set is, in effect, a list that never ends, and for that reason such a list could not possibly be committed to memory.

This "infinite scope" of language brings out an important property of the meaning of phrases and sentences in any given language. That is, meaning is *compositional*—the meaning of whole phrases and sentences is a function of the meaning of the individual parts of those phrases and sentences. For example, the meaning of the whole sentence *Kim is brilliant* is a function of the meaning of the individual words and the manner in which those words are arranged and structured within the sentence (we will have a good deal more to say about syntactic structure in the following sections of this chapter). The meaning of the sentence *Mary thinks that Kim is brilliant* is a function of the meaning of the sentence *Kim is brilliant* and the meaning of *Mary thinks,* and so on. In this fashion, larger meanings are "composed" from the meanings of smaller parts. Using familiar units (words) that are combined and recombined in new ways (into phrases and sentences), we are able to produce and comprehend an infinite number of novel expressions in our language. (In chapter 6, section 6.4, we will see in detail how a semantic theory can account for compositionality of meaning.)

Since native speakers of a language cannot have memorized each phrase or sentence of their language, given that the set of phrases and sentences is infinite, their linguistic knowledge cannot be characterized as a *list* of phrases or sentences. How, then, can we characterize the linguistic knowledge of native speakers of a language? We will say that a speaker's linguistic knowledge can be characterized as a *finite set* of procedures that form the basis for the speaker's ability to produce and comprehend the infinite number of phrases and sentences of the language. A grammar is a finite set of rules and principles for capturing the regularities in the language.

In referring to the linguistic knowledge of the native speaker, we begin to touch upon a distinction between two concepts that have figured prominently in discussions of syntax in recent years: the distinction between *competence* and *performance*. In discussing these concepts, we will be following, in general outline, the work of the linguist Noam Chomsky (see references); indeed, our general approach to syntax in this entire chapter is based on his influential work.

Competence and Performance

Consider the fact that native speakers of a language are able to make numerous *intuitive judgments* about their language. For example, as native speakers of English we can make the intuitive judgment that example (2a) is a well-formed sentence of English, whereas example (2b) is ill-formed. (Following linguistic custom, we have prefixed the ill-formed sentence with an asterisk, *.)

(2)
a.   The dog bit the horse.
b.   *Dog the horse the bit.

Notice that we do not have to consult grammar books or interview large groups of English speakers in order to determine that (2a) is well-formed, whereas (2b) is not. Rather, as native speakers we are able to make certain judgments, known as *grammaticality judgments*, about whether sentences are well-formed or not. Our ability to make such judgments concerning examples like (2a) and (2b) reflects our linguistic knowledge; by virtue of knowing English, we know that (2a) is fine, whereas (2b) is somehow "bad." This knowledge is part of our linguistic *competence* as native speakers of English.

The competence-performance distinction (see Chomsky 1965) is intended to reflect the difference between the linguistic *knowledge* of fluent speakers of a language (*competence*) and the actual production and comprehension of speech by those speakers (*performance*). To take a simple example, suppose that a fluent speaker of English has undergone extensive dental surgery on a certain day, which leaves him temporarily unable to talk. Would we want to say that he has lost his knowledge of English? Surely not. That is, in terms of *competence* we would say that the speaker still maintains a fluent grasp of the English language; however, because of *performance limitations* (aching jaw muscles and tooth pain) the speaker's vocal apparatus happens to be temporarily afflicted. Similarly, a fluent native speaker of English under the influence of alcohol may well mispronounce words, forget words, use syntactic patterns not characteristic of the language, and so forth; yet we would hardly claim that such a person had ceased to have native knowledge of the language. Competence, in the sense in which we are using that term, has not been affected in this case; rather, we would say that performance has been affected (by ingestion of alcohol).

The competence-performance distinction can also be seen if we examine carefully the actual speech of native speakers in a conversation. That is, actual speech is characterized by false starts and stops, hesitations, lapses of memory, coughing, clearing of the throat, and so on. A detailed transcription of actual speech would reveal numerous *uhh*'s and *umm*'s and other extraneous sounds. While such details reflect the actual performance of a given speaker on a given occasion, they do not necessarily reflect the competence of that speaker. In other words, a speaker's competence is his or her *linguistic capacity,* and although that capacity is reflected in actual speech, it may also be obscured by performance factors such as memory limitations, coughing, inebriation, and so on. In a similar fashion, we can say that a Lamborghini sports car has the *capacity* to travel at 150 mph, even if it happens to be sitting in the shop right now with four flat tires. The point is that we must distinguish between what it *can* do (under ideal circumstances) and what it is *actually doing* (in the given circumstances of the moment).

Our study of syntax in this chapter will be based on our intuitive judgments as native speakers of English. In the pages that follow we will be examining numerous expressions, some of which we will judge to be well-formed and others of which we will judge to be ill-formed. Hence, the primary data for our study of syntax will come from our own introspection about English sentences—that is, our own linguistic competence. Not only will the rules and principles that we discover from our study be part of the grammar of English, they will also be of a general type found in numerous other languages. We will proceed in our study of syntax first by examining the concept of *syntactic structure*. Having determined some of the central aspects of the concept of structure, we will then examine certain properties of syntactic *rules*. We will not attempt to discuss a wide range of structures or rules; rather, we will focus on a small number of structures and rules in English, in order to get a feel for how syntactic analysis is carried out. But for now, let us begin by examining what we mean by *structure*.

The Concept of Structure

In all languages, sentences are structured in certain specific ways. What is syntactic structure, and what does it mean to say that sentences are structured? Like many other questions that can be posed about human language, it is difficult to answer this one in any direct fashion. In fact, it is impossible to answer the question *What is structure?* without actually constructing a theory of syntax, and indeed one of the central concerns of current theories of syntax is to provide an answer to this question. Thus, it must be stressed that we cannot define the concept of structure before we study syntax; rather, our study of syntax will be an attempt to find a definition (however elaborate) of this concept.

To begin to find such a definition, we will adopt the following strategy: let's assume that sentences are merely unstructured strings of words. That is, given that we can recognize that sentences are made up of individual words (which we can isolate), it would seem that the minimal assumption we could make would be that sentences are nothing more than words strung out in linear order, one after the other. If we examine some of the formal properties of sentences in light of this strategy, we will quickly discover whether our unstructured string hypothesis is tenable or whether we will be forced to adopt a hypothesis that attributes greater complexity to sentences.

If we adopt the hypothesis that sentences are unstructured strings of words, then almost immediately we must add an important qualification. One of the first things we notice about the sentences of human languages is that the words in a sentence occur in a certain linear order. Although some languages display considerable freedom of word order (standard examples being Latin, Russian, and aboriginal Australian languages), in no human language may the words of a sentence occur in any random order whatsoever. No matter how free a language is with respect to word order, it will inevitably have some constraints on word order (see exercise 7). Furthermore, in many languages the linear order of words plays a crucial role in determining the meaning of sentences: in English, *The horse bit the dog* means something quite different from *The dog bit the horse,* even though the very same words are used in both. Hence, we might say that sentences are unstructured strings of words, but we must ensure that we specify at least a *linear order* for those words. (See exercise 6.)

Structural Ambiguity

Even with the important qualification just made about word order, our unstructured string hypothesis runs up against an interesting puzzle. Consider a sentence such as the following:

(3)
a. The mother of the boy and the girl will arrive soon.

This sentence is ambiguous; that is, it has more than one meaning. It is either about one person (the mother of both the boy and the girl) or about two people (the mother of the boy and, in addition, a second person, the girl). In sentences with the verbs *is* or *are,* these two possibilities are brought out clearly:

(3)
b. The mother of the boy and the girl *is* very talented.
c. The mother of the boy and the girl *are* (both) very talented.

The interesting feature of sentence (3a) is that the ambiguity cannot be attributed to an ambiguity in any of the words of the sentence. That is, we cannot attribute the ambiguity of the sentence to an ambiguity in *mother* or *boy* or *girl*. In contrast, consider a sentence such as *She's good at catching flies*. This, too, is an ambiguous sentence, but it seems clear that the ambiguity in this case is attributable to an ambiguity in the word *flies* (and possibly *catching*): it is referring either to baseball or to insects (recall chapter 3, section 3.3). For sentence (3a), however, we cannot appeal to such an explanation.

At this point, then, we are faced with a puzzle: how is it that a sentence consisting entirely of unambiguous words can nonetheless be ambiguous? Our unstructured string hypothesis does not lead us to expect this sort of sentence ambiguity, nor does it provide any mechanism for explaining the phenomenon. In order to find an explanation, it would seem that we are forced to concede that sentences are not merely unstructured strings of words and to assume instead that the words can be grouped together in various ways. If we make this assumption, we can explain ambiguous sentences such as (3a) by saying that although the sentence consists of a single set of unambiguous words, those words can in fact be grouped in two different ways:

(4)
a. The mother (of the boy and the girl) will arrive soon.
b. (The mother of the boy) and (the girl) will arrive soon.

The parentheses indicate the intuitively natural groupings of the words that correspond to the two meanings we have isolated.

By saying that words in a sentence can be grouped together, we have started to define the concept of sentence structure. Notice that by appealing to a notion of grouping, we have, even with this simple example, already gone beyond the directly observable properties of a sentence and are postulating abstract, or theoretical, properties. Although the linear order of words is something we can check by direct observation of a sentence, the grouping of words in that sentence is generally not directly observable. Rather, word grouping is a theoretical property that we appeal to in order to account for abstract characteristics of sentences—such as structural ambiguity.

Given what we have said so far, it would appear that in specifying the structure of a sentence we specify (a) the linear order of words and (b) the possible groupings of the words. Indeed, these are two important properties of the structure of sentences, but by no means are they the only important properties. Given that we have initial evidence that requires us to attribute some kind of structure to sentences, let us examine in more detail what is involved in specifying the structure of English sentences (and, more generally, the sentences of many other languages).

5.2 AN INFORMAL THEORY OF SYNTAX

One of the most important ways of discovering why and how sentences must be structured is to try to state explicitly some grammatical rules for a given language. For example, consider the following set of sentences, which consists of English declarative sentences and their corresponding question forms:

(5)
a. John can lift 500 pounds.
   Can John lift 500 pounds?
b. Mathematicians are generally thought to be odd.
   Are mathematicians generally thought to be odd?
c. They will want to reserve two rooms.
   Will they want to reserve two rooms?
d. Mary has proved several theorems.
   Has Mary proved several theorems?

Any native speaker of English knows how to form questions of the sort illustrated in (5). We will now engage in an apparently simple exercise: that is, to state as precisely as we can how such English questions are formed. We will disregard the evidence of section 5.1 and return to our earlier assumption that sentences are unstructured strings of words.

The English Question Rule

How can we describe the way the questions in (5) are formed from the declarative sentences? Possibly the simplest way to begin would be to number each word of the declarative sentence:

(6)
John can lift 500 pounds
  1   2   3   4   5

Now we can state a set of instructions for forming a question based on this sentence.

(7)
Question Rule I (QR-I)
To form a question from a declarative sentence, place word 2 at the beginning of the sentence.

Question Rule I operates in such a way that (8) is produced as an output, given (6) as input.

(8)
Can John lift 500 pounds
 2   1   3   4   5

Notice that this is the correct question form. A simple check will reveal that QR-I also works for the other examples in (5), and nothing forces us to talk about sentence structure.

    However, it should be clear that QR-I quickly runs into problems. Consider what would happen if we followed that rule faithfully with respect to the examples in (9).

(9)
a. Yesterday John could lift 500 pounds.
b. Many mathematicians are thought to be odd.
c. Those people will want to reserve two rooms.

Here, the second words are *John, mathematicians,* and *people,* respectively. If we faithfully follow QR-I and place the second word at the beginning of the sentence, we derive the following:

(10)
a.   John yesterday could lift 500 pounds.
b. *Mathematicians many are thought to be odd.
c. *People those will want to reserve two rooms.

The rule has given the wrong results in each case. Though sentence (10a) might be a possible (albeit awkward) sentence, it is certainly not the question that corresponds to (9a)—which should be *Yesterday, could John lift 500 pounds?* As for sentences (10b) and (10c), not only are they not the questions corresponding to (9b) and (9c); they are ungrammatical, or ill-formed, sentences.

    It is clear that we must reformulate QR-I so as to account for the counterexamples in (10). We see that English questions are not formed by simply moving the second word of the sentence to the beginning. After all, the second word of an English sentence can be any type of word: a noun, a verb, an adjective, an article, and so on. However, the examples in (5) show that in forming a question in English, it is always a *verb* that is moved to the front of the sentence, that is, a word such as *can, are, will,* and *has.*

In order to state the Question Rule more accurately, we are now forced to suppose that the words of a sentence are not only strung out in some linear order but are also classified into different morphological categories—what have traditionally been called *parts of speech.* (Recall from chapter 3 that in morphology we must classify words into parts of speech in order to state word formation rules properly.) If we make this assumption, then we can restate the Question Rule so that it is sensitive to this morphological information:

(11)
Question Rule II (QR-II)
To form a question from a declarative sentence, place the first verb of the sentence at the beginning of the sentence.

In an example such as *John can lift 500 pounds,* the word *can* is the first verb of the sentence; by placing it at the beginning, we derive *Can John lift 500 pounds?* Similarly, in *Many mathematicians are thought to be odd* the first verb is *are;* by placing it at the beginning of the sentence, we derive the question *Are many mathematicians thought to be odd?* Indeed, the reformulated rule gives the right results for the examples in both (5) and (9), with one exception. For sentence (9a), *Yesterday John could lift 500 pounds,* the first verb is *could;* by placing it at the beginning of the sentence, we derive **Could yesterday John lift 500 pounds?*—which seems to be unnatural. Instead we want to arrive at the form *Yesterday, could John lift 500 pounds?* We will return to this problem shortly.

We have now been forced to further assume that the words in a sentence must be classified into parts of speech. It should be stressed that this classification is not a matter of convenience or conjecture; rather, it turns out to be impossible to state the Question Rule properly if we cannot appeal to such a classification. Just as we found counterexamples to the first rule we postulated, however, we can easily find counterexamples to QR-II as well. Consider what would happen if we followed QR-II with respect to the next set of examples:

(12)
a. You *know* those women.
b. Mary *left* early.
c. They *went* to Phoenix.

Here, the first verbs are *know, left,* and *went,* respectively. Now, by applying QR-II to these examples—that is, by placing the first verb of the sentence at the beginning—we arrive at the following results:

(13)
a. *Know you those women?
b. *Left Mary early?
c. *Went they to Phoenix?

Although the English language once formed questions of this general sort (one can find similar forms in Shakespeare, for example), it is a fact that questions such as (13a–c) are ill formed in present-day English. Instead, the appropriate forms are as follows:

(14)
a. *Do* you know those women?
b. *Did* Mary leave early?
c. *Did* they go to Phoenix?

What is going on here is that contemporary English distinguishes between *auxiliary verbs* and *main verbs,* and only auxiliary verbs are involved in the question-formation process.

Auxiliary Verbs versus Main Verbs in English

The auxiliary verbs of English include the following forms:

(15)
a. Forms of the verb *be* (*is, am, are, was, were*)
b. Forms of the verb *have* (*have, has, had*)
c. Forms of the verb *do* (*do, does, did*)
d. The verbs *can, could, will, would, shall, should, may, might, must,* and a few others. Members of this group are usually referred to as *modal auxiliaries.*

The distinction between auxiliary verbs and main verbs shows up very clearly in several grammatical processes in English, among which are the following:

A. Auxiliary verbs, but not main verbs, are fronted in forming questions.
Examples: John *is* running. → *Is* John running?
             They *have* left. → *Have* they left?
             I *can* sing.   → *Can* I sing?

When a sentence contains no auxiliary verb, but has only a main verb, then the auxiliary verb *do* is used in forming questions.

Examples: You know those women. → *Do* you know those women?

Mary left early. → *Did* Mary leave early?

They went to Phoenix. → *Did* they go to Phoenix?

B. In the negative form of the verbs, the contracted negative *n't* can attach to auxiliary verbs but not to main verbs.

Examples: John is running. → John *isn't* running.

They have left. → They *haven't* left.

I can sing. → I *can't* sing.

Notice that main verbs cannot be negated in this fashion. The negative forms of sentences such as *You know those women* or *Mary left early* are not *You known't those women* or *Mary leftn't early*. When a sentence contains no auxiliary verb but has only a main verb, then the auxiliary verb *do* is used in forming the negative version.

Examples: You know those women. → You *don't* know those women.

Mary left early → Mary *didn't* leave early.

They went to Phoenix. → They *didn't* go to Phoenix.

Note, in addition, that auxiliary verbs can be followed by the uncontracted negative *not* (as in *John is not running, They have not left, I cannot sing*). Main verbs cannot be followed by uncontracted *not* in current spoken American English: expressions such as *We know not what we do* are possible only in highly stylized forms of English in which an archaic flavor is preserved (as in religious preaching styles and highly formal oratory).

C. Auxiliary verbs, but not main verbs, can appear in *tags*. A tag occurs at the end of a sentence and contains a repetition of the auxiliary verb found in that sentence:

John <u>has</u> not been here, <u>has</u> he?

    main sentence   tag

When the auxiliary verb of the main sentence is positive in form, the repeated auxiliary verb in the tag may be positive or negative in form:

Herman <u>is</u> threatening to leave, <u>is</u> he!

Herman <u>is</u> threatening to leave, <u>isn't</u> he?

The positive and negative tags are used under different circumstances (the positive tag often having the force of a challenge; the negative tag being used by the speaker to request confirmation of the main sentence). But in both cases the auxiliary verb of the tag is a repetition of the auxiliary verb of the main sentence. Notice, in addition, that when the auxiliary verb of the main sentence is negative in form, the auxiliary in the tag is always positive:

Herman isn't threatening to leave, is he?

In other words, we do not find cases like *Herman isn't threatening to leave, isn't he?*

Main verbs, unlike auxiliary verbs, cannot appear in tags. For a sentence such as *You know those women,* there is no corresponding tagged form, *You know those women, know you?* Instead, when a sentence contains no auxiliary verb, but has only a main verb, the auxiliary verb *do* is used in forming the tag.

Examples: You know those women, *do* you!
             Mary left early, *did* she!
             They went to Phoenix, *didn't* they?

Thus, auxiliary verbs and main verbs differ with respect to question formation, negation, and tag formation, as summarized in table 5.1.

Given this distinction in English verbs, and given the impossibility of question forms such as those in (13), we must now amend the Question Rule to take account of the new data:

(16)
Question Rule III (QR-III)
a. To form a question from a declarative sentence, place the first auxiliary verb of the sentence at the beginning of the sentence.
b. If there is no auxiliary verb, but only a main verb, place an appropriate form of the verb *do* at the beginning of the sentence and make appropriate changes in the main verb.

As we can verify, this amended rule covers the cases we have cited so far. For a sentence such as *Mary has left,* the first auxiliary verb is *has;* by fronting this, we derive the question form *Has Mary left?* A sentence such as *You knew those women* has no auxiliary verb; thus, we must insert an appropriate form of the auxiliary verb *do.* In this case, the appropriate form is *did* (past tense), and we must make appropriate changes in the main verb (changing past tense *knew* to tenseless *know*),

Table 5.1
Comparison of auxiliary verbs and main verbs

	Auxiliary Verbs	Main Verbs
Fronted in forming questions?	Yes: *Is* John running? *Have* they left? *Can* I sing?	No: *Know you those women? *Left Mary early? *Went they to Phoenix? Use *do*: *Do* you know those women? *Did* Mary leave early? *Did* they go to Phoenix?
Negative form can have *n't* attached?	Yes: John *isn't* running. They *haven't* left. I *can't* sing.	No: *You known't those women. *Mary leftn't early. *They wentn't to Phoenix. Use *do*: You *don't* know those women. Mary *didn't* leave early. They *didn't* go to Phoenix.
Can occur in tag sentence?	Yes: John isn't running, *is* he? They haven't left, *have* they? I can't sing, *can* I?	No: *You know those women, know you? *Mary left early, left she? *They went to Phoenix, went they? Use *do*: You know those women, *do* you! Mary left early, *did* she! They went to Phoenix, *did* they!

thus deriving the question form *Did you know those women?* And so on for the rest of the examples given. We will not be concerned with the details of the use of auxiliary *do,* and thus we leave part (b) of the Question Rule stated in a rather vague way. Since our interest from this point on will be in part (a) of the rule, we will omit further mention of part (b)—keeping in mind, however, that part (b) is to be understood as being included in further revisions of the rule.

We now have a revised version of the Question Rule, amended to take account of the distinction in English between auxiliary and main verbs. In other words, the Question Rule must be sensitive not only to the distinction among major parts of speech (such as *noun* versus *verb*) but also to the distinction(s) among *subcategories* of a major category. The Question Rule does not involve just *any* verb; it involves only a specific subcategory of verbs, namely, the auxiliaries. With this additional refinement, our Question Rule has become more adequate.

Structural Grouping: The Subject Constituent

Even Question Rule III is inadequate, though, when we consider a new class of sentences:

(17)
a. The people who are standing in the room will leave soon.
b. Many mathematicians who you will meet are thought to be odd.
c. Anyone that can lift 500 pounds is eligible for our club.

Notice that in (17a) the first auxiliary verb is *are:*

(18)
The people who <u>are</u> standing in the room will leave soon.

If we follow QR-III faithfully and place this first auxiliary verb at the beginning of the sentence, we will derive the following ungrammatical sentence:

(19)
*Are the people who standing in the room will leave soon?

Clearly, in this example it is not the first auxiliary verb that should be moved; instead, it is the second auxiliary verb, *will:*

(20)

a. The people who are standing in the room <u>will</u> leave soon.

b. Will the people who are standing in the room leave soon?

But is it really the *second* auxiliary verb, as such, that we are looking for in these cases? The answer is clearly no. In the following examples, the appropriate auxiliary verb (which is boxed) does not correspond to any particular number; it can be the third, fourth, or any other number.

(21)

a. The people who <u>were</u> saying that John <u>is</u> sick [will] leave soon.
            1   2   3

b. The people who <u>were</u> saying that Pat <u>has</u> told Mary to make
            1   2

Terry quit trying to persuade David that many mathematicians <u>are</u>
                                                   3

thought to be odd [will] leave soon.
                  4

An important point to notice here is that such examples can be extended indefinitely—as noted earlier in this chapter, there is simply no limit on the length of the sentences we can construct or on the number of auxiliary verbs we can place within them. Naturally, when sentences become this long, they become difficult to understand and remember; consequently, they would normally not occur in everyday conversation as single uninterrupted sentences. However, this is a practical problem, a problem of performance limitations on memory, and we will consider sentences such as (21b) to be appropriate data.

In (21a–b) we see that in each instance the auxiliary verb *will* is the correct verb to move. However, that auxiliary verb does not occupy any particular fixed slot in the linear order of words. Further, it is in principle impossible to specify exactly what can come between that auxiliary and the beginning of the sentence (because there is no limitation on the length of the sentence between the beginning point and the point where the appropriate auxiliary is located). It should be clear that for (21a–b), QR-III will give the wrong results if we apply it strictly. A more general rule is needed.

If we look more carefully at examples (17a–c), we see that the auxiliary verb that must be moved to the front of the sentence is the auxiliary that immediately follows an intuitively natural *grouping* of words traditionally referred to as the *subject* of the sentence:

(22)

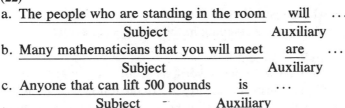

a. The people who are standing in the room   will   ...
             Subject   Auxiliary
b. Many mathematicians that you will meet   are   ...
             Subject   Auxiliary
c. Anyone that can lift 500 pounds   is   ...
             Subject   -   Auxiliary

The underlined words listed in (22) are referred to as *constituents* of a sentence. The subject constituent of the sentence (discussed further in the next section) plays an important role in the statement of the Question Rule, since it allows us to locate the appropriate auxiliary verb in the formation of questions. That is, we can now amend the Question Rule as follows, to take into account examples such as (17a–c):

(23)
Question Rule IV (QR-IV)
To form a question from a declarative sentence, locate the first auxiliary verb that *follows the subject of the sentence* and place it at the beginning of the sentence.

Given this reformulation of the Question Rule, we can now pick out the proper auxiliary verb to front in forming questions (you might want to verify that QR-IV covers all the cases discussed so far), and we will successfully avoid the problem illustrated by example (19), which plagued QR-III.

However, even QR-IV must be further modified before it will be adequate. As we have already seen, it is not the case that the appropriate auxiliary verb is in all instances moved to the front of the sentence. Recall the following examples:

(24)
a. Yesterday John could lift 500 pounds.
b. *Could yesterday John lift 500 pounds?
c. Yesterday, could John lift 500 pounds?

These examples suggest that the appropriate auxiliary verb of the sentence must be placed *immediately to the left of the subject*—not actually at the beginning of the sentence. This would lead to the following modification:

(25)
Question Rule V (QR-V)
To form a question from a declarative sentence, locate the first auxiliary verb that follows the subject of the sentence and place it *immediately to the left of the subject*.

This reformulation will cover all the cases we have examined so far.

We began with the minimal assumption that sentences are unstructured strings of words, and we attempted to state an adequate rule for forming questions in English. Successive counterexamples forced us to complicate our assumptions about how sentences are structured. For example, notice that the latest statement of the Question Rule forces us to refer to *linear order* (by referring to the *first* auxiliary verb after the subject), to categorize words into *parts of speech* (by referring to *auxiliary verbs*), and to refer to *constituent structure* (by referring to a structural grouping called the *subject*). It is important to note that at each stage the increased complexity of our assumptions was not a matter of convenience; rather, we found that we simply could not state the Question Rule of English properly without referring to notions such as part of speech and constituent structure.

The Notion "Subject"

In our latest reformulations of the Question Rule we have referred to the subject of sentences, and it would be useful here to note that subjects play an important role in other grammatical processes in English (and indeed, in many other languages). To begin with, what exactly is a *subject?* This notion has never been precisely defined, despite its significant role in linguistic analysis. Like many linguistic notions, it has an intuitive basis. The classic example of a subject comes from simple sentences with action verbs, such as *The farmer killed the duckling,* in which the subject, in this case *the farmer,* is understood as the *agent* ("the doer") of the action, while the *object,* in this case *the duckling,* is understood as that which undergoes, or suffers, the action. Not every subject is an agent; in the sentence *Mary resembles her Aunt Bettina, Mary* is the subject, but there is no action involved. In general, trying to characterize subjects in terms of meaning is an extremely complex undertaking.

In any given language we can find grammatical processes that crucially (and uniquely) involve subjects of sentences, however, and we can use these processes as tests for identifying the subject of a sentence in that language. For example, in English, tag questions provide a good test for identifying the subject of a sentence, because the pronoun in the tag *agrees with* the subject:

(26)

a. You will persuade Aunt Bettina, won't you?

b. John can't sing, can he?

c. The woman in the photo is your mother, isn't she?

d. The man who hated everybody didn't leave early, did he?

e. The students in the class voted for me, didn't they?

f. The girl and the boy are playing, aren't they?

The pronouns in the tags illustrated in (26) agree with the subjects of the main sentences in terms of *person* (1st, 2nd, or 3rd person), *number* (singular or plural), and *gender* (masculine, feminine, or neuter). For example, in (26c) the subject, *the woman in the photo,* is third person singular feminine, and these features are reflected in the pronoun *she* in the tag. The features of person, number, and gender serve to classify the personal pronouns of English, as shown in table 5.2.

In English, then, subjects of sentences have a number of properties:

(27)

a. The subject of a declarative sentence generally precedes the auxiliary and main verb in linear order.

Table 5.2
Classification of English personal pronouns in terms of person, number, and gender

	Singular	Plural
1st person	I	we
2nd person	you	you
3rd person		
Masculine	he	
Feminine	she	they
Neuter	it	

b. It forms the constituent around which an auxiliary is fronted in forming a question (see (25)).

c. It is the constituent that a pronoun in a tag agrees with in terms of person, number, and gender. (See exercise 10 for another grammatical process that makes reference to subjects.)

In languages other than English, subjects can have other grammatical properties. For example, recall the Japanese sentence discussed in chapter 3, section 3.1, *John-ga hon-o yonda* "John read the book." We noted that the subject of the sentence, *John,* has the particle *-ga* attached to it, which serves to indicate the subject function (the particle *-o* indicating the object function of *hon* "book"). Thus, in languages like Japanese, the subject is overtly *marked* in some way. In English, only the pronoun system overtly marks the difference between subjects and nonsubjects in the contrasts between *I-me, we-us, he-him, she-her,* and *they-them,* summarized in table 5.3. As the table shows, the pronoun *you* has the same form in all uses (singular and plural, subject and nonsubject), and the pronoun *it* has the same form in subject and nonsubject uses. Otherwise, pronouns in English assume two different forms to reflect their subject or nonsubject function. The subject pronouns, *I, we, he, she,* and *they,* are sometimes called *nominative case* pronouns; the nonsubject pronouns, *me, us, him, her,* and *them,* are sometimes called *accusative case* pronouns. Nonsubject pronouns can-

Table 5.3
Subject and nonsubject pronouns in English

	SUBJECT PRONOUNS	NONSUBJECT PRONOUNS	
	As subject of sentence	As object of verb	As object of preposition
1st person			
Singular	I love movies.	They like me.	She spoke to me.
Plural	We enjoy fast cars.	You follow us.	It ran from us.
2nd person			
Singular or Plural	You forgot your keys.	We can find you.	They work for you.
3rd person			
Singular	He collapsed before us. She might win the race. It will blow up!	Let's watch him. They copy her. Why not buy it?	I'll sit by him. You go after her. Look under it!
Plural	They are the enemy.	I'll hire them.	It flew over them.

not be used in subject position (except in jokes such as *Me Tarzan, you Jane*), and subject pronouns cannot be used in nonsubject positions (note the ungrammatical *You saw I*). Aside from the pronouns listed in table 5.3, no other words (noun(s)) in English change morphological form to reflect subject versus nonsubject function. Thus, in sentences such as *Mary saw the dog* or *The dog saw Mary,* the nouns *dog* and *Mary* have the same shape whether they function as subject or object.

These examples illustrate some of the ways in which subjects can be marked, or function in grammatical processes (also see exercise 11). We have not given a rigorous definition of subject, but for the purposes of this text we need not do so. In further discussions, we will use the notion in an intuitive way.

Constituent Structure and Tree Diagrams

We have now cited two kinds of evidence in favor of the hypothesis that sentences are structured. First, if we do not assume that sentences are structured—that words are grouped together into *constituents* — then we cannot explain how a sentence consisting of a set of unambiguous words can nevertheless be ambiguous. Second, it is impossible to state certain grammatical rules (such as the Question Rule for English) without appealing to constituent structure. Not only can we say that sentences are indeed structured, but we can also indicate (at least partially) how they must be structured. That is, we have found at least three important aspects of sentence structure:

(28)
a. The *linear order* of words in a sentence
b. The categorization of words into *parts of speech*
c. The grouping of words into *structural constituents* of the sentence

These three types of structural information can be encoded into what is called a *tree diagram* (or *phrase marker*) of the sort illustrated in tree 5.1.

Let us pause for a moment and study tree 5.1. Such tree diagrams can at first seem quite complicated. But in fact they represent in a simple and straightforward way the kinds of structural information summarized in (28). The trick is learning how to read them (and reading them is an important part of doing syntax). Let's begin by reading tree 5.1, in a step-by-step fashion, to see how it represents structural infor-

Tree 5.1

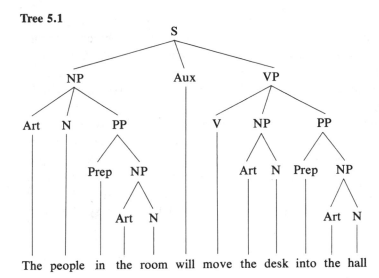

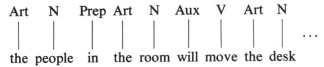

Symbols used: S—sentence; NP—noun phrase; Aux—auxiliary verb; VP—
verb phrase; PP—prepositional phrase; Art—article; N—noun; V—verb;
Prep—preposition.

mation. Learning how to decode this particular tree will give us an idea
about how to read tree diagrams in general.

Tree 5.1 represents the structure of the sentence *The people in the
room will move the desk into the hall.* Beginning at the bottom of the
tree, note that each word of the sentence is connected by a line—called
a *branch* of the tree—to a certain symbol of the tree:

Art   N   Prep Art   N   Aux   V   Art   N
 | | | | | | | | | . . .
the people   in   the   room will move the   desk

In this way, each word of the sentence is assigned to a certain *lexical
category* (part of speech). Thus, the word *the* is connected by a branch
to the symbol *Art*, standing for *Article,* indicating that *the* is an article.
The word *people* is connected by a branch to the symbol *N*, standing for
Noun, indicating that *people* is a noun. The word *in* is connected by a
branch to the symbol *Prep,* standing for *Preposition,* indicating that *in*
is a preposition. Shifting over to the right, the word *move* is connected
by a branch to the symbol *V*, standing for *Verb,* indicating that *move* is
a verb. In a similar fashion, all the words of the sentence are connected

by branches to appropriate symbols indicating their lexical category (part of speech). Notice that the words, as well as the lexical category symbols *Art, N, Prep,* and so on, are all shown in a specific *linear order* (reading the tree from left to right). Thus, tree 5.1 represents the information cited in (28a) and (28b): (a) the *linear order* of words, and (b) the *categorization* of words into parts of speech.

Now, how do tree diagrams represent *structural constituents* of a sentence? To see this, we will move up the tree a bit, focusing first on the subject phrase, *the people in the room*. Notice that this string of words is shown as having a certain constituent structure. For example, the sequence of words *the room* is shown as a *noun phrase* (NP); that is, the symbols *Art* and *N* are connected by branches to the symbol *NP:*

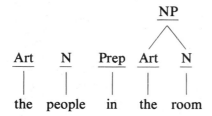

Both *Art* and *N* are connected by branches to the *same* symbol *NP;* hence, *Art* and *N* form a *single constituent.* The NP *the room* and the preposition *in* are shown as forming a prepositional phrase (PP); that is, the symbols *Prep* (*in*) and *NP* (*the room*) are both connected by branches to the symbol *PP:*

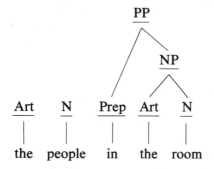

Both *Prep* and *NP* are connected by branches to the *same* symbol *PP;* hence, *Prep* and *NP* form a *single constituent.* Thus far, then, in tree 5.1 the sequence of words *the room* is a single constituent—a noun phrase (*NP*)—and the sequence of words *in the room* is a single constituent—a prepositional phrase (*PP*).

Finally, let us consider the sequence of words *the people*. This phrase is structurally similar to the phrase *the room:* it consists of an article followed by a noun, thus forming a noun phrase:

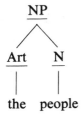

But noun phrases do not only consist of articles followed by nouns. Sometimes the noun in a noun phrase can be followed by a "modifying phrase." For example, in the phrase *the people in the room,* the prepositional phrase *in the room* is a modifying phrase: that is, it provides *additional information* about the noun *people.* To put it simply, when we use the phrase *The people in the room,* we are not talking about any random group of people; rather, we are talking about the people who are *in the room,* and in this sense the modifying phrase *in the room* provides "additional" information about the people. In tree 5.1 this modifying prepositional phrase is shown as part of the subject noun phrase:

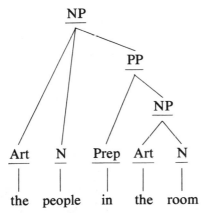

Notice that the article *the,* the noun *people,* and the prepositional phrase *in the room* are all connected by branches to the *same* symbol *NP;* hence, *Art, N,* and *PP* all form a *single constituent,* which functions as the subject of the sentence, *The people in the room will move the desk into the hall.*

Let us now turn to the verb phrase (*VP*) of tree 5.1. Notice that the symbols *V* (*move*), *NP* (*the desk*), and *PP* (*into the hall*) are all connected by branches to the *same* symbol *VP;* this means that the sequence *V-NP-PP* forms a *single constituent*—namely, the verb phrase *move the desk into the hall*. Finally, moving up to the highest level of the tree, notice that the subject *NP* (*the people in the room*), the auxiliary verb *will* (symbolized as *Aux*), and the *VP* are all connected by branches to the same symbol *S* (standing for *Sentence*); hence, the sequence *NP-Aux-VP* forms a *single constituent*, namely, a *Sentence*. A tree diagram, then, is a kind of *branching diagram* that represents syntactic constituent structure in terms of the particular way that its lines branch. The particular points in a tree that are connected by branches to other points are called the *nodes* of the tree, and these nodes are labeled with specific symbols such as *S, NP, Aux, VP, V, N, Art*, and *Prep*. Particular labeled nodes represent single constituents, made up of the items connected to them by branching lines.

In section 5.3 we will discuss how tree diagrams can be *generated* by certain kinds of rules. For the time being, however, it is sufficient merely to know how to read a tree diagram, without worrying yet where it "comes from." In decoding tree diagrams, notice that you can start from the top and work your way "down," to see how larger constituents are *broken down* into their constituent parts. For example, in tree 5.1 you can start at the top, *S*, and trace the branches down from *S* to see what constituents *S* is broken down into (and so on, for other phrases). Or you can start from the bottom of a tree and work your way "up," to see how individual words make up smaller constituents, and how smaller constituents make up larger ones, as we did in our earlier discussion. In any event, with practice you will find that reading tree diagrams becomes easy.

Tree 5.1 in effect encodes the important structural properties of a sentence. As we have seen, the various parts of the sentence are shown in a fixed linear order. Each word is assigned a part of speech: Art, N, Prep, and so on. And different elements in the sentence are shown as being grouped into successively larger constituents of the sentence: NP, Aux, and VP make up a sentence (S); V, NP, and PP make up a verb phrase (VP); and so on. What is important about this diagram is the information that it encodes, and we must note that the same information could be encoded in other (equivalent) ways. For example, the syntactic constituent structure of phrases and sentences can also be represented in terms of "box diagrams" of the sort illustrated in figure

NOUN PHRASE				
Article	Noun	Prepositional Phrase		
		Preposition	Noun Phrase	
			Article	Noun
the	people	in	the	room

Figure 5.1
Constituent structure represented by box diagram

5.1. This particular box diagram provides a structural analysis of the phrase *the people in the room:* (a) the words are represented in a linear order; (b) each word is assigned to a part-of-speech category; and (c) a hierarchical grouping is defined (the diagram indicates that a Noun Phrase can consist of an Article followed by a Noun followed by a Prepositional Phrase; the Prepositional Phrase in turn consists of a Preposition followed by a Noun Phrase, and so on). In effect, then, the box diagram of figure 5.1 encodes the same information as the tree structure in tree 5.1 with respect to the subject Noun Phrase *the people in the room*. In the tree, structural grouping is indicated by branching of the lines, rather than by levels in a box. Even though box diagrams might adequately represent constituent structure information for our purposes at this point, we will nevertheless continue to represent syntactic structure by means of tree diagrams, since in the theory of syntax we are adopting in this chapter—the theory known as *transformational grammar,* developed by the linguist Noam Chomsky (see references)— syntactic rules are traditionally defined as operating on tree structures. For present purposes, the point is that the same structural information can be encoded in a number of equivalent ways.

The same thing is true for the symbols we have chosen; although we have used the traditional names for the parts of speech, any system of labeling that made the same distinctions would be just as good for our purposes. Hence, we could call articles *Class 1 words,* nouns *Class 2 words,* and so on. As long as the right distinctions were made and similar words were assigned to similar categories, this system of naming parts of speech would be perfectly adequate.

Constituent Structure Tests: Using Rules, Clefts, and Conjunction

At this point, a natural question arises: namely, what evidence do we use to arrive at particular tree diagrams such as tree 5.1? How do we know that the sentence represented by that tree is structured as we have shown it? The answer is that tree diagrams represent hypotheses in our theory of syntax—they are not dictated by some sort of grammatical authority.

One of the ways in which we arrive at a particular formulation of a phrase marker (tree diagram) is to use certain *constituent structure tests*. Such tests usually involve stating a grammatical rule of the language, and then formulating the phrase marker (tree) in such a way as to allow the grammatical rule to be stated as simply as possible. For illustration, let us return to tree 5.1. We have good reasons for supposing that the phrase *the people in the room* forms a single NP constituent and is not merely an unstructured string of words. One important reason (but by no means the only one) is that if we represent this set of words as a single NP constituent, we can state the Question Rule in the simplest possible way: we can say simply that the auxiliary verb is to be moved to the left of the subject NP constituent of the sentence, and not, for instance, that the auxiliary verb should be moved to the left of the string of words *the people in the room*. More to the point, however, recall that since there is no limit on the length of the subject of a sentence (cf. example (21)), it is impossible to state the Question Rule in terms of the linear string of words that make up a subject: we would never be able to exhaustively list all the strings of words that could make up the subject of a sentence. Hence, we are forced to postulate an NP constituent as the subject of a sentence.

In the foregoing discussion, we have used the Question Rule in a constituent structure test. Since grammatical rules (such as the Question Rule) are stated in terms of tree structures, we formulate our tree structures in such a way as to allow the simplest statement of the rules. In a certain sense, then, grammatical rules of a language tell us what the tree structures ought to look like, and in this sense we can use such rules as constituent structure tests.

In addition to using grammatical rules of a language as constituent structure tests, we can also use certain *sentence frames*. For example, English has a construction referred to as the *cleft sentence,* with the following general form:

(29)

Cleft Sentence

It $\begin{Bmatrix} \text{is} \\ \text{was} \end{Bmatrix}$ X that Y

That is, cleft sentences consist of *it* followed by some form of the verb *to be,* followed by some constituent X, followed by a clause headed by *that:*

(30)

a. It was *the burglar* that broke the lamp.
b. It is *Mary* that I want to meet.
c. It was *under the mattress* that we found the money.
d. It is *at three o'clock in the afternoon* that they change guards.

An important fact about cleft sentences in English is that the phrase that fits into position X of the frame [*It is/was X that* . . .] is always (a) a single constituent and (b) either a noun phrase (NP) or a prepositional phrase (PP). Sentences (30a–b) have NPs in position X of the cleft frame; (30c–d) have PPs in position X of the cleft frame.

Returning to tree 5.1, we can use the cleft test to determine certain aspects of its constituent structure. Consider the sequences of words *the desk* and *into the hall.* In tree 5.1 *the desk* is shown as a single NP constituent, and *into the hall* is shown as a single PP constituent. Is there any corroborating evidence for this? Let's plug those two phrases into position X of some appropriate cleft sentences:

(31)

a. It is *the desk* that the people will move into the hall.
b. It is *into the hall* that the people will move the desk.

Given what we have said about cleft sentences, (31a) confirms that the phrase *the desk* is a single constituent (an NP) and (31b) confirms that the phrase *into the hall* is a single constituent (a PP). Tree 5.1 accurately reflects this constituent structure by representing *the desk* as an NP and *into the hall* as a PP. Continuing with tree 5.1, can we determine whether or not the sequence *the desk into the hall* is a single NP (or PP) constituent? The cleft test can help us here:

(32)

*It is *the desk into the hall* that the people will move.

Sentence (32) is ungrammatical. If the sequence *the desk into the hall* were a single NP constituent, then it would be able to occur in position X of the cleft frame [*It is X that* . . .]. But it cannot, suggesting that this sequence is not a single constituent. Tree 5.1 reflects this accurately, by representing *the desk* and *into the hall* as two distinct constituents. Those two constituents do not, in themselves, make up another constituent (however, note that those two constituents *along with* the verb *move* make up a verb phrase constituent). Hence, tree 5.1 assigns a constituent structure in which *move the desk into the hall* is a single constituent (VP) and the three phrases *move* (V), *the desk* (NP), and *into the hall* (PP) are each single constituents, but the sequence *the desk into the hall* is not a single NP constituent. Thus, the constituent structure represented by the tree seems consistent with what we know about the sentence so far.

Another test frame that has been used in linguistic analysis is the so-called *conjunction test*. The assumption underlying this test is that only single constituents of the same type can occur in the frame [____ and ____] (that is, only single constituents of the same type can be conjoined with *and*):

(33)
a. *The teacher* and *the student* argued. (NP and NP)
b. Mary *played the harmonica* and *danced a jig*. (VP and VP)
c. We moved the desk *through the door* and *into the hall*. (PP and PP)

These examples include conjoined noun phrases (*the teacher* and *the student*), conjoined verb phrases (*played the harmonica* and *danced a jig*), and conjoined prepositional phrases (*through the door* and *into the hall*); such examples have been used to show that the conjunction *and* is used to conjoin two constituents of the same type. Indeed, when we attempt to conjoin two constituents not of the same type, a decidedly odd sentence results:

(34)
a.   Sandy expects *to leave town*. (*to leave town* = VP)
b.   Sandy expects *a good time*. (*a good time* = NP)
c.   *Sandy expects *to leave town* and *a good time*.

In (34c) we have conjoined a verb phrase with a noun phrase, and the sentence is clearly much less acceptable than any of those in (33). On the basis of the conjunction test, we can establish in English such constituents as NP, PP, and VP: these are all types of expressions that can be conjoined with *and* (but see exercise 14). Given such a test for constituency, we can assume that structures such as tree 5.1 represent typical constituent structures of English.

There are other aspects of the structure shown in tree 5.1 for which we have presented little or no evidence. For example, we represent the auxiliary verb *will* as a constituent outside the verb phrase. But another, quite conceivable possibility is to consider the constituent Aux to be part of the verb phrase, as in tree 5.2. This structure may or may not be more adequate than the structure shown in tree 5.1—in the absence of any evidence bearing on the issue, we simply cannot say. We must stress that although the gross outline of the structure shown in tree 5.1 is probably correct, many fine details of the structure are, for the moment, left undetermined.

We could devote a great deal of space to attempting to justify the various features of the structure shown in tree 5.1; indeed, much work in syntax has been concerned with this sort of issue. Nonetheless, this structure provides a rough illustration of the general sort of structural diagrams used in current syntactic work, and that will suffice for our purposes at the moment. We turn now to certain important ideas about phrase markers in general.

Grammatical Relations

We have already alluded to the distinction between *structural* concepts such as noun phrase (NP) and *grammatical relations* such as subject or object. This distinction reflects the fact that we can ask two questions about any given phrase: (a) What is its *internal structure?* (b) How does it *function* grammatically within a sentence? Diagrams such as tree 5.1 can also be used to give a structural definition of the grammatical relations *subject* and *object*. In English, the *subject* of a sentence can be structurally defined as the particular NP in the structural configuration that is immediately under S and precedes Aux VP, as illustrated in tree 5.3. The *object* of a main verb can be structurally defined as the NP in

Tree 5.2

Aux V NP PP

Tree 5.3

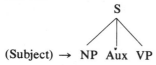

(Subject) → NP Aux VP

Tree 5.4

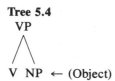

V NP ← (Object)

the structural configuration that immediately follows V under VP, as illustrated in tree 5.4.

Trees 5.3 and 5.4 illustrate that the same structural constituent in a sentence can have distinct relational functions. For example, take the phrase *the people in the room*. Structurally, this phrase is an NP, but this NP can function in different ways in different sentences. In tree 5.1 the NP *the people in the room* functions as the subject of the sentence. However, in sentence (35) this same NP functions as the object of the main verb:

(35)
The police arrested *the people in the room*.

Hence, the phrase *the people in the room* is structurally an NP and only an NP; but relationally this phrase can be either a subject or an object, depending on its position in the structure of a particular sentence.

The distinction between structural and relational concepts is crucial in determining the meaning of a sentence, as illustrated by the fact that the sentences represented by trees 5.5 and 5.6 have exactly the same structural NP constituents, but those structural constituents have quite different grammatical relations in the two sentences. (Following a common practice, we have used triangles in trees 5.5 and 5.6 to simplify the representation of the internal structure of the NPs.) These two sentences mean opposite things, and these opposite meanings result from the fact that the subject in one tree diagram is the object in the other tree diagram.

So far, then, we have isolated the following structural properties and grammatical relations, and we have shown how these can be represented in, or defined on, tree diagrams:

Tree 5.5

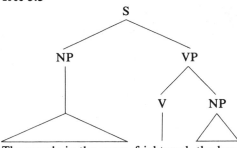

The people in the room frightened the boy

Tree 5.6

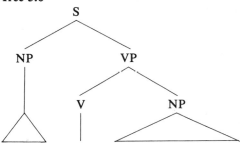

The boy frightened the people in the room

(36)
Structural Properties
a. the linear order of elements
b. the labeling of elements into parts of speech (lexical categories)
c. the grouping of elements into structural constituents (phrases)

(37)
Grammatical Relations
a. subject (structural configuration given in tree 5.3)
b. object (structural configuration given in tree 5.4)

Although definitions of subject and object (as illustrated in trees 5.3 and 5.4) are given simply in terms of *tree configurations,* we must stress once again that subjects have an important grammatical status. For instance, we have discussed grammatical processes that make reference to subject (such as the agreement of the tag pronoun with the subject of the sentence).

Finally, we must point out that the tree configurations for subject and object illustrated in trees 5.3 and 5.4 hold for certain languages (such as

English) but are irrelevant for many others. That is, not all languages have a favored "structural configuration" within a sentence for subject (or object), but instead mark subjects by some other grammatical means. Recall that in Japanese, subjects are marked with the particle -*ga,* and it is probably this feature that we would use for defining the notion "subject" in Japanese, rather than a tree structure configuration. (Also see exercise 11.)

Tree Diagrams and Structural Ambiguity

So far we have seen that tree diagrams (phrase markers) can represent a certain variety of structural and relational concepts. Now we must turn to the question of whether tree diagrams can be used to explain other important linguistic phenomena. To address this issue, let us recall the ambiguous sentence (3a), repeated here as (38):

(38)
The mother of the boy and the girl will arrive soon.

In a theory of syntax using phrase markers to represent syntactic structure, the explanation of the phenomenon of structural ambiguity is straightforward: whereas an unambiguous sentence is associated with just one basic phrase marker, structurally ambiguous sentences are associated with more than one basic phrase marker. For example, sentence (38) would be assigned two phrase markers, which we could formulate as trees 5.7 and 5.8.

As before, we have simplified the structure in the diagrams by using triangles for certain phrases rather than indicating the internal structure of those phrases. But these trees suffice to show the difference in structure that we postulate for the two phrase markers associated with sentence (38). In tree 5.7 the "head" noun of the subject, *mother,* is modified by a prepositional phrase that has a conjoined noun phrase in it: *of the boy and the girl.* In tree 5.8, on the other hand, the subject noun phrase is itself a conjoined noun phrase: *the mother of the boy* followed by *the girl.* We see, then, that a system of representation using phrase markers allows us to account for structurally ambiguous sentences by assigning more than one phrase marker to each ambiguous sentence. In this way the system of tree diagrams can be used to describe this linguistic phenomenon.

Tree 5.7

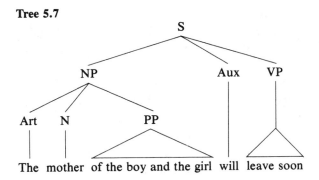

The mother of the boy and the girl will leave soon

Tree 5.8

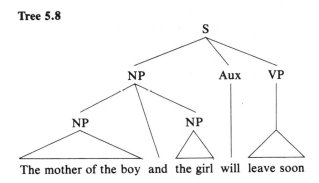

The mother of the boy and the girl will leave soon

Discontinuous Dependencies

A natural assumption to make about phrase markers is that each sentence of a language is assigned exactly one phrase marker, except for those sentences that are structurally ambiguous. In the latter case, as we have seen, we assign more than one phrase marker—one for each particular meaning of the sentence, roughly speaking. But now let us examine some sentences that are not structurally ambiguous in the sense in which we have been using that term, but that nevertheless display interesting structural properties. Consider pairs of sentences such as the following:

(39)
a. Mary stood up her date.
b. Mary stood her date up.

These sentences illustrate what is known as the verb + particle construction in English—in this particular case, the verb + particle construction *stand up* (where *stand* is the verb and *up* is the particle). The interesting feature of this construction is that the particle can occur separated from its verb, as in (39b). (Indeed, in many cases English speakers prefer the version in which the particle is separated from the verb.)

It is natural to suppose that *stood up* is a single constituent in sentence (39a). For one thing, we have used the phrase *stood up* in its idiomatic sense, synonymous with *broke a social engagement without warning,* and we have ignored the other meaning synonymous with *propped up.* In its idiomatic sense the combination *stood up* has a single meaning; neither part of the expression has the literal meaning it has in isolation. A good guess at the structure of (39a) would be that shown in tree 5.9.

Now, what phrase marker would we assign to (39b)? The most obvious candidate, in terms of what we have done so far, would be tree 5.10. Because the particle *up* comes last in the linear order of words in

Tree 5.9

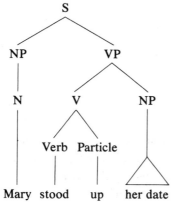

Tree 5.10

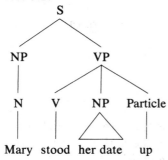

(39b), we have shown it at the end of the VP in tree 5.10. (Keep in mind that we could just as easily have placed the particle at the end directly attached by a branch to S rather than to VP—again, we have presented no evidence for choosing between these two structures.)

Tree 5.10, though accurate in representing the linear order of words, is inadequate in other ways. Given the idiomatic use of *stood up* in *Mary stood her date up,* we know that the particle *up* goes with the verb *stand:* even though the particle is separated from the verb, it is nevertheless the case in this sentence, as in (39a), that neither the verb nor the particle has the literal meaning it would have in isolation; it is still the combination of the two items that determines the single meaning. Yet tree 5.10 does not represent this affinity between verb and particle in any way; that diagram gives no indication whatever that *up* is to be associated with *stood.* Whenever a single constituent of a sentence is broken up in this way, we say that we have a *discontinuous constituent* or, more generally, a *discontinuous dependency.* It turns out that phrase markers, though very useful for representing certain kinds of information about sentences, do not adequately represent discontinuous dependencies.

For another illustration of the same phenomenon, consider a sentence whose subject contains a modifier:

(40)
Several people *who were wearing hats* came in.

In this case a phrase, *who were wearing hats,* known as a modifying *clause,* serves to supply additional information about the head noun, *several people.* We would assign this sentence a phrase marker such as tree 5.11. (Here the symbol *Mod* indicates a modifying clause; the

Tree 5.11

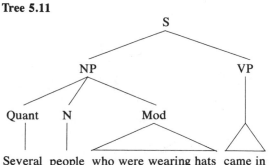

Several people who were wearing hats came in

symbol *Quant* stands for *Quantifier,* the grammatical category that includes words such as *several, many, few,* and *all.*)

In English there is a rather general grammatical process known as *extraposition,* whereby modifying clauses (and other types of clauses that need not concern us) can be shifted to the end of the sentence. Therefore, sentence (40) also has the following version:

(41)
Several people came in *who were wearing hats.*

This sentence is probably structured as in tree 5.12. This diagram correctly indicates that the linear position of the modifying clause is at the end of the sentence. However, it completely fails to show that the modifying clause goes with the subject NP, *several people*. It does not indicate in any way that *who were wearing hats* in fact modifies *several people*. In contrast, in tree 5.11 the head noun and the modifying clause are shown as part of a single syntactic constituent, indicating that the head noun and the modifier are related. It is not possible to show the relation between the two in tree 5.12, however, because the head noun and the modifier have been broken apart and separated by the verb phrase. Consequently, this is another case of a discontinuous dependency, and this dependency is not represented in any way by tree 5.12.

It turns out that discontinuous dependencies are quite common in human language; in fact, the complexity of such dependencies can be much greater than we have so far illustrated. To take just one example, note that the two processes just examined—separation of the verb particle and extraposition of the modifying clause—can interact in the same sentence. To see this, consider (42):

Tree 5.12

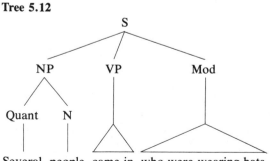

(42)

She stood up all those men who had offered her diamonds.

Recall that the particle *up* can be shifted to the end of the verb phrase:

(43)

She <u>stood</u> all those men who had offered her diamonds <u>up</u>.

This produces an awkward sentence that is difficult to understand: the particle and verb are separated by a constituent that is too long. But, since modifying clauses can be extraposed in English, we can extrapose the clause here to produce the following perfectly natural sentence:

(44)

She stood all those men up <u>who had offered her diamonds</u>.

In this example, the dependencies actually "cross" each other, as illustrated in the final line of figure 5.2. As we see, *up* goes with *stood,* and *who had offered her diamonds* goes with *all those men;* both constituents are broken up in such a way that parts of one constituent intervene between parts of the other (in particular, *up* occurs between *all those men* and its modifying clause). This is a striking example of how sentences of natural language exhibit discontinuous dependencies.

Transformational Rules as an Account of Discontinuities

The examples we have been discussing show that some properties of sentences in natural language cannot be accounted for in terms of single phrase markers alone, that is, in terms of relations between contiguous words. It turns out that we need to account for relations between items in a sentence that are connected (in some sense), dependent, or related, but that are nonetheless not contiguous in the linear order of words. One way to account for discontinuous dependencies of this sort is to devise a means by which two or more phrase markers can themselves be related to each other in a special way. This is in fact the fundamental insight of the theory of transformational grammar.

As an illustration, consider again the pair of sentences in (39), repeated here as (45):

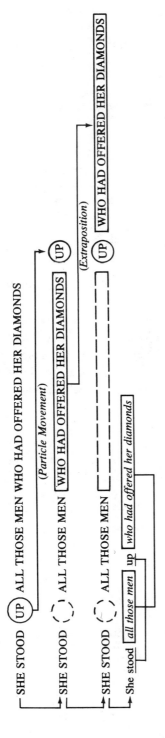

Figure 5.2
Crossing dependencies in Particle Movement and Extraposition

(45)
a. Mary stood up her date.
b. Mary stood her date up.

We will assume as before that sentence (45a) is assigned a single phrase marker, shown as tree 5.9. But what about sentence (45b)? This is the sentence with the discontinuous constituent, *stood . . . up*. In order to express the dependency between *stood* and *up* in (45b), let us suppose that this sentence derives from the same phrase marker as (45a), shown as the Input Tree in figure 5.3. Call this the *input structure* or *base structure* for sentence (45b), *Mary stood her date up*.

Now we postulate a structural operation known as a *transformation* (or *transformational rule*), which we can state informally as follows:

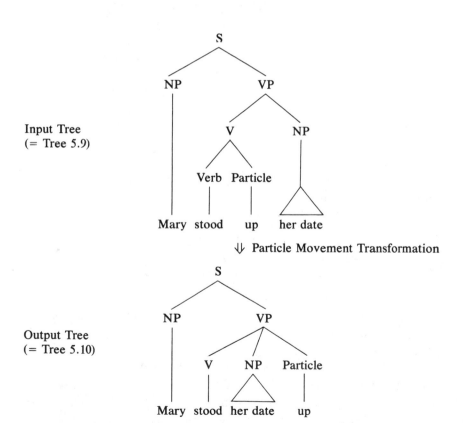

Figure 5.3
Input and output of the Particle Movement transformation

(46)

Particle Movement Transformation

Given a verb + particle construction, the particle may be shifted away from the verb, and moved immediately to the right of the object noun phrase.

Transformational rules are operations on tree structures that convert an *input* tree structure (or *base* structure) into an *output* tree structure (or *derived* structure). The operation of the Particle Movement transformation is illustrated in figure 5.3. The output structure in figure 5.3 corresponds to what is called the *surface structure* of sentence (45b); that is, this output phrase marker correctly represents the actually occurring word order and structure for the elements of sentence (45b).

We now have a way of accounting for discontinuous dependencies. The output tree in figure 5.3 is the correct surface phrase marker for the sentence *Mary stood her date up:* the particle is correctly represented as following the object NP. Nevertheless, we can account for the dependency between the particle and the verb because we are claiming that the output tree derives from the input tree in figure 5.3, and in that base phrase marker the verb and its particle are in fact contiguous and form a single constituent. Thus, the base (or "underlying") structure of the sentence shows the basic constituency of the verb and its particle, but the surface structure of the sentence correctly shows the particle as separated from its verb.

Now let us consider another case, involving the other discontinuous dependency discussed earlier: extraposition. Once again, consider pairs of sentences such as (47a–b):

(47)

a. Several people who were wearing hats came in.
b. Several people came in who were wearing hats.

As before, we would assign to sentence (47a) the phrase marker 5.11 (shown as the Input Tree in figure 5.4). This phrase marker accurately represents the word order and structure of the elements of sentence (47a).

But what about sentence (47b)? This is the sentence containing the discontinuous constituent *several people . . . who were wearing hats.* We will account for this sentence in a manner parallel to the case of particle movement, namely, by postulating that sentence (47b) derives from the base structure given as the Input Tree in figure 5.4. In that

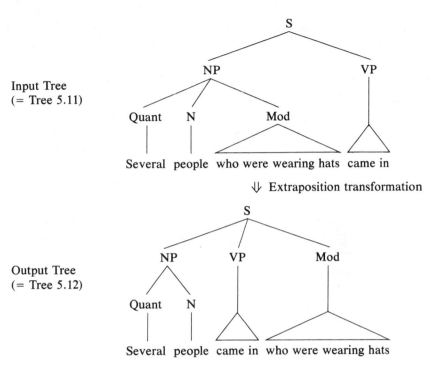

Input Tree
(= Tree 5.11)

⇓ Extraposition transformation

Output Tree
(= Tree 5.12)

Figure 5.4
Input and output of the Extraposition transformation

input structure, then, the head noun and the modifying clause form a single constituent. We will now postulate the following transformational rule:

(48)
Extraposition Transformation
Given a noun phrase containing a head noun directly followed by a modifying clause, the modifying clause may be shifted out of the noun phrase to the end of the sentence.

As shown in figure 5.4, by applying this transformation to the input tree, we derive the output tree, which is the correct surface structure for the sentence *Several people came in who were wearing hats.*

We have been able to account for the discontinuous dependency between the modifying clause and the head noun in sentence (47b) by deriving that sentence from the Input Tree in figure 5.4, in which the discontinuous elements are actually represented as a single constituent. This is another example of a transformational account of discontinuous dependency. The effect of the transformational rule of Extraposition, like that of Particle Movement, is to set up a relationship between phrase markers: it states, in effect, that for every phrase marker containing a noun phrase with a modifying clause directly following the head noun, there is a corresponding phrase marker in which that same modifying clause has been shifted to the end of the sentence. (Although this is not strictly true—in certain cases extraposition of the modifying clause is prohibited—it is nonetheless quite adequate for present purposes, and we need not add any refinements.)

The kind of analysis we have just sketched is illustrative of the transformational model of syntax. This general sort of model (including numerous variations) has dominated the field of syntax ever since the publication of Noam Chomsky's 1957 book *Syntactic Structures,* the first major work to propose the transformational approach (see Newmeyer 1980 for discussion). Even though the transformational analysis we have presented is one means of accounting for discontinuous dependencies, the question remains whether there is any reason to suppose it is the best means, or the most insightful means. It is difficult to answer this question in any definitive way, but it is possible to give additional evidence for the model that will serve to illustrate its explanatory power.

Interaction between Transformations

We have examined two cases in which a transformational analysis can account for discontinuities, but that in itself is not enough to indicate whether the transformational model is a particularly revealing account. It is time to turn to some rather striking evidence for this model. It turns out that individual transformational rules, established for independent reasons, can in fact interact with each other to account for a complex array of surface data in a straightforward and simple fashion.

Consider tree 5.13. One function of this phrase marker is to accurately represent the surface structure of sentence (49):

(49)
She stood up all those men who had offered her diamonds.

However, tree 5.13 also functions in another way, that is, as an input structure from which we can derive another surface structure. Notice

Tree 5.13

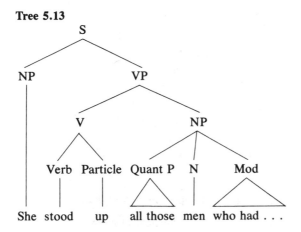

that this structure contains both a verb + particle construction and a complex noun phrase composed of a head noun and a modifying clause. Hence, this is a tree to which the Particle Movement transformation (46) may apply (see figure 5.5). If we apply Particle Movement to the top Input Tree in figure 5.5, we derive the output structure shown as the middle tree in that figure. The particle has been placed after the object noun phrase, as dictated by the rule. This derived structure is not yet a well-formed surface structure (recall the awkwardness and difficulty of the sentence *She stood all those men who had offered her diamonds up*). However, this output tree can, in turn, become a new input tree: we can now apply the Extraposition transformation to yield yet another derived structure, namely, the bottom Output Tree shown in figure 5.5. We have now arrived at the final surface structure for the sentence *She stood all those men up who had offered her diamonds*. Recall that this sentence has two discontinuous dependencies, which actually "cross" each other, as shown in figure 5.2. Yet we can account for this complicated pattern of dependencies in a simple way: we have already postulated the Particle Movement and Extraposition transformations for independent reasons. If we simply allow both rules to apply in sequence, they will automatically interact as shown in figure 5.5. We can now specify precisely what elements of the bottom Output Tree are dependent upon each other, because we have claimed that it derives from the base structure shown at the top of figure 5.5, and that structure represents the surface discontinuities as underlying constituents.

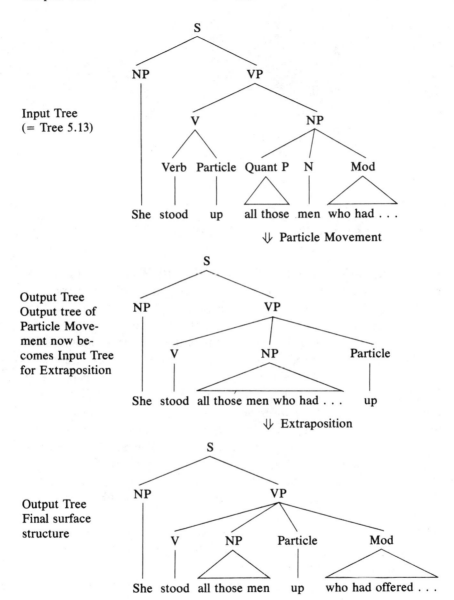

Figure 5.5
Interaction of Particle Movement and Extraposition transformations

The important point here, then, is this: individual transformations are postulated to account for certain dependencies; but even stronger evidence for the transformational model comes from the interaction of the independently established transformations. We have seen that the interaction of two transformations applying in sequence automatically leads to a simple account of a complex set of surface structure dependencies.

We began our investigation of syntactic structure by posing the questions, What is structure? and How do we know that sentences are structured? As we have seen, there is no simple answer to these questions nor any way to answer them without actually constructing a theory of syntax. We have provided a partial answer, though, by arriving at the conclusion that sentence structure involves both structural and relational aspects: specification of the linear order of words, classification of words into parts of speech, grouping of words into structural constituents, and assignment of grammatical relations to certain NPs in a sentence (such as the subject of the sentence). We did not arrive at this view for the sake of convenience, or because it was handed down to us by ancient grammatical authorities. Rather, we found it impossible to state some of the most fundamental syntactic processes of a language—such as how to form questions—without appealing to these properties. On further investigation we found that in order to account for discontinuous dependencies, we needed to postulate not just structural properties of sentences but structural relations as well (represented by transformations). In this way our view of what constitutes syntactic structure is very much determined by what phenomena we are trying to explain, and there is no doubt that theories of syntactic structure will become increasingly subtle and complex as syntactic theorists are faced with an ever-expanding range of new and heretofore unexplained data on the formal properties of sentences.

Finally, we should note that the constituent structure of sentences is not merely an artifact of syntactic theory; there is reason to think that aspects of constituent structure have some reality in the minds of speakers. On this point, see the discussion of click experiments in chapter 10.

5.3 A MORE FORMAL ACCOUNT OF SYNTACTIC THEORY

The type of transformational analysis sketched informally in section 5.2 has, in fact, been given a more precise and formal description by theorists working within the transformational framework. The references at the end of this chapter give a number of alternative accounts of the more formal theory (see Kimball 1973 and Wall 1972 for formalizations of "classical" transformational grammar). In this section we will provide only a brief description to give some idea of how transformational theory has been developed. It should be stressed that we will present here a description of some of the more basic features of standard, or classical, transformational theory, keeping in mind that at present many linguists are working on significant modifications and variations of these basic concepts (see Newmeyer 1980 and Radford 1981 for discussion).

The Formal Statement of Transformations

Recall that a single phrase marker alone cannot account for a discontinuous dependency and that transformational rules are introduced into the theory in order to express syntactic relations between pairs of phrase markers. Transformational rules have been formalized in standard transformational theory; to illustrate the formalism used, we restate the Particle Movement transformation:

(50)
Particle Movement
SD: X - Verb - Particle - NP - Y
      1 -   2 -   3   - 4 - 5 $\Rightarrow$
SC: 1 -   2 - $\emptyset$ - 4+3 - 5

A transformational rule consists, first, of an input: a *structural description* (SD), which is an instruction to analyze a phrase marker into a sequence of constituents, in this case, Verb followed by Particle followed by NP. The variables X and Y indicate that the constituents to the left of the verb and to the right of the NP are irrelevant to this transformation—they can represent anything at all. In order for a transformation to be applied, the analysis of a phrase marker must *satisfy* the SD of the particular transformation. As we can see, tree 5.14 can be analyzed—that is, can be cut up into chunks—in a way that matches exactly the sequence of constituents listed in the SD of the Particle Movement transformation. Hence, this phrase marker satisfies the SD of the rule.

    The second part of a transformational rule is the output: a *structural change* (SC), which in the case of Particle Movement is an instruction

Tree 5.14

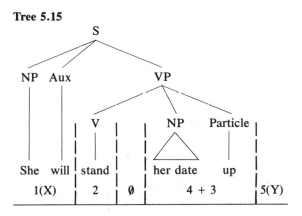

	X	Verb	Particle	NP	Y
	1	2	3	4	5

Tree 5.15

S
NP   Aux   VP
V   NP   Particle

She will stand   her date   up

| 1(X) | 2 | ∅ | 4 + 3 | 5(Y) |

to modify the structural description by shifting term 3 (Particle) immediately to the right of term 4 (NP), as illustrated in tree 5.15. The particle (term 3) has correctly been placed immediately after the NP (term 4), and the plus sign (+) between them in the SC indicates that these two constituents are to be *sisters;* that is, they are to be daughters of the same node (in this case, VP). The symbol ∅ ("zero") indicates that nothing remains in the slot where the particle had been, and marks the spot from which the particle was moved. There are many other details of transformational formalism that we cannot go into here; for these, we recommend the works listed in the references.

Phrase Structure Grammars

Within the standard transformational model it is assumed that basic phrase markers are generated by *phrase structure rules* (PS rules) of the following sort:

(51)
a. S → NP Aux VP
b. NP → Art N
c. VP → V NP

Each rule is essentially a formula, or specification, for how the constituent represented by a certain symbol—the symbol on the left of the arrow—can be constituted in a tree diagram. For example, PS rule (51a) tells us that S (sentence) can *consist of*, or can be *expanded as*, the sequence NP Aux VP. This is shown in tree form as tree 5.16. The rules also tell us that NP (noun phrase) can be expanded as Art N and that VP (verb phrase) can be expanded as V NP. These expansions are illustrated in tree 5.17. By inserting appropriate words, we derive a structure like tree 5.18.

As noted earlier, each labeled point in a tree is referred to as a *node;* thus tree 5.18 includes an S-node, an NP-node, an Aux-node, a VP-node, and so on. We say that the node *S dominates* the nodes *NP, Aux,* and *VP;* the node *NP dominates* the nodes *Art* and *N;* the node *VP dominates* the nodes *V* and *NP,* and so on. We also use a certain type of genealogical terminology when discussing the relationships between nodes in a tree. For example, the nodes *NP, Aux,* and *VP* in tree 5.18 are referred to as the *daughter nodes* of the node *S,* which is the *mother node.* Hence, *NP, Aux,* and *VP* are *sister nodes* with respect to each other. Notice that the *NP-node the sun* and the *V-node dry* are not sisters, because the *NP* is a daughter node of *S,* whereas the *V* is a daughter node of *VP.* In other words, sister nodes must be daughters of the same mother node. (We should note, in passing, that linguistic custom has settled on the mother/daughter/sister terminology, and thus we do not speak of father nodes, brother nodes, and so on.)

Returning to tree 5.17, how do we know what words to insert into that structure? We will assume that part of our grammar consists of a *lexicon,* that is, a list of the words of a language. In the lexicon, words are listed with their parts of speech: for example, *the* is listed as an *article, sun* is listed as a *noun, will* is listed as an *auxiliary verb, dry* is

Tree 5.16

Tree 5.17

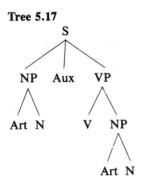

Tree 5.18

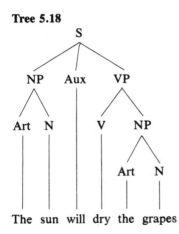

The sun will dry the grapes

listed as a *verb,* and so on. Given a tree such as tree 5.17, we can insert the word *the* under the node *Art,* the word *sun* under the node *N,* the word *will* under the node *Aux,* the word *dry* under the node *V,* and so on, as shown in tree 5.18. We could not, for example, insert the word *the* under the node *V,* because *the* is an article, and not a verb.

It is not the case that every noun phrase of English must contain an article, nor is it the case that every verb phrase must contain an object NP. We say that these are *optional constituents,* and we will indicate this by placing them within parentheses:

(52)
a. S → NP Aux VP
b. NP → (Art) N
c. VP → V (NP)

Items in parentheses *may* be chosen in generating a tree structure; other items *must* be chosen if a structure is to be well-formed. This allows us to generate structures such as tree 5.19.

As we have seen, noun phrases in English may contain various sorts of modifiers after the head noun (for instance, clauses, as in *the men who offered her diamonds*). We have seen that nouns can also be followed by prepositional phrases (PP) as modifiers:

(53)
a. the house *in the woods*
b. the weather *in England*
c. a portrait *of Mary*
d. the prospects *for peace*

In order to form such phrases—or *generate* them, to use the technical term—we can modify our NP rule as follows:

(54)
NP → (Art) N (PP)

We now add a PS rule to expand prepositional phrases:

(55)
PP → Prep NP

This set of PS rules, called a *phrase structure grammar,* now generates NPs such as the one in tree 5.20.

Tree 5.19

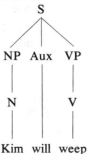

Tree 5.20

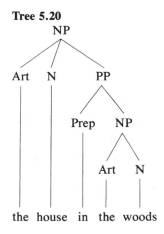

the house in the woods

Consider again the phrase structure rules in (52), in particular the rules for NP and VP. Notice that an NP must consist at least of an N, which forms the *head* of the NP; and a VP must consist at least of a V, which forms the *head* of the VP. A noun phrase is called a noun phrase because it has a noun as its head; and a verb phrase is called a verb phrase because it has a verb as its head. This has led to the suggestion that for each of the *lexical categories* N (noun), V (verb), A (adjective), and P (preposition), there is a corresponding *phrasal category* NP (noun phrase), VP (verb phrase), AP (adjective phrase), and PP (prepositional phrase). We have already seen how this works for NPs and VPs. What about PPs? Notice that in rule (55) PP is expanded as *Prep NP;* in fact, a prepositional phrase *must* contain a preposition, and we say that the preposition is the *head* of the prepositional phrase. (In our discussion, we have only omitted adjective phrases (AP); see exercise 18 for the structure of these phrases.) Generally speaking, then, if we let the symbol X stand for the lexical categories N, V, A, and P, and if we let the symbol XP stand for "phrase of the type X," then it seems that we can state a general formula for certain PS rules: $XP \rightarrow \ldots X \ldots$. This says that a phrase of the type X has a lexical category X as its head, and in this sense it seems that there is a regular relation between lexical categories and phrasal categories (see Radford 1981 (chap. 3) for further discussion).

Embedding

An interesting consequence of rules (54) and (55) is that we can generate a potentially infinite number of noun phrases. This is because the PS rule for NP may be expanded to contain a PP, which in turn contains an NP, which itself may be expanded to contain a PP; and so on, indefinitely, as in tree 5.21. This is one of the ways in which a finite set of rules—in this case, the two rules (54) and (55)—can generate an infinite set of structures. PS grammars containing pairs of rules such as (54) and (55) are said to be *recursive*.

Suppose that we now allow the rule for VP to include an optional symbol S following V:

(56)
VP → V (S)

Tree 5.21

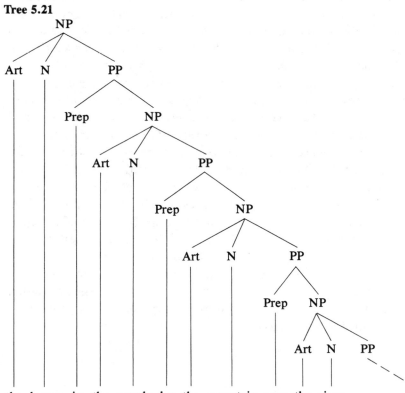

the house in the woods by the mountain near the river

If we allow such a rule, then the PS rule for S will contain a VP, and the PS rule for VP can contain an S:

(57)
a. S → NP Aux VP
b. VP → V (S)

This is another instance of recursion, as we can see by examining tree 5.22. Beginning on the very lowest level (on the far right) in this tree, notice the sentence, S, *Kim didn't leave*. This sentence is *embedded* in a VP of a larger sentence, *Bill will say Kim didn't leave*. That S in turn is embedded within the VP of an even larger sentence, *Pat may think Bill will say Kim didn't leave*. A sentence embedded within a larger sentence is referred to as an *embedded clause, subordinate clause,* or just *embedded sentence*. A sentence that contains an embedded clause is called a *matrix sentence;* in tree 5.22 the sentence *Kim didn't leave* is

Tree 5.22

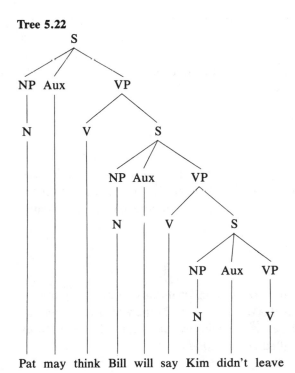

embedded within the matrix sentence that begins *Bill will say* . . . , and
the sentence *Bill will say Kim didn't leave* is embedded within the matrix sentence that begins *Pat may think*. . . . The "highest" matrix
sentence in tree 5.22 (*Pat may think* . . .) is referred to as the *main
clause*. A sentence such as *Kim didn't leave* is referred to as a *simple
sentence* because it contains no embedded sentences; a sentence such
as *Bill will say Kim didn't leave* is referred to as a *complex sentence*
because it contains a matrix sentence and an embedded sentence.

The pair of PS rules in (57) thus constitutes another example of recursion: sentences contain verb phrases, which in turn may contain
sentences, which in turn contain verb phrases, and so on. Again, we
see how a finite set of rules can generate a potentially infinite set of
sentences, and we now have an account for the kinds of examples discussed at the very beginning of this chapter.

We now have two PS rules for VP:

(58)
a. VP → V (NP)
b. VP → V (S)

In other words, our rules allow for the possibility that a verb phrase will
contain just a verb (since the NP and S are optional); or it may contain a
V followed by NP; or it may contain a V followed by S. We can collapse these two rules into a single rule by using a notation involving
braces, { }:

(59)
$$\text{VP} \rightarrow \text{V} \left(\begin{Bmatrix} \text{NP} \\ \text{S} \end{Bmatrix} \right)$$

This rule states that VP must contain at least a V, and that V may
optionally be followed by *either* an NP *or* an S. Thus, the parentheses
notation, ( ), indicates optionality; the braces notation, { }, indicates
an either-or choice.

Center Embedding

In tree 5.21, beginning at the lowest level (rightmost end), every prepositional phrase (PP) is on the extreme right branch of a noun phrase
(NP), which is itself on the extreme right branch of some PP. Structures
of this general sort are called *right-branching*.

Now consider tree 5.23 (where the symbol *Poss* stands for *Possessive Phrase*). We could generate such a tree with the following PS rules:

(60)
a. NP → (Poss) N
b. Poss → NP Poss-Affix

These rules state that an NP may have an optional possessive phrase preceding the head noun. A possessive phrase consists of an NP followed by an Affix (in this case, *'s*). Tree 5.23 once again illustrates the property of recursion, in that an NP may contain a Poss, which in turn contains an NP, which in turn may contain a Poss, and so on. In tree 5.23, beginning at the lowest level (leftmost end), every possessive phrase (Poss) is on the extreme left branch of an NP that is itself on the extreme left branch of a Poss. Structures of this general sort are called *left-branching*.

Tree 5.23

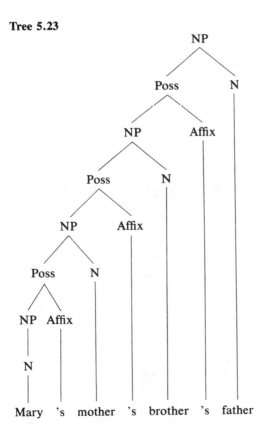

Phrases with right- or left-branching structures are relatively easy to comprehend, provided they are within memory limitations. In other words, the degree of right- or left-branching itself does not seem to lead to excessive difficulty in comprehension. Of course, if any given phrase becomes very long, we will probably forget what was at the beginning of the phrase by the time we come to the end.

In contrast, linguists have noted another class of phrases with a property known as *center-embedding,* which can pose serious problems for sentence comprehension. Let's begin with the simple sentence *The rat ate the cheese.* Noun phrases such as *the rat* can be modified by clauses (as we have seen in examples of extraposition). In this case, we can modify the NP *the rat* with a clause such as *that the cat chased,* producing the sentence *The rat that the cat chased ate the cheese.* Given that noun phrases can be modified by clauses, there is nothing in principle to prevent us from modifying the noun phrase *the cat* with a clause such as *that the dog bit:*

(61)
The rat that the cat that the dog bit chased ate the cheese.

Notice that the sentence has become extremely difficult to comprehend. If we examine these sentences schematically, a pattern appears:

(62)
a. The rat ate the cheese

b. The rat (that) the cat chased ate the cheese

c. The rat (that) the cat (that) the dog bit chased ate the cheese

(62a) is a simple sentence, *The rat ate the cheese.* (62b) is an example of center-embedding: that is, the modifying sentence *the cat chased* is embedded *within* the larger sentence *The rat ate the cheese.* With one level of center-embedding, as in (62b), the sentence remains comprehensible. However, (62c) involves two center-embeddings: the modifying sentence *the dog bit* is embedded within the matrix sentence *the cat chased,* which is in turn embedded within the main sentence *The rat ate the cheese.* We see that two (or more) levels of center-embedding (as in (62c)) renders the sentence extremely difficult to comprehend. It is not fully understood why center-embedding causes such perceptual complexity (that is, not enough is known about the psychological mechanisms underlying our perceptual abilities); nevertheless, the perceptual difficulties posed by center-embedding form an interesting feature of human language processing and comprehension (see chapter 10).

The Standard Theory

The relation between phrase structure rules and transformations in the standard transformational model is summed up in figure 5.6. The syntactic component of a transformational grammar contains a set of phrase structure rules, which generate a class of input phrase markers called *base* (or *underlying*) structures. These underlying structures in turn form the input to the transformational rules, which transform them into a class of phrase markers called *surface structures*. These surface

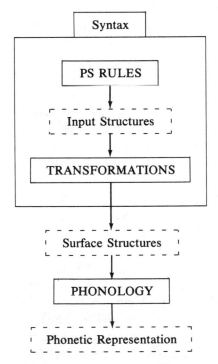

Figure 5.6
Relations between rules in a standard transformational model

structures are in turn operated on by phonological rules, and thus phonetic representations for sentences are derived. To this conception of a
grammar we must yet add a *semantic* component, which assigns representations of meaning to the underlying structures, and a *lexicon,*
which lists the words of a language with their meanings (see chapter 6).

In recent years no part of this overall picture of grammar has remained unchallenged (see Newmeyer 1980 and Radford 1981). Even
though the standard theory of transformational grammar—roughly, the
model presented in Noam Chomsky's 1965 work, *Aspects of the Theory
of Syntax*—has been challenged and modified at every level, it is still
important to have some familiarity with this model in order to understand the many changes in linguistics that have occurred since the
mid-1960s.

Natural Language Processing by Computers: Parsing with Augmented Transition Networks (ATNs) (technical section)

A grammar of a language (such as the one illustrated in figure 5.6) does
not necessarily reflect the way people process sentences in actual
speech comprehension. The study of how human beings process sentences is part of the subfield known as *psycholinguistics,* which we discuss in chapter 10. Here, however, we wish to take note of the fact that
people are not the only processors of language—computers also process language, and one very active area of contemporary research in
computer science and linguistics is the study of machine-parsing of
sentences. The term *parsing* in this context refers to the syntactic analysis of a sentence by a computer, scanning the words of the sentence in
sequence from left to right. Research on machine-parsing has been
motivated, in part, by the desire to communicate with computers in
natural language; to achieve this, a computer must be programmed
to integrate a sequence of words into a syntactically well-formed
sentence.

Among the current approaches to natural language processing, one
of the most popular (and one, incidentally, that has found favor with
psychologists concerned with the processing problem; see Wanner and
Maratsos 1978) is the *Augmented Transition Network* (ATN). The basic
idea behind the ATN approach is that parsing a sentence can be viewed
as moving through a network, scanning the words in a sentence from
left to right, in an attempt to find a "path" that will indicate what the
syntactic structure of the sentence is. We will illustrate this with the

example shown in figure 5.7, which represents a simple ATN consisting of a Sentence network (A) and a Noun Phrase network (B). This ATN analyzes simple declarative sentences and noun phrases in a way we will illustrate shortly.

In addition to the networks illustrated in figure 5.7, we must also assume that the ATN system has access to a lexicon, a simple example of which is given in table 5.4. The lexicon is a list of English words, each associated with specific kinds of information. In the oversimplified example given in the table, note that each word is listed with its lexical category (part of speech). With access to such a lexicon, the ATN system is able to recognize English words and provide a lexical category for each word. Given this information, let us examine how the ATN shown in figure 5.6 will parse (provide a syntactic structure for) the following simple sentence of English:

(63)
John kisses Mary.

Focusing first on the Sentence network (A) of the ATN in figure 5.7, the device starts on the left (see "START"), in state 1 (= S_1), and moves progressively to the right through each successive state, only if it can find a word that matches the specification above each arrow. When such a match occurs, the device assigns the structural description specified directly beneath each arrow. Imagine now that sentence (63) is being scanned from left to right by the ATN beginning at S_1. To arrive at a complete structural description of this sentence, each major transition of the ATN system will be recorded in a table of structural descriptions (of a sort illustrated in table 5.5).

The first word of the sentence is *John,* and the first task of the ATN is to find a Noun Phrase: satisfying that instruction is the only way the device is allowed to move on to S_2. The analysis of Noun Phrases is

Table 5.4
Sample lexicon for ATN

Word	Lexical Category
John	Noun (N)
the	Article (A)
boy	Noun (N)
kisses	Verb (V): transitive
girl	Noun (N)
interesting	Adjective (Adj)

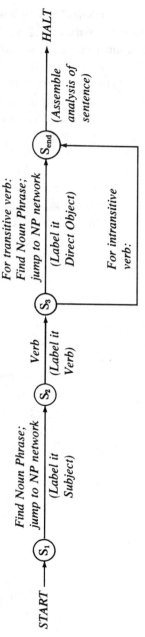

A. Sentence Network of ATN

B. Noun Phrase Network of ATN

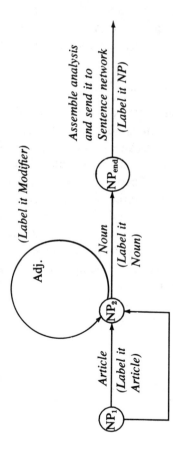

Figure 5.7
Augmented Transition Network (ATN) for an elementary sentence of English

carried out by the Noun Phrase network (B) of the ATN in figure 5.7, and so the Sentence network seeks out the Noun Phrase network at this point and lands in state NP_1. There are now two valid moves the device can make in order to get from state NP_1 to state NP_2: either (a) find an article and label it as such; or (b) jump directly to state NP_2. In our particular example, the word *John* is not an article (but rather a noun); this information is supplied by the lexicon given in table 5.4. Thus, the device cannot label *John* as an article, and so it takes the arc that allows it to jump directly to state NP_2. At state NP_2 there is a loop for labeling adjectives; but again, the word *John* is simply a noun (with no modifying adjectives), and so the device can take the "Noun" path to the end-state, NP_{end}. In making this move, the parser labels *John* as a noun (in accordance with the instruction beneath the Noun arc), giving a representation such as $[John]_N$. In order to return to the Sentence network (A), the device now must leave NP_{end}, labeling the item(s) analyzed in NP_{end} as a Noun Phrase, thus giving a representation such as $[[John]_N]_{NP}$. This Noun Phrase is now sent back to state S_1 of the Sentence network.

The parser can now move from state S_1 to state S_2, because it has found a Noun Phrase (the one just supplied by the Noun Phrase network, $[[John]_N]_{NP}$). In moving to state S_2, the device now labels *John* as the Subject, in accordance with the instruction directly beneath the arc linking S_1 and S_2. To sum up so far, the major transitions of the ATN system are illustrated in lines 1–4 of table 5.5.

The ATN must now move to state S_3, but in order to do so it must find a verb. The word after *John* in left-to-right sequence is the word *kisses* (see example (63)), and in the lexicon (table 5.4) this word is indeed listed as a verb. The device now moves into state S_3, labeling *kisses* as a verb: $[kisses]_V$ (see line 5, table 5.5).

There are two possible paths leading from S_3 to the end-state S_{end}, one for transitive verbs and one for intransitive verbs. Since *kisses* is listed in the lexicon as a transitive verb, the device now takes the transitive verb arc to S_{end}; in order to land there, it must find a Noun Phrase. The next word in example sentence (63) being *Mary,* the parser jumps to NP_1 and runs the word *Mary* through the Noun Phrase network (B) (just as it did for the word *John*), labeling it as a noun $[Mary]_N$. In the transition from NP_{end} back to S_3, the parser labels $[Mary]_N$ as a Noun Phrase $[[Mary]_N]_{NP}$ (see lines 5–7 of table 5.5). In going from state S_3 to the end-state S_{end}, the device now labels the Noun Phrase as Di-

Table 5.5
Table of structural descriptions, recording transitions of ATN system

	Transition from State to State	Input Item	Output: Categorization or Function
1	S_1 (Start) — (Jump to NP network)		
2	NP_1 → NP_{end} (Return)	John	$[John]_N$
3	S_1	$[John]_N$	$[[John]_N]_{NP}$
4	S_2	$[[John]_N]_{NP}$	*Subject*
5	S_3 (Jump to NP network)	kisses	$[kisses]_V$
6	NP_1 → NP_{end} (Return)	Mary	$[Mary]_N$
7	S_3	$[Mary]_N$	$[[Mary]_N]_{NP}$
8	S_{end}	$[[Mary]_N]_{NP}$	*Direct Object*
9	*Halt:* $[[John]_N]_{NP} [kisses]_V [[Mary]_N]_{NP}$ ⟶ $_S[[[John]_N]_{NP} [kisses]_V [[Mary]_N]_{NP}]_S$		

rect Object and finally arrives at S_{end}. The major transitions of the ATN system are recorded in table 5.5.

The output representation of the sentence *John kisses Mary,* given at the right in line 9 of table 5.5, is in a form known as *labeled bracketing.* Important structural information concerning linear order, categorization (into parts of speech), and hierarchical grouping (into constituent structure) has been encoded into the bracketing format. In fact, for every labeled bracketing there is a corresponding representation in tree diagram form (and vice versa), illustrated here with example sentence (63):

(64)

a. Labeled bracketing

$_S[[[John]_N]_{NP} [kisses]_V [[Mary]_N]_{NP}]_S$

b. Corresponding tree diagram

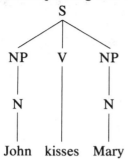

John   kisses   Mary

Notice that the labeled bracketing and the tree diagram have not been constructed with a verb phrase (VP) constituent; for the sake of simplicity, we have omitted discussion of how this constituent structure could be built up by an ATN. But the point is that a computer ATN system, scanning the words of a sentence in left-to-right sequential order, can assign the same structural analysis to simple sentences that a tree-generating phrase structure grammar can. Of course, an ATN that can parse more complex sentences of English (or any other natural language) must be a good deal more complicated than the simple one illustrated in figure 5.7, and no ATN system exists at the present time that can process all of English.

Key Words

competence
performance
structure
structural ambiguity
tags
tree diagrams
phrase markers
discontinuous dependencies
transformational rules
phrase structure grammars
embedding

Exercises

1. The following tree structures have been left incomplete, in the sense that no
words have been filled in. For each structure, list an appropriate sentence that
would fit the structure (that is, supply an appropriate word for each blank):

a.

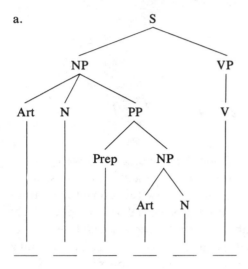

b.

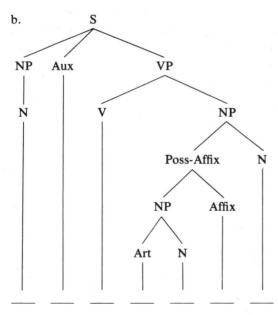

c.

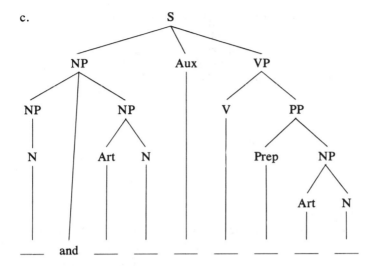

2. Figure 5.1 illustrates a "box diagram" for representing constituent structure. Take tree 5.1 (from the text) and convert the VP of that tree structure into an equivalent box diagram.

3. Using tree 5.1 as your reference, answer the following questions:

A. What are the daughter nodes of the node VP?

B. The subject NP, *the people in the room,* contains a PP node. What are the *sister* nodes of that PP?

C. The phrase structure rule for VP given in example (52c) of the text will not generate the VP shown in tree 5.1. Why not (that is, what constituent is missing from rule (52c))? How would you reformulate rule (52c) so that it will generate the VP in tree 5.1?

D. Is the sequence of words *the room will move* represented as a *single* constituent in tree 5.1?

4. Draw tree diagrams for the following noun phrases:

a. the weather in England

b. John's uncle in England

c. John's uncle in England's company

5. The sequence of words *light, house, keeper* is structurally ambiguous.

A. How many meanings can you detect for this sequence?

B. What structural groupings would you assign to the phrase, to represent each meaning you have found? (Use parentheses, in the manner of example (4) of the text.)

6. Basic word order for English is *Subject-Verb-Object,* as in *Gorillas eat bananas.* For the following two languages, isolate and identify the different words and determine what the basic word order is.

Language #1: Navajo (Native American language of the Southwest)

a. Łį́į́' dzaanééz yiztał   "The horse kicked the mule"
b. Dzaanééz łį́į́' yiztał   "The mule kicked the horse"
c. Ashkii at'ééd yiztsǫs   "The boy kissed the girl"
d. At'ééd ashkii yiztsǫs   "The girl kissed the boy"
e. Ashkii łį́į́' yo'į́   "The boy saw the horse"

horse _____

mule _____

boy _____

girl_____

kicked_____

kissed_____

saw_____

Basic word order: _____

Language #2: Lummi (Native American language of the Pacific Northwest)

a. x̌čits cə-swəy²qə² sə-słeni²   "The man knows the woman"
b. x̌čits sə-słeni² cə-swəy²qə²   "The woman knows the man"
c. leŋnəs cə-sčətxʷən cə-swəy²qə²   "The bear saw the man"
d. leŋnes sə-słeni² cə-swi²qo²əł   "The woman saw the boy"

man _____

woman _____

bear _____

boy _____

know _____

saw _____

Basic word order: _____

7. As noted in the text, in some languages word order is quite free, as, for example, in Papago, a Native American language of southern Arizona and northern Mexico. To see the possibilities for word order, consider the following sentence (data from Zepeda 1983):

(i)

Huan   'o   wakon   g-ma:gina.
Subject Aux   Verb   Object
"John" "3rd person" "washing" "the car"
"John is/was washing the car."

Sentence (i) can have the word order shown, or any of the following word orders:

(ii)

a. Huan 'o g-ma:gina wakon.
b. Wakon 'o g-ma:gina g-Huan.
c. Wakon 'o g-Huan g-ma:gina.
d. Ma:gina 'o wakon g-Huan.
e. Ma:gina 'o g-Huan wakon.

The auxiliary *'o* (which we label Aux) indicates a third person subject (in this case, *Huan* "John") and is used in sentences that describe ongoing or incompleted actions. (In the Papago sentences, the symbol : is used to indicate a long vowel, and a "prefix" *g-* sometimes appears with nouns and sometimes does not. Both of these features can be ignored in this exercise.) Now answer the following questions:

A. For each sentence in (ii), indicate what the word order is. Use the labels Subject (= *Huan*), Aux (= *'o*), Verb (= *wakon*), and Object (= *ma:gina*), in the manner shown in the first example below:

Sentence	Word Order
a. Huan 'o g-ma:gina wakon.	Subject-Aux-Object-Verb
b. Wakon 'o g-ma:gina g-Huan.	_____
c. Wakon 'o g-Huan g-ma:gina.	_____
d. Ma:gina 'o wakon g-Huan.	_____
e. Ma:gina 'o g-Huan wakon.	_____

B. As your answer to question A will have shown, word order in Papago appears to be free, except for one particular constituent of the above sentences, which occurs in the same relative position in every sentence. What is this constituent, and in what position of a sentence must it appear?

C. Given your answer to question B, consider the following ungrammatical sentences of Papago:

(iii)

a. *Huan g-ma:gina 'o wakon.

b. *Huan g-ma:gina wakon 'o.

Why are these sentences bad?

8. In American English, the word *so* can be used as an intensifier, or emphasizer, as in the following example:

(i)

a. I can lift this weight.

b. I can *so* lift this weight!

In the second example, *so* functions to indicate emphasis. The following examples show that there is a restriction on the placement of *so* in a sentence:

(ii)

a. I will pass the test.

b. I will *so* pass the test!

(iii)

a. I know the answer.

b. *I know *so* the answer! (ill-formed)

c. I do *so* know the answer.

(iv)

a. Mary is running in tomorrow's race.

b. Mary is *so* running in tomorrow's race!

(v)

a.   They took our money.

b.   *They took *so* our money! (ill-formed)

c.   They did *so* take our money!

(vi)

a.   He is nice.

b.   He is *so* nice.

What is the restriction on the placement of *so?* That is, where can *so* be inserted within a sentence, and when is it impossible to insert *so?* Use yes/no questions, tag formation, and negative placement to support your answer.

9. Example (27) of the text describes a number of properties of the *subject* constituent of English sentences. For example, the pronoun in a tag will agree with the subject of a sentence in person, number, and gender (see (26) in the text). Now consider the following sentences:

a.   That John arrived late annoyed Bill.

b.   There were three men in the park.

c.   It was Mary who solved the problem.

d.   The car, truck, and train collided with each other.

e.   Thirty or forty bees have built a hive.

f.   That movie, the boys really like a lot.

A. For each sentence, construct an appropriate tag.

B. For each case, indicate what constituent of the main sentence the pronoun in the tag *agrees* with. Do this by underlining the constituent and connecting it to the tag pronoun (as in example (26) of the text).

C. Based on your results in questions A and B, what is the subject of each sentence?

10. In the text we noted a number of grammatical properties of subjects in English (summarized in (27)). Now consider the following sentences, focusing in particular on the form of the italicized *verb:*

(i)

a.   The boy *likes* that cake.

b.   The boys *like* that cake.

c.   The boy and girl *like* that cake.

d.   *The boy and the girl *likes* that cake.

(ii)

a.   That cake, the boy *likes*.

b.   That cake, the boys *like*.

c.   *That cake, the boys *likes*.

Many verbs in English *agree in number* with some preceding constituent. That is, the verbs take on a singular form (*likes*) or a plural form (*like*) in the present tense (in the manner illustrated above), depending on whether certain preceding constituents are singular or plural. This process, illustrated in (i) and (ii), is known as *verb agreement*. Now consider the following hypothetical verb agreement rules, and answer the questions associated with each:

A. The verb agrees in number with the noun immediately to its left.
Question: Why is this rule inaccurate? Use the data in (i) to show that the rule makes a false prediction.
B. The verb agrees in number with the noun phrase that comes at the very beginning of the sentence.
Question: Why is this rule inaccurate? Use the data in (ii) to show that the rule makes a false prediction.
Finally, after answering parts A and B, answer the following question: what constituent of a sentence does the verb agree with in number? That is, what is the proper way to state the verb agreement rule?

11. As we saw in examining the notion "subject," in English the subject of a sentence can be identified by its structural position (see tree 5.3), among other things, and in Japanese by a special marking on the subject noun phrase (*-ga*). There are also languages in which the subject of a sentence can be identified by means of a special marking on the main verb. For example, in Navajo there are two verbal prefixes, *yi-* and *bi-*, illustrated in the following examples:

a. Łį́į́' dzaanééz *yi*ztał   "The horse kicked the mule"
b. Łį́į́' dzaanééz *bi*ztał   "The mule kicked the horse"

(The translations of the words *łį́į́'* and *dzaanééz* can be derived from exercise 6.)
A. In Navajo, for sentences of the form $NP^1 \; NP^2 \; yi + Verb$, which NP is interpreted as the subject and which as the object?
B. For sentences of the form $NP^1 \; NP^2 \; bi + Verb$, which NP is interpreted as the subject and which as the object?

12. In English we find many pairs of corresponding active and passive sentences:
a. Mary hit John. (active sentence)
b. John was hit by Mary. (passive sentence)
Hypothesis: To form a passive sentence from an active sentence,
(i)
interchange the first and last words of the sentence (make the first word the last word and the last word the first word),
(ii)
add *by* before the last word and insert the proper form of the verb *be* into second position of the sentence.

Why is the hypothesis wrong? Cite specific examples from English to support your answer. Show why it is necessary to refer to syntactic constituents in the rule for forming passive sentences. (Hint: Review the discussion of the English Question Rule in section 5.2.)

13. Consider the sentence *I kicked the ball into the basket*. Is *the ball into the basket* a single constituent? Show how the cleft construction can be used to answer this question. (Review the discussion of examples (30)–(32).)

14. The conjunction test, discussed in connection with examples (33) and (34), is not foolproof, and in fact there are certain problems with it. For example,

consider the sentence *They moved the desk into the hall and the table into the office*.

A. In this example, what two phrases seem to be conjoined by *and?*

B. Are these two phrases *single* constituents? (Hint: Check tree 5.1 again.)

15. Example (39) provides one instance of a verb + particle construction: *stood up*. Cite five additional verb + particle constructions, showing for each example how the particle occurs both adjacent to the verb and separated from the verb (as in example (39)).

16. Under certain circumstances, the Particle Movement transformation seems to be obligatory; that is, the particle *must* be separated from the verb:

(i)

a. *She stood up them.

b. She stood them up.

(ii)

a. *I wrote down it.

b. I wrote it down.

(iii)

a. *The bartender kicked out him.

b. The bartender kicked him out.

Under what circumstances must the particle be separated from its verb?

17. The following sentences illustrate cases of extraposition similar to ones discussed in the text:

(i)

a. A review *of the new book by Chomsky* will soon appear.

b. A review will soon appear *of the new book by Chomsky*.

(ii)

a. Several theories *about the structure of language* were presented last night.

b. Several theories were presented last night *about the structure of language*.

The phrases *of the new book by Chomsky* and *about the structure of language* are single constituents that can be shifted to the end of a sentence by the Extraposition transformation.

A. Draw a tree structure for each of the following phrases:

a. a review of the new book by Chomsky

b. several theories about the structure of language

B. Now draw a tree structure for sentence (ia) and a tree structure for sentence (iia) (you will naturally incorporate the structures you have drawn in question A). If you are unsure about details of the verb phrase, simply use triangles to abbreviate the structure, as in trees 5.7, 5.8, 5.11, and 5.12.

C. Finally, draw tree structures for sentences (ib) and (iib). These will be the output trees of Extraposition. (Hint: A careful study of trees 5.11, 5.12, 5.20, and 5.21 should clear up any problems you might have in drawing your trees for this exercise.)

18. In discussing phrase structure rules, we mentioned that adjective phrases have a structure parallel to that of noun phrases, verb phrases, and preposi-

tional phrases (recall the discussion of what constitutes the *head* of a phrase). Now consider the following italicized adjective phrases:

a. Kim is *angry at Bill's sister.*
b. We're *proud of the invention.*

Now answer the following questions:
A. What is the structure of the adjective phrase *angry at Bill's sister?* Draw a tree diagram for this adjective phrase; use the symbol *AP* to stand for *adjective phrase,* and *Adj* to stand for *adjective.*
B. What is the structure of the adjective phrase *proud of the invention?* Follow the same procedure as in part A.
(Hint: A careful study of tree 5.20 should give you the clue you need to draw tree structures for adjective phrases.)

19. *For open discussion.* As noted in the text, tags can occur in positive or negative forms:

a. Herman is threatening to leave, *is* he!
b. Herman is threatening to leave, *isn't* he?

When the main sentence is itself negative in form, then the tag is always positive:

c. Herman isn't threatening to leave, *is* he?
d. *Herman isn't threatening to leave, *isn't* he?

For the purposes of this exercise, concentrate just on examples (a) and (b).
A. How do the positive and negative tags differ in their use? That is, when would you use the positive tag but not the negative tag, and vice versa?
B. Provide additional examples like (a) and (b) in order to support your answer.

20. *For open discussion.* Speakers of English have considerable difficulty in providing tags for certain sentences. For example, the following sentences seem to have no appropriate tag (for many speakers):

a. Either John or Mary will buy tickets.
b. John, or possibly Mary, will buy tickets.

Discuss why sentences (a) and (b) might present problems for speakers in deciding how to form appropriate tags. In your answer, consider the fact that sentences very similar in structure to (a) and (b) do not present problems for tag formation:

c. Both John and Mary will buy tickets.
d. John, and Mary too, will buy tickets.

21. *For extra credit (difficult!).* Consider the following ungrammatical sentence:

a. *You gave liquor to.

There is a gap—something is missing—after the preposition *to,* and this gap must apparently be filled in order for the sentence to be grammatical:

b. You gave liquor to the boy.

However, when a question word such as *which (boy)* is present, a gap can occur:

c. Which boy did you give liquor to ____?

In other words, we understand that the phrase *which boy* in fact "fills" the gap at the end of the sentence; thus, there is a dependency between the initial question word and the final gap.

A. Cite specific examples from English to show that there is in principle no limit on the length of the sentence that can intervene between the initial question phrase and the final gap. (Hint: Think of sentences such as *Which boy did Mary say you gave liquor to?*)

B. Propose a transformational rule that will explain the discontinuous dependency. A clue for what this rule might be comes from observing the position of the question phrase, *which boy*, in the following two sentences:

d. You gave liquor to *which boy?*

e. *Which boy* did you give liquor to?

Bibliography

Akmajian, A., and F. W. Heny (1975). *An Introduction to the Principles of Transformational Syntax*, MIT Press, Cambridge, Mass.

Bach, E. (1974). *Syntactic Theory*, Holt, Rinehart and Winston, New York.

Baker, C. L. (1978). *Introduction to Generative-Transformational Syntax*, Prentice-Hall, Englewood Cliffs, N.J.

Chomsky, N. (1957). *Syntactic Structures*, Mouton, The Hague.

Chomsky, N. (1965). *Aspects of the Theory of Syntax*, MIT Press, Cambridge, Mass.

Chomsky, N. (1976). *Reflections on Language*, Pantheon Books, New York.

Chomsky, N. (1979). *Language and Responsibility*, Pantheon Books, New York.

Chomsky, N. (1980). *Rules and Representations*, Columbia University Press, New York.

Culicover, P. (1983). *Syntax*, Academic Press, New York.

Greenberg, J. H., ed. (1966). *Universals of Language*, MIT Press, Cambridge, Mass.

Kimball, J. P. (1973). *The Formal Theory of Grammar*, Prentice-Hall, Englewood Cliffs, N.J.

Newmeyer, F. J. (1980). *Linguistic Theory in America: The First Quarter-Century of Transformational Generative Grammar*, Academic Press, New York.

Radford, A. (1981). *Transformational Syntax: A Student's Guide to Chomsky's Extended Standard Theory*, Cambridge University Press, Cambridge.

Stockwell, R. P., P. Schachter, and B. H. Partee (1973). *The Major Syntactic Structures of English*, Holt, Rinehart and Winston, New York.

Wall, R. (1972). *Introduction to Mathematical Linguistics,* Prentice-Hall, Englewood Cliffs, N.J.

Wanner, E., and M. Maratsos (1978). "An ATN approach to comprehension," in M. Halle, J. Bresnan, and G. A. Miller, eds., *Linguistic Theory and Psychological Reality,* MIT Press, Cambridge, Mass.

Zepeda, O. (1983). *A Papago Grammar,* University of Arizona Press, Tucson.

Chapter Six

SEMANTICS: THE STUDY OF MEANING AND REFERENCE

6.1 SEMANTICS AS PART OF A GRAMMAR

The study of linguistic units and their principles of combination would not be complete without an account of what these units mean, what they are used to talk about, and what they are used to communicate. The study of communication is a part of pragmatics, to which we will return in chapter 9. In this chapter we will take up the first two topics, which constitute a major portion of *semantics*.

In the field of linguistics, semantics is generally considered to be the study of *meaning* (and related notions) in languages, while in the field of logic, semantics is generally considered to be the study of *linguistic reference* and *truth conditions* in languages. Other disciplines, such as philosophy, psychology, and computer science, sample freely from both traditions. Although there is sometimes tension between these conceptions of semantics, the dispute is really one of emphasis: in the end, an adequate semantic description of natural languages must record facts of meaning, linguistic reference, and truth conditions. In chapter 3 we discussed some semantic notions at the word level. But semantic analysis also applies to those expressions that are made up of words: phrases and sentences. Indeed, traditionally, phrases and sentences have received more attention than the words that make them up.

Semantics has not always enjoyed a prominent role in modern linguistics. From World War II to the early 1960s semantics was viewed, especially in the United States, as not quite respectable: its inclusion in a grammar was considered by many as either a sort of methodological impurity or an objective to be reached only in the distant future. But as Katz and Fodor pointed out in their influential article "The structure of a semantic theory" (Katz and Fodor 1963), there is as much reason to consider semantics a part of grammar as syntax or phonology. It is often said that a grammar describes what fluent speakers know of their language—their *linguistic competence* (recall chapter 5). If that is so, we can argue that whatever fluent speakers know of their language is a proper part of a description of that language. Given this, then the description of meaning is a necessary part of the description of a speaker's linguistic knowledge (that is, the grammar of a language must contain a component that describes what speakers know about the semantics of the language). In other words, if appealing to what fluent speakers know about their language counts as motivation for including a phonological fact or a syntactic fact in the grammar of that language, then the same sort of consideration motivates the inclusion of semantic facts.

A more general consideration also motivates us to include semantics in the grammar of a language. A language is often defined as a conventional system for communication, a system for conveying messages. Moreover, communication can be accomplished (in the system) only because words have certain meanings, so to characterize this system—the language—it is necessary to describe these meanings. Hence, if a grammar describes a language, part of it must describe meaning, and thus it must contain a semantics. Taking these two considerations together, it seems reasonable to conclude that semantic information is an integral part of a grammar.

In reading this chapter, though, bear in mind that the subfield of semantics is in a greater state of diversification than phonology or syntax; much that we will discuss is a cautious selection from among possible alternatives. There is no shortage of semantic theories, but it is widely acknowledged that serious open questions still lie at the very foundations of semantics. We would suggest consulting the works listed in the reference section of this chapter, in order to get a general idea of the range and scope of semantics.

6.2 WHAT ARE MEANING AND REFERENCE?

It would take a whole semantic theory to answer the questions raised here, but in the history of semantics a few "leading ideas" have emerged about the nature of meaning and reference, and a brief look at some of these conceptions is instructive.

Meaning

In everyday English, the word *mean* has a number of different uses, many of which are not relevant to the study of language:

(1)
a. That was no mean (insignificant) accomplishment.
b. They are so mean (cruel) to me.
c. This will mean (result in) the end of our regime.
d. This means so much (is so important) to me.
e. I mean (intend) to help if I can.
f. Keep Off the Grass! This means (refers to) you.
g. His losing his job means (implies) that he will have to look again.
h. Lucky Strike means (indicates) fine tobacco.
i. Those clouds mean (are a sign of) rain.
j. She doesn't mean (believe) what she said.

These uses of the word *mean* can all be paraphrased by other expressions (indicated in parentheses above). None of them is appropriate for our discussion of word meaning. Rather, we will use the terms *mean* and *meaning* as they are used in the following examples:

(2)
a. *Procrastinate* means "to put things off."
b. In saying that, she meant that we should leave.

These two uses of the word *mean* exemplify two important types of meaning: *linguistic meaning* and *speaker's meaning*.

This distinction can be illustrated with an example. Suppose that you've been arguing with another person, who exclaims, "The door is right behind you!" You would assume, quite rightly in this context, that the speaker, in uttering this sentence, means that you are to leave—although the speaker's actual words indicate nothing more than the location of a door. This illustrates how a speaker can mean something quite different from what his or her words mean. In general, the *linguistic meaning* of an expression is simply the meaning or meanings of that expression in the language. In contrast, the *speaker's meaning* can differ from the linguistic meaning, depending on whether the speaker is speaking *literally* or *nonliterally*. When we speak literally, we mean what our words mean, and in this case there is no important difference between speaker's meaning and linguistic meaning. But when we speak nonliterally, we mean something different from what our words mean.

Nonliteral uses of language include sarcasm or irony, as when someone says of a film, "That movie was a real winner!", uttered in such a way that we understand the speaker to mean that the movie was a real flop. Metaphorical uses of language (some of which we discussed in chapter 3) are also examples of nonliteral language use, as, for example, when someone is described as having raven hair, ruby lips, emerald eyes, and teeth of pearl. Taken literally, this description would indicate that the person in question is an inorganic monstrosity; taken metaphorically, it is quite a compliment. As we shall see in part three of this text, a crucial feature in human communication is the ability to determine whether a speaker is speaking literally or nonliterally.

Returning now to the question of linguistic meaning, whenever we talk about the meaning of an expression, it is useful to keep in mind the distinction between the linguistic meaning of the expression and a given speaker's literal or nonliteral use of the expression. Furthermore, in talking about the linguistic meaning of an expression, we must note that meanings can vary across dialects and across individual speakers. To recall an example from chapter 3, in American English the word *bonnet* refers to a type of hat, whereas in British English it refers to the hood of a car. Hence, for a word such as *bonnet* we cannot isolate a single meaning valid for all forms of English; rather, our discussion of the meaning of the word will be relative to a specific dialect of English.

The matter is further complicated when we note that meanings of words can vary across individual speakers within the same dialect. For example, the word *infer* seems to have different meanings for different speakers. For some speakers, it has roughly the same meaning as *surmise* or *conclude,* as in *I infer from what you say that you are sick.* For other speakers, it has roughly the same meaning as *imply,* as in *He inferred that he was fed up with us.* The language of a particular individual is referred to as that person's *idiolect* (see chapter 7), and it is clear that the idiolectal meaning of a word can differ from one person to another (even among people who can be said to speak the same dialect). The varieties of meaning we have specified so far are summarized in figure 6.1.

At this point we might ask, How can so many varieties of meaning exist? Isn't it the case, after all, that "official" dictionaries of a language tell us what the meaning of a word is? And isn't it the case that the only "valid" meanings for a word are those listed in the dictionary? In answering these questions, it is important to recall the distinction made in chapter 1 between prescriptive and descriptive grammar. Cur-

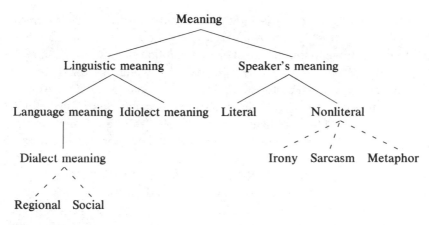

Figure 6.1
Some varieties of meaning

rent dictionaries of English (and many other languages as well) derive from a tradition of prescriptive grammar, and almost invariably have focused on the written language. You can probably think of numerous words and uses of words in current spoken, informal English that do not appear in dictionaries. From a prescriptive point of view these un-listed words and uses might be termed "incorrect" or "improper." From a descriptive point of view, however, the spoken language forms a central source of data for linguistic theory, and linguists are very much concerned with discovering meaning properties and relations in forms of spoken language actually used by speakers (rather than forms of language that prescriptive grammar dictates speakers "should" use). Hence, although dictionaries might be useful in providing certain basic definitions of common words, they do not, by and large, reflect accurately enough the meaning and variations in meaning of words in cur-rent use in everday spoken language.

The descriptive point of view is sometimes misinterpreted as ad-vocating "linguistic freedom"—that is, a situation in which speakers are free to use words any way they like and are allowed to "get away with" breaking the rules of proper English. This is, of course, an absurd parody of the descriptive point of view. It turns out that, quite aside from dictionaries and prescriptive grammar books, speakers are indeed not free to use words any way they like (despite Humpty-Dumpty's assertion to the contrary in Lewis Carroll's *Through the Looking Glass*). There is tremendous social pressure for speakers of a language to use words in similar ways—successful communication depends on this, in fact—and the need to communicate effectively provides constraints on how "creative" an individual speaker can be in the use of words.

What Is Meaning?

Historically, the most compelling notion concerning meaning has been that it is some sort of entity or thing. After all, we do speak of words as "having" a meaning, as meaning "something," as having the "same" meaning, as meaning the same "thing," as "sharing" a meaning, as having many "meanings," and so forth.

What sort of entity or thing is meaning? Different answers to this question give us a selection of different conceptions of meaning, and a selection of different types of semantic theory.

The Referential Theory of Meaning

If one focuses on just some of the expressions in a language—for instance, proper names such as *de Gaulle, Chris Evert, Italy,* or definite descriptive noun phrases such as *the present president of the United States, the first person to walk on our moon,* and so forth—one is likely to conclude that their meaning is the thing they refer to. For convenience we will formulate this conception of meaning as the following slogan:

(R)

The meaning of each expression E is the (actual) object it refers to, its *referent*.

Although (R) does reflect the fact that we use language to talk about the world, there are serious problems with the identification of meaning as reference.

For instance, if we believe that the meaning of an expression is its referent, we are committed to at least the following additional claims:

(3)

a. If an expression E has a meaning, then it must have a referent.

b. If two expressions have the same referent, then they have the same meaning.

c. Anything that is true of the referent of an expression is true of its meaning.

Each of these consequences of (R) is false, and so the Referential Theory of meaning must be modified.

For instance, (3a) requires that for any expression having a meaning there is an actual object that it refers to. But this is surely wrong. What, for instance, is the (actual) object referred to by such expressions as *Pegasus, the, empty, and, hello, very,* and *Leave the room?* Next, consider (3b). This says that if two expressions refer to the same object, then they mean the same thing; that is, they are synonymous. But many expressions that can be correctly used to refer to a single object do not mean the same thing. For instance, *the morning star, the evening star,* and *Venus* all can refer to the same planet, but they are not synonymous. Nor are the expressions *the first person to walk on our moon* and *Neil Armstrong* synonymous, but they refer to the same person. Finally, consider (3c). As far as we know, Sir Edmund Hilary was the first European to climb Mt. Everest, and as a consequence he was knighted by the Queen. But by (3c) we must conclude that it is the meaning of the words *Edmund Hilary* that climbed Mt. Everest and was knighted by the Queen. Since this is absurd, we conclude instead that the Referential Theory will have to be either rejected or modified in some significant way.

Mentalist Theories of Meaning
Well, we might say, if meanings are not actual objects, perhaps they are mental objects; even if there is no real flying horse for *Pegasus* to refer to, there is surely such an *idea,* and maybe this idea is the meaning of *Pegasus.* A typical example of this view can be seen in the following quotation from Glucksberg and Danks (1975, 50): "The set of possible meanings of any given word is the set of possible feelings, images, ideas, concepts, thoughts, and inferences that a person might produce when that word is heard and processed." As with the Referential Theory, this conception of meaning can be formulated as a slogan:

(M)
The meaning of each expression E is an idea (or ideas), *I,* associated with E in the minds of speakers.

This sort of theory has a number of problems, but the most serious one can be put in the form of a dilemma: either the notion of an idea is too vague to allow the theory to predict anything specific and thus the theory is not testable; or if the notion of an idea is made precise enough to test, the theory turns out to make false predictions. The quotation from Glucksberg and Danks illustrates the first problem. How, with such a view of meaning, could one ever determine what an expression means? With such a view, could two expressions be synonymous, or would there always be feelings and thoughts associated with one expression that are not associated with the other?

Turning to the second problem, suppose we sharpen the notion of an idea by saying that ideas are *mental images*. While this might work for words like *Pegasus* and perhaps *the Eiffel Tower,* it is not obvious how it would work for nouns such as *dog* and *triangle,* or a verb such as *kick.* For instance, if one really does form an image of a dog or a triangle, more than likely the dog will be of some particular species and will not comprise both a Chihuahua and a Saint Bernard; the triangle will be isosceles or equilateral but will not comprise all triangles. Similar problems arise with *kick.* If one really forms an image of X kicking Y, then that image probably will have properties not essential to kicking, such as the sex of the kicker, which leg was used, the kind of thing being kicked, and so forth. In general, mental images are just not abstract enough to be the meanings of even common nouns and verbs. But suppose for the moment that appropriate images could be found for these nouns and verbs. What about other kinds of words? What images are the meanings of words such as *only, and, hello,* and *not?* Worse still, can the theory apply to units larger than words, such as the sentence *She speaks French and Navajo?* How, for instance, does an Image Theory of meaning differentiate this sentence from *She speaks French or Navajo?*

One way around this problem of the excessive specificity of images is to make the relevant notion of an idea be a *concept.* Even though this way of making the theory testable has promise, there is as yet no theory in cognitive psychology that is detailed enough to test as a theory of meaning. To succeed, such a theory must be capable of identifying and distinguishing concepts independently of meaning, which they at present fail to do (see chapter 10 for more on concepts). In short, theories of meaning as entities, whether they be objects referred to, images in the mind, or concepts, all face various difficulties. Perhaps the trouble lies with the initial assumption that meaning is an entity.

The Use Theory of Meaning

One of the last theories of meaning to emerge has been the (nonentitative) Use Theory of meaning. Advanced by Wittgenstein in the 1930s, it has more or less taken over Anglo-American theorizing about meaning for the past forty years. Properly construed, it is, we think, a promising theory. Like the previous theories of meaning, this one can be formulated as a slogan:

(U)
The meaning of an expression E is determined by its use in the language community.

Notice that this theory does not suffer all the weaknesses of entitative theories. We can just as easily speak of the use of *hello* as of the use of *table* or *Pegasus*. The main problem with the Use Theory of meaning is that the relevant conception of *use* must be made precise, and the theory must say how, exactly, meaning is connected to use. Such a theory is being developed by various authors (see the works of Grice and Schiffer, cited in the bibliography), and we will say more about language use in chapter 9.

   In conclusion, it is fair to say that we do not have a very good idea about what meaning is and that all of the theories we have surveyed are in various states of disarray. The situation is not hopeless, as there are still promising avenues for future research. The student should not be deterred by this limitation on our present understanding, but should consider it an opportunity to make a contribution. Roughly the same situation holds for the theory of reference.

Reference

In the case of reference we can also distinguish speaker's reference from linguistic reference. Terminology varies here. Often the word *refer* is reserved for what speakers do, and the terms *denote* or *semantic reference* are used for what words or phrases do. Under this terminology, the object (or objects) referred to by a person is called the *referent,* and the object (or objects) semantically referred to by a word or phrase is called the *denotation* of that word or phrase.

   Speaker's reference involves what the speaker is referring to in uttering an expression, and the speaker's reference may coincide with what the speaker's words denote. For instance, this happens when one refers to George Washington by using the phrase *the first president*. However, it can happen that what the speaker is referring to is not the same as the semantic reference or denotation of the words used. For instance, suppose that Jones believes himself to be the world's most famous linguist—much to the amusement of his friends. We might well refer to Jones in saying, "Well, here comes *the world's most famous linguist*," even though our words denote, say, Noam Chomsky.

It is important to emphasize that denotations are things and events in the world (or groups of them); what words or phrases denote are the things and events that the words correctly describe. For example:

(4)

a. *desks*
b. *is a desk* } denote each and every desk

c. *the first man to walk on our moon:* denotes Neil Armstrong

d. *Richard Nixon:* denotes those named Richard Nixon (including the former president of the United States)

These examples reveal a distinction that is important for more advanced work in semantics and for pragmatics: the distinction between "general" expressions such as (4a) and (4b) and "singular" expressions such as (4c) and (4d). General expressions—such as common nouns, verbs, adjectives, and phrases that contain them—correctly describe potentially many different things or events. Thus, *red* applies to any red thing (and so denotes them all) and *table* applies to any table (and so denotes them all). Singular expressions include proper names, such as *Julius Caesar* and *Paris;* definite descriptive phrases such as *the first man to walk on our moon* and *the dents on the fender;* and pronouns such as *she, he,* and *they.* Singular denoting expressions have the property that they are used, on particular occasions, to refer to one single thing or collection of things. Even though there are many persons we can speak of as "she," and many collections of dents that can be referred to as "the dents on the fender," and even several different people named "Richard Nixon," when we use these singular denoting expressions in normal discourse we are still taken to have just one person or collection of dents in mind. Thus, the language makes available different types of expressions to do these different types of jobs in connecting words to the world.

What Is Reference?

At present there are two major competing theories of reference: the Description Theory and the Historical Chain Theory. The basic idea behind the Description Theory is that an expression refers to its referent because it describes the referent, either uniquely or uniquely enough to be identified. For instance, the phrase *the first person to walk on our moon* refers to Neil Armstrong by virtue of the fact that the description fits him uniquely. What about other kinds of referring expressions, such as the pronouns *he, she, that,* or proper names such as *Charles de Gaulle, America,* or *Fido?* These do not seem to describe anything uniquely, so how does the Description Theory handle them? It handles them by saying that people using these expressions have *in mind* some description of the object they intend to refer to. At this point the theory becomes one of speaker's reference, not linguistic reference, and belongs to pragmatics.

The Historical Chain Theory says, in effect, that an expression denotes its referent by virtue of there being a certain historical relation between the words uttered and some initial dubbing or christening of the object with that name. For instance, when a speaker uses the name *Charles de Gaulle,* it refers, in this view, to the person christened by that name, provided there is a chain of uses linking the current speaker's reference with the original christening. This view proposes no unique description to pick out the proper referent; rather, it proposes that referential uses are handed down from speaker to speaker, generation to generation, from the original dubbing or christening. Clearly, this theory works best for the kinds of referring expressions that function as names, which can be given to persons, places, and things.

Both theories of reference have strengths and weaknesses. The Description Theory works best for various uses of such descriptions as *the first person to walk on our moon* and perhaps also for most common nouns and adjectives. However, the Historical Chain Theory seems to work best for proper names, and can be extended to expressions such as *he, she, that,* and so forth. There is no reason to think that some mixture of these two views might not turn out to be correct, but much work needs to be done in the area of the theory of reference.

6.3 AIMS AND CLAIMS OF A SEMANTIC THEORY

The foregoing discussion indicates that there are facts for a semantic theory to describe, and it leads us to consider what kinds of information are central to the description of the semantics of a language.

Words and Phrases

Meaning Properties

Having noted some of the types of meaning that we must remain aware of, we can turn our attention to certain *meaning properties* of words that play an important role in the description of human languages. Perhaps the most central semantic property of words is the property of being *meaningful* or being *meaningless*. Any adequate account of the lexicon of a language must specify the meaningful words of the language, and must represent the meaning of those words in some fashion. For example, at the very least an adequate account of the English lexicon must tell us that *procrastinate* means "put things off," *bachelor* means "unmarried adult male," *mother* means "female parent," and so on for numerous other words of the language. In learning our native language, we obviously learn a large set of words that we know to be meaningful in the language, and at the same time we come to distinguish between meaningful words and meaningless expressions. A young child who uses the expression *wawa* to refer to water soon learns that *wawa* is not a meaningful word of the language (even if it has functioned as a useful term in communication with the parents). Thus, in learning one's native language, the semantic property of meaningfulness versus meaninglessness is a crucial one in acquiring vocabulary.

Another important semantic property of words is *ambiguity,* in particular what is referred to as *lexical ambiguity,* as illustrated in the following examples:

(5)
a. He found a *bat*.
   (*bat:* baseball bat; flying rodent)
b. She couldn't *bear* children.
   (*bear:* give birth to; put up with)

In each case, the italicized word is ambiguous in that it has more than one meaning. The ability to detect ambiguity is crucial in the communicative process, and successful communication can depend on both speaker and hearer recognizing the same meaning for a potentially ambiguous word.

Another important semantic property of words, in particular words put together in larger expressions, is *anomaly*. An expression is anomalous when the meanings of its individual words are incompatible:

(6)
a. strawberry truth
b. colorless green idea
c. dream diagonally

Of course, it is almost always possible to impose a meaning on such expressions—indeed, certain forms of poetry demand that the reader impose a meaning on anomalous expressions. For example, *to dream diagonally* might be taken to mean "to lie diagonally in a bed while dreaming," but this is the result of a special (and forced) interpretation, which speakers could argue about at length. The point is that expressions like (6) have no conventional interpretation in English. It is important to notice that a semantically anomalous expression can nevertheless be syntactically well-formed (for example, *colorless green idea* is formed on a regular syntactic pattern of English exemplified by phrases such as *colorful red flower*), and this may be the factor that makes it feasible for speakers to invent meanings for such anomalous expressions.

Meaning Relations
Not only do words have *meaning properties* (such as ambiguity, or having a meaning), they also bear various *meaning relations* to one another. Just as words can be related morphologically (for example, by word formation rules such as the *-able* rule), so they can also be related semantically, and words related by virtue of meaning form subgroups within the lexicon of a language. For example, one central meaning relation is *synonymy,* or "sameness" of meaning. Thus, we say that *automobile* is synonymous with *car, plane* (in one of its senses) is synonymous with *aircraft, kid* (in one of its senses) is synonymous with *child,* and so on. Synonymy is a relation that structures the lexicon of a language into sets of words sharing a meaning.

Words may also be *homophonous;* that is, they may have identical pronunciations but different meanings. An often-cited example of homophony is the word *bank* referring to the side of a river, versus the word *bank* referring to a financial institution. (Homophonous words often have distinct spellings in the written language, and we will see in chapter 9 how the homophony in this case forms the basis for a certain type of humor—the pun.) Of course, certain questions immediately arise. Is there a single word *bank* with two distinct meanings? Or are there two distinct, but homophonous, words, each with a single meaning? It is by no means easy to resolve such issues, and we can provide no firm solutions here. We raise the matter simply to introduce the term homophony, since it often appears in the linguistic literature.

Another important meaning relation is *meaning inclusion*, illustrated in examples such as (7a–c):

(7)
a. The meaning of *sister* includes the meaning of *female*.
b. The meaning of *murder* includes the meaning of *illegal*.
c. The meaning of *kill* includes the meaning of *dead*.

When we put words together that are related by meaning inclusion, we derive expressions that are *redundant* (such as *female sister, illegal murder*) and idiomatic expressions (such as *She killed him dead*).

Even if two expressions are not synonymous and the meaning of one does not include the meaning of the other, they still may be semantically related in that they *overlap*, or *share* some aspect of meaning:

(8)
a. *Father, uncle, bull,* and *stallion* all express the property "male."
b. *Say, speak, whisper, yell, shout,* and *scream* all express the property "vocalization."
c. *Fortunately, luckily, happily,* and *fortuitously* all express the property "good for" something or someone.

Sometimes words can share an aspect of meaning but be "opposite" in some other aspect of meaning. We say that such sets of words are *antonymous*. Typical examples of word antonymy include the following:

(9)
a. *Small, medium-sized,* and *large* share the notion "size" but differ in degree.
b. *Cold, warm,* and *hot* share the notion "temperature" but differ in degree.

The sense in which words such as *hot* and *cold* are "opposites" is not just that they are incompatible in meaning. Many words are semantically incompatible in the sense that they cannot both be true of something at the same time. For example, the words *cat* and *dog* are semantically incompatible (they cannot both be true descriptions of the same thing at the same time); nevertheless, they are not "opposites" in the sense of being antonyms. The examples in (9) are antonyms essentially because there is a scale containing the "opposites" at either end, with a midpoint (or midinterval) between them:

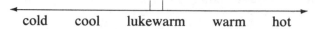

cold   cool   lukewarm   warm   hot

Thus, the words *hot* and *cold* can be said to be antonyms ("opposites") since they define the *extremities* of a scale (of temperature, in this case) that has a midinterval between them (in this case, represented by the word *lukewarm*, a word that can be used to refer to things that are neither hot nor cold). (See Lehrer and Lehrer 1982.)

Finally, groups of words in the lexicon can be semantically related by being members of a set known as a *semantic field* (see Lehrer 1974). On a very general and intuitive level, we can say that the words in a semantic field, though not synonymous, are all used to talk about the same general phenomenon. Classical examples of semantic fields include color terms (*red, green, blue, yellow*), kinship terms (*mother, father, sister, brother*), and cooking terms (*boil, fry, bake, broil, steam*). The notion of a semantic field can be extended intuitively to any set of terms with a close relation in meaning, all of which can be subsumed under the same general label. Thus, in addition to the specific semantic fields cited, we could also refer to labels such as "nautical terms," "plant names," "animal names," "automobile terms," and so on, as specifying semantic fields. The kinds of semantic fields found in the lexicon of any given language (that is, the kinds of general labels that define the particular semantic fields) may vary from culture to culture, and in fact anthropologists have found the study of semantic fields useful in investigating the nature of belief systems and reasoning in different cultural groups.

At this point we have completed our initial survey of semantic properties and relations in the area of word meaning. We note, once again, that the study of word meaning reveals that the lexicon of a language is not simply a random list of words. Semantic relations such as synonymy, antonymy, and the relation defined by semantic fields all serve to link certain words with other words, indicating that the overall lexicon of a language has a complex internal structure consisting of subgroups, or "networks," of words sharing significant properties.

Sentences

Since sentences are composed of words and phrases, we can expect that certain semantic properties and relations of words and phrases will carry over to sentences as well. However, as traditional grammarians put it, a sentence (as opposed to a single word or phrase) expresses a "complete thought." This is not a very useful definition of a sentence, but it does suggest that sentences have a unique function, and thus we might expect to find semantic properties and relations that are unique to sentences.

Meaning Properties and Relations

Among the meaning properties and relations of words and phrases that carry over to sentences are ambiguity and synonymy:

(10)
a. Ambiguity
   She visited a little girl's school.
b. Synonymy
   A man, in a car, just pulled up.
   A man in an automobile just pulled up.

However, sentences also exhibit meaning properties and relations that words and phrases lack. One important property of a sentence is its *communicative potential*. Sentences with different structures often have different communicative functions (see chapter 9). Thus, if a speaker wants to assert or state that something is true, then the normal type of sentence to utter is a declarative sentence such as *Snow is white*. On the other hand, if the speaker wants to issue an order, request, or command, then an imperative sentence such as *Leave the room!* is in order. Finally, if a speaker wants to ask a question, then the obvious choice is an interrogative sentence such as *What time is it?* As a first approximation we could diagram these facts as follows:

(11)
a. Declarative sentence → Used to assert, state, declare, etc.
b. Imperative sentence → Used to order, request, command, etc.
c. Interrogative sentence → Used to ask questions, etc.

It seems to be a part of the semantics of these structural types (declarative, imperative, interrogative) that they have the distinct communicative functions cited above. In any event, no one could be said to understand sentences of these types if they did not understand the differences in communicative function.

That some types of sentences are used literally to assert that something is *true* is an important semantic fact. That an imperative sentence is normally used to request a hearer to do something (to *comply with* the request) and that an interrogative sentence is used literally to *ask a question* are also important semantic facts. However, the field of semantics has traditionally concentrated on the assertive function of language, concerning itself mainly with the properties and relations that sentences have regarding truth.

Truth Properties

Not only do expressions in a language have meaning, and often reference, they are also used to say things that are true or false. Of course, no semantic theory can predict which sentences are used to say something true and which are used to say something false, in part because truth and falsity depend upon what is being referred to, and because the same words can be used in identical sentences to refer to different things. For instance, if two speakers utter the sentence *I took your picture last night,* then what one of them says may be true, while what the other says may be false. Furthermore, if the sentence is ambiguous, it may be used to say something true when taken one way but false when taken another way:

(12)

a. I removed your painting last night.

b. I photographed you last night.

Does this mean that the semantics of natural language cannot deal with truth and falsity? The answer is no, because some truth properties and truth relations hold regardless of reference, provided meaning is held constant.

Consider first the property of being *linguistically true* (also called *analytically true*) or *linguistically false* (also called *contradictory*). A sentence is linguistically true (or linguistically false) if its truth (or falsehood) is determined solely by the semantics of the language and it is not necessary to check any facts about the nonlinguistic world in order to determine its truth or falsehood. A sentence is *empirically true* (or *empirically false*) if it is not linguistically true or false—that is, if it is necessary to check the world in order to verify or falsify it. Most of the claims of common sense and science are of this latter sort. If some-

one says that the glottis was discovered last year, this claim is true (or
false) just in case the glottis was, as a matter of fact, discovered (or not
discovered) last year; knowledge of the language alone does not settle
the matter. Semantics is not concerned with empirical truths and false-
hoods but with those sentences that are linguistically true or false. In
each of the groups (13), (14), and (15) it is possible to determine truth
values (true = T, false = F) without regard to the actual state of the
world.

(13)
a. Either it is raining here or it is not raining here. (T)
b. If John is sick and Mary is sick, then John is sick. (T)
c. It is raining here and it is not raining here. (F)
d. If John is sick and Mary is sick, then John is not sick. (F)

(14)
a. All people that are sick are people. (T)
b. If every person is sick, then it is not true that no person is sick. (T)
c. Some people that are sick are not people. (F)
d. Every person is sick, but some person is not (sick). (F)

(15)
a. If John is a bachelor, then John is unmarried. (T)
b. If John killed the bear, then the bear died. (T)
c. If the car is red, then it has a color. (T)
d. John is a bachelor, but he is married. (F)
e. John killed the bear and it's (still) alive. (F)
f. The car is red, but it has no color. (F)

Again, knowing the language seems to be sufficient for knowing the
truth or falsity of these sentences, and this being so, the semantics of
these sorts of sentences will be relevant to a semantic theory.

Truth Relations
We have noted that there are truth relations as well as truth properties
that fall within the scope of semantics. The most central truth relation
for semantics is *entailment*. One sentence S is said to entail another
sentence S' when the truth of the first guarantees the truth of the second and the falsity of the second guarantees the falsity of the first, as in
(16):

(16)

a. *The car is red* entails *The car has a color.*

b. *The needle is too short* entails *The needle is not long enough.*

We can see that the first sentence in each example, if true, guarantees the truth of the second; and the falsity of the second sentence in each example guarantees the falsity of the first.

Closely related to entailment is another truth relation, *semantic presupposition*. The basic idea behind semantic presupposition is that the falsity of the presupposed sentence causes the presupposing sentence not to have a truth value (T or F). Furthermore, both a sentence and its denial have the same semantic presupposition. Although this truth relation is somewhat controversial, (17) and (18) show typical examples of semantic presupposition in which both the positive (a) and the negative (b) sentences have the same presupposition (c):

(17)

a. The present King of France is bald.

b. The present King of France is not bald.

c. There is a present King of France.

(18)

a. John realizes that his car has been stolen.

b. John does not realize that his car has been stolen.

c. John's car has been stolen.

In sum, there are at least two truth relations that an adequate semantic theory must explain, or explain away, entailment and semantic presupposition, and these must be added to the truth properties already discussed.

Logical Form and Analytic Sentences (technical section)
There are some important differences between examples (13), (14), and (15). In (13) the truth value (T or F) is determined solely by the connectives *or, and, if . . . then,* and the word *not* (which sometimes abbreviates *it is not the case that*). Since these sorts of words are often dubbed *logical words,* these sentences are also called *logical truths* (of English). It can be seen that the *form* of these sentences makes them true regardless of how the world is. For instance, the logical form of (13a) and (13b) in terms of logical words is:

(19)
a. Either S or not-S.   (T)
b. If S and S', then S.   (T)

No matter what (grammatical) declarative sentences we may pick for S and S', the resulting compound sentence will be true. The same holds for the falsity of (13c) and (13d), which also is attributable to their logical form:

(20)
a. S and not-S.   (F)
b. If S and S', then not-S.   (F)

The same remarks hold for (14), except that the relevant logical words are *some, every,* and *no.* The first two of these sentences are true in virtue of their logical form; the last two are false in virtue of their logical form:

(21)
a. All X's that are P are X's.   (T)
b. If every X is P, then it is not true that no X is P.   (T)
c. Some X's that are P are not X's.   (F)
d. Every X is P, but some X is not P.   (F)

   This procedure of deriving the logical form of a sentence yields very different results when applied to the sentences in (15). This is because the words relevant to the linguistic truth or falsehood of these sentences are not logical words, which can be used in discussing any subject matter, but descriptive words such as *bachelor, kill,* and *red* used in discussing certain kinds of subject matter—bachelors, killings, colors, and so on. If we follow the procedure of replacing descriptive words with letters in (15a–c), thereby converting them into their logical forms, the result is (22a–c):

(22)
a. If John is a B, then John is U.
b. If John K-ed the bear, then the bear D-ed.
c. If the car is R, then the car has a C.

It is easy to see that such forms as those in (22) need not always result in sentences that are true, as was the case with previous examples of linguistic truth, since these forms can yield sentences that are false:

(23)

a. If John is a bachelor, then John is unhappy. (F)
b. If John kicked the bear, then the bear died. (F)
c. If the car is repossessed, then the car has a carburetor. (F)

Even if such sentences as (23a–c) are not true by virtue of their logical form, sometimes they can be converted into logical truths by substituting into them definitions for these descriptive words. For instance, suppose that the following definition is correct:

(Def. 1)
bachelor = Def. "unmarried and adult and male"

If we replace the word *bachelor* in (15a) with the right-hand side of Def. 1, the result is sentence (24):

(24)
If John is unmarried and adult and male, then John is unmarried.

What is interesting about (24) is that it has the form of a logical truth, namely, (25):

(25)
If John is *U* and *A* and *M,* then John is *U.*

Thus, certain sentences that are not logical truths can be converted into logical truths by replacing the crucial descriptive words with their definitions. Sentences that can be converted into logical truths by this sort of substitution are often called *analytic* sentences, and since they are true by virtue of their semantic structure, they are considered to fall within the scope of a semantic theory.

In sum, there are a variety of truth properties that a semantic theory should account for, including those of linguistic truth and linguistic falsehood and, among these, logical and even analytical truth (or falsehood).

Goals of a Semantic Theory

We now come to the question of the goals of a semantic theory. What should a semantic theory do, and how?

The short answer to the first question is that a semantic theory should attribute to each expression E in the language the semantic properties and relations that it has; moreover, it should define those properties and relations. Thus, if an expression E is meaningful, the semantic theory should say so. If E has a specific set of meanings, the semantic theory should specify them. If E is ambiguous, the semantic theory should record that fact. And so on. Moreover, if two expressions are synonymous, or if one entails the other, the semantic theory should mark these semantic relations. We can organize these demands on a semantic theory by saying that an adequate semantic theory of a language must generate every true instance of the following schemes:

(26)
a. Meaning Properties and Relations
   E is literally used to ____ .
   E means ____ .
   E is meaningful.
   E is ambiguous.
   E is anomalous (nonsense).
   E is redundant.
   E and E' are synonymous.
   E includes the meaning of E'.
   E and E' overlap in meaning.
   E and E' are antonymous.
b. Denotational Properties and Relations
   E is a singular denoting expression.
   E is a general denoting expression.
   E and E' are codenotational (coextensive).
c. Truth Properties and Relations
   E is logically true (or false).
   E is analytic.
   E is contradictory.
   E entails E'.
   E semantically presupposes E'.

We can say in sum that the domain of a semantic theory is at least the set of properties and relations listed in (26); we should not be satisfied with a semantic theory of English that fails to explain them (or to explain them away).

The second question concerning the goals of a semantic theory is, How should the theory handle these semantic properties and relations? What kinds of constraints on a semantic theory are reasonable to impose? We will mention just two. First, it is generally conceded that even though a natural language contains an infinite number of phrases and sentences (recall chapter 5), a semantic theory of a natural language should be *finite:* people are capable of storing only a finite amount of information, but they nevertheless learn the semantics of natural languages. The second constraint on a semantic theory of a natural language is that it should reflect the fact that, except for idioms, expressions are *compositional*—in other words, that the meaning of a syntactically complex expression is determined by the meaning of its constituents and their grammatical relations. Compositionality rests on the fact that a finite number of familiar words and expressions can be combined and recombined to form an infinite number of novel phrases and sentences; hence, a finite semantic theory that reflects compositionality can describe meanings for an infinite number of complex expressions.

The existence of compositionality is most dramatic when compositional expressions are contrasted with expressions that lack compositionality. In (27a) the expression *kick the bucket* has two meanings:

(27)
a. John kicked the bucket.
b. John kicked the wooden pail.
c. John died.

One of the meanings of (27a) is compositional: it is determined on the basis of the meaning of its constituent words and is synonymous with (27b). The other meaning of (27a) is idiomatic and can be paraphrased as (27c). Idiomatic meanings are not compositional in the sense of being determined from the meaning of the constituent words and their grammatical relations. One could not determine the idiomatic meaning of (27a) by knowing just the meaning of the words and recognizing familiar grammatical structure—an idiomatic meaning must be learned separately as a unit. Idioms behave as though they were syntactically complex words whose meaning cannot be predicted, since their syntactic structure is doing no semantic work.

It would be a mistake to think of the compositionality of a complex expression as simply adding up the meanings and references of its parts. For adjective + noun constructions like that in (28a), adding up sometimes works:

(28)
a. He was a *bearded Russian soldier.* =
b. He was Russian and bearded and a soldier.

But even in such constructions the contribution of syntax can be devious, as in (29), where we cannot simply add up the meanings of *occasional* and *sailor:*

(29)
a.   An occasional sailor walked by. $\neq$
b.   *Someone who is a sailor and occasional walked by.

Modifiers can create other complications for compositionality, which must also be reflected in a semantic theory of the language. Contrast the arguments in (30) and (31):

(30)
a. That is a *gray* elephant.   (T)
b. All elephants are animals.   (T)
c. So, that is a *gray* animal.   (T)

(31)
a. That is a *small* elephant.   (T)
b. All elephants are animals.   (T)
c. So, that is a *small* animal.   (F)

In (30) the premises (a) and (b) jointly entail the truth of (c), but in (31) the premises (a) and (b) do not jointly entail (31c). The only difference between (30) and (31) is the occurrence of *gray* in (30) and *small* in (31), so clearly there is some difference in the semantics of these two words.

More complicated and interesting examples of the interaction of semantics and syntax come from the functional relations of subject and object in a sentence. In sentences like (32a) and (32c) the words are the same, but the entailments (32b) and (32d) are importantly different.

(32)
a. John killed the snake.
b. The snake died.
c. The snake killed John.
d. John died.

This further illustrates the degree to which a semantic theory must be integrated with a syntactic theory in an adequate description of a natural language.

6.4 A SAMPLE SEMANTIC ANALYSIS

The goal of a semantic theory is to correctly describe the semantic properties and relations of every expression in the language. The theory must also define what these semantic properties and relations are. Furthermore, since the scope of a semantic theory will be infinite (there being an unlimited number of phrases and sentences in the language), the theory itself will have to make use of the structure and categories in the language. That is to say, just as a grammar attempts to state a finite number of principles that reveal structure at various levels (phonological, morphological, syntactic), so a semantic theory attempts to state a finite number of principles that will account for the unlimited number of possible phrases and sentences. A semantic theory with this property is said to be "compositional."

We turn now to the problem of outlining a semantic theory. It is traditional to do this in two stages: first, to represent the semantics of words and idioms; second, to represent the semantics of phrases and sentences. The reason for this division is that syntactic relations such as subject and object are used in the second stage of representation but not in the first.

Words and Idioms

Semantic Representation and Decomposition
Most semantic theories have one component that represents the semantics of the syntactically unstructured expressions of the language, the words, as well as the semantics of those expressions whose internal syntactic structure is semantically irrelevant, the idioms. It also describes the semantic relations between words and idioms. This component is variously called the *dictionary* or the *lexicon*. We will first look at the sorts of information that are represented at this level. We will call whatever information is recorded at this point the *lexical entry* for a word or idiom.

Beginning with the syntactic information associated with words, note that we need to represent the part of speech of each expression. For instance, the word *run* can be either a verb or a noun:

(33)
a. Run on now, I run this place. (verbs)
b. He scored nine runs in one inning and got a run in his sock. (nouns)

Since a semantic theory must represent the meaning of each (meaningful) expression and represent nonsynonymous expressions as different in meaning, a lexical entry will have to associate the verb *run* with its verbal meanings and the noun *run* with its nominal meanings. Each occurrence of *run* in (33) means something different, and the syntactic categories noun and verb distinguish the first two from the last two. Thus, the first piece of information needed to describe the semantics of a word is its syntactic category.

The situation is similar for idioms, some of which correspond to intransitive verbs (34a), some to transitive verbs (34b), and some to noun phrases (34c):

(34)
a. NP kicks the bucket: NP dies
b. NP reads the riot act to NP: NP bawls out NP
c. That stick-in-the-mud: that old fogy

Though the syntactic category is necessary for correctly representing the semantics of an expression, it is not sufficient; many nonsynonymous expressions have the same syntactic categorization, as we saw in the case of *run*. To account for the full range of semantic properties and relations set out in section 6.3, lexical entries for words and idioms will have to represent enough semantic information to predict these properties and relations at the lexical level. How can this be accomplished? First, by the representation of meaning (and occasionally reference) of words and idioms; and second, by the representation of various semantic relations between words and idioms.

The problem of how to represent the semantics of words and idioms is complicated by our inability to say exactly what meaning is, but the representation problem is not thereby made impossible. For instance, in mathematics we are able to describe various properties and relations between numbers, as in (35):

(35)
a. The number 2 is an even prime.
b. For any number there is a larger number.

Yet we have no generally accepted theory of what numbers are. Similarly, it can be argued that in semantics one can represent meaning and reference without committing oneself to stating exactly what meaning and reference are. In order to do this, though, semantics must be fairly abstract and formal. We will not attempt a detailed discussion of

semantic representation here. In spite of this, we believe that our informal presentation will provide some insight into the nature of semantic representation.

Consider typical descriptive words and idioms such as *boy, girl, father, mother, kill,* and *kick the bucket.* It has seemed clear to many
theorists that such words are not the most basic semantic units but are
actually semantically complex items, composed or made up of more
primitive semantic components. Semantic theories that decompose
lexical items into more basic semantic components are called *decompositional* (or sometimes *componential*) semantic theories. In effect, a
decompositional theory of word meaning extends compositionality to
the level of the internal structure of lexical items. Let us consider, as an
example of lexical decomposition, the following definition:

(Def. 2)
boy = Def. HUMAN(X) AND MALE(X) AND NOT-ADULT(X)

The basic idea in such a representation is that the symbols in capital
letters represent the semantic components in the meaning of the word
and the variable X stands for whoever is being spoken of. According to
Def. 2, saying (36a) amounts to saying (36b):

(36)
a. That's a boy.
b. That's a human male who is nonadult.

A lexical entry for *girl* would look like Def. 2 except for having FE-
MALE(X) instead of MALE(X).

The word *father*, unlike *boy*, is a relational noun. To be a father is to
be a male parent of someone—it is to bear a special relation to another
person, the relation of fathering or begetting. Relations are usually represented with variables standing for the objects that are related. For
instance, *father* is understood as "X is the father of Y," where X represents the father, Y the child. We can represent *father* at this level as in
Def. 3:

(Def. 3)
father = Def. MALE(X) AND X PARENT OF Y

Clearly, *mother* is like Def. 3 but with FEMALE(X) instead of
MALE(X).

Transitive verbs are like relational nouns in requiring variables to
indicate the various roles of the participants. Thus, *kill* is understood as

"X kill *Y."* This is indicated by the fact that if there was a killing, then someone or something did the killing, and someone or something was killed; that is, if *X* killed *Y*, then *Y* died, and *X* caused this. We can represent this as in Def. 4, letting X_s indicate the subject and X_o the direct object:

(Def. 4)
kill = Def. X_s CAUSE(X_o CHANGE TO (NOT-ALIVE(X_o)))

Thus, at this level we can be said to have represented important aspects of the meaning-structure of these words.

It is easy to grasp how to do decompositional semantics, though the details can become complicated (see Katz 1972 and Kempson 1977). The question now arises, What is the evidence for positing these semantic components out of which meaning representations are constructed? Probably the central form of linguistic argument in favor of lexical decomposition is based on simplicity of predictions concerning the various semantic properties and relations. Just as syntactic rules, such as transformations, capture syntactic generalizations that might otherwise be missed, so it could be claimed that systems of semantics without decomposition fail to reflect certain generalizations concerning semantic properties and relations.

To see this, consider some additional kinship terms such as *mother, brother,* and *sister,* with their decompositional definitions:

(Def. 5)
mother = Def. FEMALE(X) AND X PARENT OF Y

(Def. 6)
brother = Def. MALE(X) AND X SIBLING OF Y

(Def. 7)
sister = Def. FEMALE(X) AND X SIBLING OF Y

On the basis of these representations we can predict a number of semantic properties and relations concerning these and related words. For instance, we can predict that *father* and *brother* (as well as the potentially infinite set including *son, uncle, nephew, grandfather, great-grandfather, great-great-grandfather,* and so on) all share the aspect of meaning MALE, and so are similar in meaning in expressing the property of being male. The same holds for the analogous set containing FEMALE. That is, the decompositional representation of this potentially infinite set of kinship words can be given in terms of a very small

number of repeatable semantic primitives. If we then add a general
definition of *similarity in meaning* (in terms of repeated semantic primitives), it is possible to predict that each of these sets contains words
that are similar (in meaning) with respect to maleness and femaleness.

Moreover, given a definition of *contradictory* (in terms of incompatible semantic primitives), it is possible to make certain predictions as
an automatic consequence of decompositional representation. For
instance, we can predict that each of the examples in (37) is contradictory:

(37)

$$X \text{ is a} \left\{ \begin{array}{l} \text{father} \\ \text{uncle} \\ \text{grandfather} \\ \text{great-grandfather} \\ \text{. . . great-grandfather} \end{array} \right\} \text{ and female}$$

But with *male* substituted for *female,* each example is noncontradic-
tory. Furthermore, such a theory can predict simply and directly that
the members of each pair in the following potentially infinite list of
pairs are *synonyms* (both members having identical semantic representations):

(38)

$$\begin{array}{r} \text{father} = \text{Def. male parent} \\ \text{mother} = \text{Def. female parent} \\ \text{grandparent (of)} = \text{Def. parent of parent (of)} \\ \text{great-grandparent (of)} = \text{Def. parent of parent of parent (of)} \end{array}$$

This form of prediction can be carried out for each semantic property
and relation, covering huge parts of the vocabulary of a language.
Without lexical decomposition, each of these semantic predictions
would have to be made separately for each of these words. Analogously in syntax, grammars without rules having the power of transformations could deal only clumsily, or not at all, with discontinuous
constituents and other dependency relations, at the cost of adding
many separate but clearly related rules. It might be concluded, then,
that grammars excluding decomposition, as well as grammars excluding rules such as transformations, miss obvious generalizations in their
respective domains.

Again, then, the basic argument in favor of decomposition is
simplicity of theory. Such theoretical elegance requires stronger con-

ditions of adequacy on a semantic theory in that decompositional theories demand definitions of meaningful words. These definitions not only must provide necessary and sufficient conditions for correct application, but also must be identical for synonyms and nonidentical for nonsynonyms. Some theorists have found such constraints highly desirable in principle but too strong in fact, a contention we will return to toward the end of this chapter.

Semantic Restrictions and Relations

Words and idioms combine with, and bear various semantic relations to, other words and idioms. So far our dictionary represents intrinsic meaning, but it does not represent semantic restrictions between words. For instance, it can be claimed that there is something anomalous about (39), if it is taken literally:

(39)
The table is a parent of the chair.

This could be accounted for by saying that the variables X and Y in the analysis of *parent* are restricted to animate objects. Ordinary dictionaries often put such restrictions in terms of what such words are "said of":

(Dcf. 8)
addled = Def. confused, *said of* minds; rotten, *said of* eggs

In decompositional semantics, we can represent these semantic restrictions by using angle brackets, $\langle \ \rangle$, as in the complete definition of *father:*

(Def. 9)
father = Def. MALE(X) AND X PARENT OF Y AND $\langle$ANIMATE(X) AND ANIMATE(Y)$\rangle$

The angle brackets enclosing ANIMATE(X) AND ANIMATE (Y) in Def. 9 restrict the application of *father* to animate things when it is used literally. The same device can be used to represent the semantic restrictions on *kill:*

(Def. 10)
kill = Def. X_s CAUSE(X_o CHANGE TO (NOT-ALIVE(X_o))) AND $\langle$ANIMATE (X_o)$\rangle$

This representation makes the claim that whatever is killed must be animate and so predicts that when this restriction is violated, the compound expression will be (literally) anomalous, as in (40):

(40)
John killed the table.

Still, none of these definitions is more than a first approximation to a correct one. We will return in the exercises to the question of how they can be improved.

If we consider again the meaning representation of *boy*, we can see that there are semantic relations that the dictionary entry alone does not represent. For instance, if X is a boy, then X is not female, and if X is a boy, then X is animate, and so forth. How can we supplement the lexicon so as to account for these and similar facts?

One way would be to add such components as NOT-FEMALE(X) and ANIMATE(X) to our lexical entry for *boy* (as well as for other words such as *father, brother,* and *grandfather*). However, this would seem to miss the generalization that if a word contains MALE as one of its components, then that in itself guarantees that it will also contain ANIMATE and will not contain FEMALE, and so forth. How can each of these conditions be stated once as a single fact? Theorists all agree that some kind of a meaning rule is needed here that connects these semantic components, but they do not agree on the exact nature of such devices, which have been called *redundancy rules* by Katz (1972) and *meaning postulates* by Carnap (1956). For neutrality, we will call such principles *inference rules,* and they will be added to the lexicon as information concerning semantic relations between words and idioms, separate from any particular lexical entry. For example, the following rules by which one can infer what is on the right-hand side of the arrow from what is on the left-hand side would account for the facts already mentioned about *boy:*

(IR 1)
MALE(X) $\rightarrow$ NOT-FEMALE(X) ("Infer NOT-FEMALE(X) from MALE(X)")

(IR 2)
MALE(X) $\rightarrow$ ANIMATE(X) ("Infer ANIMATE(X) from MALE(X)")

So far it may seem that the addition of inference rules to the lexicon is a matter of theoretical simplicity and that their job of recording certain semantic relations between words could be done, albeit less economically, by decomposition. There are semantic relations between words suggesting that inference rules are not simply elegant ways of stating certain facts, however, but are required. Some semantic relations between words cannot plausibly be represented by decomposition:

(41)

a. John likes pizza and Mary likes pizza.

b. John likes pizza.

c. Mary likes pizza.

Although (41b) and (41c) can be inferred from (41a), it makes no sense to speak of the decomposition of *and*. Similarly, in the following examples the second member of each pair does not seem to be the result of decomposing the first:

(42)

a. *Someone* likes ice cream.

b. It is *not* true that *everyone* does not like ice cream.

(43)

a. It is *possible* that someone likes okra.

b. It is *not necessarily* true that *not* anyone likes okra.

(44)

a. His window is *red*.

b. His window has a *color*.

Examples (41)–(44) suggest that inference rules such as the following must be a part of the lexicon:

(IR 3)

X AND $Y \rightarrow \begin{Bmatrix} X \\ Y \end{Bmatrix}$ ("From (X and Y) one may infer X and one may infer Y")

(IR 4)

RED(X) $\rightarrow$ COLORED(X)

With both lexical entries and inference rules, our semantic theory can account for a number of semantic properties and relations, for example, that (45a) entails (45b):

(45)
a. Someone is a boy.
b. Someone is not female.

This entailment can be accounted for by our semantic theory in the following way:

(46)
a. According to Def. 2, *Someone is a boy* means something like SOME$_x$(X) IS HUMAN(X) AND MALE(X) AND NOT-ADULT(X).
b. Then, according to IR 3, we may infer that MALE(X).
c. Then, according to IR 1, we may infer that NOT-FEMALE(X).
d. Since the English expression *not female* can be represented as NOT-FEMALE(X), we may conclude that SOME$_x$(X) IS NOT-FEMALE(X).

According to this explanation, we show that one sentence entails another sentence when the second can be inferred from the first by decomposition and inference rules.

So far, then, we can represent the following three kinds of information in our semantics: meaning (lexical entry), semantic restrictions (lexical entry), and some entailments (inference rules). We certainly have not shown that *all* semantic properties and relations can be represented in this format (see exercises). Indeed, it is still an open question in the field of semantics what a descriptively adequate format will look like.

Phrases and Sentences

So far we can account for the semantics of only words and idioms. We have not yet attempted to account for the semantics of syntactically *complex expressions*. For this we need a syntactic description of the strings of words that involves more than the parts of speech. We need to know the linear order of the words, the grouping of the words, and the grammatical relations that the various expressions in the phrase or sentence bear to each other. These are properties specified by the syntactic component of a grammar, and the relation between the syntactic component and the semantic component in the standard transformational grammar is shown in figure 6.2.

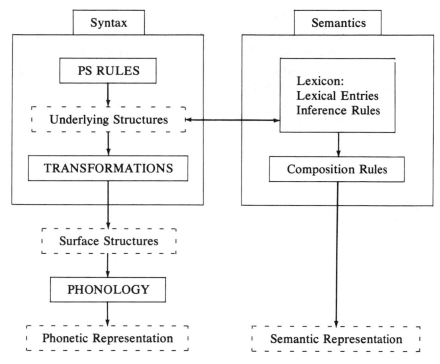

Figure 6.2
Model of the Standard Theory of transformational grammar

Composition

An adequate semantic theory must reflect the compositionality of natural language, and to do this it must contain rules that are sensitive to the syntactic structure of phrases and sentences. We call these *composition rules* (also called *projection rules*). To illustrate them and their mode of operation, we consider a simple sentence such as (47):

(47)
A boy kills a dog.

The syntax of (47) will be simplified somewhat and represented as tree 6.1, which reflects only semantically relevant structure. Given the meaning of (47), we want to be sure that in the semantic representation of this sentence it is the case that the dog dies, not the boy; whereas in the sentence *A dog kills a boy,* it is the boy who dies and not the dog. How can this be accomplished? The first thing that the semantic component of the grammar does is to represent the meaning of each word by simply inserting its semantic representation from the lexicon—where *dog* is represented as CANINE(X) AND ANIMATE(X)—as illustrated in tree 6.2. This completes the semantic representation of the sentence for meaning at the lexical level.

We will turn first to the phrase level and then to the whole sentence. The basic idea is to start combining, or composing, semantic represen-

Tree 6.1

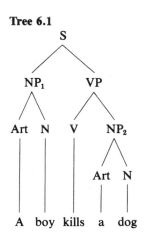

Tree 6.2

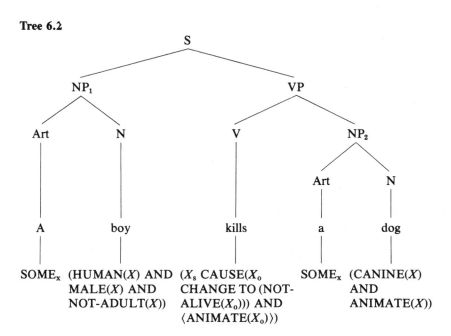

tations of different words that are grouped together under a single node in the tree, starting at the bottom and working our way up to the S-node. But to compose semantic representations, we need rules of composition to derive representations of complex expressions from representations of simpler ones. The nature and full variety of composition rules are still unresolved, so we will merely illustrate the process with the following three composition rules:

(CR 1)
Variables in lexical entries that are not categorized for subject or object are given the number index from their dominating NP.

(CR 2)
Lexical variables that are categorized for subject or object are given the number of the NP they are categorized for.

(CR 3)
Semantic components are joined with AND, provided semantic restrictions are not violated.

Let us see how these rules work. Recall that we apply the rules from the bottom of the tree up, starting with CR 1, then CR 2, and finally CR 3. Both NP_1 and NP_2 are at the bottom of tree 6.2, but we will begin with the more deeply embedded one. So the first step is to apply CR 1 to the phrase *a dog* under NP_2. The result is to subscript the lexical variable X with a 2 (see tree 6.3). Since CR 2 and CR 3 cannot apply, we move to the next higher node, which is NP_1. The result of applying CR 1 here is illustrated in tree 6.4. Again, since CR 2 and CR 3 cannot apply, we move to the next higher node, VP.

Tree 6.3

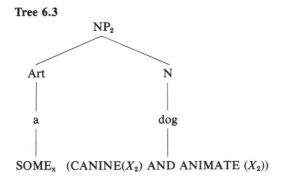

SOME$_x$ (CANINE(X_2) AND ANIMATE (X_2))

The last two composition rules apply at VP; we will illustrate their application in order. First, notice that in the semantic representation for *kill*, the variable X is categorized for subject, X_s, and then for direct object, X_o. However, tree 6.5 shows that only the direct object is a constituent at the VP node, so only it, NP_2, can be composed at this point. Since CR 1 does not apply and CR 2 does, the result is as shown in tree 6.5. Note that the semantic representation of NP_2 meets the semantic restriction on *kill*, and for simplicity we will henceforth omit the restriction $\langle \text{ANIMATE } (X_o) \rangle$ in the representation of *kill*.

Now we need only connect the semantic representation of *kill* to the semantic representation of *a dog* to derive the semantic representation of the VP *kills a dog* (see tree 6.6).

Tree 6.4

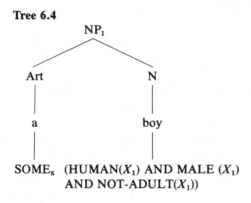

$$\text{SOME}_x \; (\text{HUMAN}(X_1) \text{ AND MALE } (X_1) \\ \text{AND NOT-ADULT}(X_1))$$

Tree 6.5

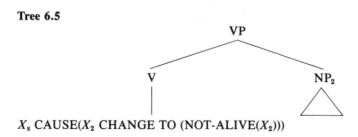

$$X_s \text{ CAUSE}(X_2 \text{ CHANGE TO (NOT-ALIVE}(X_2)))$$

Tree 6.6

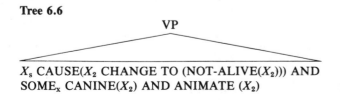

$$X_s \text{ CAUSE}(X_2 \text{ CHANGE TO (NOT-ALIVE}(X_2))) \text{ AND} \\ \text{SOME}_x \text{ CANINE}(X_2) \text{ AND ANIMATE } (X_2)$$

Finally, we move to the highest node in the sentence, the S-node. So far our semantic representations have been at the word or phrase level. To compose at the S-node is to say how the meaning of the whole sentence is determined by the meaning of its constituent phrases and their grammatical relations. Since CR 1 does not apply and CR 2 does, the result is tree 6.7, where the subject variable in *kill* is indexed as X_1. This leaves only CR 3 to apply to connect the semantic representation of NP_1 with the semantic representation of VP within the sentence, producing tree 6.8.

Although tree 6.8 is not perfect as a semantic representation of the original sentence *A boy kills a dog,* further refinements are not necessary for our purposes here (see Bierwisch 1969, 1971). As we can see, some desired semantic properties and relations are captured. For instance, the fact that sentence (47) receives a semantic representation at all predicts that the expression is meaningful, and tree 6.8 represents (imperfectly) its meaning. Also note that the component NOT-ALIVE(X_2) in tree 6.8 is attached to the same variable, X_2, that the reading for *dog* is attached to—CANINE(X_2) AND ANIMATE(X_2)—indicating that the dog, not the boy, died. However, had the sentence been (48), then *a boy* would have been the direct object:

(48)
A dog kills a boy.

Tree 6.7

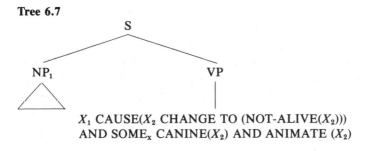

X_1 CAUSE(X_2 CHANGE TO (NOT-ALIVE(X_2)))
AND SOME$_x$ CANINE(X_2) AND ANIMATE (X_2)

Tree 6.8

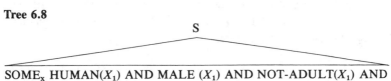

SOME$_x$ HUMAN(X_1) AND MALE (X_1) AND NOT-ADULT(X_1) AND X_1 CAUSE(X_2 CHANGE TO (NOT-ALIVE(X_2))) AND SOME$_x$ CANINE(X_2) AND ANIMATE(X_2)

So *a boy* would have been NP$_2$ and the reading for *boy* would have been attached to X_2, thereby representing the fact that if (48) were true, it would be a boy who dies, not a dog. Other semantic properties and relations are captured as well (see exercises). But, more importantly, we can see how a semantic theory can be *compositional:* how the semantic representation of a syntactically complex expression can be determined by the semantic representation of its constituent words and their grammatical relations by means of rules of composition.

Finally, we might ask ourselves how this compositional theory might define some of the semantic properties and relations set out earlier. First of all, the theory will, if adequate, generate a semantic representation for every well-formed expression in the language: if the expression is a word or idiom, its meaning is represented in the lexicon; if the expression is a phrase or sentence, its meaning is represented on the basis of syntactic structure plus composition rules. Since one way or another every meaningful expression will receive a semantic representation in an adequate theory, we can say that an expression is meaningful if it has a semantic representation; an expression is ambiguous if it is given more than one semantic representation; two expressions are synonymous if they are given the same semantic representation; two expressions overlap in meaning if they share a semantic component; and, finally, one expression entails another if the second can be inferred from the first on the basis of decomposition and inference rules.

Notice that although these definitions do capture something essential to the notions of ambiguity, synonymy, overlap of meaning, and so forth, they in effect reduce these notions to the nature and number of semantic representations given by the lexicon and composition rules. But the question, Why does expression E mean what it means? is not yet answered. It may well be that *bachelor* means HUMAN(X) AND ADULT(X) AND MALE(X) AND UNMARRIED(X), but what are we saying about the word *bachelor* when we say that this is what it means? Which brings us back to the original question: What is meaning? That is, what is it for something to have a meaning? We concluded earlier that currently the most promising account of meaning is in terms of use. If this conclusion is correct, the question of what meaning is leads us to pragmatics, the topic of chapter 9.

Semantic Representation: Some Issues (optional sections)

In a short survey it is impossible to cover all issues exercising semantic theorists, but two particular areas can be mentioned because they are both far-reaching and active topics of investigation.

Decomposition vs. Inference Rules
One topic of current research and controversy is the relative importance of lexical decomposition and inference rules. On the one hand, Katz (1972) and Katz and Nagel (1974) view a substantial portion of the lexicon as susceptible to decomposition; on the other hand, Jackendoff (1972) and Fodor, Fodor, and Garrett (1975) view decomposition as a marginal phenomenon, with inference rules being the predominant piece of semantic machinery. To see the pervasiveness of inference rules, consider again the fact that (47), *A boy kills a dog,* entails (49a), which has (49b) as its semantic representation:

(49)
a. A dog dies.
b. $SOME_x$ ANIMATE(X) AND CANINE(X) AND (CHANGE TO (NOT-ALIVE(X)))

To infer (49b) from (47), we must first apply IR 3 to (47) to derive (50):

(50)
X_1 CAUSE (CHANGE TO (NOT-ALIVE(X_2))) AND $SOME_x$ CANINE(X_2) AND ANIMATE(X_2)

But to infer (49a) from (47), we still need the principle that causing X to change to being not alive entails that X be not alive. In other words, we need another inference rule:

(IR 5)
X_1 CAUSE (CHANGE TO (NOT-ALIVE(X_2))) $\rightarrow$ NOT-ALIVE(X_2)

When IR 5 applies to (50), it gives (49a) as an entailment. We can see that even with this amount of decomposition, we still need inference rules to account for the entailments of *kill.*

A further challenge to decomposition comes from another quarter, from what are called *natural-kind terms.* These are words such as *dog, water, gold,* which refer to things (or stuff) that form a "kind," or species, in nature and are governed by particular laws of nature, such as the laws of biology, chemistry, or physics. Some authors—Kripke

(1981) and Putnam (1975) are two—have suggested that these sorts of words function semantically in the language very much like proper names and that both proper names and natural-kind terms should receive an historical chain analysis of their meaning and reference. If that suggestion is correct, then the meaning of such terms would not be represented by decomposition. On the historical chain view, something is gold, for example, if it is the same kind of thing, obeying the same physical laws, as the matter originally dubbed *gold* when the word was introduced into the language. If such a view is correct (see Schwartz 1977 for a survey discussion), then decomposition is an even more restricted phenomenon than has been supposed.

Anaphora and Reference

One phenomenon that has interested linguists and logicians for some time is the relation between pronouns (or noun phrases) and a set of "antecedent" noun phrases (see Chomsky 1981 and references cited). Such relations are known as *anaphoric relations,* and can be illustrated as follows:

(51)
Co-linked
a. Reflexives: John shaves himself

b. Reciprocals: The men liked each other

c. Idioms: I lost my way

d. *Wh*-Antecedent: Who thinks that they have been cheated?

e. Quantified-Antecedent: Everyone said that he was tired

f. Epithets: He stepped on my foot, the creep!

(52)
Disjointly Linked
a. Robert saw Michael

b. He likes Sam

c. John believes him to be rash

d. John believes that she is rash

e. Sam believes that Sam is rash

In each case the second item is linked to the first item in some way that is relevant to how a speaker and hearer communicate (there would be a misunderstanding if the speaker intended one linking, but the hearer understood another).

What sorts of linking are these? This is a difficult question and any answer at present would have to be considered tentative, but it seems likely that some of these links are semantic, whereas others are pragmatic (see chapter 9 for further discussion). One way of getting a feel for which is which is to ask whether the sentence would be used nonliterally if the link were actually broken. For instance, in (52a) *Robert* and *Michael* are disjointly linked, and thus are considered to be distinct in reference. But is this semantic reference or speaker reference? Well, imagine a person named both *Robert* and *Michael,* who sees himself in a mirror at an arcade. If a speaker were to say *No one saw Michael,* it would be possible to answer literally *That's not so, Robert saw Michael.* Although it can be true that Robert is Michael, it is still an odd way of *saying* what we want to say. Why is this so? Probably there is a pragmatic presumption to the effect that unless otherwise indicated, subject and object positions of verbs are to be taken as disjoint in speaker reference. This same principle would account for (52b). A case where the linkage is semantic, and so cannot be overridden pragmatically without being nonliteral, is given in (51a). Here the reflexive pronoun *himself* marks the fact that *him* has the same semantic reference as the subject of the verb, *John.* If *himself* is changed to *herself,* either one must assume that the speaker is speaking nonliterally in virtue of using the pronoun *her,* or one must assume that *John* is being used to refer to some female. These remarks extend to complex cases such as (52d). Notice that if the name *John* in these examples is changed to one without gender associations, as in (53), one has to know whether *Lee* is being used to refer to a male or a female in order to determine whether *she* is linked with *Lee* or not, preserving literality.

(53)
Lee believes that *she* is rash.

In some of the above cases, the linking is optional, in that there is another way of construing the sentence literally that does not involve the indicated links. For instance, (51d) and (51e) seem to admit the interpretation indicated below:

(54)
a. Who thinks that they have been cheated? (Those people over there)

b. Everyone said that he was tired. (That man over there)

Finally, notice that we can put more than one anaphoric device into a sentence and thereby affect its linking. For instance, (55) allows *he* either to be linked to *John,* or to refer demonstratively to someone else:

(55)
John said that he was tired. (That man over there)

However, if we add *as for himself* to the sentence, we block the latter possibility.

(56)
John said that, as for himself, he was tired.

How can the phrase *as for himself* contribute to establishing the link between *John* and *he?* These are still matters of current research, but the above examples should serve to illustrate that anaphora is a topic rich in connections between morphology, syntax, semantics, and pragmatics.

How might we represent these kinds of facts in a semantic theory? Clearly, we will not want our semantics to represent information that is nonsemantical, but since the distinction is difficult to determine at times, we will give an illustration of how a semantic case might work and also how a pragmatic case might work.

For a semantic case consider *Everyone shaves himself*. This sentence would receive roughly the syntactic and semantic analysis shown in tree 6.9. Combining NP_2 with the verb yields the result shown in tree 6.10, and combining this result with NP_1 in turn yields tree 6.11. Again,

Tree 6.9

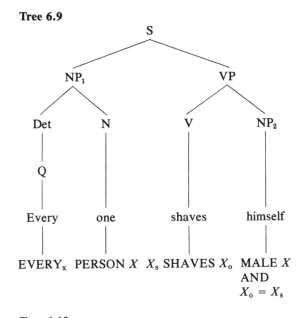

EVERY$_x$ PERSON X X_s SHAVES X_o MALE X
                                            AND
                                            $X_o = X_s$

Tree 6.10

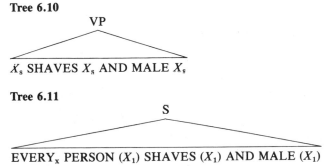

X_s SHAVES X_s AND MALE X_s

Tree 6.11

EVERY$_x$ PERSON (X_1) SHAVES (X_1) AND MALE (X_1)

the semantic rendition of our original sentence is imperfect, but the effect of the semantics is clear, and the result entails that all the people shave themselves and they are all males—which is what the original entails.

For a pragmatic case consider (52e), *Sam believes that Sam is rash*. This sentence has roughly the syntactic structure shown in tree 6.12. When a noun phrase (such as NP$_1$) precedes another noun phrase that is a proper name (such as NP$_2$), and is also "higher" in the tree structure (as in tree 6.12) than the second NP, then the two NPs will be subject to the following presumption:

Tree 6.12

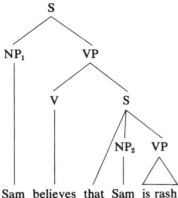

Sam believes that Sam is rash

(57)
Presumption of Disjoint Reference
If a speaker utters a sentence with a structure such as that shown in tree 6.12, then the hearer may assume that the speaker intends to refer to two distinct persons (or things), unless there is some reason to think the same person or thing is being referred to.

Given the PDR, sentence (52e) will be understood by a hearer to involve references to two distinct persons, unless the context of utterance overrides it. This can happen in cases like the following:

(58)
Speaker A: Everybody believes Sam is rash.
Speaker B: But does Sam believe *himself* to be rash?
Speaker A: Sure, since *everybody* believes Sam is rash, so Sam (pointing to Sam) must believe that Sam is rash.

This example illustrates again the important difference between semantic constraints and these sorts of pragmatic constaints. If the speaker chooses to override semantic constraints, then he or she will be speaking nonliterally. However, if the pragmatic constraint is overridden, the speaker can still be speaking literally; however, the hearer will now have to figure out what the speaker is referring to, given that the most obvious presumption is not in effect. In this way we can see that all levels of a grammar can be called upon to explain related aspects of language structure and communication.

Key Words

meaning
reference
denotation
antonymy
truth
entailment
presupposition
logical form
compositional
decomposition
anaphora

Study Questions

1. What are two reasons for a grammar to include a representation of semantic information?

2. What is the Referential Theory of meaning? What is one objection to it?

3. On the Referential Theory of meaning (R), if an expression has a referent, it has a meaning. Give at least one example of a kind of expression for which this is false.

4. What is the Mentalist Theory of meaning? What two versions of it are discussed in the text? What are the problems with each version?

5. What is the Use Theory of meaning? What is its major weakness?

6. Consider the following dialogue:

Speaker A: What chances do I have for a raise?
Speaker B: Two, slim and fat.

Does *fat* mean the same thing as *slim* in the language, or is one of these words being used nonliterally? Defend your answer.

7. Why should a semantic theory be finite?

8. What is it for a semantic theory to be compositional?

9. Anaphora involves which two kinds of linking?

10. What is the difference between semantic and pragmatic linking?

Exercises

1. Think of a reason, not given in the text, why semantics might be considered a part of a grammar.

2. Can you think of a reason why semantics should not be included in a grammar? Discuss.

3. What is *ambiguity* on the Referential Theory of meaning? How might this semantic property be a problem for the theory? Defend your answer.

4. What is ambiguity on the imagist version of the Mentalist Theory of meaning? How might this be a problem for the theory? Discuss.

5. Interpret the following sentences. What are the principles of interpretation?
a. Ralph may not be a communist, but he's at least a *pinko*.
b. He traded his hot car for a *cold* one.
c. John is studying sociology and other *soft* sciences.
d. Who *killed* Lake Erie?

6. Think of five words, write down what you think they mean, then look them up in a good dictionary. Is your idiolect at variance with the dialect called Standard English?

7. Suppose someone said that a grammar must describe what a *speaker* means in uttering an expression from the language, and that it must do this for every meaningful expression. What problems are there for this proposal?

8. Entailment relations are transitive: If *cat* → *mammal*, and *mammal* → *animal*, then *cat* → *animal*. Now consider the "part of" relation. Is it transitive? Defend your answer.
a. A second is part of a minute.
   A minute is part of an hour.
   An hour is part of a day.
   Is a second part of an hour? part of a day?
b. The toenail is part of the toe.
   The toe is part of the foot.
   The foot is part of the leg.
   Is the toenail part of the leg?
c. Henry's toe is part of Henry.
   Henry is part of the 23rd Battalion.
   Is Henry's toe part of the 23rd Battalion?

9. Consider the following sentences and state what the referring expression refers to:
a. *The chair you are sitting on* sells all over France for $200.
b. *Time Magazine* was bought out by Hearst, so now *it's* good for wrapping your garbage.

10. The words *mother, father, sister,* and *brother* all have religious as well as biological meanings. How would one represent the religious senses of each word?

11. Provide a semantic analysis of the form given in the text for five more kinship terms including *uncle, grandmother,* and *niece*.

12. Given Def. 4, what would the semantic representation of the idiomatic sense of *kick the bucket* be?

13. Find another word like *addled* in Def. 8 that changes its meaning depending on what it is applied to.

14. Are there any more restrictions on the (literal) meaning of *kill* in Def. 10? (Hint: Can the number 2 kill someone?)

15. The word *kill* has a related figurative sense, as in *The bill was killed in Congress*. How would you represent that figurative sense?

16. How many different meanings can you see in the following sentences? (Hint: If you think of the possible meanings of the words in isolation, you may come up with more meanings.)
a. My dogs are very tired today.
b. The green giant is over the hill.
c. Time flies.

17. At the lexical level, how might the ten meaning properties and relations schematized in (26a) be defined? (Hint: Some of these were defined in the text.)

18. Work out a derivation of the reading for sentence (48), *A dog kills a boy*, on the model of the derivation given in trees 6.3 through 6.8.

19. Suppose someone were to claim the following: "Given some combination of phonemes, we can *never* predict the meaning of the combination; given some combination of morphemes, we can *sometimes* predict the meaning of the combination; given some combination of words into a sentence, if we know the words and their grammatical relations, we can *always* predict the meaning of the sentence." Criticize or defend this claim in terms of evidence based on the information presented in chapters 3 through 6.

Bibliography

Alston, W. (1967). "Meaning," in P. Edwards, ed., *The Encyclopedia of Philosophy*, vol. 5, Macmillan, New York.

Bierwisch, M. (1969). "On certain problems of semantic representation," *Foundations of Language* 5, 153–184.

Bierwisch, M. (1970). "Semantics," in J. Lyons, ed., *New Horizons in Linguistics*, Penguin Books, Baltimore, Md.

Bierwisch, M. (1971). "On classifying semantic features," in D. D. Steinberg and L. A. Jakobovits, eds., *Semantics*, Cambridge University Press, Cambridge.

Carnap, R. (1956). *Meaning and Necessity*, University of Chicago Press, Chicago.

Chomsky, N. (1965). *Aspects of the Theory of Syntax*, MIT Press, Cambridge, Mass.

Chomsky, N. (1981). *Lectures on Government and Binding*, Foris Publications, Dordrecht, Holland.

Dillon, G. (1977). *Introduction to Contemporary Linguistic Semantics*, Prentice-Hall, Englewood Cliffs, N.J.

Dowty, D., et al. (1981). *Introduction to Montague Semantics*, Reidel, Dordrecht, Holland.

Evans, G. (1983). *Varieties of Reference,* Oxford University Press, Oxford.

Fodor, J. D. (1977). *Semantics: Theories of Meaning in Generative Grammar,* Crowell, New York.

Fodor, J. D., J. A. Fodor, and M. F. Garrett (1975). "The psychological unreality of semantic representations," *Linguistic Inquiry* 6, 515–531.

Glucksberg, S., and J. Danks (1975). *Experimental Psycholinguistics,* Lawrence Erlbaum, Hillsdale, N.J.

Grice, H. P. (1957). "Meaning," *Philosophical Review* 66, 377–388.

Grice, H. P. (1968). "Utterer's meaning, sentence-meaning, and word-meaning," *Foundations of Language* 4, 225–242.

Grice, H. P. (1969). "Utterer's meaning and intentions," *Philosophical Review* 78, 147–177.

Jackendoff, R. (1972). *Semantic Interpretation in Generative Grammar,* MIT Press, Cambridge, Mass.

Katz, J. (1972). *Semantic Theory,* Harper and Row, New York.

Katz, J. (1980). *Propositional Structure and Illocutionary Force,* Harvard University Press, Cambridge, Mass.

Katz, J., and J. Fodor (1963). "The structure of a semantic theory," *Language* 39, 170–210.

Katz, J., and R. Nagel (1974). "Meaning postulates and semantic theory," *Foundations of Language* 11, 311–340.

Kempson, R. (1977). *Semantic Theory,* Cambridge University Press, Cambridge.

Kripke, S. (1977). "Speaker's reference and semantic reference," reprinted in P. French, et al., eds., *Contemporary Perspectives in the Philosophy of Language,* University of Minnesota Press, Minneapolis, 1979.

Kripke, S. (1981). *Naming and Necessity,* Harvard University Press, Cambridge, Mass.

Lehrer, A. (1974). *Semantic Fields and Lexical Structure,* North-Holland, Amsterdam.

Lehrer, A., and K. Lehrer (1982). "Antonymy," *Linguistics and Philosophy* 5, 483–501.

Lehrer, K., and A. Lehrer, eds. (1970). *Theory of Meaning,* Prentice-Hall, Englewood Cliffs, N.J.

Lyons, J. (1977). *Semantics,* 2 vols., Cambridge University Press, Cambridge.

McCawley, J. (1981). *Everything that Linguists Have Always Wanted to Know about Logic,* University of Chicago Press, Chicago.

Miller, G. (1978). "Semantic relations among words," in M. Halle, J. Bresnan, and G. A. Miller, eds., *Linguistic Theory and Psychological Reality,* MIT Press, Cambridge, Mass.

Platts, M. (1979). *Ways of Meaning,* Routledge & Kegan Paul, London.

Putnam, H. (1975). "The meaning of 'meaning'," in K. Gunderson, ed., *Language, Mind and Knowledge,* University of Minnesota Press, Minneapolis.

Schiffer, S. (1972). *Meaning,* Oxford University Press, Oxford.

Schwartz, D. (1979). *Naming and Referring,* Walter de Gruyter, New York.

Schwartz, S., ed. (1977). *Naming, Necessity and Natural Kinds,* Cornell University Press, Ithaca, N.Y.

Chapter Seven

LANGUAGE VARIATION

7.1 LANGUAGE STYLES AND DIALECTS

No human language is fixed, uniform, or unvarying: all languages show internal variation. Actual usage varies from group to group, and speaker to speaker, in terms of the pronunciation of a language, the choice of words and the meaning of those words, and even the use of syntactic constructions. To take a well-known example, the speech of Americans is noticeably different from the speech of the British, and the speech of these two groups in turn is distinct from the speech of Australians. When groups of speakers differ noticeably in their language, they are often said to speak different *dialects* of the language.

Dialectal Variation

It is notoriously difficult, however, to define precisely what a dialect is, and in fact the term has come to be used in various ways. The classic example of a dialect is the *regional* dialect: the distinct form of a language spoken in a certain geographical area. For example, we might speak of Ozark dialects or Appalachian dialects, on the grounds that inhabitants of these regions have certain distinct linguistic features that differentiate them from speakers of other forms of English. We can also speak of a *social* dialect: the distinct form of a language spoken by members of a specific socioeconomic class, such as the working class dialects in England or the ghetto languages in the United States (to which we will return). In addition, certain *ethnic* dialects can be distinguished, such as the form of English sometimes referred to as Yiddish English, historically associated with speakers of Eastern European Jewish ancestry.

It is important to note that dialects are never purely regional, or purely social, or purely ethnic. For example, the distinctive Ozark and Appalachian dialects are not merely dialects spoken by any of the inhabitants of those geographical areas. Rather, they are dialects used primarily by a certain social class in these regions, namely, low-income rural inhabitants. As we shall see, regional, social, and ethnic factors combine and intersect in various ways in the identification of dialects.

In popular usage the term *dialect* refers to a form of a language that is regarded as "substandard," "incorrect," or "corrupt," as opposed to the "standard," "correct," or "pure" form of a language. In popular terms, to speak a dialect is to be uneducated and ignorant. In sharp contrast, the term *dialect,* as a technical term in linguistics, carries no value judgment and simply refers to a distinct form of a language. Thus, for example, linguists refer to so-called Standard English as a dialect of English, which, from a linguistic point of view, is no more "correct" than any other form of English. From this point of view, the monarchs of England and teenagers in Los Angeles and New York all speak dialects of English.

Although dialects are often said to be regional, social, or ethnic, linguists also use the term *dialect* to refer to language variations that cannot be tied to any geographical area, social class, or ethnic group. Rather, this use of *dialect* simply indicates that speakers show some variation in the way they use elements of the language. For example, some speakers of English are perfectly comfortable using the word *anymore* in sentences such as the following:

(1)
a. Tools are expensive anymore.

Here, *anymore* means roughly the same as *nowadays* or *lately*. Other speakers of English can use *anymore* only if there is a negative element, such as *not,* in the sentence:

(1)
b. Tools are not cheap anymore.

As far as we can tell, this difference between speakers cannot be linked to a particular region of the country or to a particular social class or ethnic group.

Language variation does not end with dialects. For each recognizable dialect of a language is itself subject to considerable internal variation: no two speakers of a language, even if they are speakers of the same dialect, produce and use their language in exactly the same way. We are able to recognize different individuals by their distinct speech and language patterns; indeed, a person's language is one of the most fundamental features of self-identity. The form of a language spoken by a single individual is referred to as an *idiolect,* and every speaker of a language has a distinct idiolect.

Once we realize that variation in language is pervasive, it becomes apparent that there is no such thing as a single language used at all times by all speakers. There is no such thing as a single English language; rather, there are many English languages (dialects and idiolects) depending on who is using the language and what the context of use is. Consider the well-known phenomenon of variation in vocabulary words that exists among speakers of English:

(2)
a. *Dope* means "cola" in some parts of the South.
b. *Pocketbook* means "purse" in Boston and in parts of the South.
c. *Fetch up* means "raise" (children) in the South.
d. *Pavement* means "sidewalk" in eastern Pennsylvania and in England.
e. *Happygrass* means "grasshopper" in eastern Virginia.
f. *Bubbler* means "water fountain" in Wisconsin.
g. *Knock up* means "to wake someone up by knocking" in England.
h. *Bonnet* means "hood" (of a car) in England.
i. *Fag* means "cigarette" in England.

As the last three examples indicate, vocabulary differences between American and British English are common and often amusing. Indeed, the Bell Telephone System has published a pamphlet entitled "Getting Around the USA: Travel Tips for the British Visitor," which contains a section entitled "How to Say It." In this section we find the following correspondences:

(3)

British	American
car park	parking lot
coach	bus
garage	service station
lay by	rest area
lift	elevator
lorry	truck

petrol	gasoline
underground (or tube)	subway
call box	telephone booth
telephonist	switchboard operator
gin and French	dry martini
minerals	soft drinks
suspenders	garters
vest	undershirt

These examples are typical of the sort of dialectal variation found in the vocabulary of British and American English.

Mutual Intelligibility

Given the existence of dialectal and idiolectal variation, what allows us to refer to something called English, as if it were a single, monolithic language? A standard answer to this question rests on the notion of *mutual intelligibility*. That is, even though native speakers of English vary in their use of the language, their various languages are similar enough in pronunciation, vocabulary, and grammar to permit mutual intelligibility. A New Yorker, a Texan, and a Californian may recognize differences in each other's language, but they can understand each other (despite all the jokes to the contrary) and they recognize each other as speaking the "same language." Hence, speaking the "same language" does not depend on two speakers speaking identical languages, but only very similar languages.

In discussing the notion of mutual intelligibility, it is interesting to note, by way of contrast, cases that might be called *one-way intelligibility*, involving speakers of different, but historically related, languages. For example, speakers of Brazilian Portuguese who do not know Spanish can often understand the forms of Spanish spoken in neighboring countries. The analogous Spanish speakers, however, find Portuguese largely unintelligible. A similar situation holds between Danish and Swedish: speakers of Danish can (more or less) comprehend Swedish, but the reverse situation is much less common. Even if one group of speakers can understand another group, they cannot be said to speak the same language unless the second group also understands the first, and thus the notion of *mutual* intelligibility is crucial in specifying when two languages are the "same" language.

Although the notion of mutual intelligibility seems like a reasonable criterion in defining dialects, the situation can be considerably complicated by social and political factors. In China, for example, a northern Chinese speaker of the Beijing dialect (also known as Mandarin) cannot understand the speech of a southern Chinese speaker of Cantonese, and vice versa. For this reason, a linguist might well label Mandarin and Cantonese as two distinct "languages." Nevertheless, in traditional studies of the Chinese language, both Mandarin and Cantonese are regarded as "dialects" of Chinese, given that they are historically related (that is, they may have been offshoots of several closely related dialects that existed earlier in the history of the Chinese language). Moreover, both Mandarin and Cantonese are spoken in the same nation (they are not languages of two different countries with different governments), and speakers of both "dialects" can use the written language (in the form of Chinese characters) as a common language of communication. For such reasons, the tendency has persisted to use the term "dialect" to refer to various mutually unintelligible forms of the Chinese language.

Historical and political factors can also give rise to the opposite situation, namely, where two mutually intelligible forms are not considered dialects of the same language, but rather two distinct languages. For example, Papago and Pima are two Native American languages spoken by members of tribal groups living in the state of Arizona and in northern Mexico. In fact, Papago and Pima are mutually intelligible and are extremely close phonologically and grammatically, with only minor linguistic differences in pronunciation and syntax (the differences between them being less radical than the differences between American and British English). For this reason, a linguist could well consider Papago and Pima to be two dialects of the same language. Nevertheless, the two tribal groups, for historical and political reasons, consider themselves distinct political entities, and consider their languages as distinct languages rather than dialectal variations of a single language.

Having examined some of the complications involved in the term *dialect,* how can we define it? No satisfactory definition of *dialect* has yet been proposed, but for our purposes we will ignore complications and settle on a very general one. A dialect is simply a distinct form of a language, possibly associated with a recognizable regional, social, or ethnic group, differentiated from other forms of the language by specific linguistic features (for example, pronunciation, or vocabulary, or grammar, or any combination of these). This rough definition is intended to do no more than capture a certain intuitive idea of the term *dialect,* but one that seems useful. In any event, it must be kept in mind that from a linguistic point of view *dialect* is a theoretical concept. In reality, variation in language is so pervasive that each language is actually a continuum of languages from speaker to speaker, and from group to group, and no absolute lines can be drawn between different forms of a language.

Dialects and the Interplay of Regional and Social Factors: New York City /r/

As we have mentioned, the classic example of a dialect is the regional dialect, the assumption being that speakers of the dialect form a coherent speech community living in relative isolation from speakers outside the community. Such relative isolation between geographical areas is becoming increasingly more rare in the contemporary world, and in the United States the population as a whole is so geographically and socially mobile that it is becoming increasingly more difficult to speak of regional dialects in any pure sense. Especially in large urban areas, a particular linguistic feature of a regional dialect might well be influenced by social factors.

An interesting example of the effect of "social prestige" on a regional dialect is found in the pronunciation of /r/ in New York City speech. The so-called *r*-less dialect of New York City is so well known that it is often the subject of humor, especially on the part of the New Yorkers who themselves speak it. It is commonly thought that speakers of the dialect completely lack /r/ in words such as *car, card, four, fourth,* and so on, but this is a misconception, as an intriguing study by the sociolinguist William Labov (1972) reveals.

Labov began with the hypothesis that New York City speakers vary in their pronunciation of /r/ according to their social status. Labov interviewed salespeople at several New York City department stores that differed in price range and social prestige. Assuming that salespeople tend to "borrow prestige" from their customers, Labov predicted that the social stratification of customers at different department stores would be mirrored in a similar stratification of salespeople. These assumptions led him to hypothesize that "salespeople in the highest-ranked store will have the highest values of (r); those in the middle-ranked store will have intermediate values of (r); and those in the lowest-ranked store will show the lowest values" (1972, 45).

Labov chose three stores: Saks Fifth Avenue (high prestige), Macy's (middle level), and S. Klein (low prestige). He interviewed salespeople by asking them a question that would elicit the answer *fourth floor:*

The interviewer approached the informant in the role of a customer asking for directions to a particular department. The department was one which was located on the fourth floor. When the interviewer asked, "Excuse me, where are the women's shoes?" the answer would normally be, "Fourth floor."

The interviewer then leaned forward and said, "Excuse me?" He would usually then obtain another utterance, *"Fourth floor,"* spoken in careful style under emphatic stress. (1972, 49)

The phrase *fourth floor* has two instances of /r/, both of which are subject to variation in the pronunciation of New York City speakers, and Labov was able to study both casual and careful pronunciations of this phrase.

The result turned out to correlate in an interesting way with the hypothesis. For example, Labov found that at Saks, 30 percent of the salespeople interviewed always pronounced both /r/'s in the test phrase; at Macy's 20 percent did so; and at Klein's only 4 percent did. In addition, Labov found that 32 percent of the interviewed salespeople at Saks had variable pronunciation of /r/ (sometimes /r/ was pronounced and sometimes not, depending on context); at Macy's 31 percent of the interviewees had variable pronunciation; and at Klein's only 17 percent did. These overall results do suggest that pronunciation of /r/ in New York City is correlated, at least loosely, with social stratification of the speakers.

What about the differences in pronunciation between the casual and the emphatic styles? It turns out that in the casual response the /r/ of *floor* was pronounced by 63 percent of the salespeople at Saks, 44 percent at Macy's, and only 8 percent at Klein's. In contrast, in the careful, emphatic response the /r/ of *floor* was pronounced by 64 percent at Saks, 61 percent at Macy's (note the jump from 44 percent), and 18 percent at Klein's. In other words, at Saks there was very little difference between casual and careful pronunciations, whereas at Macy's and Klein's the difference between these styles was significantly larger. This suggests that speakers at the middle and lower levels of the New York City social scale are perfectly aware that a final /r/ occurs in words such as *floor*. Even though they omit this /r/ in casual pronunciation, it reappears in careful speech:

In emphatic pronunciation of the final (r), Macy's employees come very close to the mark set by Saks. It would seem that r-pronunciation is the norm at which a majority of Macy employees aim, yet not the one they use most often. In Saks, we see a shift between casual and emphatic pronunciation, but it is much less marked. In other words, Saks employees have more *security* in a linguistic sense. (1972, 51–52)

As we will see again in section 7.2, the difference between casual and careful language styles is important in syntactic variation as well.

Hypercorrection

In connection with the pronunciation of New York City /r/, it is interesting to note that some New York City speakers insert /r/ in words where it does not actually occur in spelling. One can hear *Cuba* pronounced [kyuwbr̩], *saw* pronounced [sɔr], *idea* pronounced [aydiyr̩], and so on. It seems that the very speakers who drop out /r/ in some words and positions will insert an /r/ in other words and positions. The cause of this phenomenon is sometimes thought to be *hypercorrection* (that is, overcorrection): speakers who have been persuaded that it is "incorrect" to drop /r/ will overcompensate or overcorrect for this by inserting the sound where it does not actually occur in spelling. (Overcompensation can be seen in syntax with speakers who say *between you and I* instead of *between you and me* on the grounds that *I* is more "correct" and "cultured" than *me*.)

However, we might question whether, for given speakers, inserting /r/ involves only hypercorrection. For one thing, even those speakers who insert /r/ do not always pronounce words such as *idea* with a final /r/: the insertion of /r/ on such words happens only when the next word begins with a vowel (hence, we could hear phrases such as *the idear I heard about* but not *the idear John told me about*). The insertion of /r/ is thus at least partially governed by a phonological principle. In the second place, hypercorrection often involves imitating what is thought to be prestige language. For example, a hypercorrect phrase such as *It is I* is thought to sound more prestigious than *It's me,* even though there is nothing grammatically incorrect about the latter phrase. Returning to words such as *idear,* speakers who insert /r/ in *idear* may not think that such a pronunciation is prestigious. Since insertion of /r/ is governed partially by a phonological principle, and since it may not involve imitation of prestige language, for some speakers this insertion of /r/ is not strictly a case of hypercorrection.

The Labov study illustrates once again that there is often no absolute or simple distinction between one dialect and another: we cannot simply say that the New York City dialect is *r*-less. Rather, the pronunciation of /r/ in that dialect is variable, and this variation seems to be correlated both with social factors and with the casual or careful context. Thus, just as no language can be said to be unvarying or fixed, so no dialect of a language can be said to be unvarying or fixed either. Finally, not even the language of an individual speaker is unvarying: an individual New Yorker may well show variation in pronouncing /r/.

"Standard" versus "Nonstandard" Language

A pervasive phenomenon of societies in the contemporary world is the designation of one dialect of a language as the "standard," "correct," or "pure" form of the language. In the contemporary United States, Standard American English (or SAE, for short) is a form of the language used in news programs in the national media (often referred to as "Network English"); it is the language of legal and governmental functions; and it is the language used in the schools as a vehicle for education.

As noted earlier, in linguistic terms no one dialect of a language is any more correct, any better, or any more logical than any other dialect of the language: all dialects are equally effective forms of language, in that any idea or desire that can be expressed in one dialect can be expressed just as easily in any other dialect. The idea that SAE is the correct form of the language is a social attitude—more precisely, a language prejudice—which is just as irrational as social prejudices involving race or sex. In America the so-called standard language is perhaps most widely identified with the educated white middle class; hence, a good case can be made that the reverence for the standard language in our schools and official functions is a reflection of the far more general bias in the United States toward considering the white middle-class value system the correct or best value system. It is important to realize at the outset that labeling one particular dialect as standard and others as inferior reflects a sociopolitical judgment, not a linguistic judgment. Indeed, in countries throughout the world, the standard national language is the dialect of the subculture with the most prestige and power.

Black English and the Verb *Be*

A well-known example of a social dialect that has been labeled as nonstandard is Black English. In a certain sense the term Black English (or BE, for short) is misleading in that it suggests that all Black Americans speak the same dialect and use it all the time. Both impressions are incorrect. Black Americans show as much linguistic variation as any other social group in the nation; language is not determined by race. Further, even those who can be said to use BE do not necessarily use this dialect at all times. Essentially, BE refers to an informal style of language typically (though not exclusively) used by Black residents of low-income ghettos in large urban areas of the United States. Although BE is also used by certain Latinos and Whites who live in the same ghetto areas, BE is stereotypically associated with Black residents of the ghetto.

In recent years, BE has attracted a good deal of attention from linguists (see references), whose investigations have shown quite clearly that BE is every bit as rule-governed and as logical as SAE. In a series of important studies Labov (see references) has demonstrated that there are several important and highly systematic relationships between BE and SAE. To take what is perhaps the best-known example, consider the frequently noted fact that in BE present tense forms of the verb *to be* are often dropped in casual speech (examples taken from Labov 1969a).

(4)
a. She the first one started us off.
b. He fast in everything he do.
c. I know, but he wild, though.
d. You out the game.
e. We on tape.
f. But everybody not black.
g. They not caught.
h. Boot always comin' over my house to eat.
i. He gon' try to get up.

The omission of the verb *to be* in Black English can easily be misinterpreted by those untrained in linguistics as evidence that BE is a kind of defective dialect that violates rules of grammar or, worse yet, has no rules of grammar. As Labov (1969b) notes, this has even led to the mistaken view on the part of certain educators and psychologists that Black children entering school have a language deficit and are culturally deprived. Even though the omission of forms of the verb *to be* may at first appear to make BE quite distinct from SAE, Labov (1969b, 203) points out that

The deletion of the *is* or *are* in [BE] is not the result of erratic or illogical behavior: it follows the same regular rules as standard English contraction. Wherever standard English can contract, [BE can] use either the contracted form or (more commonly) the deleted zero form. Thus, *They mine* corresponds to standard *They're mine,* not to the full form *They are mine.* On the other hand, no such deletion is possible in positions where standard English cannot contract: just as one cannot say *That's what they're* in standard English, *That's what they* is equally impossible in the vernacular we are considering.

In the examples already cited, the correspondence between SAE and BE is as follows:

SAE: Contraction	BE: Deletion
She's the first one . . .	She the first one . . .
He's fast . . .	He fast . . .
You're out . . .	You out . . .
They're not caught.	They not caught.

Both dialects have contraction, but only BE has the further option of deleting a contractible form of *to be*.

What appears at first to be a significant difference between SAE and BE actually turns out to be rather minor. Indeed, in both dialects the same general phenomenon is taking place: the verb *to be* (as well as other auxiliary verbs) becomes *reduced* in casual speech when it is unstressed. One dialect reflects the reduction process by contraction alone, the other dialect by contraction or deletion. As we shall see, in fact, the deletion of the verb *to be* (and other auxiliary verbs) is by no means limited to BE, but happens quite generally in the informal style in all dialects of American English.

Another grammatical feature of Black English that has been noted in linguistic studies is a certain use of the verb *to be* illustrated by examples such as the following (taken from Fasold 1972 (chap. 4)):

(5)
a. I get a ball and then some children *be* on one team and some *be* on another team.
b. Christmas Day, well, everybody *be* so choked up over gifts and everything, they don't *be* too hungry anyway.

c. My father *be* the last one to open his presents.
d. Yes, there always *be* fights.
e. On Saturdays, I like to watch cartoons, but I *be* out working.

This use of *be* has been termed *invariant be* (since it does not vary either to reflect past or present tense, or to agree with the subject), and it indicates a habitual and repeatable action, state, or event. Thus, invariant *be* is typically used in general descriptions (as in (5a), a description of a game) and to indicate customary or typical states of affairs. Given this, note that it is unacceptable in Black English to say **He be working right now,* since the time expression *right now* does not have a habitual interpretation, but rather refers to the specific present. In addition, whereas one can say *He my brother* (SAE *He's my brother*), it is unacceptable to say **He be my brother,* since the sibling relation is permanent over time; that is, it is not repeatable over time (invariant *be* is used to indicate actions, states, or events that can be repeated). The use of invariant *be* has been cited as a grammatical feature unique to BE, representing what seems to be a genuine difference between BE and other American dialects.

In discussions of Black English, there has been an all too unfortunate tendency to compare BE to SAE without paying sufficient attention to the level of formality of the languages being compared. That is, BE refers to an *informal*-style language used in the ghetto by ghetto residents (within the culture of the Black ghetto there are more formal styles of language as well: for example, Afro-American religious preaching styles—see Smitherman 1977). BE has been compared with *formal*-style SAE, and thus an informal oral language has been compared with an "official" language of news broadcasts, governmental functions, and school settings. It is no surprise that significant differences have been found. However, when we examine *informal* styles of American English, we find similar features across all dialects, and it turns out that certain features of BE are simply part of the general linguistic features of informal English. It is crucial to distinguish between formal and informal styles of language before one can compare dialects in an accurate way.

Formal and Informal Language Styles

Without being aware of it, each speaker of any language has mastered a number of language styles. To illustrate, in a formal setting someone might offer coffee to a guest by saying *May I offer you some coffee?* or perhaps *Would you care for some coffee?* In an informal setting the same speaker might well say *Want some coffee?* or even *Coffee?* This shift in styles is completely unconscious and automatic; indeed, it takes some concentration and hard introspection to realize that we each use a formal and an informal style on different occasions.

The clearest cases of formal speech occur in social contexts that are formal, serious, often official in some sense, in which speakers feel they must watch their language and in which the *manner* of saying something is regarded as socially important. These contexts would include a formal job interview, meeting an important person, and standing before a court of law. Informal speech in our use of that term occurs in casual, relaxed social settings in which speech is spontaneous, rapid, and uncensored by the speaker. Social settings for this style of speech would include chatting with close friends and interacting in an intimate or family environment or in similar relaxed settings.

Some speakers of English, notably self-styled educated speakers, often equate the formal language style with the so-called standard language; the informal style, if discussed at all, is dubbed a form of sloppy speech or even slang, especially in language classes in public schools. But on closer investigation of the actual details of informal language, it turns out that the informal style, far from being merely a sloppy form of language, is governed by rules every bit as precise, logical, and rigorous as the rules governing formal language. (Of course, the informal style also has idiosyncrasies and irregularities—but, then, the formal style does too.) In section 7.2 we will concentrate on some of the rules of the informal style because a detailed study of the syntactic differences between formal and informal language styles reveals a number of important ideas about language variation in general, and about the question of standard versus nonstandard language in particular.

7.2 SOME RULES OF THE GRAMMAR OF INFORMAL STYLE IN ENGLISH

A well-known difference between formal and informal language styles in English (and indeed in many other languages) is that the informal style can be characterized as having a greater amount of abbreviation, shortening, contraction, and deletion. Compare the formal *Would you care for some coffee?* with the informal *Want some coffee?* The formal style is often redundant and verbose, whereas the informal style is brief, to the point, and grammatically streamlined. In this section we will concentrate on two important grammatical features of the informal style, (a) the dropping of the subject of the sentence and (b) the dropping of the auxiliary verb, these being two central features of the *abbreviated* style.

The abbreviated style we will describe here is based on the language of the authors of this book, and all grammatical judgments will be based on our own speech. We have tested and confirmed our judgments with those of numerous other speakers, however. Furthermore, it seems clear that the abbreviation processes we describe are quite general within American English. Some readers may find that their own judgments differ from ours at certain points, and this will be entirely natural; indeed, there could be no better illustration of the topic of this chapter. The important point is that every speaker of English has an abbreviated style in casual speech. Consequently, readers will be able to judge for themselves how accurate we are in describing the abbreviated style in general.

Tag-controlled Deletion

To begin, let us consider sentences that end in tag questions:

(6)
a. You've been hitting the bottle again, *haven't you?*
b. He wants me to pay the bill, *does he!*
c. She likes her new house, *does she!*
d. He's failing his courses, *isn't he?*
e. They'll steal my money, *will they!*
f. You're getting pretty excited, *aren't you?*
g. You're not ready to swim fifty laps, *are you?*

As we saw in chapter 5, tag questions—*haven't you, does he,* and so on—reflect at least two important properties of a sentence: (a) the tag contains the auxiliary verb found in the main sentence or (in the case of *do*) the auxiliary appropriate to the main sentence, and (b) the pronoun in the tag agrees with the subject of the sentence. The tag question thus contains, in part, a repetition of some of the information found in the main sentence.

In the informal, abbreviated style, the subject and the auxiliary of the main sentence can in fact be dropped out when these elements are identical with the pronoun and auxiliary of the tag:

(7)
a. Been hitting the bottle again, haven't you?
b. Wants me to pay the bill, does he?
c. Likes her new house, does she?
d. Failing his courses, isn't he?
e. Steal my money, will they?
f. Getting pretty excited, aren't you?
g. Not ready to swim fifty laps, are you?

Let us refer to the process illustrated here as Tag-controlled Deletion, described as follows: given a sentence with a tag question, the subject and the auxiliary (if any) of the main sentence may be deleted if they are identical with the pronoun and the auxiliary of the tag question. Tag-controlled Deletion is a rule of the abbreviated style in informal language.

Notice that there is nothing incomplete about the sentences in (7). Even though the subjects and auxiliaries are missing from the main clauses, we can easily *recover* this information from the tag question. The sentences are formed by a regular rule. Further, they show another regularity: if the subject is deleted, then the auxiliary must be deleted also. Consider the following examples, which, as far as we know, are not possible for any speakers:

(8)
a. *Have been hitting the bottle again, haven't you?
b. *Is failing his courses, isn't he?
c. *Will steal my money, will you?
d. *Are getting pretty excited, aren't you?

We can make a firm judgment that these sentences are bad, indicating that there is a rule at work here that is being followed strictly. The abbreviation process is hardly sloppy.

How can we account for the fact that the auxiliary verb may not remain behind if the subject of the sentence has been deleted? Labov's observations on contraction suggest that we consider the fact that subjects and auxiliaries are often contracted. Along with *You have been hitting the bottle* (*have* uncontracted) goes *You've been hitting the bottle* (*have* contracted as *'ve*). If the rule is that the subject of the sentence can be deleted only if the auxiliary verb is contracted onto it, sentences such as those in (8) will never occur: the auxiliary will always be deleted along with the subject, since it is contracted onto the subject and forms a single unit with it. To form a sentence such as *Been hitting the bottle again, haven't you?*, we do not delete the two separate elements *you* and *have,* but the single contracted element *you've.*

What happens when the auxiliary verb of the sentence cannot be contracted onto the subject? For example, consider what happens when the auxiliary is negative:

(9)
You haven't been hitting the bottle again, have you?

Even though the sequence *you have* can be contracted to *you've,* the sequence *you haven't* cannot be contracted to **you'ven't*—no such form exists in English. For a sequence such as *you have not been,* we can either contract the subject and auxiliary, as in *you've not been,* or we can contract the auxiliary and the negative, as in *you haven't been,* but we cannot contract both (**you'ven't*).

It is striking that negative auxiliaries, unlike positive auxiliaries, can remain behind if the subject is deleted:

(10)
a. Haven't been hitting the bottle again, have you?
b. Aren't getting too excited, are you?
c. Doesn't like all these rules, does he?
d. Won't take too much time, will it?

We now have an interesting explanation for the contrast in the following sentences:

(11)
a. *Have been hitting the bottle again, haven't you?
b. Haven't been hitting the bottle again, have you?

Example (11a) is not a possible sentence, but (11b) is. On the surface this might seem at first to indicate randomness, irregularity, or sloppiness in the abbreviated style. But a more careful consideration of the details reveals that *have* in (11a) is a contractible auxiliary, whereas *haven't* cannot be contracted. This suggests the following revision in our Tag-controlled Deletion rule:

(12)

Tag-controlled Deletion (revised)

Given a sentence with a tag question, the subject of the main sentence may be deleted, under the following conditions:

a. the subject must be identical with the pronoun in the tag, and

b. if the main sentence contains an auxiliary, it *must* be contracted onto the subject if it *can* be contracted onto the subject.

Since *have* in (11a) can be contracted onto the subject, it must be, before the subject can be deleted. Since this has not happened, (11a) is a bad sentence. However, in (11b) *haven't* cannot in any event be contracted onto the subject; thus, condition (b) of the rule is not relevant and the subject can be deleted.

Notice that the Tag-controlled Deletion rule, as stated in (12), has some interesting consequences. Auxiliary *will* has a contracted form, *'ll;* compare *It will get on your nerves* and *It'll get on your nerves*. In contrast, however, an auxiliary such as *could* has no such contracted form: from the sentence *It could get on your nerves* we cannot derive another in which *could* is contracted or shortened. Rule (12) now makes a prediction: since *will* can contract with the subject, it should not be possible to leave *will* behind if the subject is deleted; since *could* has no contracted form, it should be possible to leave *could* behind after the subject is deleted. This prediction seems to us to be true: it seems fine to say *Could get on your nerves, couldn't it?*, but **Will get on your nerves, won't it?* seems bad. Further, negative *won't* (a contraction of *will* + *not*) differs from positive *will* in that it can remain behind, as in *Won't get on your nerves, will it?* But, then, *won't* has no further contracted form: the sequence *it won't* cannot be contracted in any way. Again, the uncontractible auxiliary can remain after the subject has been deleted.

We have now set up a system wherein the deletion of the subject is dependent upon contraction of the subject with the auxiliary, wherever this is possible. As we saw, in Black English the link between contraction and deletion is crucial, and it turns out that this link is just as crucial in the general abbreviated style of American English.

We have by no means exhausted the topic of Tag-controlled Deletion. However, the tag cases are only one part of the general deletion processes that affect subject and auxiliary in abbreviated style. We now turn to some other cases.

Abbreviated Questions

Deletion of Subject and Auxiliary *Do*
Let us continue our study of informal style by noting again sentences of a sort discussed earlier:

(13)
You want some coffee?

(14)
Want some coffee?

We will refer to questions such as (13) and (14) as *abbreviated questions,* inasmuch as certain elements are missing or deleted. Such abbreviated questions occur quite commonly in the informal speech style and are one of the more interesting features of that style. In example (14) the subject of the sentence, *you,* has been dropped. In example (13) another deletion process seems to be at work: the deletion of the auxiliary verb *do.* We propose that a sentence such as (13) derives from a sentence such as (15):

(15)
Do you want some coffee?

When the auxiliary verb *do* is dropped, the result is the abbreviated question (13). Do we have further evidence for this hypothesis? After all, we need not assume that these examples involve a deletion of *do.* We could just as easily say that *You want some coffee?* is the declarative sentence *You want some coffee* with a rising question intonation placed on it. Why should we assume any involvement of the verb *do* in this process?

When we examine a new set of examples drawn from a wider range of data, the *do*-deletion hypothesis is confirmed. Consider the following:

(16)
Last night's party go well?

(17)
She like her new house?

These are perfectly good examples of the informal speech style that we are discussing; we would suggest repeating them (perhaps aloud) to get a feeling for how they would sound in rapid informal speech. The point to notice is the form of the verbs in (16) and (17): they are the infinitive ("tenseless") forms *go* and *like*. Now examine the simple declarative sentences corresponding to these questions:

(18)
Last night's party *went* well.

(19)
She *likes* her new house.

In these examples the verbs reflect tense (past tense *went*) and number (third person *likes*). If we placed a question intonation on the declarative sentences in (18) and (19), we would simply get the questions *Last night's party went well?* and *She likes her new house?* We would *not* derive (16) and (17).

The verbs in (16) and (17) show no tense or number agreement. This is precisely the form such verbs take in questions with *do:*

(20)
Did last night's party *go* well?

(21)
Does she *like* her new house?

If we now assume that in informal speech the verb *do* (*did, does*) can be dropped, we will arrive at just the right verb form for abbreviated questions:

(22)
Did last night's party go well → _____ Last night's party go well?

(23)
Does she like her new house → _____ She like her new house?

Hence, to account for the verb forms in (16) and (17), we assume that *do* is deleted from these abbreviated questions and that they are not regular declarative sentences with rising intonation.

Of course, as already noted, along with (16) and (17) we do have such declarative sentences in the form of questions: *Last night's party went well?* and *She likes her new house?* It is interesting that these differ from (16) and (17) not only structurally (in terms of the verb forms) but also in terms of their use. For example, a declarative sentence with question intonation such as *Last night's party went well?* seems to be used in a conversation only if the questioner expects that the party did go well and is asking for confirmation of that expectation. In other words the question *Last night's party went well?* is used in much the same way as the question *So, I take it that last night's party went well, right?*

In contrast, an abbreviated question such as *Last night's party go well?* could be used even if it is a genuine request for information and does not imply that the questioner has any expectations either way about the party. It is striking that such subtle differences in use should be associated with the simple, and apparently trivial, difference between *go* and *went*. Given what we have said, it is interesting to note that (13)—*You want some coffee?*—could be either an abbreviated question from which *do* has been deleted or a simple declarative sentence with question intonation. Although it could be either, our concern here will be with its use as an abbreviated question with missing *do*.

Turning now to a second piece of evidence that auxiliary *do* drops out from questions in the abbreviated style, consider examples such as the following:

(24)
Last night's party not go too well?

Let us concentrate here on the negative word, *not*. In a simple declarative sentence *not* cannot appear unless an auxiliary verb appears as well; that is, (25) is impossible. Rather, the verb *do* turns up in such examples, as in (26) (recall the discussion of auxiliary verbs in chapter 5):

(25)
*Last night's party not went too well.

(26)
Last night's party *did* not go too well.

One question form of (26) is as follows:

(27)
Did last night's party not go too well?

Given (27), we again see that dropping the verb *do* (*did*) gives just the right form for abbreviated questions such as (24). Thus, there are at least two good reasons to assume that such informal questions as *You want some coffee?* and *Last night's party go well?* are derived by deleting the auxiliary verb, in this case *do*.

We have seen that two deletion processes are at work to produce abbreviated questions: deletion of *do* and deletion of the second person subject *you*. Hence, from *Do you want some coffee?* we can get *You want some coffee?* and *Want some coffee?* However, note the following restriction, already encountered in Tag-controlled Deletion: even though it is possible to delete the auxiliary verb without deleting the subject *you,* it is never possible to delete the subject *you* without also deleting the auxiliary verb *do,* as (28) illustrates.

(28)
Do you want some coffee? →
*Do want some coffee?

We have derived the impossible form *Do want some coffee?* by deleting the subject *you* but failing to delete the auxiliary verb as well. Again it is important to note that even in the abbreviated informal style, precise grammatical rules must be followed.

At this point, what can we add to our account in order to guarantee that whenever the subject *you* is deleted, the auxiliary verb will be deleted as well?

It is not only in declarative statements that auxiliary verbs in English undergo processes of reduction and contraction; contraction happens in questions as well. Consider the following facts:

(29)
The sequence *do you* in a question is often pronounced *d'you* [dyuw] or *d'ya* [dyə] or *ja* [jə]: *D'you like dancing? D'ya like dancing?* or *Ja like dancing?*

(30)
The sequence *did you* in a question is often pronounced *didja* [dɪjə] or *djou* [juw]: *Didja like the party?* or *Djou like the party?*

These processes of reduction and contraction are common enough among speakers of English that one even hears abbreviated exchanges such as

(31)
a. Jeet?   (= Didja eat? = Did you eat?)
b. No, djou?   (= No, did you?)

We can now make use of these contraction facts to explain the nonexistence of *Do want some coffee? just as we did in the case of Tag-controlled Deletion.

Once again, suppose that we begin with the full question form, *Do you want some coffee?*. At this point let us assume that either contraction of the auxiliary verb *do* with the subject *you* can occur (producing *d'you, d'ya,* or *ja*) or deletion of auxiliary verb *do* can occur.

(32)

Do you want some coffee?

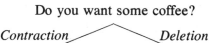

Contraction   *Deletion*

D'ya want some coffee?   You want some coffee?

Notice that once the verb *do* is contracted with the subject *you,* the result is the form *d'ya* (or *ja* or *d'you*), which is a single word (inasmuch as contraction is the process of taking independent morphemes and fusing them into a single word unit). If we assume that *you* is deleted only if the auxiliary verb is contracted onto it, it will automatically be the case that whenever the subject is deleted, the auxiliary verb is too: they are deleted together as a single contracted unit. Hence, it is not *you* that is deleted, but some contracted form such as *d'you, d'ya, ja,* or *djou*. The undesirable case *Do want some coffee? never arises because *you* will not delete if *do* is not contracted onto it.

At this point we have refined our account sufficiently to posit the following two rules in the grammar of the informal abbreviated style:

(33)
Abbreviated Question Rules
Rule 1. To form an abbreviated question, the auxiliary verb (*do*) can be deleted, or else it can be contracted onto the subject *you*.
Rule 2. In forming an abbreviated question, the second person subject *you* can be deleted as long as an auxiliary verb is contracted onto it.

These rules correctly describe the cases we have dealt with so far.

Deletion of *Have*
Let us now ask whether *do* is the only auxiliary verb that can be deleted in abbreviated questions. As it turns out, the following data indicate that the auxiliary verb *have* can be deleted as well:

(34)

a. (You) seen John lately?
   (= Have you seen John lately?)
b. (You) picked up your laundry yet?
   (= Have you picked . . .)
c. She been sick these days?
   (= Has she been . . .)
d. Your job been getting you down?
   (= Has your job been . . .)

In these cases auxiliary *have* has been deleted and, as before, *you* can be dropped out. Notice once again that even though *have* and *you* can both be deleted, it is impossible to delete *you* without also deleting *have:*

(35)

a. *Have seen John lately?
b. *Have picked up your laundry yet?

In this respect *have* behaves just like *do*. And just as *do* contracts with *you,* so also *have* contracts with *you;* that is, the sequence *have you* can be pronounced *'vyou* ([vyuw], rhyming with the word *view*) or *'vya* ([vyə]):

(36)

a. 'vyou seen John lately?
b. 'vyou picked up your laundry yet?

Once again, we will assume that *you* can drop out only if it is contracted with an auxiliary, in this case *have;* hence, it is not *you* that deletes, but rather *'vyou.* It will automatically follow that we cannot derive **Have seen John lately?,* since *you* can delete only if *have* is contracted onto it and deleted also.

In English there is a distinction between auxiliary *have,* as in *I have seen him,* and main verb *have,* as in *I have some wool.* Stated simply, auxiliary *have* is followed by a verb (*seen*) and main verb *have* is followed by a noun phrase (*some wool*). Now consider the following question, made famous by a nursery rhyme:

(37)

Have you any wool?

In our speech (that is, in the speech of the authors) this instance of main verb *have* cannot be deleted to form an abbreviated question:

(38)
*You any wool?

Furthermore, in our speech the main verb *have* also lacks a contracted form with *you*. The following type of question is never found:

(39)
*'vyou any wool?

This lends further plausibility to the idea that contraction is crucial for deletion: only a contractible verb can be deleted in an abbreviated question. This now leads to a prediction: if for some speakers of English it is possible to contract main verb *have*, as in (39), then for those speakers it should also be possible to delete main verb *have*, as in (38).

Deletion of *Be*
Continuing our exploration into which auxiliary verbs can be dropped in abbreviated questions, we find the following data indicating that the verb *be* can be deleted:

(40)
a. (You) running a fever?
   (= Are you running . . .)
b. (You) finally rich now?
   (= Are you finally rich . . .)
c. Your car in the garage?
   (= Is your car . . .)
d. Satisfied?
   (= Are you satisfied?)
e. John a drug addict or something?
   (= Is John a drug addict . . .)
f. (You) gonna leave soon?
   (= Are you going to leave soon?)
g. (You) sposta do that?
   (= Are you supposed to . . .)

Our data show that deletion of auxiliary *be* and the subject *you* is possible, and by now it should not be surprising to note that the subject *you* cannot be deleted unless the auxiliary verb is deleted as well:

(41)
a. *Are running a fever?
b. *Are finally rich now?

And, once again, the verb in question is a contractible verb. For example, the various forms of *be* can contract with various subjects:

(42)

am I   = 'my [mɑy]
are you   = 'ryou [ṛyuw]
is he   = 's he [ziy]
is she   = 's she [zšiy]
is it ⌣ = 's it [zɪt]
is John   = 's John [zǰan]
are we   = 'r we [ṛwiy]
are they = 'r they [ṛðey]

As noted in chapter 3, *am* shortens and contracts as /m/, *are* contracts as /r/, and *is* as /z/, showing that *be* is a contractible verb and hence can delete. Since the subject *you* is deleted only if *be* is contracted onto it, such ungrammatical cases as *Are running a fever?* can never arise. So far, our account of the verb *be* is completely parallel to our account of *do* and *have*.

There are some interesting differences, however. Recall the distinction between auxiliary *have* and main verb *have*. A similar distinction holds for the verb *be:*

(43)
a. Auxiliary *be:*   You *are* running a fever.
b. Main verb *be:*   The car *is* in the garage.
                       John *is* a drug addict.

Stated simply, auxiliary *be* is followed by a verb, whereas main verb *be* is followed by a nonverb category: noun phrase, prepositional phrase, and so on. But main verb *be*—unlike main verb *have*—can be deleted in abbreviated questions: cases such as *Your car in the garage?* and *John a drug addict?* are both possible. This difference between main verb *have* and main verb *be* is matched by another difference between them: main verb *be* has contracted forms (those listed in (42)), whereas main verb *have* does not (recall (39)). Thus, what appears on the surface to be an irregularity—main verb *be* can delete, but main verb *have* cannot—turns out to be a consequence of a regular principle governing the formation of abbreviated questions.

Summary of Deletion in Abbreviated Questions
We are now in a position to summarize our discussion of abbreviated questions. We have seen that the second person subject (*you*) can be deleted in the formation of abbreviated questions. The auxiliary verbs that can be deleted are the contractible forms of the auxiliaries *do, have,* and *be,* and these are the only forms that can delete. The processes involved in the formation of abbreviated questions are summarized in figure 7.1.

Deletion in Declarative Sentences

So far, we have examined deletion processes only in questions. For simple declarative statements (without tag questions) the deletion possibilities are quite different from those in questions.

For example, in declarative statements the auxiliary *do* appears only when the sentences are negative or emphatic:

(44)
a. I don't know that man.
b. You *DO* know that man.

Neither emphatic nor negative *do* can delete, under any circumstances. And unemphatic positive *do* never appears: the unemphatic positive sentence is *I know that man,* with no overt auxiliary. Hence, the question of the deletion of auxiliary *do* in statements is simply irrelevant.

Deletion of auxiliary *have* in declarative statements is possible, although some speakers have unclear judgments about *have*. The situation is variable in our own speech. We find the following deletions of *have* quite natural when *have* is followed by *been:*

(45)
a. I been sick lately.
    (= I have been . . .)
b. You sure been doin' good work these days.
    (= You sure have been . . .)

However, we find the following cases unacceptable:

(46)
a. *I gone there many times.
    (= I have gone . . .)
b. *I seen that film.
    (= I have seen . . .)

Some dialects of American English accept sentences such as those in (46). Hence, even though in questions *have* can delete quite generally (for all dialects), in declarative statements the deletion of *have* is more complicated, being variable for speakers in a single dialect and variable across different dialects.

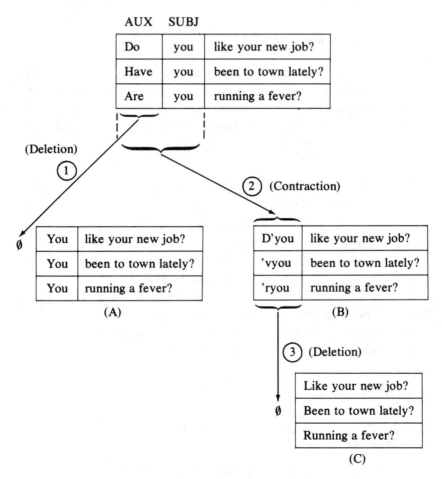

Figure 7.1
Processes involved in the formation of abbreviated questions. The auxiliary can be either deleted (arrow 1), producing forms such as those in (A), or contracted onto the subject (arrow 2), producing forms such as those in (B). Finally, the auxiliary + subject contracted unit can be deleted (arrow 3), producing forms such as those in (C). The symbol Ø stands for deletion.

What about the verb *be?* The answer is that for our own style of speech, deletion of *be* in statements is generally not possible (but see the exercises for some examples of *be*-deletion in statements). We do not have sentences such as *He a doctor, Your car in the garage, You running a fever,* and so on, in contrast with the pattern cited for Black English.

We can summarize the results for our own speech as follows:

(47)

	In questions	In statements
do	can delete	(irrelevant)
have	can delete	can delete, but variable
be	can delete	generally cannot delete

Deletion and Recoverability of Information

We have seen that abbreviated questions are formed by deleting certain elements (auxiliaries and subjects), and we have posited certain rules to characterize these processes. It is important to realize that other apparent abbreviations also occur in the informal style in English. For example, in a situation where we might use the abbreviated question *Want some coffee?,* we might also be able to ask, simply, *Coffee?* To take another example, suppose you see a friend wearing shoes you haven't seen before. You might point to them and ask, "New?" These single-word utterances are quite common in casual styles and are perfectly appropriate and comprehensible. The point is that there is no reason whatsoever to suppose that such single-word utterances are derived from whole sentences from which all the other words have been deleted. It is simply that we can use many kinds of short expressions (including single words), as long as the context (linguistic or nonlinguistic) makes it clear what we are talking about.

In sharp contrast, the deletion of subjects and contractible verbs in abbreviated questions is governed by a *systematic rule,* with strict conditions. Not just any kind of deletion of subject and verb is possible, even if the context would make the abbreviation perfectly clear. For example, recall the impossible form in (28), **Do want some coffee?* There is nothing incomprehensible about this question: its meaning is clear and nothing in the context of conversation would rule it out. However, the expression has violated a systematic grammatical rule: if the subject has been deleted, the auxiliary must also be deleted. An important point about grammatical rules is that expressions that violate those rules are ill-formed and generally cannot be rescued, or made good, by appealing to meaning or to pragmatic context. In other words, such rules do not have to have logical or commonsensical reasons for existing: it is a plain and simple fact that when grammatical rules are violated, an ill-formed expression results. For these various reasons, then, we say that an abbreviated question such as *Want some coffee?* is in fact the result of a systematic deletion rule, whereas expressions such as *Coffee?* are not.

Notice that the interpretation of abbreviated questions is also highly systematic. For example, a question such as *Want some coffee?* is always interpreted as *Do you want some coffee?* and not as, say, *Don't you want some coffee?* A question such as *Drive your car much?* is interpreted as *Do you drive your car much?* and not as, say, *Must you drive your car much?* Morphemes such as negative auxiliaries and modal auxiliaries carry important information that would be unrecoverable—lost—if they were deleted from abbreviated questions: the resultant abbreviated forms would carry no clue about the presence of these items.

It turns out that the formation of abbreviated questions involves reference to a small, highly specific set of elements: the subject *you* and the contractible forms of *do, have,* and *be.* It would appear that native speakers of English, as they learn how to form abbreviated questions, come to learn the specific elements that can be missing from these questions. Given that the set of elements is small, we already know what information to "look for" in interpreting abbreviated questions, and in cases of potential ambiguity the conversational (or linguistic) context can resolve the matter.

Thus, we have seen two ways in which "recoverability" of information can be guaranteed in cases where deletion is involved:

A. By *deletion under identity* (as with Tag-controlled Deletion), so that elements to be deleted must be identical to other elements that will be "left behind" in the sentence. This means that information about the missing elements will still be encoded in remaining elements.
B. By deletion involving a *small,* and highly *specific,* set of elements, so that elements that are deleted could only be drawn from that small set.

Such mechanisms in natural language allow speakers to properly infer "missing" information, and thus to properly interpret expressions in the abbreviated style.

Black English in Relation to Other American Dialects

Returning now to the features of Black English that we discussed earlier, it is important to note that certain features of BE are in fact part of
the general set of features for American dialects in the informal style.
In particular, it appears that deletion of the verb *to be* is a property of
all dialects in informal style. The difference is that BE allows deletion
of *to be* in declarative sentences as well as abbreviated questions,
whereas other dialects limit the deletion of the verb *to be* to abbreviated questions. Hence, BE has generalized a pattern that other
dialects leave incomplete. These results are summarized in table 7.1.

Other features of BE seem distinctive, however (for instance, recall
the use of invariant *be* in examples such as those given in (5)). Hence,
not all the features of BE can be shown to be part of the general features of informal style, and we can speak of BE as a dialect with certain
unique features. Regardless of whether features of BE turn out to be
distinct or part of more general features of American dialects, the point
to be stressed is that this dialect, and other dialects of American English, are in no way defective or illogical.

Table 7.1
Comparison of formal and informal styles with regard to contraction and deletion of the verb *be*. The informal style sentences in the chart are variations of
the formal style sentences at the top. Examples such as *You sick?*, spoken with
the rising intonation pattern characteristic of questions, shows that deletion of
the verb *be* (and other auxiliary verbs) is a feature of all American dialects, not
just Black English. However, in Black English deletion of *be* is allowed in
declarative sentences, a possibility not found in other dialects. Thus, Black
English actually completes a pattern left incomplete in the informal style of
other dialects.

	Questions	Declarative Sentences
Formal Style	Are you sick?	You are sick.
Informal Style:		
All Dialects	'Ryou sick?	You're sick.
Informal Style:		
Black English (Deletion)	You sick?	You sick.
Other Dialects	You sick?	(not possible)

Where Phonology, Morphology, Syntax, and Pragmatic Context Meet

The rules for the abbreviated informal style that we have discussed here not only provide insight into the nature of language variation; they also provide a concrete example of how different subfields of linguistics are integrated and unified at a broader level. The rules for the abbreviated style must refer to *phonological* information: the deletion process is dependent on the phonological process of contraction. *Morphological* information also plays a crucial role, since only certain kinds of morphemes can be (phonologically) contracted and then deleted. For example, only contractible verbs can delete, whereas other types of verbs may not; and both the information about the part of speech and the information about specific words are types of morphological information. The deletion process itself is a *syntactic* process, broadly speaking, since it concerns the way sentences are formed in the abbreviated style. Finally, in order to understand sentences that have undergone deletion, we must be able to infer, or recover, the missing information. The pragmatic context in which the abbreviated sentences are actually used plays a crucial role in this inference process, and hence *pragmatic* information is necessary in our overall account of the abbreviated style.

In other words, linguistic explanations are rarely purely syntactic, or purely morphological, or based on any single component of the grammar. More often than not, to account for linguistic phenomena we require diverse kinds of information from different components of a grammar. Even though various subfields of linguistics are presented in separate chapters of this book—reflecting the need to break down the broad questions about language into more manageable ones—we must not forget that these areas are ultimately integrated when we seek to give complete explanations for linguistic phenomena.

7.3 OTHER LANGUAGE VARIETIES

We have so far examined the phenomenon of language variation in terms of dialects and styles of American English. In this section we will examine certain additional examples of language variation (from other languages, as well as from English) that are of interest to linguists. In our brief survey, we will not attempt to be comprehensive; rather, we will focus on a small number of selected examples in order to give a basic idea of some of the significant ways in which forms of language can vary.

Lingua Francas, Pidgins, and Creoles

For various reasons, groups of people speaking diverse languages are often thrown into social contact. When this occurs, a common language must be found, to serve as a medium of communication. Sometimes, by common agreement, a given language (not necessarily a native language of anyone present) known to all the participants will be used, and a language used in this fashion is known as a *lingua franca*. The term *lingua franca* derives from a trade language of this name used in Mediterranean ports in medieval times, consisting of Italian with elements from French, Spanish, Greek, and Arabic. Until about the eighteenth century, European scholars used Latin as a lingua franca—a common language for treatises on science and other scholarly subjects. In the contemporary world, English serves as a lingua franca in numerous social and political situations where people require a common language. For example, English has become a lingua franca for international scientific journals and international scientific meetings—it is, by common agreement, the language in which scientific results are presented. Thus, at a conference of, say, Spanish, Hungarian, German, Japanese, and Chinese scientists, English is very likely to be the lingua franca used for presentation and discussion of scholarly papers.

Historically, there has been another kind of situation in which people come into contact, sharing no common language whatever, where one group has been politically and economically dominant over the other. This has been typical of colonial situations, in which the dominant group desires trade with, or colonialization of, the subordinate group. In such situations, *pidgin languages* (or *pidgins*) have developed, having the following important properties:

A. The pidgin has no native speakers, but is used as a medium of communication between people who are native speakers of other languages.
B. The pidgin is based on linguistic features of one or more other languages, and is a *simplified* language with *reduced* vocabulary and grammatical structure.

There have been pidgins based on English, French, Dutch, Spanish, Portuguese, Arabic, and Swahili, among others. Pidgin languages are sometimes called *contact languages* (reflecting the fact that such languages often arise when social groups come into contact) or *marginal languages* (reflecting the reduced grammar and vocabulary of the pidgin).

The word *pidgin* itself is said to derive from the English word *business* as pronounced in Chinese Pidgin English. Pidgin languages have limited vocabulary (most often drawn from the "dominant" language), and in terms of grammatical features they typically lack inflectional morphemes (nouns have no endings to indicate plurality, and verbs have no endings to indicate tense or subject agreement). In addition, forms of the verb *to be* are often entirely lacking in pidgins, and prepositions are often limited to a reduced set that serves multiple functions.

In an interesting discussion of Hawaiian Pidgin English, Bickerton (1981) notes that although the vocabulary of the pidgin comes primarily from English, its syntax may vary depending on the original native language of the individual user. For example, Bickerton cites cases such as the following (1981, 11):

(48)

a. da pua pipl   awl poteito it   (pidgin form)
   the poor people only potatoes eat   (English gloss)
   "The poor people ate only potatoes."   (translation)

b. wok had dis   pipl   (pidgin form)
   work hard these people   (English gloss)
   "These people work hard."   (translation)

Example (48a) is from a Japanese speaker using Hawaiian Pidgin; note that the verb (*it* "eat") is final in the sentence, just as it is in Japanese. Example (48b) is from a Filipino user of the pidgin; note that the verb (*wok* "work") is initial, just as it is in Philippine languages of the sort this speaker used natively. Although word order in Hawaiian Pidgin is by no means fixed for any given group of speakers, Bickerton notes that the original language of the user of the pidgin is a significant influence on grammatical features of the pidgin. Thus, a pidgin language is not based exclusively on a single language, such as English. It may well have significant features of more than one language.

Although pidgin languages are said to have limited uses, as well as reduced vocabularies and grammars, they can be used in highly expressive ways. Bickerton (1981, 13) cites a striking example from Hawaiian Pidgin English, uttered by a retired bus driver:

(49)

samtaim gud rod get, samtaim, olsem ben get, enguru ["angle"] get, no? enikain seim. olsem hyuman laif, olsem. gud rodu get, enguru get, mauntin get—no? awl, enikain, stawmu get, nais dei get—olsem. enibadi, mi olsem, smawl taim.

"Sometimes there's a good road, sometimes there's, like, bends, corners, right? Everything's like that. Human life's just like that. There's good roads, there's sharp corners, there's mountains—right? All sorts of things, there's storms, nice days—it's like that for everybody, it was for me, too, when I was young."

Although we have not given a word-by-word English gloss of the pidgin, we suggest using the English translation as a basis for isolating words of the pidgin (the translation should also give some hints about how to pronounce the pidgin words). It is striking to see how a pidgin—a language with reduced vocabulary and structure—can be used as a vehicle of serious thought.

Certain pidgins have become well established, the most notable case being *Tok Pisin,* a pidgin widely used in Papua New Guinea. Tok Pisin has a writing system, a literature (including comic books), and even radio programs.

As we have already noted, pidgins are generally used by native speakers of other languages as a medium of communication. Under certain circumstances, however, children may learn a pidgin as their first language. When a pidgin begins to acquire native speakers who use it as their primary language, it is referred to as a *creole language.* Creole languages are said to develop in situations where the adults in a community speak mutually unintelligible native languages and must rely on a pidgin to communicate with each other. As children acquire the pidgin, they probably use it with playmates and other children in the peer group. Such situations often arose on slave plantations in the Americas, where Africans from linguistically diverse backgrounds could only communicate in a pidgin. Their descendants began to use the pidgin as a first language, and from this sort of development came such creoles as Haitian Creole, certain forms of Jamaican English, and Gullah (or Sea Island Creole, spoken by descendants of African slaves living on the Sea Islands off the coast of Georgia and South Carolina). Some scholars believe that current Black English may have had its origins as a creole language (see Dillard 1972 for discussion), but this is by no means a firmly established conclusion.

When a pidgin becomes creolized—that is, when it comes to be used as a primary language of a group of speakers—it undergoes considerable *expansion* of its vocabulary and grammar and begins to acquire rules comparable in nature and complexity with the rules of any other human natural language. To take one example, Crowley and Rigsby (1979) have described an interesting English-based creole spoken in the northern part of the Cape York Peninsula in Australia. Some typical vocabulary words of this creole are listed in table 7.2. Among the grammatical features of this creole, common to many other creoles as well, Crowley and Rigsby note a system of marking verb tenses:

(50)
a. Im bin ran.
   "He ran."   (*bin* used to mark past)
b. Im ran.
   "He is running."
c. Im go ran.
   "He will run."   (*go* used to mark future)

Within the noun system, there are mechanisms for distinguishing singular from plural:

(51)
a. Wan dog i bin singaut.
   "*A* dog was barking."
b. Plenti dog i bin singaut.
   "*Some* dogs were barking."

Wan (originally from the English word *one*) is generally equivalent to the indefinite article *a* in English; and *plenti* (originally from the English word *plenty*) is generally equivalent to the English *some*. Possession is marked with the preposition *blong* (from the English word *belong*):

(52)
a. stik blong olmaan
   "the old man's stick"
b. dog blong maan
   "the man's dog"

Table 7.2
Some vocabulary words of Cape York Creole. In the Cape York Creole orthography, the vowel *i* is pronounced [ɪ]; *e* is pronounced [ɛ]; *a* is pronounced [ə]; *aa* is pronounced [ɑ]; *o* is pronounced [ɔ], with *oo* having greater length; and *u* is pronounced [ʊ]. (See chapter 4 for explanation of phonetic symbols.) (From Crowley and Rigsby 1979, 206–207.)

English	Cape York Creole
bad	nogud (from "no good")
diarrhea	beliran (from "belly run")
cold (the illness)	koolsik (from "cold sick")
on your back	beliap (from "belly up")
live, stay	stap
a lot	tumach (from "too much")
beach	sanbich (from "sand beach")
return	kambek (from "come back")
other	nadha(wan) (from "another one")
the best	nambawan (from "number one")
the same	seimwei (from "same way")
shout	singaut (from "sing out")
stand	staanap (from "stand up")
sit	sidaun (from "sit down")
run away in anger	stoomwei (from "storm away")
grab, take, get	kech-im (from "catch him")
stingray	tingari
stop a vehicle for a lift	beil-im ap (from "bail it up")
throw	chak-im (from "chuck him")
deaf	talinga nogud (from "telling no good")
blind	ai nogud (from "eye no good")
smoke	faiasmouk (from "fire smoke")
be drunk	spaak (from "spark")
urine, urinate	pipi (from "pee-pee")
lie (tell a lie), pretend	geman (from "gammon")
cheat	blaf (from "bluff")
hide	stoowei (from "stow away")
father's elder brother	big ankl
father's younger brother	litl ankl
maternal grandmother	greni blo madha
Thursday Island	tiai (from "T.I.")
bow of canoe	foored (from "forehead")
Red Island Point	araipi (from "R.I.P.")

Certain morphemes, known as concord particles, precede the verb of the sentence and agree with the subject. For example, when the subject is a third person noun, the concord particle is *i:*

(53)

a. Dog i singaut.

   "The dog is barking."

b. Olmaan i kam ia.

   "The old man is coming here."

Concord particles such as *i* perform the function of "agreement" with the subject, and in this way are very similar to the English third person singular morpheme *-s,* which is suffixed to verbs in the present tense (as in *She/he runs* versus *I, you, we, they run*). The difference is that concord particles precede the verb, whereas *-s* is an inflectional suffix on the verb.

To sum up, then, grammatical features such as those illustrated in (50)–(53) often come into existence as a creole evolves from a pidgin.

This evolutionary process has sometimes been described in terms of a broader "creole continuum" (Bickerton 1975). In his study of Guyanese Creole, Bickerton noted that between the pure creole (the *basilect*) and the local variety of Standard English (the *acrolect*), there are a series of *mesolects:* language varieties that form a continuum beginning at the creole and gradually shifting toward Standard English, each successive mesolect approximating Standard English more closely. Individual speakers can often use a range of mesolects from the continuum and are not necessarily limited to a single mesolect. The evolutionary process of pidginization and creolization is concisely summed up by Naro (1979, 888):

In the broadest possible terms, many specialists accept a cyclic concept of pidgin/creole evolution. The start is some sort of reduction process in both inner and outer form (PIDGINIZATION); this leads to a non-standard linguistic system (a PIDGIN) different from any of the ingredients (SOURCE or SUBSTRATA) existing previously. The middle stage is achieved by re-expansion (CREOLIZATION) to a less-limited linguistic system (a CREOLE). The end of the cycle is a stage in which a standard language exerts influence on the creole (DECREOLIZATION), producing a result that can range up to a regional variety of the standard.

What "guides" the process of creolization? How can children acquiring a pidgin "expand" the pidgin so that it comes to have grammatical structures on a par with those of other human languages? Some scholars have suggested that the increased complexity of the creole reflects an innate "faculty of language"—that is, a biologically innate linguistic capacity (see Bickerton 1981 for discussion of a "bioprogram" along these general lines). Thus, speakers expanding a pidgin language into a creole are in some intuitive sense constrained by their innate linguistic capacity, and for this reason, perhaps, all creoles have very similar structures regardless of where they have developed.

Jargon, Secret Languages, and "Mother-in-Law" Language-Varieties

In virtually every recognized profession, a special vocabulary evolves to meet the special needs of the profession. This special, or technical, vocabulary is known as *jargon*. To take well-known examples, physicians and health professionals use medical jargon; lawyers use legal jargon; and linguists use a technical linguistic jargon with vocabulary items such as *phoneme, morpheme, transformation,* and so on. Jargon is not limited to professional groups, but also exists in what we might term "special-interest" groups. For example, sports enthusiasts, amateur rock-climbers, jazz and rock-and-roll fans, custom car hobbyists, art lovers, and many other groups all make use of technical jargons that are specially suited to the particular interests of the group. The jargon of the criminal underworld is often referred to as *argot*.

Despite its mysterious nature to an "outsider," jargon is not intended to be secret, but, for purely practical reasons, particular jargons are largely incomprehensible to those outside the particular profession or group that uses the jargon. For example, the jargon of the computer industry is largely beyond the grasp of the general public, not because it is intended to be secret, but rather because most people cannot spend the time, money, and effort required to learn computer science. The shared use of jargon is often the basis for a feeling of group solidarity, with the accompanying feeling that those who do not use the jargon are not part of the "elite" (see discussion of "slang" below).

There is, however, another situation similar to that in which jargon is used, where a given variety of language is consciously intended to be *secret,* with cultural rules determining who is to be allowed to use the secret language and who is to be excluded from using it. Secret language-varieties exist in cultures the world over, and anthropologists have reported on a number of these. One of the most interesting, and most unusual, cases is that described by Hale (1971), in a study of the Warlpiri aboriginal culture in Central Australia. All the males of the culture undergo certain initiation rituals when they are young adolescents (roughly around age 13, shortly after circumcision). Part of a boy's initiation into male society is to learn a secret form of language, spoken only in the context of initiation rituals and only by those involved in the ritual. This language-variety is intended to be kept secret from anyone not involved in the rituals—that is, from women and children.

The secret language is described by its users as an "Upside-Down" language—that is, the ordinary language turned "upside-down." The basic rule for the Upside-Down ritual language is this: replace each noun, verb, and pronoun of the ordinary language with an *antonym* (a word "opposite" in meaning). The actual linguistic data are fairly complex (see Hale 1971 for details), but the basic idea can be illustrated by using English sentences. For example, in an English version of the Upside-Down ritual language, a sentence such as *I am short* would be used to mean "You are tall"; *That one is small* would be used to mean "This one is big"; *I am thirsty* would be used to mean "You are quenched"; and the sentence *He is standing in the sky* would be used to mean "I am sitting on the ground."

The idea, then, is that for words of the ordinary language, one must find "opposing" words for the Upside-Down language. For some words, finding an antonym is straightforward, as for polar opposites such as *good/bad, large/small, long/short, strong/weak,* and so on. For other kinds of words, finding an antonym is not so obvious. For example, how does one determine opposing words for any given plant name or animal name? As it turns out, pairs such as *whistling eagle/hawk* or *red-gum tree/ghost gum tree* are regarded as opposing terms, indicating that with plant and animal names members of a class are opposed to members of the same immediate class. Thus, predatory birds will be contrasted with other predatory birds, eucalyptus trees will be contrasted with other types of eucalyptus trees, and so on.

With kinship terms, the oppositions are based on factors such as seniority and generation. For example, the opposite of *older brother* is *younger brother,* and the opposite of *older sister* is *younger sister* (these terms, incidentally, are single morphemes in Warlpiri). There are also oppositions that are culturally based: *fire* and *water* are regarded as opposites. The principles that determine antonymy for the Upside-Down language are quite abstract and reveal a complex and sophisticated semantic classification system (see Hale 1971 for further discussion). Despite the superficial complexity of the Upside-Down language, speakers who have mastered it can apparently use it with great ease and can carry on conversations in rapid speech.

The Upside-Down language is used in the context of a special ritual. But not all ritual language-varieties are secret: many ritual uses of language are open and known to all speakers in a community. For example, in certain parts of the world special forms of language must be ritualistically used in the presence of certain relatives, specifically one's in-laws. Once again, we will draw our examples from the aboriginal cultures of Australia, not because these are the only cultures with ritual uses of language, but because these are among the best-studied and most interesting cases. As Haviland (1979, 163–164) puts it:

Aboriginal Australians are celebrated for their highly complex social organization, in which people reckon their relationships to one another largely in terms of kinship. Amidst a complicated calculus of social identities that divided everyone into kin or spouse's kin, into friends, neighbors and strangers, or into elders and juniors, many groups of these original Australians observed elaborate etiquette, treating some classes of people with extreme respect and caution and enjoying unrestrained and often ribald relations with others. Not surprisingly, this social complexity is mirrored in correspondingly complex speech practices.

As a specific case, Haviland goes on to note (1979, 211):

Typically, throughout Aboriginal Australia a man was obliged to behave with extreme deference to his wife's mother or simply to avoid contact with her altogether.

Indeed, special forms of language, known as *"mother-in-law"* language-varieties, would be used by a man when he spoke in the presence of his mother-in-law.

One such language is described by Dixon (1971), in his study of Dyirbal, an aboriginal language of North Queensland. Speakers of Dyirbal used two distinct forms of the language: one was the "everyday" language, known as Guwal, and the other was the special "mother-in-law" language-variety, known as Dyalŋuy. A man and his wife would use everyday language when they were conversing alone, but a man had to use the mother-in-law variety when he was talking within hearing distance of his mother-in-law. The everyday and mother-in-law language-varieties were alike in grammar and pronunciation, but the vocabularies of the two languages were entirely distinct—they shared no words in common.

To take an example, the everyday language has a number of names for types of grubs: *dʸambun* "long wood grub," *bugulum* "small round bark grub," *mandidʸa* "milky pine grub," *gidʸa* "candlenut tree grub," *gaban* "acacia tree grub." The everyday language has no generic term covering all five types of grub. In the mother-in-law language-variety, however, there is only a single general term *dʸamuy* "grub," corresponding to the five terms of the everyday language. The only way to become more specific in the mother-in-law variety is to use descriptive phrases with the single general term, referring to color, habitat, and behavior of various grubs. As Dixon (1971, 437) notes, the mother-in-law language-variety contains many fewer words than the everyday language (roughly one-fourth as many). The mother-in-law variety is no longer in active use (having been dropped roughly around 1930), but it is still remembered by older speakers.

Along similar lines, Haviland (1979) describes a "brother-in-law" language-variety that is part of an aboriginal Australian language known as Guugu Yimidhirr, spoken in Cooktown in North Queensland. Among the Guugu Yimidhirr speakers, a man used the brother-in-law variety to speak to his brothers-in-law, father-in-law, and certain other kin. He did not use it with his mother-in-law, because he was never supposed to speak to her at all. As with the mother-in-law language-variety of Dyirbal, the brother-in-law variety of Guugu Yimidhirr consists of a special set of vocabulary words, distinct from everyday vocabulary words. The size of the brother-in-law vocabulary is relatively small, and again a single term in the brother-in-law language-variety often corresponds to a number of terms in the everyday language. For example, Haviland (1979, 218) cites a number of motion verbs in the everyday language: *dhadaa* "go," *dhaarmbil* "float, sail, drift," *yaalgal* "limp," *gaynydyarr* "crawl," *biilil* "paddle," and *daabal* "wade." Corresponding to all these terms is a single general term in the brother-in-law variety: *balil* "go." To be more specific when using the brother-in-law variety, speakers used descriptive phrases to add distinguishing details.

As with the mother-in-law variety of Dyirbal, the brother-in-law variety of Guugu Yimidhirr is now out of use, and remains only in the memory of certain older speakers.

Language and Sex Roles: Male and Female Speech

We have already seen one example in which the language of men and women can differ: the mother-in-law language-variety of Dyirbal was used by a man when speaking in hearing distance of his mother-in-law. As Haviland (1979, 211) notes, in Australian aboriginal culture women were apparently not required to use special in-law forms of language, and thus the use of such forms seems limited to men.

The distinction between men's and women's speech shows up in various ways in languages of the world. Perhaps the most salient examples are those in which men and women use distinct vocabulary words. A well-known study of this phenomenon is that of Haas (1944), who examined men's and women's speech in Koasati, a Native American language once spoken in the state of Louisiana. There was a rule-governed difference between the forms of words used by men and women, illustrated by these data:

(54)

Women's Form	Men's Form	
lakáw	lakáws	"he is lifting it"
lakáwwitak	lakáwwitaks	"let me lift it"
mól	móls	"he is peeling it"
í:p	í:ps	"he is eating it"
tačílw	tačílws	"you are singing"

As the data indicate, the basic rule is that the men's forms of the words given above have a final /s/, whereas the women's forms do not. The linguistic data are somewhat more complex, in fact, since there are certain circumstances under which the men's and women's forms are identical. For example, words ending in a nonnasal vowel and words ending in the affricate /č/ have identical forms for men and women (thus, words such as *iskó* "he drank" and *hí:č* "he is looking at it" are used by men and women alike). There are some additional minor complications, (see Haas 1944 for details), but the general idea is that for a large part of the vocabulary, men and women used distinct forms of the words of the language, and the distinction can be described by a rule governing the presence or absence of a final /s/.

Haas (1944) notes that members of both sexes were quite familiar with both forms of speech and could use either form:

Thus if a man is telling a tale he will use women's forms when quoting a female character; similarly, if a woman is telling a tale she will use men's forms when quoting a male character. (1944, 144)

Thus, men and women used distinct vocabulary forms in ordinary speech, but their shared linguistic knowledge allowed them to speak in the manner of the opposite sex.

At the time of Haas's study (1944), only the middle-aged and elderly Koasati women were using the women's forms, while younger women were using the men's forms in their speech.

In the case of Koasati, there is a regular morphological and phonological correspondence between men's forms and women's forms (governed by the rule for final /s/), but in other languages men's and women's vocabulary can be entirely distinct in certain areas. For example, Thai has distinct forms of the first person pronoun for males and females: *phŏm* "I" is used by men, and *díchăn* "I" is used by women. In Japanese, there is a general set of first and second person pronouns, used by both men and women: *watashi* "I" and *anata* "you." However, there is a special set of first and second person pronouns used only by men in casual styles: *boku* "I" and *kimi* "you." In general, it is likely that the differences in men's and women's speech in the world's languages involve pronunciation and vocabulary words, rather than strict distinctions in major grammatical constructions of a language.

Can we detect any differences between men's and women's language in contemporary American English? The question is complicated by various factors, but generally speaking it seems difficult to pick out any single linguistic feature of contemporary American English as being restricted to male speakers or female speakers. The distinctions between male and female speech for contemporary American English seems minimal, and are probably best viewed as matters of degree (for example, female speakers might use certain vocabulary words and grammatical constructions more often than men do, or vice versa), rather than matters of strict linguistic convention, as in the case of Koasati or Japanese. (See Thorne and Henley 1975 for further examples and discussion.)

The topic of male and female speech often raises the question of "sexism" in language. For example, is the English language "sexist" because it has terms such as *policeman, fireman,* and *chairman,* where the morpheme *man* is used in words denoting professions? Is the English language "sexist" because grammar books tell us that *he* is the "correct" pronoun to use in the following type of sentence?

(55)

a. When a student arrives, *he* must register at once.

b. If anyone needs a book, *he* can get one here.

There is no doubt that the English language *reflects* certain sexist attitudes (the male bias in our previous cultural history), but the language
itself is not intrinsically sexist. For example, *policeman* can be replaced
with *police officer,* *fireman* can be replaced with *firefighter,* and *chairman* can be replaced with *chair*. The sentences of (55) are in fact
found primarily in grammar books and hypercorrect forms of English,
whereas the following are the most acceptable in natural speech (see
Bodine 1975 for discussion):

(56)

a. When a student arrives, *they* must register at once.

b. If anyone needs a book, *they* can get one here.

In other words the English language (like all languages) is constantly
changing, and changes in the language reflect (among other things)
changes in social attitudes. As this chapter and the next chapter make
abundantly clear, there is no such thing as a fixed or unvarying language. If English now has features that are perceived as "sexist," it
seems clear that these features can change, and the language will continue to evolve in new ways to reflect the new attitudes and needs of its
speakers.

Slang and Taboo Language

It has been said that slang is something that everyone can recognize but
no one can define. Speakers show enormous creativity in their use of
slang (it is, indeed, one of the most creative areas of language use), and
it is often the source of a good deal of humor. Although a precise
definition of slang seems extremely difficult (if not impossible), there
are, nevertheless, some salient features of this form of language:

A. Slang is part of casual, informal styles of language use. Further, the
term *slang* has traditionally carried a negative connotation: it is often
perceived as a "low" or "vulgar" form of language and is deemed to be
out of place in formal styles of language.

B. Slang, like fashions in clothing or popular music, changes quite
rapidly. Slang terms can enter a language rapidly, then fall out of fash-

ion in a matter of a few years or even months. This rate of turnover is much greater than for other areas of the vocabulary of a language.

C. Specific areas of slang are often associated with a particular social group, and hence one can speak of teenage slang, underworld (criminal) slang, the slang of the drug culture, and so on. In this respect slang is a kind of jargon, and its use serves as a mark of membership and solidarity within a given social group. To use outdated slang, or to use current slang inappropriately, is to be hopelessly "out of fashion" and excluded from an "in-group."

Slang is sometimes referred to as *vernacular* (especially when it is associated with a particular social group), and some forms of slang fall under the term *colloquialism,* referring to informal conversation styles of language. These terms do not carry negative connotations; however, for convenience we will continue to use the popular term *slang*.

Slang vocabulary often consists of regular vocabulary used in specific ways. For example, the words *turkey* and *banana* are regular vocabulary items in English (and can be used in formal styles with their literal meaning), but in slang they can be used as insults (referring to stupid or foolish people). In addition to the use of regular vocabulary words, however, slang also makes use of regular word formation devices (of the sort discussed in chapter 3) to create new words. For example, new slang words can be coined, as was the case for forms such as *diddleysquat* (as in *He doesn't know diddleysquat* meaning "He knows nothing") and *grody* (as in *grody to the max,* a phrase made popular by the 1982 hit song "Valley Girl," with a meaning something like "maximally repulsive"). Blends are common in slang, as with forms such as *absotively* and *posilutely* (both words being blends based on the words *absolutely* and *positively*). Affixes can be used also, as with the slang suffix *-ski* (or *-sky*), found on such words as *brewski* ("beer"), *tootski* ("a puff on a marijuana cigarette"), and *buttinski* ("one who butts in"). It is interesting to note that *brew* and *toot* (with the same meanings as *brewski* and *tootski*) are recent slang words that may have been becoming stale or outmoded; the addition of the slang suffix *-ski* "rejuvenates" the words. The origin of this slang use of *-ski* is unknown, but it may be a linguistic parody on Polish or Russian words that end in a similar phonetic sequence.

An interesting, and quite amusing, phenomenon in American slang is the use of the forms *city* and *ville* to create various compound expressions such as those illustrated in the following examples:

(57)

city

a. We're in *fat city*.

b. What a bummer! It was, like, *depresso city*.

c. You shoulda seen all the cars—I mean, *lowrider city!*

d. She cried all night . . . you know, *heartbreak city*.

(58)

ville

a. This place was out in the boonies; I mean, *hicksville*, you know?

b. What a boring place . . . talk about *nowheresville*.

c. You shoulda seen it: those people were so stoned, it was like *drugsville* all the way.

d. That guy's really strange—totally *weirdsville*.

The interpretation of expressions with *city* and *ville* is clear enough in specific contexts, but not so easy to explicate in general. Such expressions all seem to refer to situations where some maximum concentration or extreme degree is reached: *depresso city* means "extremely depressing"; *lowrider city* means something like "lowriders [modified automobiles] everywhere"; *heartbreak city* means something like "maximum heartbreak"; *nowheresville* means something like "really nowhere"; *weirdsville* means something like "very weird." These are only rough paraphrases, and we leave the finer details to the brave reader. Both *city* and *ville* refer to locations, and it is interesting to note that other words denoting locations can be used in similar ways:

(59)

a. We're on easy *street*.

b. He's in fantasy-*land*.

c. I'm in chocolate *heaven*.

In any event, although this area of slang is as yet relatively unexplored, it seems that slang "place names" are fairly commonly used in current American English.

In addition to individual vocabulary items, and expressions on the pattern of *fat city*, there are also longer expressions (with idiomatic meanings) that are characteristic of slang usage, such as the following examples (all used in describing someone who appears unintelligent, foolish, or crazy):

(60)

a. He's got a few screws loose.
b. She doesn't have all her marbles.
c. He's not playing with a full deck.
d. Her elevator doesn't go all the way to the top.
e. He's running a quart low.

These examples contain no grammatical or morphological features that are uniquely slang-related (such as *-ski* or *ville*). Rather, their use as insults seems to place them most naturally as slang expressions.

Such examples serve to emphasize the fact that a significant portion of slang is concerned with name-calling, insults, and generally what might be termed verbal abuse. Speakers are often quite creative in this area. A recent example brought to the attention of the authors involves a car club in the Phoenix (Arizona) area, whose members are said to use the word *Pluto* (the name of the Walt Disney cartoon dog) as an insult referring to someone who is stupid, clumsy, and foolish. In addition, something that is stupid or foolish can be called *Plutonious,* and a person who does something really stupid or foolish can exclaim, *I really Pluted out!*

Discussion of verbal insults invariably raises the question of obscenity, profanity, "cuss words," and other forms of *taboo language*. Taboo words are those that are to be avoided entirely, or at least avoided in "mixed company" or "polite company." Typical examples involve common swear words such as *Damn!* or *Shit!* Even though these are heard in mixed company (both men and women use the words openly), the words are still felt to be inappropriate in "polite" or formal contexts. Instead, certain *euphemisms*—that is, polite substitutes for taboo words—can be used, including words such as *darn* (a euphemism for *damn*), *heck* (a euphemism for *hell*), *gee* or *jeez* (a euphemism for the exclamation *Jesus!*), and so on. An amusing example is the current expression, *the "F" word,* which is a euphemism for that notorious English word that many newspapers spell as *f---.* Euphemisms are often quite indirect and roundabout ways of communicating, especially about things related to bodily functions: if you ask someone, "Where is the bathroom?", chances are you are not merely interested in the physical location of a certain room, nor do you necessarily want to take a bath. Euphemisms for words pertaining to death and dying are still common, including such expressions as *to pass away* or the idiom *to kick the bucket.*

Taboo language is not limited to obscenity—sacred language can also be taboo, that is, language to be avoided outside the context of sacred ritual. In many societies the language of religious or magical rites can only be used by certain members of the society (priests or shamans).

What counts as taboo language is something determined by culture, and not by anything inherent in the language itself. There is nothing inherent in the sounds of the expression *Shit!* that makes it "obscene"—it is simply that in our cultural history the word has come to be known and used as a "swear word." Foreigners learning English as a second language will at first find nothing unusual about the word, and will not experience the "emotional charge" that often accompanies the use of a taboo word. For Americans learning French, there will be nothing intrinsic in the expression *Merde!* (meaning "Shit!") that will seem obscene.

It is interesting to note, however, that bilingual (or multilingual) speakers will sometimes avoid words in one language that accidentally resemble taboo words in another language. This phenomenon of *interlingual word taboos* (Haas 1957) can be illustrated in various ways. For example, American students learning Brazilian Portuguese are often embarrassed in learning the word *faca,* meaning "knife," since its pronunciation in Portuguese comes uncomfortably close to sounding like the tabooed English word *fuck.* Haas (1957) cites a case in which a Creek Indian informant avoided using certain words of the Creek language when whites were around. One of the words was *fákki,* meaning "soil, earth, clay." A particularly interesting case cited by Haas (1957) involved a group of Thai students in the United States, who noticed that the Thai word *phríg* (the sequence *ph* pronounced as an aspirated /p/, not as /f/), meaning "pepper," resembled the American English slang word *prick.* It was necessary to use this word frequently when dining in public, and not wanting Americans to overhear a word that sounded like a tabooed word of English, the students sought another term in Thai that could replace *phríg.* The substitute that they hit upon was the Thai word *lyŋ,* which, ironically, means "phallus," but secondarily came to mean "pepper" in the context of their dining out. Thus, the students found a term in Thai that did not sound like a tabooed American slang word (thus, they could freely talk about pepper with Americans in hearing distance); yet their substitute term had the same meaning as the tabooed English word they were trying to avoid!

Code-switching and Borrowing

The term *code-switching* refers to a situation in which a speaker uses a *mixture* of distinct language varieties as discourse proceeds. This occurs quite commonly in everyday speech with regard to levels of style, as, for example, when speakers mix formal and informal styles:

(61)
We must not permit the State of California to deplete the water supply of the State of Arizona. Ain't no way we're gonna give em that water.

The speaker (in this case an Arizona politician) is mixing styles for a certain rhetorical effect: the juxtaposition of formal speech-making style with informal colloquial style adds emphasis to the speaker's position on the water issue; and the use of the informal style in this context is intended by the speaker to increase a feeling of solidarity with the audience.

Code-switching can often happen within a single sentence (and at numerous points within a sentence). Among the most interesting cases of this sort of code-switching are those in which a speaker mixes distinct (mutually unintelligible) languages, a situation that often arises in bilingual or multilingual areas such as the American Southwest. In the following example, Spanish is mixed with English (the Spanish forms are italicized, with the English glosses in parentheses):

(62)
It's now *ocho y media* ("eight-thirty") on a Saturday night, and we're gonna hear a new artist *con* ("with") his new group. You're in tune with *la máquina rítmica* ("the rhythm machine").

This example (taken from a radio broadcast on station KXEW, "Radio Fiesta," Tucson, Arizona) is predominantly based on English, with a mixture of Spanish words. The reverse situation is also common, where a predominantly Spanish utterance has a mixture of English, as in the following example (where the English word, *leak,* is italicized):

(63)
Está *leak*iando.
"It is leaking."

This sentence, used by a Spanish-speaking mechanic to a fellow Spanish speaker in reference to a leaking radiator, shows an interesting morphological pattern in which the verb stem is the English verb *leak* to which the Spanish progressive ending *-ando* has been added.

In cases of code-switching, the speaker is in effect using two distinct language-varieties at the same time. We can contrast this situation with that of *borrowing*. When speakers of one language borrow words from another language, the foreign words come to be used as regular vocabulary items and are not code-switching substitutions for regular vocabulary items. For example, when a speaker of English says, "They have a great deal of *savoir-faire*," we might well recognize that the term *savoir-faire* was originally a borrowed word (or *loanword*) from French, but it has come to be used as a vocabulary item in English (in fact, it is listed in Webster's). In contrast, the Spanish phrase *ocho y media* in (62) is not a borrowed vocabulary item that English speakers now use, but rather is a result of code-switching between English and Spanish.

Conclusion

In this chapter we have covered several aspects of variation in language. We would like to conclude with the observation that variation, far from being a "defect" of language, actually reveals its true nature: human language is basically a rule-governed system within which an enormous amount of flexibility or creativity is possible. Variation is linguistically neutral, and there is no evidence that the powers of "nonstandard" dialects *themselves* are weaker than the so-called standard dialect. In other words, variation in language does not entail any inferiority in language. One should not assume that "different is dumber." Instead the problem is with the *attitudes* of the language community toward the *speakers* of these forms. The community as a whole socially ranks the various forms of language, thereby elevating some speakers and stigmatizing others to the point where listeners frequently perform on-the-spot assessments of a speaker's background and abilities based on the selection and pronunciation of a few words! To repeat, then, the fact that dialects occur readily is a natural consequence of humans using language in a creative manner. The force of variation and change in language is such that differentiation within a language will eventually lead to the formation of different languages, a topic to which we turn in the next chapter.

Key Words

dialect
hypercorrection
Standard English
Nonstandard English
formal styles
informal styles
lingua franca
pidgins
creoles
jargon
slang
taboo language
code-switching

Exercises

1. If you are acquainted with a regional, social, or ethnic dialect, list as many features as you can that distinguish this dialect from the so-called standard language. What are some significant differences in pronunciation, vocabulary words, and syntax?

2. The following types of sentences (originally made famous by *Mad Magazine*) are frequently used in the informal style of English:

a. What, me worry?
b. What, John get a job? (Fat chance!)
c. My boss give me a raise? (Are you joking?)
d. Him wear a tuxedo? (He doesn't even own a clean shirt!)

How would you express each of these sentences in formal English? Do these informal sentences express any feeling or idea that is not expressed in the formal style?

3. Several acquaintances who were raised in Brooklyn inform us that the following sentences are good:

a. Let's you and him fight—how about it?
b. Let's you guys shut up, all right?

How does this informal use of *let's* differ from its use in formal English?

4. In the informal style it is quite common to hear sentences such as the following:

a. There's three cars in the garage.
b. There's a lot of problems with this car.
c. There's many ways to do this.

How would these sentences be expressed in formal English, and how do the formal and informal styles differ in the use of *there's?*

5. Sports announcers on TV and radio use a style of English that is both color-ful and unique. Listen to a variety of sports broadcasts, paying careful attention to the language, and try to characterize as precisely as you can how this lan-guage differs from the formal style or standard language. To get started, you might consider the following sample of sportscaster language: "Smith on third. Jones at bat. Mursky winding up for the pitch." (This language should be rem-iniscent of the informal style discussed in this chapter.) Don't forget to include differences (if any) in pronunciation and vocabulary words, as well as syntax.

6. In this chapter we considered abbreviated questions of one type, namely, questions without question words (or *wh-words*) such as *who, what, where,* etc. The following sets of sentences illustrate the differences between *wh*-questions and the abbreviated questions we examined:

(i)
a.   Where have you been lately?
b.   Where've you been lately?
c.   *Where've been lately?
d.   Where ya been lately?
e.   *Where been lately?

(ii)
a.   Who are you taking to the prom?
b.   Who're you taking to the prom?
c.   *Who're taking to the prom?
d.   Who ya takin' to the prom?
e.   *Who takin' to the prom?

(iii)
a.   What do you want to do?
b.   Whattaya wanna do?
c.   *Whatta wanna do?
d.   Whatcha wanna do?
e.   *What want to do?

How do these abbreviated *wh*-questions differ from the abbreviated questions studied in the chapter? That is, what are the differences in the rules for forming the two types of abbreviated questions? In answering, pay careful attention to (a) the fact that certain of the examples here are ungrammatical and (b) the way contraction works in these cases.

7. It is not quite true to say that *be* can never be deleted in declarative state-ments in the informal speech style of the authors, for the following sentences are good:

a. Odd that Mary never showed up.
b. Good thing you fixed your engine.
c. Too bad (that) she had to leave town so soon.
d. Amazing that he didn't spot that error.

What has been deleted from these sentences? Is this deletion general?

8. Questions typically come from a first person speaker and are addressed to a second person hearer. Can you relate this *use* of questions to the fact that *you* is deleted from abbreviated questions? Can *any* subject be deleted from abbreviated questions as long as use and context make the deletion recoverable?

Bibliography

Bailey, R. W., and J. L. Robinson, eds. (1973). *Varieties of Present-Day English,* Macmillan, New York.

Bickerton, D. (1975). *The Dynamics of a Creole System,* Cambridge University Press, Cambridge.

Bickerton, D. (1981). *Roots of Language,* Karoma Publishers, Ann Arbor, Mich.

Bodine, A. (1975). "Androcentrism in prescriptive grammar: Singular 'they', sex-indefinite 'he', and 'he' or 'she'," *Language in Society* 4, 129–146.

Burling, R. (1973). *English in Black and White,* Holt, Rinehart and Winston, New York.

Crowley, T., and B. Rigsby (1979). "Cape York Creole," in T. Shopen, ed., *Languages and Their Status,* Winthrop Publishers, Cambridge, Mass.

Dillard, J. L. (1972). *Black English: Its History and Usage in the United States,* Random House, New York.

Dixon, R. M. W. (1971). "A method of semantic description," in D. D. Steinberg and L. A. Jakobovits, eds. (1971).

Fasold, R. W. (1972). *Tense Marking in Black English,* Urban Language Series, Center for Applied Linguistics, Arlington, Va.

Folb, E. A. (1980). *Runnin' Down Some Lines: The Language and Culture of Black Teenagers,* Harvard University Press, Cambridge, Mass.

Giglioli, P. O., ed. (1972). *Language and Social Context,* Penguin Books, Baltimore, Md.

Glissmeyer, G. (1973). "Some characteristics of English in Hawaii," in R. W. Bailey and J. L. Robinson, eds. (1973).

Haas, M. R. (1944). "Men's and women's speech in Koasati," *Language* 20, 142–149. Reprinted in D. H. Hymes, ed. (1964).

Haas, M. R. (1957). "Interlingual word taboos," *American Anthropologist* 53, 338–341. Reprinted in D. H. Hymes, ed. (1964).

Hale, K. (1971). "A note on a Warlpiri tradition of antonymy," in D. D. Steinberg and L. A. Jakobovits, eds. (1971).

Haviland, J. B. (1979). "How to talk to your brother-in-law in Guugu Yimidhirr," in T. Shopen, ed., *Languages and Their Status,* Winthrop Publishers, Cambridge, Mass.

Hudson, R. A. (1980). *Sociolinguistics,* Cambridge University Press, Cambridge.

Hymes, D. H., ed. (1964). *Language in Culture and Society,* Harper and Row, New York.

Hymes, D. H., ed. (1971). *Pidginization and Creolization of Language,* Cambridge University Press, Cambridge.

Labov, W. (1966). *The Social Stratification of English in New York City,* Center for Applied Linguistics, Washington, D.C.

Labov, W. (1969a). "Contraction, deletion, and inherent variability of the English copula," *Language* 45, 715–762.

Labov, W. (1969b). "The logic of nonstandard English," in *Report of the Twentieth Annual Round Table Meeting on Linguistics and Language,* Georgetown University Press, Washington, D.C. Reprinted in R. W. Bailey and J. L. Robinson, eds. (1973) and P. O. Giglioli, ed. (1972).

Labov, W. (1972). "The social stratification of (r) in New York City department stores," in *Sociolinguistic Patterns,* University of Pennsylvania Press, Philadelphia.

Labov, W. (1973). "Some features of the English of Black Americans," in R. W. Bailey and J. L. Robinson, eds. (1973).

Lakoff, R. (1973). "Language and woman's place," *Language in Society* 2, 45–79.

Naro, A. (1979). Review of Valdman (1977), *Language* 55, 886–893.

Pride, J. B., and J. Holmes, eds. (1972). *Sociolinguistics,* Penguin Books, Middlesex, England.

Smitherman, G. (1977). *Talkin and Testifyin, The Language of Black America,* Houghton Mifflin, Boston, Mass. (Chapter 5.)

Steinberg, D. D., and L. A. Jakobovits, eds. (1971). *Semantics: An Interdisciplinary Reader in Philosophy, Linguistics, and Psychology,* Cambridge University Press, Cambridge.

Thorne, B., and N. Henley, eds. (1975). *Language and Sex: Difference and Dominance,* Newbury House, Rowley, Mass.

Valdman, A., ed. (1977). *Pidgin and Creole Linguistics,* Indiana University Press, Bloomington.

Williams, F., ed. (1970). *Language and Poverty,* Markham, Chicago.

Chapter Eight
LANGUAGE CHANGE

8.1 SOME BACKGROUND CONCEPTS

In the last chapter we observed that no language is fixed or unvarying: all languages show considerable linguistic variation at any given point in time. Just as all languages show such internal variation, so too all languages undergo constant change over time. Contemporary speakers of English find the language of Shakespeare's plays more or less comprehensible, but they can detect numerous differences between the language of *Hamlet* and the current English language. When Shakespeare used the expression "pigeon-livered" in *Hamlet,* what might he have meant? Modern readers will immediately detect here a phrase no longer in use (although we have a contemporary counterpart in "chicken-livered"). In this and countless other ways English has undergone many changes over the centuries (in section 8.3 we will discuss some of these), and indeed all human languages change relentlessly and unavoidably.

Historical linguistics is the subfield of linguistics that studies language change. Sometimes the term *diachronic linguistics* is used instead of historical linguistics, as a way of referring to the study of a language (or languages) at various points in time and at various historical stages. The term *diachronic* is often used in contrast to the term *synchronic,* which refers to the study of a language (or languages) at a single point in time, without reference to earlier (or later) stages. For example, our study of syntax in chapter 5 is a synchronic study of current American English, but section 8.3 is a brief diachronic study of syntax, that is, a study of the historical development of certain sentence constructions in English.

In considering the history and development of particular languages, one of the most fascinating questions—and indeed, a question that has intrigued scholars throughout the ages—concerns the origin and evolution of language in the human species in general. When in the history of our species did language originate? What was the nature of the first language(s)? As with many questions in linguistics, the most fascinating ones are often the very ones we cannot answer in any definitive way. Let us see why questions concerning the origin of language have so long resisted efforts to find clear answers.

The Origin and Evolution of Human Language

Considerable evidence suggests that the capacity for language is a species-specific, biologically innate trait of human beings (see chapter 11 for a brief discussion of this evidence). The question then naturally arises how this capacity may have originated and evolved in the species. Unfortunately, we have little, if any, solid evidence to indicate when language might have originated, why it might have developed in our particular species, and how it evolved from its early stages.

Over the centuries there has been endless speculation on these questions, and numerous guesses have been advanced. According to one type of speculation, humans began to mimic the sounds of nature and the cries of animals (sometimes dubbed the *"bow-wow"* theory). The existence of onomatopoeic words (recall section 3.1 of chapter 3) such as *bow-wow, meow, crash, boom,* and so forth, might be taken as evidence of such mimicking. But onomatopoeic words invariably form a very small portion of the words of any given language; and even if "imitation of nature" accounts for some words, we still have no explanation of how the rest of human language evolved.

According to another speculation, vocal language gradually evolved from spontaneous cries of pain, pleasure, or other emotions. Once again, absolutely no evidence has been advanced to show how a full-blown language—complete with phonology, morphology, and syntax, and so on—could evolve from simple emotional cries. To this day all humans use response cries of pain, pleasure, and other emotions; what is left unexplained is why they have language as well.

It has been suggested that a *gestural language*—that is, a system of hand gestures and signals—may have preceded vocal language (see Hewes 1976). This might well be true, but again we are faced with the problem of understanding how gestural language came to be supplanted by vocal language as well as when and why this might have happened.

In addition, it is sometimes speculated that human language gradually evolved from the need for humans to communicate with each other in coordinating certain group tasks. The idea here is that people working in groups can cooperate more efficiently if they can use a vocal language to communicate. But such "functional" theories of the origin of language seem quite dubious. For one thing it has never been shown that the carrying out of group tasks requires a *vocal* language. Why couldn't a sign language or gestural language suffice as a communication system in the context of groups at work? Further, it has never been shown that group tasks require a communication system anywhere near as complicated as human language. For example, wolf packs are extremely efficient hunting groups and yet have no complex language; further, many farming tasks carried out by humans require no language and are learned by imitation. Generally speaking, "functional" theories of the origin of language all suffer from a similar defect: human language is vastly more expressive and more powerful than would be dictated by any given functional task involving groups at work. Of course, once human language did evolve, it came to be exploited fully for all sorts of social functions; but the needs involved in such functions cannot be identified as the cause of language evolution.

At the present time the most reasonable suggestion about the origin and evolution of human language is that it was intimately linked with the evolution of the human brain. We know, for example, that over roughly the last 5 million years there has been a striking increase in brain size, ranging from about 400 cc. in our distant hominid ancestors to about 1,400 cc. in modern *Homo sapiens* (see Miller 1981 for a useful summary). The mere increase in brain size would not necessarily have led to superior intelligence and the evolution of language—since dolphins, for example, have brains of a size comparable to that of humans, yet (as we saw in chapter 2) they have only a rudimentary communication system. Furthermore, even a mere increase in general intelligence might not necessarily have led to the evolution of language. Dolphins and primates, for example, are considered to be more intelligent than birds, yet their communication systems seem to be no more sophisticated or complex than that of birds. Indeed, as Lenneberg (1964) has pointed out, mentally retarded humans with IQ levels significantly below normal can nevertheless grasp the rudiments of language. Obviously, brain size is only one factor that may have played a role in the evolution of language; changes in the organization and complexity of the brain must also be supposed to have played a crucial role. At what point in time language may have originated is far from clear: guesses range from 50,000 to 100,000 years ago and even earlier, but such figures are speculative at best. In any event it seems likely that language is a relatively recent development in the human species. Given the complexity and uniqueness of many aspects of the structure of language (seen in the previous chapters), one quite plausible hypothesis is that human language came into being more or less full blown, as the result of a genetic mutation.

The crucial problem in determining the answer to questions concerning the origin and evolution of human language is that we have so little solid evidence on which to base any claims. Although attempts have been made to reconstruct the vocal tract of Neanderthal man (see Lieberman 1975 for discussion) and to show (indirectly) that Neanderthal man had only a limited capacity for speech, these efforts have been somewhat controversial, and we still have no clear evidence whether human language had earlier, more "primitive" stages, and if so, what these "primitive" stages might have been like. In the biological world it is frequently possible to find earlier forms of life existing simultaneously with more evolved forms. For example, the coelacanth was a biologically primitive fish known only in fossil form until a living species was discovered and identified in 1938. Might it be possible to discover a language being spoken today that represents an earlier form of human language?

Small, previously unknown groups of people are indeed discovered from time to time in jungle areas in New Guinea and the Philippines. These groups have apparently been isolated from other humans for long periods of time and have no knowledge of the modern world. Their existence, then, often gives rise to speculation that they may speak a more primitive language that could be an earlier form of modern human languages. But despite the fact that the technology of such people is often at a Stone Age level, their languages appear to be as developed and as complex as any other human language. So far, then, no natural language (with the possible exception of the pidgin languages discussed in chapter 7) has been shown to be more primitive than any other language in terms of grammatical organization, expressiveness, and so forth.

Hence, it may seem that we are limited to studying language on the basis of written records that date back only approximately 6,000 years, in order to investigate the earliest known forms of language. It turns out, however, that because languages change over time, some languages that are now different can be shown to have come from the earlier "parent" language. Not only is it possible to discover the historical developments that a language has undergone, but it is even possible to learn something about the grammatical properties of an original parent language that antedates written records. We now turn to this topic.

8.2 THE RECONSTRUCTION OF INDO-EUROPEAN, THE NATURE OF LANGUAGE CHANGE, AND LANGUAGE FAMILIES OF THE WORLD

Similarities among Languages

The discovery in the early nineteenth century that modern European languages, such as English, German, French, and so forth, were historically related to the languages of antiquity, such as Latin, Greek, and Sanskrit (an ancient language of India), led to a revolution in our understanding of the nature and history of language. Actually, linguistic similarities among different languages had not gone entirely unnoticed in Europe earlier. Italian and Sanskrit had been compared by Filippo Sassetti as early as the sixteenth century, and the philosopher Leibnitz had later pointed out that Persian and German were grammatically similar. A true understanding of the nature of the relationships in question did not come, however, until the early part of the nineteenth century. The person who is credited with the first and clearest statement concerning the relationships among the classical and other ancient languages was Sir William Jones, who wrote in 1786 that

The Sanskrit language, whatever be its antiquity, is of a wonderful structure; more perfect than the Greek, more copious than the Latin . . . yet bearing to both of them a stronger affinity, both in the roots of verbs and in the forms of grammar, than could possibly have been produced by accident; so strong indeed, that no philologer could examine them all three, without believing them to have sprung from some common source, which, perhaps, no longer exists. There is a similar reason, though not quite so forcible, for supposing that both the Gothic and the Celtic . . . had the same origin with the Sanskrit; and the Old Persian might be added to the same family. . . . (Lehmann 1967, 15)

This language, "which no longer exists," is called *Proto-Indo-European* in the English-speaking world, a term reflecting the (earlier)

geographical distribution of the speakers of this language family from India to Europe. Note that if it is possible to learn about an earlier form of a language for which no written records exist, then we may also be able to learn about the history of the world's languages and perhaps even something about the geographical origin of language itself. How can we learn about this language that no longer exists and for which no written records are available? In order to see how linguists establish historical relationships among languages and learn about earlier forms of language, consider first the words in (1):

(1)

Language A	Language B	Language C
uno	ɫááʔii	eka
dos	naaki	dva
tres	tááʔ	tri
cuatro	díɲʔ	catur
cinco	ashdlaʔ	pañca
seis	hastą́ą́	ṣaṣ
siete	tsostsʔid	sapta
ocho	tseebíí	aṣṭa
nueve	náhástʔéí	nava
diez	neeznáá	daśa

You may know (or be able to guess) that these are the words for the numerals one through ten in each of the three languages. You will also notice that languages A and C have some phonological similarities: six out of ten words begin with the same (or a similar) consonant; the words for *one* and *eight* are the only ones that begin with vowels; nine of the words have the same number of syllables; and so forth. Thus, we have some initial evidence that languages A and C (Spanish and Sanskrit, respectively) might be related in some way; but neither of these two seems to be related to language B (Navajo). This brief exercise raises the central questions to be dealt with in this section: (1) How do we establish with a reasonable degree of certainty that two or more languages are related? (2) If languages are related but no longer the same in grammar and vocabulary, how and why did they change? and (3) Does language change involve an improvement or a decay in expressive ability? In attempting to answer these questions, we will be examining some of the most important aspects of *historical* or *comparative linguistics*.

Based on the similarities between Spanish and Sanskrit in the words
for *one* through *ten,* we could hypothesize that Spanish and Sanskrit
are related languages (that they both derive from a common ancestor
language), in spite of the fact that 2,500 years separate the written records of ancient Sanskrit and Modern Spanish. However, in order to
establish a *genetic relationship* between or among languages—that is,
in order to prove that languages are descended from a common ancestor—more is needed than the discovery of similarities in sound. In
fact, we can contrast the relationship obtaining between Sanskrit and
Spanish with two other types of relationships that linguists are bound to
encounter. Consider the words in (2) and (3).

(2)

Language A	Language B
cuprum	copper
planta	plant
cuppa	cup
discus	dish
coquīna	kitchen
cāseus	cheese

(3)

Language A	Language B	Meaning
bhanem	ban	"woman"
alnoba	allaban	"person, immigrant," respectively
lhab	lion-obhair	"netting"
odana	dun	"town"
haʔlwiwi	na h-uile	"everywhere"
kladen	claden	"frost, snowflake"
pados	bata	"boat"
monaden	monadh	"mountain"
aden	ard	"height"
cuiche	cuithe	"gorge"

The languages in (2) are Latin (language A) and, of course, Modern
English (language B). The meanings of the Latin words are the same as
those of their English counterparts, although the pairs of words differ
somewhat in pronunciation.

The languages in (3) are Scots Gaelic (language B) and Northeastern
Algonquian (language A). Scots Gaelic is a Celtic language of Western
Europe, whereas Algonquian is a Native American language of the

northeastern United States. Based on similarities such as those in (3), it has been proposed by Fell (1977) that the words of the Algonquian language are related to the corresponding words of Scots Gaelic, with the further conclusion that there were European (Celtic) settlements in North America more than 2,000 years ago. Below we will take a closer look at this conclusion.

Examples (1), (2), and (3) illustrate three situations in which languages can share a set of words that are individually similar both in sound and in meaning. These similarities can be the result of a true historical relationship, borrowing, or chance overlap in sound and meaning. We will discuss these three possibilities in reverse order.

Chance Overlap in Sound and Meaning

The fact that languages often have similarities in sound structure and have words for common objects yields a significant probability that there will be overlaps in sound-meaning correspondences between them. For example, all languages have the /a/ vowel, and most have /i/ and/or /u/ vowels; most languages have *t, k,* and *p* and the nasal consonants *m* and *n.* Moreover, most languages have words referring to water, the numbers, male and female parents, and so forth. In the Lummi language, a Native American language spoken in northwestern Washington State, the word for "father" is /mæn/. In Navajo the word for "mother" is /-má/, as in /shi-má/ "my mother." Thus, there are a few words in both Navajo and Lummi that are phonetically and semantically similar to words in English, but this is insufficient evidence to demonstrate that either Navajo or Lummi is genetically related to English.

Likewise, there is insufficient linguistic evidence that the languages in (3), Scots Gaelic and Algonquian, are genetically related. The meanings of the phonologically similar words shared by Scots Gaelic and Algonquian are typical of the type of vocabulary that would suggest a genetic relationship, in that the words generally refer to common objects. The number of words, however, is very small; more important, there are no systematic sound correspondences of the sort that we will discuss. We must conclude, therefore, that the similarities between Scots Gaelic and Algonquian are due to an accidental overlap in the sound-meaning associations of some of their words. Accidental overlaps must be ruled out when establishing historical relatedness among languages.

Borrowing

Many terms relating to Western technology and culture have become part of the vocabulary of the world's languages, and English speakers in turn have borrowed many words from other languages. The vocabularies of Modern Japanese and English, for example, share a significant number of common words, such as *hibachi, karate, sushi, beer,* and *computer.* This common and shared vocabulary might lead a naive linguist to hypothesize that English and Japanese are somehow related—perhaps they are descended from a common language? (It may be that Japanese and English are in fact descended from a common language, but this is unprovable given our present state of knowledge.) In establishing *genetic relationships* among languages, then, one must exclude words that may have been borrowed and are therefore not part of a common inheritance. Borrowed words tend to be those dealing with categories such as religion, culture, technology, government, and cuisine. Less likely to be borrowed are words for common objects and activities, numerals, and so forth. The Latin words in (2) were borrowed by English speakers, and although this vocabulary seems to refer to rather common objects, it does reflect the cultural influence of the Roman civilization in England.

Having introduced the term *genetic relationship* to refer to relatedness among languages, we will make explicit what this term means. We will show that for some languages with words that are similar in their sound-meaning association a valid historical connection between the languages can be established.

Establishing Historical Relationships

The study of language history and the relationships among languages is one of the tasks of *comparative linguistics.* The traditional procedure that linguists use in determining a true historical (genetic) relationship is called the *comparative method.* Comparative method is not really a term referring to a fixed procedure that is to be followed rigidly. Rather, it is a general term covering the analytical techniques linguists employ in reconstructing the history of languages that are hypothesized to be members of the same language family. We will demonstrate some of the aspects of the comparative method by considering a set of words that are phonetically and semantically similar, the similarities suggesting a historical relationship:

(4)

English	Latin	Greek	Sanskrit
ten	decem	deka	daśa
two	duo	duo	dva
heart	cordia	kardía	hṛd-

Limiting ourselves to the word-initial and -final *t* of English, we note that this sound corresponds to the *d*'s of the other languages. The term *correspond* used here means that a particular sound occurring in some position in words of one language appears in the same relative position in semantically similar words of the other languages.

In the case of the forms in (4), we can establish the phonological correspondence set given in (5):

(5)

English	Latin	Greek	Sanskrit
t	d	d	d

Whenever extensive correspondence sets of sounds such as the one in (5)—which could be greatly expanded, if space permitted—can be established among groups of words in different languages, a historical phonological relationship among these languages can be inferred because of the combination of two principles:

(6)

a. Phonological changes are generally regular; that is, within the limits of certain conditions, the changes are exceptionless.

b. The relationship between sound and meaning in a word is arbitrary.

Principle (6a) expresses the fact that speakers of a language can modify their pronunciation in a systematic way. Linguists describe this type of change as the result of the *addition of a phonological rule to a speaker's grammar*. In the case of the examples in (4), the *t*'s in English that correspond to the *d*'s in other languages are the result of some speakers' adding a rule that caused all the original *d*'s to change into *t*'s in their grammars. That the regular correspondence occurs in words that are the same or similar in meaning is crucial also. When different languages have large numbers of phonologically similar words bearing the same or similar meanings, then it is likely that such arbitrary sound-meaning relationships (principle (6b)) were inherited by each of them from an historically earlier language, because such far-reaching similarities could hardly be due to chance.

Linguists surmise, then, that Latin, Greek, and Sanskrit have preserved an original *d* articulation, whereas at some point in the history of
English, certain speakers changed the pronunciation of their *d*'s to *t*'s.
English is not the only language that appears to have undergone the
change from *d* to *t*, however. German, Dutch, and the Scandinavian
languages also participated in this change. These languages, including
English, are all members of what is called the *Germanic language family,* and the change of *d* to *t* most likely occurred within a single Germanic linguistic community before the community separated into
different groups. The Germanic languages, then, share several innova-
tions, such as the change of *d* to *t,* that differentiate this group from the
other Indo-European languages.

Grimm's Law
The set of correspondences given in (4) is in fact only a part of a larger
set of correspondences that can be established between English on the
one hand and Latin, Greek, and Sanskrit on the other hand. The underlined portions of the words in (7) indicate the critical consonants
involved in the correspondences.

(7)

Germanic (English)	Other Languages
a. sli**pp**ery	lū**b**ricus (Latin) "slippery"
ten	**d**ecem (Latin) "ten"
yo**k**e	iu**g**um (Latin) "yoke"
b. **f**ather	**p**ater (Latin) "father"
three	**t**rēs (Latin) "three"
horn	**c**ornū (Latin) "horn"
c. **b**rother	**bh**rátar (Sanskrit) "brother"
bin**d**	ban**dh** (Sanskrit) "bind"
guest	**h**ostis (Latin) "enemy"

As noted earlier, the consonants of Latin and Sanskrit are for the
most part closer to what is reconstructed as the original Indo-European
pronunciation. It is hypothesized that Sanskrit and Latin preserve the
original *d, b,* and *g* pronunciation of Proto-Indo-European and that
these sounds all became voiceless in Germanic. But not all consonants
are preserved in their original form in Sanskrit and Latin, or in any
member of the Indo-European language family for that matter. For example, the *g* in English *guest* corresponds to the *h* in Latin *hostis*.
Many linguists have hypothesized that the original Proto-Indo-Euro-

pean sound was close to a voiced aspirated velar stop, symbolized *gh.
(An asterisk used with transcriptions indicates here that they are hypothetical forms for which no written records are available.) Thus, the
original Proto-Indo-European *gh became g in Germanic and h in the
language that was ultimately to become Latin. We display in (8) the set
of changes that have been hypothesized based on the correspondences
represented in (7):

(8)
Grimm's Law
a. b → p
   d → t
   g → k
b. p → f
   t → θ
   k → x(> h)
c. bh → b
   dh → d
   gh → g

The changes in (8) are known collectively as *Grimm's Law,* because
their systematic law-like character was first stressed by Jacob Grimm
(one of the Brothers Grimm, best known in this country for their collection of German fairy tales). There is some controversy over whether
Grimm should be credited for discovering this set of "laws," since the
correspondences had already been published by a Dane, Erasmus
Rask. Because of his emphasis on their law-like properties, however,
Grimm is usually given credit for the discovery.

The changes that occurred were indeed law-like, in that all words
containing the relevant phonemes underwent the rules, and the changes
that occurred applied to natural classes of phonemes, in the sense
defined in chapter 4. For example, the class of phonemes that underwent the changes in (8b) is the class of voiceless stops. Thus, after the
Germanic languages split off from the other languages, they were subject to a rule that changed all voiceless stops into fricatives (with some
minor restrictions that are not important here). This rule would presumably have had the following form:

(9)
$$\begin{bmatrix} +\text{consonant} \\ -\text{voice} \end{bmatrix} \rightarrow [+\text{continuant}]$$

After rule (9) had applied, words that formerly had p, t, and k then had j, θ, and h, respectively. For Germanic children acquiring their language after rule (9) had changed the consonants, there would be no evidence for the earlier p's, t's, and k's, and they would simply learn the new consonants. Thus, without evidence from other languages, it would be impossible to tell that Germanic f, θ, and $x(> h)$ had earlier been p, t, and k. To summarize the thrust of this example, then, we can rephrase the principles in (6) as (10) and state the conditions under which languages can be said to be historically related on the basis of their sound systems.

(10)
A group of languages is historically (or genetically) related if large groups of words can be found in each of the languages such that:
a. they are made up of phonemes that can be shown to derive from the (hypothesized) phonemes of the parent language by the result of regular phonological rules that have applied at some point in the history of each of the languages, and
b. the words that are hypothesized to come from a common parent word are the same or are related in meaning.

The Indo-European Language Family
The languages of the Indo-European family can be shown to be related because the conditions expressed in (10) are satisfied in sets of shared words. To illustrate how the principles are satisfied, we can begin by considering the words and stems in (11).

(11)
Words and stems for "brother" and "bear" (to carry)

English	Sanskrit	Greek	Latin
brother	bhrátar	phrātēr	frāter
bear	bhar-	pher-	fer-

Based on forms such as those given in (11), among others, scholars have *reconstructed* the original Proto-Indo-European forms for "brother" and "bear" to be *bhráter-* and *bher-*, respectively. Reconstructed forms such as *bhráter* are frequently referred to as *proto-forms*. Likewise, a reconstructed "parent" language is often referred to as a *proto-language*. A reconstructed form is the most plausible hypothetical source from which all the forms in all the descendent (daughter) languages can be derived. Thus, starting from reconstructed forms such as *bhráter and *bher, each of the daughter languages has undergone its own separate and regular changes from Proto-Indo-European. Some of these changes are given in figure 8.1. It is important to stress that, when certain conditions are met, *all* Proto-Indo-European *bh*'s change to *ph* in Greek and *b* in Germanic. Thus, it is the consistency (regularity) of the correspondences among the daughter languages of the Indo-European language family (due to rule-governed phonological change) that is decisive in establishing their historical relatedness. Note that none of the descendent languages preserves all of the phonetic features of the hypothesized (parent) proto-language for the words under consideration. Sanskrit turns out to be more conservative in terms of the consonants, whereas the other three languages have undergone changes in the consonants, but have maintained the original *e* vowel.

The considerations that lead to positing original *e* instead of *a* in forms such as *bher* go beyond the scope of this introductory text, but the list of references at the end of this chapter includes several books on historical linguistics in which such issues are discussed.

Although language reconstruction and the establishment of language relatedness involve many additional complications beyond those discussed here, much has been learned about the Proto-Indo-European language family in the nearly two centuries of research that has been

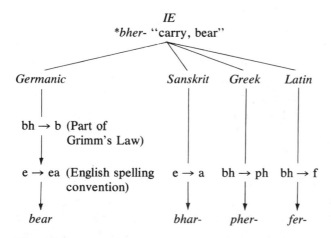

Figure 8.1
The descendent forms from a reconstructed (hypothesized) Indo-European *bher-* "carry, bear." Each of the "daughter" languages has changed from the "parent" form in a different way, and thus their common ancestry has been obscured.

devoted to them. Most of the languages in Europe, for example, have been shown to be related to each other historically. We have displayed many of these languages in figure 8.2. Languages on the same "branch" of the tree in the figure share certain changes not shared by languages on the other branches of the tree. For example, all the Indic languages underwent the change of short *e* and *o* to *a*, and all the Germanic languages shared the Grimm's Law changes in their consonants. Hence, figure 8.2 reflects a classification system similar to ones used by biologists for plants and animals.

Using techniques of reconstruction such as those discussed here, linguists have worked out a fair idea of the original Proto-Indo-European language. Many questions remain, however, concerning the original homeland of the Proto-Indo-European speakers and the time at which Proto-Indo-European began to split up. The Indo-European community of speakers had split into very different languages more than 4,500 years ago, so that the original language could not have been a single language fewer than 5,000 to 6,000 years ago. To answer the question of whether this earlier language was more primitive than its descendents, we can state confidently that there is no evidence that Indo-European was in any sense more primitive than the languages that descended from it. Ironically, when the details of Proto-Indo-European were first being worked out, it was commonly believed that the daughter languages were "decayed" versions of the pristine original language. (The quotation from Sir William Jones at the beginning of this section shows traces of this prejudice.) However, it simply does not appear that we can gain any important information about the origin of language from the analytical techniques of reconstructing earlier languages. All reconstructed languages appear to be full-fledged human languages, and there is no evidence that languages have become more expressive or have "improved" in some sense during the past ten thousand years, the most remote time to which we can reconstruct language.

Languages of the World

Although we cannot answer the question of the ultimate origin of human language through analytical techniques such as the comparative method, we can learn about the more recent origins of the world's languages in that we can show that many languages should be grouped together as members of a larger family. As noted earlier, most of the languages of Europe are members of the Indo-European language family. Among those that are not members are Finnish, Estonian, and

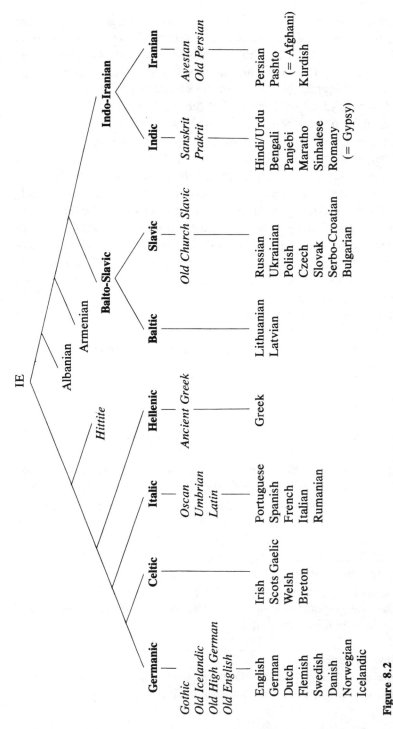

Figure 8.2
The Indo-European language family. Families are listed in boldface type. The oldest attested forms of each family are given in italics, and currently spoken languages are listed in plain roman type at the end of each vertical branch.

Hungarian, members of the *Finno-Ugric* family. The Basque language has not been shown to be related to any other language and is thus termed an *isolate*. Some scholars have speculated, however, that Basque is distantly related to the Caucasian languages, a group of non-Indo-European languages spoken in the southern USSR.

The grouping of other languages of the world into families is much less clear. It is not even settled how many different languages there are, so that estimates vary greatly. Part of the problem lies in the differing definitions of dialect, which have a political basis just as often as a linguistic one (see chapter 7). A commonly cited estimate of the number of the world's languages varies between four and five thousand, with half of the world's population speaking Indo-European languages. The large number of speakers of Indo-European languages is due in part to the European settlement of the New World. The individual language with the most speakers is, of course, Mandarin Chinese. The most common second language—that is, the language learned most frequently as a foreign language—is currently English. Thus, a Japanese pilot landing in Paris communicates with other planes and the control tower in English.

Very few of the world's languages are unrelated to other spoken languages; most can be grouped into families. In table 8.1 we list some of the world's languages, giving an approximate number of speakers for each.

Why Languages Change and How Language Change Spreads

Having answered our first question, concerning how to establish historical relationships among languages, we now turn to the second—namely, what are the causes and mechanisms of language change?

Surprisingly perhaps, linguists currently have little understanding of the exact causes of language change. For purposes of discussion, we may divide the topic of language change into two areas: individual and community. By individual change we refer to a spontaneous change in a language on the part of a single speaker. Community change we may define as the transmission and ultimate sharing of changes among speakers in a linguistic community.

Individual Change
One type of individual change that spontaneously occurs is *grammar simplification*. Modern English has a small class of exceptional nouns in

Table 8.1
Some non-Indo-European languages of the world

Family	Language	Principal Area Where Spoken	No. of Speakers in Millions
Afro-Asiatic	Hausa	West Africa	23
	Amharic	East Africa	10
	Arabic	North Africa	155
	Hebrew	Israel	3
Altaic	(Khalkha) Mongolian	Mongolia	2
	Turkish	Turkey	45
Austro-Asiatic	Vietnamese	Vietnam	45
Austronesian	Indonesian-Malay	Indonesia, Malaysia	115
Caucasian	Georgian	Caucasus (South-eastern USSR)	3
Dravidian	Kannada	India	32
	Malayalam	India	31
	Tamil	India, Sri Lanka	59
	Telugu	India	60
Finno-Ugric	Finnish	Finland	5
	Hungarian	Hungary	13
Japanese	Japanese	Japan	119
Korean	Korean	Korea	60
Niger-Congo	Swahili	East Africa	32
	Igbo	West Africa	12
	Yoruba	West Africa	14
Sino-Tibetan	Cantonese	Southern China	55
	Mandarin	Northern China	726
	Burmese	Burma	26
	Tibetan	Tibet	6

which the final voiceless fricative must be voiced in the plural form (for example, *leaf* versus *leaves*). With respect to the regular Plural Rule of English, this change to a voiced fricative is an exception and represents a *complication* of the regular process of plural formation. Many speakers of English are now regularizing these forms and use plurals such as *handkerchiefs* and *hoofs* instead of previously used *handkerchieves* and *hooves*. Also, with words derived from the exceptional nouns, speakers will form the plural according to the regular rule if the derived word differs significantly in meaning. For example, the National Hockey League team located in Toronto is known as the Toronto *Mapleleafs* (not "Mapleleaves"). In other words the pressure to simplify and regularize is quite strong, and regularization is probably carried out a great deal in language acquisition by children. Adults may also be a source of change, however, although very little is known at present about the possible contribution of adults to language change. We simply do not know why a rule such as Grimm's Law applied in Germanic, or why in more recent English, rules for flapped and glottal stop variants of *t* have been added (recall chapter 4). Once a small group of speakers have changed their grammar, however, the change can then spread to other speakers.

Community Change

If a change begins in one area, it is sometimes possible to follow its progress through time and space as it moves *wave-like* through a community of speakers. Although some areas tend to be more active in innovating than others, changes will often spread in an overlapping fashion. For example, a difference has been noticed (Joos 1942) in the pronunciation of the word *typewriter* in two dialects of Canadian English: /tʌyprayDər/ and /tʌyprʌyDər/. This difference can be explained in terms of the interaction of two rules, the rule for flapped D discussed in chapter 4 and the Vowel Centering Rule illustrated in problem A of exercise 16, chapter 4. Vowel Centering applies in some dialects of American English, so that the diphthongs /ay/ and /aw/ become /ʌy/ and /ʌw/ before voiceless consonants. The pronunciation of the word *typewriter* in the two Canadian dialects can be accounted for by an interesting interaction of the following two rules:

(12)

a. Flap Rule

$$\begin{bmatrix} t \\ d \end{bmatrix} \rightarrow D \, / \, \acute{V} \underline{\quad\quad} V$$

b. Vowel Centering

$$\begin{bmatrix} ay \\ aw \end{bmatrix} \rightarrow \begin{bmatrix} \Lambda y \\ \Lambda w \end{bmatrix} \, / \, \underline{\quad\quad} \begin{bmatrix} voiceless \\ consonant \end{bmatrix}$$

Imagine two geographical areas, A and B. In area A, Canadian speakers have rule (12a) in their dialect, but not rule (12b). In area B, on the other hand, speakers have rule (12b), but not rule (12a). What effect might this have on speakers who are located between these two groups? How might their pronunciation be influenced by their neighbors in areas A and B? Suppose that speakers are gradually influenced by neighboring speakers, so that a rule of pronunciation can be said to "move" or "spread" through successive groups of speakers located in close proximity. Given this, it turns out that two rules could originate in different areas, but gradually spread. They would eventually "meet"

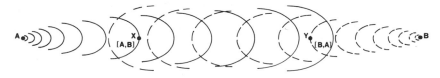

Figure 8.3
Geographic spread of two intersecting rules

and "cross," creating areas where their effects overlap, as shown in figure 8.3.

Figure 8.3 represents the general geographic spread of two rules. At point X, which is close to area A, rule (12a) "arrives" first; however, since X is farther away from area B, rule (12b) "arrives" later. In contrast, point Y is closer to area B, the area of rule (12b), and thus rule (12b) "arrives" at Y *before* rule (12a) does. This difference in the order of arrival of the rules yields the difference in the pronunciation of the word *typewriter* in the two Canadian dialects, as shown in (13):

(13)

	X-dialect		Y-dialect
	taypraytər		taypraytər
First rule (12a):	tayprayDər	First rule (12b):	tʌyprʌytər
Next rule (12b):	tʌyprayDər	Next rule (12a):	tʌyprʌyDər

This example gives a good indication of how a change can "move" among dialects. The same type of phenomenon happens also with lexical, morphological, and syntactic change, and thus a widespread language change can take place. If one group of speakers of a language becomes isolated from another group of speakers of the same language, however, each group will undergo its own changes without necessarily spreading them, and after enough time has passed the dialects that have arisen may differ so extensively that one is forced to say that new languages have been created.

Spread of Changes among Different Languages
An interesting feature of language change is that grammatical properties, especially phonological ones, can spread between adjacent but *different* languages. For example, the *uvular-r* (an *r*-like sound pronounced in the uvular region of the vocal tract (see figure 4.5, chapter 4)) has been replacing the tongue-tip-*r* in many of the languages of Europe. Uvular-*r* is characteristic of French, but it is now common in

many dialects of German as well; it is also replacing the tongue-tip-*r* in dialects of southern Sweden and northern Italy. There is much dispute, however, about where this change started.

One of the more remarkable cases of the spread of a phonological change is found in the Native American languages of the northwestern United States. In Washington State, three distinct language groups were geographically adjacent before contact with Europeans. These groups are represented by Makah (a language of the Wakashan family), Quileute (a language of the Chemakuan family), and several members of the Salish language family. The relative geographic locations of these languages are indicated in figure 8.4, in which (A) is the Makah region, (B) is the Quileute region, and (C) is the Salish language region.

What is remarkable about these different languages is that they *all* lost their nasal consonants by changing them to voiced stops: *m* became *b*, *n* became *d*, and *ŋ* became *g*. Although it is not possible to establish in which language the change began, it is noteworthy that this far-reaching change (indicated by shading in figure 8.4) spread throughout these distinct languages. Almost all of the world's languages have nasal consonants, but these three different languages are among the few exceptions. Notice, though, that the name *Makah* has a nasal consonant—thus appearing to contradict the claim that these languages have no nasals. Also, one of the Puget Sound Salish languages,

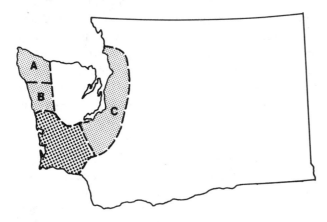

Figure 8.4
Geographical proximity of three distinct language families in the northwestern United States

Snohomish, another nasalless language, has *two* nasals in its name. The solution to this apparent contradiction is that the names *Makah* and *Snohomish* were given to these people by neigboring groups that do have nasals in their languages. The Snohomish actually call themselves *sdǝhóbš*, in which *d* corresponds to *n* and *b* corresponds to *m*, according to the regular changes mentioned above.

Language Change: Decay or Improvement?

We now turn to the third question that was posed earlier: does language change lead to a gain or a loss in expressiveness?

In the past, language change has been viewed variously as decay and as progress, but at present neither of these views seems appropriate or true. Languages seem to maintain a balance in expressiveness and grammatical complexity over time. If a particular grammatical feature is lost (say, because of a phonological change), some feature may be added in another portion of the grammar (say, in the syntax). For example, when English lost most of its inflectional endings (see section 8.3) due, it is often claimed, to the deletion of unstressed final syllables as an effect of phonological rules, it was no longer possible to identify the functional role (subject or object) of nouns by their inflectional endings. However, the functional notions of subject and object are now indicated in part by the syntactic position of nouns, that is, by their position in the linear order of words. In the next section we will discuss the loss of a morphological rule that created causative verbs from adjectives. But speakers of English did not lose the notion of causation when this word-building rule was lost. In fact, we can still say "to cause to be red" or "to cause to be blue." Thus, the expressive possibilities of a language do not seem to be limited by the lack of an overt grammatical structure that carries a particular notion. For example, Chinese has no overt past tense marker, but this does not mean that the Chinese do not have a notion of past time. The idea of past time can be quite clear either from context or from the presence of an adverb that refers to past time.

In this section we have referred several times to the changes that occurred between Old and Modern English. These extensive changes are the subject of the next section.

8.3 THE LINGUISTIC HISTORY OF ENGLISH

Background

The English language has undergone extensive changes between the Old and Modern English periods, although speakers of Modern English are still able to recognize Old English as a relative of Modern English. An example will illustrate this point:

(14)
a. Old English
   In þām tūne wǣron þæt hūs and þæt būr þæs eorles.
b. Modern English
   In the town were the house and chamber of the chief.

In (14b), a word-for-word Modern English translation of (14a) that ignores some meaning differences, many of the words show a strong similarity to the Old English words. Nevertheless, subsequent grammatical and vocabulary changes have made Old English no longer understandable to the speaker of Modern English.

As noted earlier, the English language is part of the Germanic family of languages and is thus historically related to Modern German, Dutch, Swedish, Norwegian, Danish, and Icelandic. The English language began its own separate development in the middle of the fifth century A.D. after a series of invasions of England by Germanic-speaking tribes from what is now northwestern Europe. The invading groups included Saxons, Angles, and Frisians, among others. The invaders fought against Celtic-speaking inhabitants who, after fierce battles, were overcome. These were not the first Europeans to invade England and do battle with the Celts, however. The Romans had colonized England during the first century A.D., before the migrations of the Angles and Saxons began. As the Roman Empire began to collapse, however, the Roman legions withdrew, making possible the conquest of England by the Germanic tribes. The Celtic tribes who spoke Scottish were confined to the north, and the remaining Celtic speakers were pushed into Wales and Cornwall. Of the original Celtic languages spoken in Britain, only Welsh (still spoken in Wales) survives. The original Celtic language in Scotland became extinct, although Gaelic speakers from Ireland moved to Scotland in the fifteenth century and there developed their own dialect, Scots Gaelic, which is still spoken today by a small population. The Irish Gaelic language is also still spoken in Ireland, but by a minority of its inhabitants.

During the sixth century, the Germanic invasions ended and England entered a period of relative political stability. The island became covered with a patchwork of kingdoms, and during this period of political stability several dialect areas arose. The major dialects were West Saxon, Kentish, Mercian, and Northumbrian, the West Saxon dialect eventually becoming the most important. The differences among these dialects, which mainly involved pronunciation, were similar to differences among dialects in the present-day United States. The language of this period, called Old English (or Anglo-Saxon), was in many ways grammatically similar to Modern German. For instance, the nouns, adjectives, and verbs were highly inflected, as the examples in (15) show.

(15)
Typical Old English Nouns, Adjectives, and Verbs
a. Noun: *cyning* "king"

Singular:	Nominative	cyning
	Accusative	cyning
	Genitive	cyninges
	Dative/Instrumental	cyninge
Plural:	Nominative	cyningas
	Accusative	cyningas
	Genitive	cyninga
	Dative/Instrumental	cyningum

b. Adjective: *gōd* "good" (weak declension)

		Masculine	Feminine	Neuter
Singular:	Nominative	gōda	gōde	gōde
	Accusative	gōdan	gōdan	gōde
	Genitive	gōdan	gōdan	gōdan
	Dative/Instrumental	gōdan	gōdan	gōdan
	(Same plural endings in all genders)			
Plural:	Nominative	gōdan		
	Accusative	gōdan		
	Genitive	gōdra		
	Dative	gōdum		

c. Verb: infinitive *dēman* "judge" (cf. *deem, doom*)

Present Tense:	Singular	1	dēme
		2	dēmst, dēmest
		3	dēmþ, dēmeþ
	Plural	1,2,3	dēmaþ
Past Tense:	Singular	1	dēmde
		2	dēmdest
		3	dēmde
	Plural	1,2,3	dēmdon

The words in (15) consist of two parts, a base and one of a set of inflectional suffixes. The inflectional morphology of Old English was in fact much more complicated than (15) indicates. The noun *cyning* is an example of a so-called *masculine* noun, but there were two other genders, *feminine* and *neuter,* both of which had different endings. Each of the nominal genders had different subclasses, associated with different sets of inflectional endings. There were, then, about two dozen different types of inflectional endings that could be added to nouns alone. Since adjectives and verbs were also divided into classes that required different endings, there were altogether dozens of different classes of inflectional endings that were added to Old English words. One of the major changes between Old English and Modern English, then, was obviously the loss of almost all of these nominal, adjectival, and verbal endings—for the language has very few such suffixes today (recall the discussion of morphology in chapter 3). In the nouns, only the regular genitive ending *-s/-es* (now the possessive) and the plural ending *-s/-es* have survived. Plurals such as *children* carry on an earlier *-en* plural ending, and plurals such as *geese* also reflect an earlier class of inflectional ending. (We will discuss the origin of the stem vowel alternation between *goose* and *geese* later.) The adjective endings have also been completely lost, although archaic spellings and phrases such as *ye olde shoppe* or *in the olden days* are relics of them.

Another indicator of English language history is found in words spelled with an initial *sk-* sequence. This sequence, found in words such as *sky* and *skirt,* is the result of borrowings from the Scandinavian languages. The Danes, in fact, controlled northeastern England in the ninth and tenth centuries. By far the greatest influence on English from another language, however, came as a result of the Norman Conquest and the victory of William the Conqueror in 1066. The Normans brought with them the French language, and French remained the language of the ruling class for a considerable period. Under its influence the English language changed in terms of vocabulary, phonology, and morphology, as we will see.

Although the changes from Old English to Modern English were continuous and gradual, linguists traditionally distinguish three major periods in this development: the Old English period (fifth to eleventh centuries), the Middle English period (eleventh to fifteenth centuries), and the Modern English period (fifteenth century to the present). Scholars studying the history of English are fortunate in that there are written documents spanning more than 1,200 years that enable them to trace many of the changes English has undergone during this time. These changes are typical of the changes that all languages undergo. In discussing them, we will concentrate on the three structural components of language—phonology, morphology, and syntax—as well as on vocabulary changes that have occurred between Old and Modern English. Each of these four components can undergo the three major types of changes: addition, loss, and change in structure. To illustrate how languages change in these ways, we will discuss examples of these changes from the history of English.

Lexical Change

Addition

From Old English times to the present, new words have continuously been added to the English language. Surprisingly, only a few Celtic words have found their way into Modern English, in spite of the fact that English speakers have been continuously in contact with Celtic speakers in Wales, Ireland, and Scotland. Personal names such as *Lloyd* and its variant *Floyd* are Celtic borrowings.

By far the greatest number of new words came from French as a result of the Norman invasion. These French words did not always replace Old English words, but in many instances expanded an already existing vocabulary. For example, the words *pork, beef, veal, mutton,* and *venison* are all French words referring respectively to the edible meat of the *swine, cow, calf, sheep,* and *deer,* the latter being Old English words. Formerly, the Anglo-Saxon words were used to refer to both the meat and the animals. Interestingly, the words *beef* and *cow* are descendents of the same common Indo-European word $*g^{wh}ow\text{-}$, which, because of different historical changes in the Germanic and Italic families, has given rise to quite different-sounding words.

Although English has borrowed most heavily from French, other languages have also contributed words. During the Renaissance, for example, a large number of so-called learned words from Latin and Greek became part of English (*reverberate* from Latin and *polygon* from Greek are typical examples). From Spanish we have words such as *mesa, lariat,* and *taco.* From Russian we have *sputnik* and *vodka;* from German we have many common words such as *kindergarten, hamburger,* and *gesundheit. Woodchuck* is ultimately an Algonquian word, and *tomato* comes to us from Aztec (via Spanish). English has thus borrowed freely from other languages, a habit that at least partially accounts for its enormous vocabulary.

In chapter 3 we also noted the many ways that new words can be introduced into English via abbreviations and word formation rules, producing such words as *TV, finalize, laser,* and so forth. Consequently, the number of words that can be added to our language—by borrowing or otherwise—is in principle unbounded.

Loss

Conversely, many words have been lost since the Old English period, though a surprising number of the lost words are still present in compounds. One example is OE *wer* "man." This word is historically related to the Latin word *vir,* also meaning "man," forms of which (for example, *virile*) have been borrowed into English. The form *wer,* even though lost as an independent word, still exists in *werewolf,* which originally meant "man-wolf" or "wolfman." The OE word *rice* "realm, kingdom" has a similar history. This word, which was originally borrowed from a Celtic language, has been lost in the modern language. In contrast, the German language, which also borrowed this word, has preserved it in the word *Reich.* The only relic of this word in Modern English is in the compound word *bishopric,* which originally meant "bishop's realm," a sense close to its present-day meaning.

Change

Many examples of meaning change have already been discussed in chapter 3, which focused on narrowing, broadening, and metaphorical extension of meaning. Another example of semantic narrowing that occurred between Old English and Modern English is seen in the word *hound* (OE *hund*). This word once referred to any kind of dog, whereas in Modern English the meaning has been narrowed to a particular breed. The word *dog* (OE *docga*), on the other hand, referred in Old

English to the mastiff breed; its meaning now has been broadened to include any dog. The meaning of *dog* has also been extended metaphorically in modern casual speech (slang) to refer to a particularly unattractive person.

Semantic Change and Semantic Fields

We have seen examples of individual words undergoing a meaning change. But semantic change at the word level is not limited to single words—rather, entire groups of words can undergo parallel semantic changes. In her study of *semantic fields* (see chapter 3), Lehrer (1974) has noted that words belonging to the same semantic field undergo similar semantic changes. To take an example (Lehrer and Battan 1983), consider the following set of words, drawn from the semantic field of bird names: *goose, cuckoo, pigeon, coot, turkey*. In addition to its literal meaning, each of these words has a metaphorical use indicating "foolishness." According to the *Oxford English Dictionary*, the words *goose, cuckoo,* and *pigeon* were the first of this set to be used in the metaphorical sense in question, and all three acquired their metaphorical meaning at roughly the same time (the first recorded instances dating from the mid-sixteenth century). This could be due to coincidence; but it seems plausible to assume that the simultaneous metaphorical extension of the three words was based on their membership in the same semantic class. Later, the words *coot* and *turkey* came to have the same metaphorical use, again underscoring the idea that words in the same semantic field can undergo similar semantic changes. (The word *pigeon,* incidentally, had a metaphorical use indicating "cowardice" in Shakespeare's time—recall *pigeon-livered*—but this use later became obsolete.)

It is also the case that the structure of a semantic field plays a role in semantic change. For example, the words *hot* and *cold* are antonyms that describe physical temperature. With pairs of antonyms, if one member undergoes a metaphorical extension, the other tends to change in a parallel fashion. Thus, just as *hot* and *cold* are opposites in describing temperature, so they are also opposites in their metaphorical extension in phrases such as *hot news* (news that is just breaking) versus *cold news* (news that has become stale). In colloquial styles, we can speak of a *hot car* (stolen car); hence, we would not be surprised if speakers began using the phrase *cold car* (one that is not stolen), on the grounds that semantic change tends to affect entire semantic fields in a parallel fashion, and not just single members of the field (for discussion, see Lehrer 1974).

Phonological Change

Rule Addition

There have been many phonological changes between Old English and Modern English, and the rules discussed in chapter 4 (for example, the rules governing flapped and glottal stop variants of *t*) have been *added* to American English relatively recently. Of course, rules that are added to a language can later be lost as living rules, and only certain effects of the rules remain. For example, an important set of extensive sound changes affecting the long (tense) vowels occurred at the end of the Middle English period, and these changes are the cause of one of the major discrepancies between the spelling of Modern English and its current pronunciation. Known as the *Great Vowel Shift,* this change had the effects shown in figure 8.5 (where the arrows indicate the direction of the changes).

The long (or tense) mid vowels of Middle English, which we can represent by /ē/ and /ō/ (where the bars over the vowels indicate length), both were raised and diphthongized to yield the current high vowels /iy/ and /uw/, respectively. The earlier pronunciation of these long mid vowels is still reflected in the spelling of words such as *feet* (once pronounced /fēt/, now pronounced /fiyt/) and *mood* (once pronounced /mōd/, now pronounced /muwd/). The high vowels of Middle English, in turn, became diphthongs, the first part of the vowel "mov-

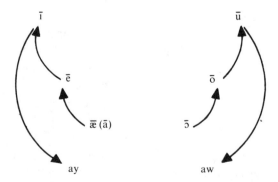

Figure 8.5
The Great Vowel Shift

ing down" to become a low vowel. As part of the Great Vowel Shift, then, /ī/ became /ay/ and /ū/ became /aw/. Again the current orthography reflects the former pronunciation in spellings such as *five* (once pronounced /fīv/, now pronounced /fayv/). Note also the spelling of OE *tune* for "town" in (14), which was the pronunciation before the diphthong was created.

Two of the long low vowels, /æ/ and /ɔ/, were also raised to yield a new set of mid vowels, /ey/ and /ow/, respectively. Thus, Modern English *mate* /meyt/ was formerly pronounced /mæt/, and the word *goat* /gowt/ was formerly pronounced /gɔt/. The addition of these phonological rules, then, caused a significant change in the pronunciation of English words, and even though the Great Vowel Shift has now been lost from English as a purely phonological rule, its effects are still revealed in the discrepancy between the pronunciation of Modern English and its spelling system.

Rule Loss

Early in the history of English a rule called *i-Mutation* (or *i-Umlaut*) existed that turned back vowels into front vowels when an /i/ or /y/ followed in the next syllable. For example, in a certain class of nouns in the ancestor of Old English, the plural was formed not by adding -*s*, but rather by adding -*i*. Thus, the plural of *gōs* "goose" was *gōsi* "geese." Later, when the *i*-Mutation rule was added, the *i*-ending of the plural conditioned the change of *gōsi* to *gǣsi*. The *ǣ* phoneme is a combination of the *o* and *e* phonemes; it is a mid front vowel like *e* but has lip rounding like *o*. Hence, the effect of *i*-Mutation was to cause back vowels to move forward, but the newly fronted vowels kept the rounding that they had had when they were back vowels. Still later, the lip rounding was lost, and the plural of *gōs* became *gēs(e)*. When *gōs* and *gēs* finally underwent the Great Vowel Shift, the current pronunciations /guws/ and /giys/ resulted. Thus, *i*-Mutation is an example of a rule that was once present in Old English, but has since dropped out of the language, and thanks to the Great Vowel Shift even the effects of *i*-Mutation have been altered.

Change in Rule Applicability

In Old English, fricatives became voiced when they occurred between voiced sounds (that is, $f \rightarrow v$, $\theta \rightarrow ð$, $s \rightarrow z$). Since the most common plural ending was formerly -*as*, all nouns ending in fricatives underwent this rule in the plural. The rule causing this voicing is no longer present in Modern English, but its effects can still be observed in pairs such as singular *wife* /wayf) and plural *wives* /wayvz/. This change of the stem in the plural is still the result of a rule, but the form of the rule is quite different from the form that it had in Old English. In Old English the rule was *phonologically conditioned:* it applied whenever fricatives occurred between voiced sounds. In contrast, the alternation between voiced and voiceless fricatives in Modern English is not phonologically conditioned, but *morphologically conditioned:* the voicing rule applies only to certain words and not to others. Thus, a particular (and now exceptional) class of nouns must undergo voicing of the final voiceless fricative when used in the plural (for example, *wife/wives, knife/knives, hoof/hooves*). Other nouns, however, do not undergo this process (for example, *proof/proofs*). Thus, the fricative voicing rule of Old English has changed in status from a phonologically conditioned rule to a morphologically conditioned one.

Differences in Phonemic Inventory

Addition of Phonemes
The phonemic system of Old English was similar to that of Modern English, although several differences can be noted. For example, the voiced labiodental fricative /v/ was not an independent phoneme in Old English. The *v*'s that did occur were voiced allophonic variants of the phoneme /f/. As a result of subsequent changes between Old English and Middle English, /v/ has become an independent phoneme.

Loss of Phonemes
As noted in the previous section, the mutated (or umlauted) vowels *œ* and *y* (front rounded vowels) lost their rounding during the Old English period. The word *thimble,* for example, probably was originally pronounced as *þymbıl* in very early Old English. Later the *y* became unrounded to *ı*. (Knowing that the suffix *-ıl* was used to form nouns with diminutive meaning from other nouns, what can you surmise about the origin of the word *thimble?*)

Morphological Change

Rule Addition
The *-able* rule discussed in chapter 3 is an example of a rule that has been added to English since the Old English period. As a result of the

influx of a large number of *-able* words from French into the English language, English speakers were (and are still) able to extract a rule from these words that is productive in current English. Words such as *doable* and *washable* have been formed by adding *-able* to the Germanic roots *do* and *wash*.

Rule Loss

An example of a morphological rule that has been lost is the Causative Verb Formation rule of Old English. At one time causative verbs could be formed by adding the suffix /-yan/ to adjectives. The verb *redden* meaning "to cause to be or make red" is a carry-over from the time when the Causative Verb Formation rule was present in English, in that the final *-en* of *redden* is a reflex of the earlier *-yan* causative suffix. However, the rule adding a suffix such as *-en* to adjectives to form new verbs has been lost, and thus we can no longer form new causative verbs such as **green-en* "to make green" or **blue-en* "to make blue." (Do you now see how *awake* (adjective) and *awaken* (verb) are related?)

Rule Change

New nouns could be formed in Old English by adding /-ing/ not only to verbs, as in Modern English (*sing* + *ing* = *singing*), but also to a large class of nouns. For example, the word *viking* was formed by adding /-ing/ to the noun *wic* "bay." (Why might the word for "bay" be used to describe the Vikings?) It turns out that the /-ing/ suffix can still be added to a highly restricted class of nouns, carrying the meaning "material used for," as in such nouns as *roofing, carpeting,* and *flooring.* Thus, the rule for creating new nouns with the /-ing/ suffix has changed by becoming more *restricted* in its application, so that a much smaller class of nouns can still have /-ing/ attached.

Syntactic Change

Rule Addition

A syntactic rule that has been added to English since the Old English period is the Particle Movement rule discussed in chapter 5. Thus, sentence pairs of the type *John threw out the fish* and *John threw the fish out* did not occur in Old English.

Rule Loss

A syntactic rule that has been lost from English is the morphosyntactic rule of Adjective Agreement. At one time adjectives had endings that had to agree with the head noun in case, number, and gender. This rule is no longer found in English, since for the most part these inflectional endings have been lost.

Syntactic Change: Auxiliary Verbs versus Main Verbs

Recall from chapter 5 that contemporary English makes a distinction between auxiliary verbs and main verbs, a distinction reflected in questions (only auxiliary verbs can be fronted in questions, as in *Can you leave?*), negative sentences (only auxiliary verbs can take the contracted negative *n't,* as in *You can't leave*), and tag questions (only auxiliary verbs can appear in tags, as in *You can leave, can't you?*). Focusing now only on so-called modal verbs (*can, could*), it is interesting to note that prior to the sixteenth century these syntactic distinctions between main verbs and auxiliary verbs did not exist.

At that time it was possible for main verbs to take *not,* and examples such as the following can be found in Shakespeare's writings:

(16)
a. I deny it *not.*   ("I don't deny it.")
b. Forbid him *not.*   ("Do not forbid him.")

Similarly, main verbs could be fronted in forming questions:

(17)
a. Revolt our subjects?   ("Do our subjects revolt?")
b. Gives not the hawthorn-bush a sweeter shade? ("Does the hawthorn-bush not give a sweeter shade?")

However, by Shakespeare's time such patterns were already beginning to disappear as a series of grammatical changes was taking place in the mid-1500s (see Lightfoot 1979 for a summary and discussion). After the sixteenth century the grammar of English had changed so that auxiliary verbs—and never main verbs—had to be used in negation, questions, and other patterns we have noted.

The changes that took place between Old English and Modern English are typical of the kinds of changes that all human languages undergo over time, and after enough years have passed the descendent language (or languages) can be very different from its (their) ancestor language. Moreover, language change offers important indirect evidence about the nature of human language—namely, that it is rule-governed. We have seen that the major changes that the English language underwent between the Old English and Modern English periods are best viewed as changes in the sets of rules characterizing the two stages of English. Over time, grammatical rules can be added, lost, or changed; so language has always changed, and it will continue to change.

8.4 THE GRAPHIC REPRESENTATION OF LANGUAGE
(optional section)

That human language can be represented as a sequence of discrete symbols standing for individual speech sounds was not known to the people who first attempted to represent speech graphically. Because writing systems have existed for only about 6,000 years, and because some of the earliest written records have been preserved, it is possible to follow the developments that eventually led to the modern alphabet.

Systematic writing developed in the Near East and was originally *pictographic* or *ideographic*. Pictographs represent objects and are thus *iconic,* whereas ideographs represent ideas or sets of related ideas and are thus *symbolic*. For example, a circle ○ used as an ideograph might represent the sun, summer, light, heat, and so forth. What is crucial is that this type of writing system did not represent either individual words or the sounds making up the words. When the individual symbols come to be associated with certain words in a standardized fashion, the writing system is said to be *logographic*. A logographic writing system is today in use in China. For the most part the Chinese characters represent concepts that can be associated with the words and do not have a consistent or fixed sound value (see figure 8.6). This lack of a sound-meaning association has an advantage in China because there exist so many different dialects of spoken Chinese. Mandarin, a form of Chinese spoken in the north, and Cantonese, a form spoken in the south, are for the most part mutually unintelligible. But since Mandarin speakers associate the Mandarin words (pronunciations) with the individual characters that stand for them, whereas Cantonese speakers associate the Cantonese words (pronunciations) with these same characters, Mandarin and Cantonese speakers can communicate via their common writing system (which functions as a lingua franca; see chapter 7). European languages share some logographic symbols, the Arabic numerals being perhaps the most common example. For the numbers 3,

				Keys:		
	工	kung¹	'work'			
1.	仁	hung²	'big belly'	1.	人	'human being'
2.	忊	k'ung¹	'impatience'	2.	心	'heart'
3.	扛	k'ang²	'carry on the shoulders'	3.	手	'hand'
4.	杠	kang⁴	'sedan chair'	4.	木	'wood'
5.	江	kiang¹	'river'	5.	水	'water'
6.	紅	hung²	'red'	6.	糸	'silk'
7.	訌	hung⁴	'quarrel'	7.	言	'word'
8.	汞	hung³	'quicksilver'	8.	水	'water'

Figure 8.6

Chinese characters, an example of logographic writing. These "compounds" have the form of a puzzle and are to be interpreted according to the following instruction: What is a word that sounds like *kung* "work" and is associated with the key word? Thus, *hung* "big belly" is a word that sounds like *kung* and can be associated with a human being. These Chinese compounds show that the Chinese writing system is not purely logographic. (Pedersen, *The Discovery of Language*, 1962. Reprinted by permission of Harvard University Press.)

4, and 5, for example, French speakers say *trois, quatre, cinq,* German speakers *drei, vier, fünf,* and English speakers *three, four, five.*

An extension of the logographic system occurs when a symbol that represents a word comes to be associated with the sound (pronunciation) of that word and is used to represent other words that contain the same sound. We can illustrate this type of writing with an example from English. Noting that the symbol *4* is pronounced /fɔr/, we can use this symbol to represent the preposition *for* in the expression *4 me* "for me." It can even be used to form part of a longer word, as in *4-ground* "foreground." This type of writing is found in Egyptian hieroglyphics and is still used today in the type of children's puzzle called the *rebus.*

As soon as symbols became associated with sounds, new possibilities for representing language became available. A common writing system, one that many languages still use, is *syllabic writing.* The earliest writing of this type is called *cuneiform* (from Latin *cuneus* "wedge"). The name reflects the fact that a wedge-shaped stylus was used to make marks on soft clay tablets that were later dried or even baked in kilns. The cuneiform symbols (see figure 8.7) were derived from pictographs and ultimately came to represent combinations of sounds and in some cases single sounds. The Sumerians first developed this writing system more than 5,000 years ago, and it soon spread to other people such as the Babylonians and Akkadians, who used these symbols to write their own languages. Some early writing systems of Semitic (the language family that includes Arabic and Hebrew) were basically syllabic, but they did not represent the vowels (Sch sntncs cn stll b ndrstd).

Egyptian hieroglyphics are also basically syllabic even though they appear to be ideographic or even pictographic. A Frenchman, Jean François Champollion, is credited with the earliest comprehensive decipherment of these Egyptian symbols. Using the Rosetta stone, on which a bilingual inscription in Greek and two forms of Egyptian writing, hieroglyphic and demotic, were found, Champollion discovered that the hieroglyphics represented sounds (see figure 8.8). *Hieroglyphics* are a very ornate writing system that eventually became limited to use in writing religious inscriptions on monuments. For common religious writing, a script called *hieratic* was developed, a simplified form of the original hieroglyphics. The hieratic script was better suited for writing quickly with pen on papyrus. The hieratic script remained in general use for religious writing, and from it an even simpler form, *demotic,* was developed for everyday use. Examples of the three writing systems are given in figure 8.9.

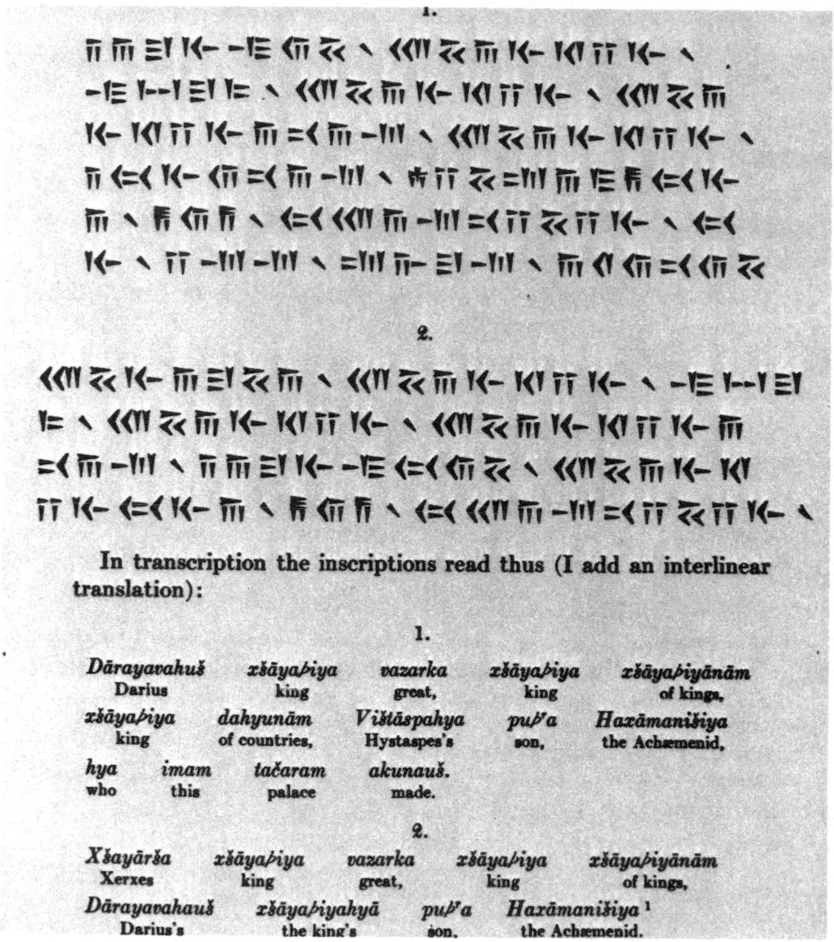

1.

𒋡 𒈩 𒀹 𒆠 𒀹 𒂖 𒄑 𒌋 𒀸 𒐏 𒌋 𒈩 𒆠 𒅗 𒅆 𒆠 𒀸

𒂖 𒐊 𒀹 𒈪 𒀸 𒐏 𒌋 𒈩 𒆠 𒅗 𒅆 𒆠 𒀸 𒐏 𒌋 𒈩

𒆠 𒅗 𒅆 𒆠 𒈩 � 𒈩 𒐍 𒀸 𒐏 𒌋 𒈩 𒆠 𒅗 𒅆 𒆠 𒀸

𒋡 𒌷 𒆠 𒄑 𒄷 𒈩 𒐍 𒀸 𒌋 𒅆 𒌋 𒐐 𒈩 𒋬 𒐬 𒄰 𒆠

𒈩 𒀸 𒌋 𒄑 𒀸 𒄰 𒐏 𒈩 𒐍 𒄑 𒅆 𒌋 𒅆 𒆠 𒀸 𒄰

𒆠 𒀸 𒅆 𒐍 𒐍 𒀸 𒐐 𒒀 𒂖 𒐍 𒀸 𒈩 𒍝 𒄷 𒄰 𒄷 𒌋

2.

𒐏 𒌋 𒆠 𒈩 𒀹 𒌋 𒈩 𒀸 𒐏 𒌋 𒈩 𒆠 𒅗 𒅆 𒆠 𒀸 𒂖 𒐊 𒀹 𒈪

𒐊 𒀸 𒐏 𒌋 𒈩 𒆠 𒅗 𒅆 𒆠 𒀸 𒐏 𒌋 𒈩 𒆠 𒅗 𒅆 𒆠 𒈩

𒄑 𒈩 𒐍 𒀸 𒋡 𒈩 𒀹 𒆠 𒀹 𒂖 𒄑 𒄷 𒌋 𒀸 𒐏 𒌋 𒈩 𒆠 𒅗

𒅆 𒆠 𒄑 𒆠 𒈩 𒀸 𒐬 𒄑 𒄰 𒀸 𒄑 𒐏 𒌋 𒈩 𒐍 𒄑 𒅆 𒌋 𒅆 𒆠 𒀸

In transcription the inscriptions read thus (I add an interlinear translation):

1.

Dārayavahuš	*xšayaþiya*	*vazarka*	*xšayaþiya*	*xšayaþiyānām*
Darius	king	great,	king	of kings,
xšayaþiya	*dahyunām*	*Vištāspahya*	*puþ'a*	*Haxāmanišiya*
king	of countries,	Hystaspes's	son,	the Achæmenid,
hya	*imam*	*tačaram*	*akunauš.*	
who	this	palace	made.	

2.

Xšayārša	*xšayaþiya*	*vazarka*	*xšayaþiya*	*xšayaþiyānām*
Xerxes	king	great,	king	of kings,
Dārayavahauš	*xšayaþiyahyā*	*puþ'a*	*Haxāmanišiya* [1]	
Darius's	the king's	son.	the Achæmenid.	

Figure 8.7
Cuneiform, one of the earliest writing systems. The above transcription, dated from about 2400 b.p., is Old Persian, a language distantly related to English. What punctuation can you see in this example of cuneiform writing? (Pedersen, *The Discovery of Language*, 1962. Reprinted by permission of Harvard University Press.)

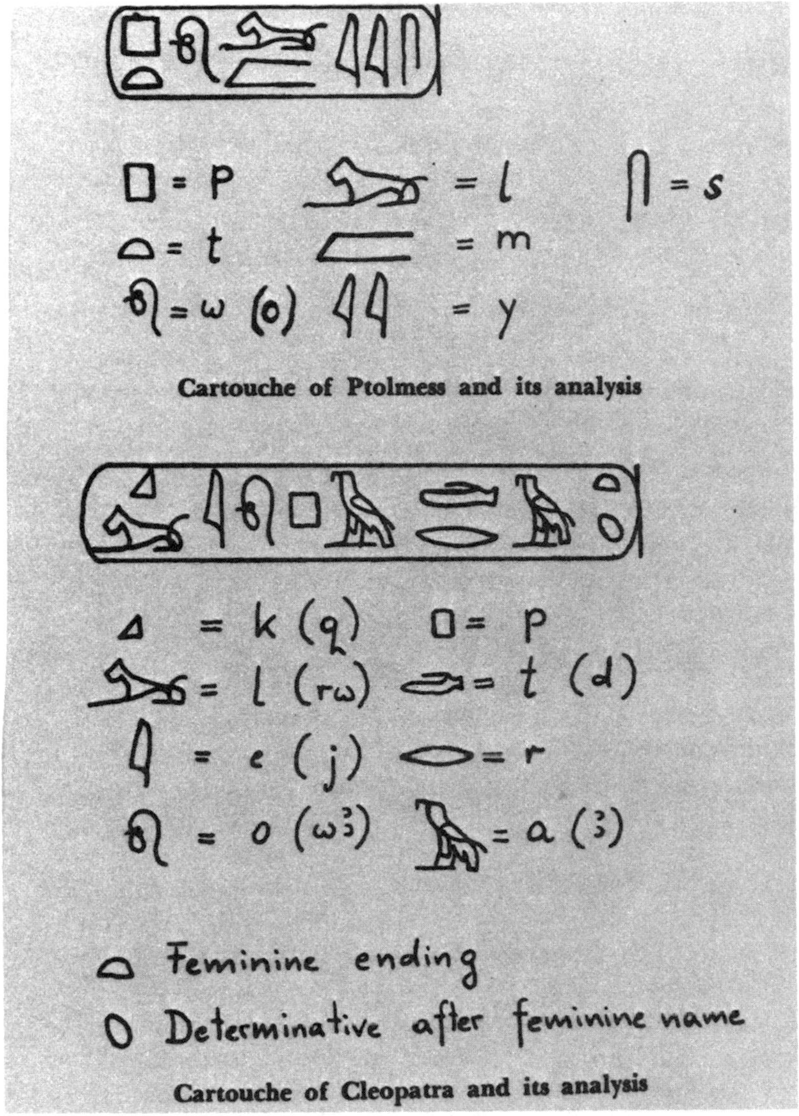

Cartouche of Ptolmess and its analysis

Cartouche of Cleopatra and its analysis

Figure 8.8
Examples of Egyptian hieroglyphic writing with accompanying sound-symbol correspondences. What does the hieroglyph for *l* look like that would help you remember this symbol? (From Ober 1965. Courtesy of the Peabody Library of the Johns Hopkins University.)

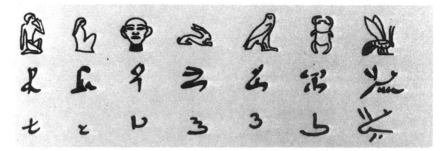

Figure 8.9
Examples of the three kinds of script used in ancient Egypt, hieroglyphic (top), hieratic (center), and demotic (bottom). Note the increasing abstractness that accompanies the evolution of Egyptian writing. (From Ober 1965. Courtesy of the Peabody Library of the Johns Hopkins University.)

Another type of syllabic writing system uses a different symbol for each consonant + vowel combination. Such a system was invented by Sequoia in the nineteenth century for use in writing his native Cherokee language (see figure 8.10). Yet another variant of syllabic writing uses a single symbol for each consonant and a different diacritic (a mark added to the symbol) to indicate which vowel occurs with the consonant (see figure 8.10). An example of this type of syllabic writing is in the *Devanāgarī* script that was used to write ancient Sanskrit and is still used in writing languages of India. The Devanāgarī syllabary is generally believed to be descended from an early Semitic writing system.

The ancient Greeks were the first people to create an alphabet as we know it today—a set of symbols representing vowels as well as consonants. In fact, the word *alphabet* is formed by combining the names for the first two letters of the Greek alphabet: *alpha* and *beta*. The Greeks adopted and revised the writing system of the Phoenicians, a Semitic people who were sea-traders in the Mediterranean. Thus, we can trace the development from ideographic to alphabetic writing, each step representing an increased economy in the inventory of symbols needed. Whereas logographic writing requires thousands of different symbols, alphabetic writing requires from as few as 12 (for Hawaiian) to at most several dozen.

The Greek alphabet, then, is the ultimate source for all the alphabets used today to write modern European languages, including English. There is still controversy on what the alphabetic symbols should represent, however. Should English be written with symbols that are pho-

SPECIMEN OF DĒVANĀGARĪ

सा मा दि श त्पि ता पुत्रं लि ख ले खं म मा ज्ञ य

sa mā di śa tpi tā pu traṁ li kha lē kham ma mā jña yั

न ते न लि खि तो ले खः पि तु रा ज्ञा न ख ण्डि त

na tē na   li khi tō lē khaḥ pi tu rā jñā na kha ndi tั

Figure 8.10
Two examples of syllabic writing systems. The Cherokee syllabary (top) uses a
different symbol for each consonant + vowel combination. The Devanāgarī
system (bottom) has a single symbol for each consonant, but adds diacritics
(extra marks) to indicate the various vowels following the consonant. (Cherokee syllabary from Sloat, Taylor, and Hoard 1978. Devanāgarī syllabary from
Pedersen, *The Discovery of Language*, 1962. Reprinted by permission of Harvard University Press.)

netic? In this case, the word *democrat* /dɛməkræt/ would have different vowels from the word *democracy* /dəmɔkrəsiy/, a word to which it is closely related. Likewise, insisting that English be written with purely phonetic symbols would require that the plural morpheme be written as either *s, z,* or *ɨz,* depending on the nature of the final phoneme of the noun to which the plural morpheme is attached (see chapter 4). Another type of writing system, the *morphophonemic* system, would allow (actually, require) the plural morpheme to be written in a single shape, in spite of the fact that it occurs in different phonemic shapes. Though a discussion of morphophonemic writing goes beyond the scope of an introductory text, further information on the relative merits of different types of writing systems, including the morphophonemic system, are to be found in Reed 1970.

We conclude this chapter with the observation that writing systems do not seem to be able to halt language change. On the contrary, language change has been one of the historical causes of revisions in alphabetic writing systems. Even though spellings such as *thru* for *through* are becoming much more common, it cannot be foreseen whether the current writing system of American English will be revised in the near future. Such revisions are as much a political issue as a practical one. In sum, the fact that sound-based writing systems become archaic is a reflection of the fact that language change is inexorable.

Key Words

diachronic linguistics
comparative method
Indo-European
reconstruction
proto-language
Grimm's Law
rule addition/loss/change
Old English

Study Questions

1. Discuss the various theories for the origin of human language.

2. What is the Indo-European language family?

3. What is one way to establish that languages are historically related (descendents of a common ancestor for which no written records exist)?

4. What is Grimm's Law? Illustrate its effect with some comparisons between English and Latin or Greek words.

5. What does it mean to say that some language changes move "wave-like" through a community of speakers?

6. What was the Great Vowel Shift? What consequences did this sound change have on contemporary English? Give examples in your answer.

7. What different kinds of semantic changes can words undergo? Give concrete examples.

Exercises

1. How can knowledge of Grimm's Law help one remember that a *podiatrist* is a *foot doctor?*

2. The Indo-European word **ghostis* corresponds to the Latin word *hostis* "enemy" and to the English word *guest*. What is a plausible meaning of *ghostis* in Proto-Indo-European that would account for the different meanings in Latin and English?

3. Using the accompanying chart, explain the relationships among the italicized words in the following English sentence: I turned up the *thermostat* on my *furnace* to get *warm*.

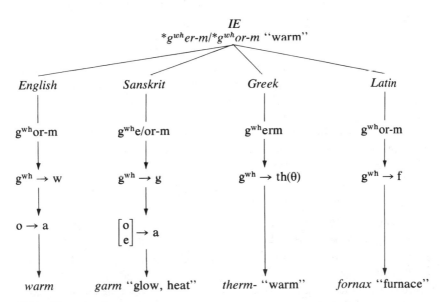

Chart (Exercise 3)

Changes that original IE **g^{wh}erm/*g^{w}horm* underwent in several daughter languages. The *n* found in Latin *fornax* is not from IE **m*, but instead is a different suffix that was added to the stem **g^{wh}or-*.

4. Each of the Indo-European words below has a cognate in English. Apply Grimm's Law (refer back to (8)) if applicable to the reconstructed Proto-Indo-European form (slightly altered for these exercises) and, making the appropriate changes in the vowels, determine which English word is related to the forms in Latin or Greek. Note if the meaning of the word has been *narrowed* or *broadened*.

Indo-European	Classical Languages
1. *$g^hw\bar{e}n$	1. Greek *gun-* "woman" (appears in English in the borrowed word *gynecologist*)
2. *$m\bar{u}s$	2. Latin *mūs* "mouse"
3. *$dek\underset{.}{m}$	3. Latin *decem* "ten"
4. *$gn\bar{o}$-	4. Greek *gnō-* "know" (appears in English in the borrowed word *agnostic*)
5. *$deiwos$ (corresponds to a day of the week)	5. Latin *deus* "god," Greek *Zeus*

Bibliography

Anttila, R. (1972). *An Introduction to Historical and Comparative Linguistics,* Macmillan, New York.

Bloomfield, L. (1933). *Language,* Holt, Rinehart and Winston, New York.

Bynon, T. (1977). *Historical Linguistics,* Cambridge University Press, Cambridge.

Fell, B. (1977). *America B.C.: Ancient Settlers in the New World,* Demeter Press Book, New York Times Book Company, New York.

Harnad, S., H. Steklis, and J. Lancaster (1976). *Origins and Evolution of Language and Speech,* Annals of the New York Academy of Science, Vol. 280, New York.

Hewes, G. (1976). "The current status of the gestural theory of language origins," in S. Harnad, H. Steklis, and J. Lancaster, eds. (1976).

Joos, M. (1942). "A phonological dilemma in Canadian English," *Language* 18, 141–144.

Lehmann, W. (1967). *A Reader in Nineteenth-Century Historical Linguistics,* Indiana University Press, Bloomington.

Lehmann, W. (1973). *Historical Linguistics: An Introduction,* 2nd. ed., Holt, Rinehart and Winston, New York.

Lehrer, A. (1974). *Semantic Fields and Lexical Structure,* North Holland, Amsterdam.

Lehrer, A., and P. Battan (1983). "Semantic fields and semantic change," *Coyote Papers 4,* Department of Linguistics, University of Arizona, Tucson.

Lenneberg, E. (1964). "A biological perspective of language," in E. Lenneberg, ed., *New Directions in the Study of Language,* MIT Press, Cambridge, Mass.

Lester, M. (1970). *Readings in Applied Transformational Grammar,* Holt, Rinehart and Winston, New York.

Lieberman, P. (1975). *On the Origins of Language: An Introduction to the Evolution of Human Speech,* Macmillan, New York.

Lightfoot, D. (1979). *Principles of Diachronic Syntax,* Cambridge University Press, New York.

Miller, G. (1981). *Language and Speech,* W. H. Freeman and Company, San Francisco.

Moore, S., and T. Knott (1963). *The Elements of Old English,* George Wahr Publishing Co., Ann Arbor, Mich.

Ober, J. (1965). *Writing: Man's Great Invention,* The Peabody Institute, Baltimore, Md.

Pedersen, H. (1962). *The Discovery of Language,* University of Indiana Press, Bloomington.

Reed, D. (1970). "A theory of language, speech, and writing," in M. Lester, ed. (1970).

Sloat, C., S. Taylor, and J. Hoard (1978). *Introduction to Phonology,* Prentice-Hall, Englewood Cliffs, N.J.

Traugott, E. (1972). *A History of English Syntax,* Holt, Rinehart and Winston, New York.

Part Three

COMMUNICATION AND
COGNITIVE SCIENCE

Introduction

In the previous chapters we have explored human language as an abstract system with numerous structural (morphological, phonological, syntactic, and semantic) properties. We have seen that human language can be fruitfully analyzed in terms of various units of representation (features, phonemes, morphemes, words, phrases, sentences, concepts, etc.), along with rules that capture regularities and generalizations among these units. Thus, various "levels" in the description of a language (the morphological, phonological, syntactic, and semantic levels) represent regularities in the behavior of the units at that level, and such levels in linguistics are like the levels in other sciences. For instance, chemists describe substances in terms of elements and their principles of combination: water is two parts hydrogen and one part oxygen, combined in a certain way. A physicist might then describe oxygen and hydrogen in terms of their atomic structure, atomic weight, and principles of atomic interaction. Furthermore, it is an important fact about human languages that they are susceptible to variation and change (we do not view the principles that govern the world of physics as varying or changing, though our knowledge of them surely will), and we have seen that often such variation and change is itself principled in interesting ways.

It is now time to remind ourselves, theoretically, of the importance of the fact that languages are *used* and *learned* by human beings (and many would say *only* by human beings). How could a language change or vary if it were not? Thinking of languages as being used and learned by humans raises still more questions, such as, How do people use language to communicate? How is this knowledge represented in and utilized by the mind/brain? How is it learned?

In chapter 9 we explore the nature of linguistic communication. Speaking a language involves producing sounds for others to hear, understand, and act upon. How is it possible for a speaker to put thoughts into words and for a hearer to understand them? This, it turns out, is not a trivial or simple accomplishment; a rich and subtle system of principles underlies this apparently facile skill.

It is an important fact about human beings that virtually all of them learn to speak a language. Placed in a minimal linguistic environment, all human children with normal brain function will quickly and almost effortlessly acquire the language spoken around them. Thus, we should expect that human language and its use will be interestingly related to human cognition. So far this has proved to be true, and a richly diverse new field called *cognitive science* has developed, incorporating aspects of linguistics, philosophy, psychology, neurology, and computer science. The basic idea behind cognitive science is that the study of human cognition (perception, memory, thought, and action) should be a unified subject of research, drawing on the expertise of many traditional disciplines. For instance, in computer science one learns how to write programs that can perform certain tasks. One also learns how machines can be built that will execute these programs and actually display the capacity written into them. Cognitive science draws on these activities of computer science, using them as an analogy that helps to unify our picture of the human mind. What if the human mind is like a mental "program" and neurons are our "hardware"? Knowing how programs and hardware are related in computer science might help us better understand, by analogy, how our knowledge and our thoughts might be related to the neuron structure of our brains. In particular, we might understand better how our knowledge of language and our ability to speak and understand might be related to the structure of our brain.

One of the most active areas of psychology is the study of linguistic knowledge, how it is acquired, and how it is used in the production and comprehension of speech. In chapters 10 and 11 we investigate some significant results in *psychology of language* (also called *psycholinguistics*). Chapter 10 is devoted to exploring issues in the production and comprehension of speech. Here we consider how linguistic knowledge might be represented in the mind and how this information can be put to use in speaking and understanding. Following the flow of information from speaker to hearer, we will both review broad theoretical options and report interesting experimental results.

Chapter 11 is devoted to the study of the acquisition of language. Here we examine the character of normal language development in the (human) child, and the implications this process might have for better understanding human biological endowment. For instance, are human beings preprogrammed to learn (or create) the kind of language system we have been describing? Can the young of another species (such as primates) acquire human language, and if so do they acquire it in the same way? To begin to answer these questions, we first explore the normal course of human language development. We then survey some recent and controversial attempts to teach American Sign Language to chimpanzees. Do they learn as human children do, or are there important differences?

Given that human language is clearly unique among communication systems in its richness and complexity, and given the natural disposition human children have for mastering it, it is quite reasonable to suppose that there is something special about the human brain, either in capacity or in its structural organization, that makes this distinctively human achievement possible. In spite of the splendid work in the last few decades of a highly dedicated group of neuroscientists, we are still quite ignorant about the structure and functioning of the human brain. In fact, the study of the human brain has often been described as the next intellectual frontier. It is certainly true that we understand the rest of the human body a great deal better than we understand the brain. Chapter 12 is devoted to some of the central ideas and controversies to come out of *neurolinguistics,* the study of the neural basis of language. Since it is hardly feasible to perform experiments on the neuroanatomy of speakers' brains, a crucial source of data about how language might be represented and used by the brain is the experience of patients suffering some loss of speech or comprehension due to brain injuries.

All in all, it seems that linguists will gain a deeper perspective on their subject matter by seeing exactly how it is related to the neighboring concerns of psychology, neurology, and biology. Likewise, these neighboring areas of research can gain something from linguistics; languages constitute the richest and most rigorously described domain of human expertise yet. The structures and regularities discovered by linguists in their analyses of human languages pose a unique challenge to psychological, neurological, and biological theories of human capacities.

Chapter Nine

PRAGMATICS:
THE STUDY OF
LANGUAGE USE AND
COMMUNICATION

9.1 LINGUISTIC COMMUNICATION: SOME BACKGROUND CONCEPTS

Probably the most pervasive characteristic of human social interaction, so pervasive that we hardly find it remarkable, is that we talk. Sometimes we talk to particular persons, sometimes to anyone who will listen; and when we cannot find anyone to listen, we even talk to ourselves. Although human language fulfills a large variety of functions, from waking someone up in the morning with a cheery *Wake up!* to christening a ship with a solemn *I hereby christen this ship "H.M.S. Britannia,"* we will be focusing here on those uses of language that are instrumental for human communication. Fluent speakers of English, for instance, know facts such as:

(1)
a. *Hello* is used to greet.
b. *Goodbye* is used to bid farewell.
c. The phrase *that desk* can be correctly used by a speaker on a given occasion to refer to some particular desk.
d. The phrase *is a desk* can be correctly used on a given occasion to characterize any number of desks.
e. *Pass the salt, please* is used to request some salt.
f. *How old are you?* is used to ask someone's age.
g. *It's raining* is used to state that it is raining.
h. *I promise I will be there* is used to promise.

From the above list we get a glimpse of the wide variety of possible uses of language, but before we survey these various uses, we must first distinguish between using language *to do* something and using language *in doing* something. It is certainly a very important fact about human beings that we use language *in* much of our thought. It is likely that we could not think some of the thoughts we think, especially abstract thoughts, if we did not have language at our disposal. Central as this fact may be to our cognitive life, it is not central to the pragmatic notion of language use, the use of language to *do* things. When we focus on what people use language to do, we focus on what a person is doing with words in particular situations; we focus on the intentions, purposes, beliefs, and desires that a speaker has in speaking.

When Charles Morris proposed his famous trichotomy of syntax, semantics, and pragmatics, he defined the last as "the study of the relation of signs to interpreters" (1938, 6), but soon generalized this to "the relation of signs to their users" (1938, 29). One year later Rudolf Carnap proposed to "call *pragmatics* the field of all those investigations which take into consideration . . . the action, state, and environment of a man who speaks or hears [a linguistic sign]" (1939, 4). This tradition continues; both linguists and philosophers (see Gazdar 1979, Bach and Harnish 1979) have taken the term *pragmatics* to cover the study of language use in relation to context, and in particular the study of linguistic communication.

As common and effortless as it is to talk, using language successfully is a very complex enterprise, as anyone knows who has tried as an adult to master a second language. Moreover, much goes into using a language besides knowing it and being able to produce and recognize sentences in it. Communication is also a social affair, usually taking place within the context of a fairly well defined social situation. In such a context we rely on one another to share our conception of what the situation is. With people we know, rather than spell everything out, we rely on shared understandings to facilitate the problem of communicating.

The Problem

What sort of process is this? Linguistic communication is easily accomplished but, as it turns out, not so easily explained; any theory of linguistic communication worth the title must attempt to answer the following question:

(2)

How does successful communication work? For example, suppose that
a speaker, S, has an *intention* to report to a hearer, H, that conditions
on the road are icy. What makes it possible for S to communicate this
to H?

Strangely enough, this question has not received intensive consideration in the literature of any major discipline. Linguistics, focusing on
structural properties of language, has tended to view communicative
phenomena as outside its official domain. Likewise, it seems possible to
pursue philosophical concerns about meaning, truth, and reference
without investigating the details of communication. Traditional psychology has focused on the processing of sentences, but without much
concern for the specifics of communicative phenomena. Finally, some
sociologists and anthropologists have begun to concern themselves
with conversations, but have bypassed (or assumed an answer to) the
question of the nature of communication itself. Thus, what is needed is
an integrated approach to communication, where the question of its
nature is the focus of investigation. Only recently has the general shape
of an adequate theory of communication begun to emerge, and more
time and research will be required to explore it in detail.

The Message Model of Linguistic Communication

For the last thirty years the most common and popular conception of
human linguistic communication has been what we will term the *Message Model*. This theory is simply a specific version of the general
communication model presented in chapter 2 (recall figure 2.1) in the
discussion of animal communication. When the Message Model is
applied to human linguistic communication between speakers of a language, the speaker acts as a "transmitter," the hearer acts as a "receiver," and the vocal-auditory path (the sound wave) is the relevant
channel. The Message Model for human communication is illustrated in
figure 9.1.

This model accounts for certain commonsense features of talk-
exchanges: it predicts that communication is successful when the
hearer decodes the same message that the speaker encodes; and as a
corollary it predicts that communication breaks down if the decoded
message is different from the encoded message. Likewise, it portrays
language as a bridge between speaker and hearer whereby "private"

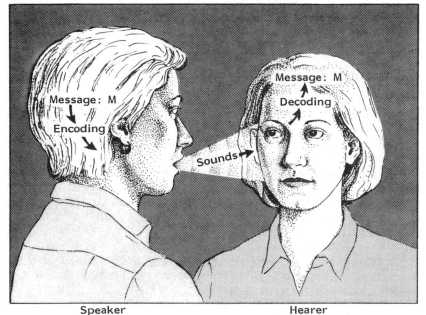

Figure 9.1
The Message Model of talk-exchanges. A speaker has some message in mind
that she wants to communicate to a hearer. The speaker then produces some
expression E from the language that encodes the message as its meaning. Upon
hearing the beginning of E, the hearer begins a decoding process that sequentially identifies the incoming sounds, syntactic categories, and meanings, then
composes these meanings in the form of the successfully decoded message.

ideas are communicated by "public" sounds, which thereby function as
the vehicle for communicating the relevant message.

Though it has a modern ring, the Message Model goes back at least
three centuries to the philosopher John Locke, who wrote in 1691 that

Man, therefore, had by nature his organs so fashioned, as to be fit to
frame articulate sounds, which we call words. But this was not enough
to produce language; for parrots, and several other birds, will be taught
to make articulate sounds distinct enough, which yet by no means are
capable of language.

Besides articulate sounds, therefore, it was further necessary that he
should be able to use these sounds as signs of internal conceptions; and
to make them stand as marks for the ideas within his own mind,
whereby they might be made known to others and the thoughts of
men's minds be conveyed from one to another.

The comfort and advantage of society not being to be had without communication of thoughts, it was necessary that man should find out some external sensible signs, whereof those invisible ideas, which his thoughts are made up of, might be made known to others.

There are, moreover, many contemporary statements of essentially this same idea:

The speaker, for reasons that are linguistically irrelevant, chooses some message he wants to convey to his listeners: some thought he wants them to receive or some command he wants to give them or some question he wants to ask. This message is encoded in the form of a phonetic representation of an utterance by means of the system of linguistic rules with which the speaker is equipped. This encoding then becomes a signal to the speaker's articulatory organs, and he vocalizes an utterance of the proper phonetic shape. This, in turn, is picked up by the hearer's auditory organs. The speech sounds that stimulate these organs are then converted into a neural signal from which a phonetic representation equivalent to the one into which the speaker encoded his message is obtained. This representation is decoded into a representation of the same message that the speaker originally chose to convey by the hearer's equivalent system of linguistic rules. Hence, because the hearer employs the same system of rules to decode that the speaker employs to encode, an instance of successful linguistic communication occurs. (Katz 1966, 103–104)

There can be little doubt that this model has fascinated many who are interested in human communication, and it is entrenched, to some extent, in our language. For example, Reddy (1979, 311–316) lists some 80 metaphors built on the idea of language as a "conduit for ideas," among which are the following:

(3)
a. Try to *get* your thoughts *across* better.
b. You still haven't *given* me any idea of what you mean.
c. Try to *pack* more thoughts into fewer words.
d. The sentence was *filled* with emotion.
e. Let me know if you *find* any good ideas *in* this essay.

According to Reddy (1979, 290), the major ideas structuring this metaphor are:

(1) language functions like a conduit, transferring thoughts bodily from one person to another; (2) in writing and speaking, people insert their thoughts or feelings in the words; (3) words accomplish the transfer by containing the thoughts or feelings and conveying them to others; and (4) in listening or reading, people extract the thoughts and feelings once again from the words.

These are clear analogues of the major tenets of the Message Model, and this suggests that our language has come to reflect this conception of communication.

Problems with the Message Model

In order to determine the meaning of expressions, the hearer must be able to mentally process sentences that reflect complex structural properties of human language (such as structural ambiguity and discontinuous dependencies). The decoding of the meaning(s) of a sentence is certainly a crucial part of linguistic communication, but the communicative process does not end with processing structural properties and decoding meaning. Indeed, there is considerably more to the process, and it is here that the Message Model encounters a number of problems. We will briefly outline six typical problems faced by the Message Model, and in so doing we hope to give an idea of how complex the communication process is.

First, since many expressions are linguistically ambiguous, the hearer must determine which of the possible meanings of an expression is the one the speaker intended as operative on that occasion. Thus, as far as the Message Model is concerned, disambiguation is a process that is not governed by any principles, and the Message Model certainly does not supply any such principles. But in actuality, contextual disambiguation is not unprincipled and random; rather, it is usually quite predictable. Although humorous cases of misunderstanding do arise from time to time, in general we do a good job of picking the appropriate reading of an ambiguous expression. To overcome ambiguity, the hearer presumes the speaker's remarks to be *contextually appropriate*. For example, at an airport zoning meeting the sentence *Flying planes can be dangerous* would naturally be taken as a remark about the danger of planes flying overhead; but at a meeting of the Pilot's Insurance Board it would naturally be taken as a reminder of occupational risk. To take another example, imagine the following conversation:

(4)
A: We lived in Illinois, but we got Milwaukee's weather.
B: Which was worse

Notice that without some extra optional cue (such as intonation), A does not know whether B was making an assertion or asking a question:

(5)
Assertion: It was worse getting Milwaukee's weather!
Question: Which weather was it worse to get?

Hence, the Message Model must be supplemented by principles of contextual appropriateness to compensate for the pervasive ambiguity of natural language.

Second, the Message Model does not account for the fact that the message often contains information about particular things being referred to, and reference is rarely uniquely determined by the meaning of expressions. For example, the phrase *the shrewd politician* in the sentence *The shrewd politician won the election* can be used on different occasions to refer to different people such as Winston Churchill, Richard Nixon, and Franklin D. Roosevelt. Yet the phrase always means one thing ("politician who is shrewd"). A hearer who thinks of Richard Nixon when the speaker's intended referent is Franklin Roosevelt will not have understood the message correctly. So the Message Model must be supplemented by mechanisms for successfully recognizing the intention to refer.

Third, the Message Model represents successful communication as simply producing, hearing, and understanding meaningful expressions. But this is not all there is to communication—after all, parrots, tape recorders, and sleep-talkers can play the speaker's role in the Message Model, yet they cannot be said to communicate in any interesting sense. What is missing in the model so far is an account of the speaker's *communicative intention,* which is not, in general, uniquely determined by the meaning of the expression uttered. For example, *I'll be there tonight* might be a prediction, a promise, or even a threat, depending upon the speaker's intentions in the appropriate circumstances. Despite these various intentions on the part of the speaker, the sentence has only one relevant meaning.

One of the most interesting facts about communicative intentions is that they are intended to be recognized. When given speakers intend to communicate something, they intend to be recognized as trying to communicate it, and communication is successful only if the hearer recognizes that intention. Thus, if a speaker utters the sentence *I'll be there tonight,* intending it as a threat, and if the hearer fails to recognize the speaker's intention and takes the utterance as a simple prediction, then communication has broken down.

Fourth, the Message Model does not account for the additional fact that we often speak *nonliterally;* that is, we do not mean what our words mean. Common cases of this are irony, sarcasm, and figurative uses of language such as metaphor. Thus, a speaker who says *Oh, that's just great* can, in the appropriate context, be taken to mean the opposite of what the words mean. (Think of discovering a flat tire on your way to class in the morning.) Nonliteral cases are especially difficult for the Message Model to accommodate, since in nonliteral communication the message conveyed by the speaker does not incorporate the literal meaning at all. Rather, the hearer is intended to *use* the literal meaning in figuring out what the speaker actually intends to communicate.

Fifth, the Message Model does not account for the fact that we sometimes mean to communicate more than what our sentences mean. We sometimes speak *indirectly;* that is, we sometimes intend to perform one communicative act by means of performing another communicative act. For example, it would be quite natural to say *My car has a flat tire* to a gas station attendant, with the intention that he repair the tire: in this case we are *requesting* the hearer to *do* something. But how can the speaker mean that the hearer is to do something if the sentence he utters merely reports on the state of his car? The answer is that in uttering the sentence the speaker is (literally and) *directly* reporting a state of affairs presumed to be unsatisfactory and is *indirectly* requesting the hearer to rectify the situation. How does a hearer know if a speaker is speaking indirectly as well as directly? Again, the answer is contextual appropriateness. In the above case, it would be contextually inappropriate to be only reporting a flat tire at a gas station. In contrast, if a police officer asks why a motorist's car is illegally parked, a simple report of a flat tire would be a contextually appropriate response. In the latter circumstance, the hearer (the police officer) would certainly not take the speaker's words as a request to fix the tire. Again, we see the surprisingly pervasive role that presumptions of contextual appropriateness play in successful communication. A speaker can use the very same sentence to convey quite different messages depending on the context.

The final problem with the Message Model is that communicating a message is not always the purpose of our remarks. For example, there are "institutional" acts such as firing or baptizing someone, whose function is to change the institutional status of that person. There are also "institutional" speech acts such as calling a base runner out or finding a defendant guilty, which involves judgments of truth with institutional and social consequences. Communicative success is not the point of such "ritual" utterances since the runner is out, the employee is fired, and the baby is baptized, whether or not they recognize it at the time. Thus, it is not necessary to recognize any communicative intention for these acts to succeed. Likewise, there are speech acts (called *perlocutionary acts*) involving the causing of an effect in a hearer. For instance, a speaker might say things with an intent to persuade, impress, or deceive an audience, but the members of the audience may well not be persuaded, impressed, or deceived if they happen to recognize the speaker's intention to do these things. In contrast, communicative intentions are always intended to be recognized.

To summarize, the Message Model would answer question (2) as follows:

(6)
Linguistic communication is possible because messages have been conventionalized as the meaning of expressions, and by sharing knowledge of the meaning of an expression E, the hearer can recognize a speaker's message—the speaker's communicative intention.

We have seen that this answer to the central question of communication is seriously defective, in that it does not accommodate most of the common cases of linguistic communication. For instance, the Message Model of communication assumes that (1) the language is unambiguous, (2) what the speaker is referring to is determined by the meaning of the referring expressions uttered, (3) the communicative intention is determined by the meaning of the sentence, (4) speakers only speak literally, and (5) speakers only speak directly; and it suggests that (6) speakers use words only to communicate.

The six problem areas discussed above show why the simple Message Model of talk-exchanges does not even begin to be adequate to account for the full richness of normal human language use. Clearly, more than just a common language is required to enable the hearer to identify the speaker's communicative intentions on the basis of the speaker's utterances. A *shared system of beliefs and inferences* must be operating, which function in effect as communicative strategies.

9.2 AN INFERENTIAL APPROACH TO COMMUNICATION

If the connection between a speaker's communicative intention (message) and a sentence is *not* one of conventional coding of the message into the sentence via its meaning, then what is it? What is the connection between sounds and communicative intentions that makes communication in all its forms possible?

Basically, the connection is *inferential*. According to the theory of communication to be presented here (see Bach and Harnish 1979, Harnish 1983), linguistic communication is successful when the hearer, upon hearing an expression, recognizes the speaker's communicative intention. Thus, we propose the following inferential answer to the question in (2):

(7)
Linguistic communication is possible because the speaker S and hearer H share a system of inferential strategies leading from the utterances of expression E to H's recognition of S's communicative intent.

If this is the correct approach to take to communication, then we need to know more about the system of inferential strategies; we want to know how such a system can account for successful communication, while avoiding the limitations of the Message Model. In particular, we want to know how it (i) incorporates the notion of communicative intentions, (ii) does not make these communicative intentions uniquely determined by the meaning of the expression uttered, and (iii) accounts for literal, nonliteral, direct, and indirect ways of communicating. We take up these matters in the next three sections.

Direct and Literal Communication

The Message Model of linguistic communication applies, if at all, only to a highly idealized form of communication—which may not ever actually take place! However, if one tries to construct a theory of actual, normal communication, then the idea that *rules* or *conventions* of language connect sounds with messages is replaced by the idea that systems of *intended inference* and *shared beliefs* are at work, and that therefore the real job of the communicative part of pragmatics is to investigate these systems.

In what follows we will do just that. The basic idea is quite simple: linguistic communication is a kind of problem solving. The speaker faces the problem of getting the hearer to recognize certain communicative intentions; so the speaker must choose an expression that will facilitate such recognition, given the context of utterance. From the hearer's point of view the problem is to successfully recognize the speaker's communicative intent on the basis of the words the speaker has chosen and the context of utterance. If the speaker and hearer had to solve these problems from scratch, there is no way communication could succeed as often as it apparently does.

The Inferential Model of communication proposes that in the course of learning to speak our language we also learn how to communicate in that language, and learning this involves acquiring a variety of shared beliefs or *presumptions,* as well as a system of inferential *strategies.* The presumptions allow us to presume certain helpful things about potential hearers (or speakers) and the inference strategies provide communicants with short, effective patterns of inference from what someone utters to what that person might be trying to communicate. Taken together, the presumptions and strategies provide the basis for an account of successful linguistic communication.

We first introduce the presumptions and the strategies in a preliminary, simplified form (see the Appendix for a more detailed formulation):

Presumptions

Linguistic Presumption (LP)
The hearer is presumed capable of determining the meaning and the referents of the expression uttered.

Communicative Presumption (CP)
Unless there is evidence to the contrary, a speaker is assumed to be speaking with some identifiable communicative intent.

Presumption of Literalness (PL)
Unless there is evidence to the contrary, the speaker is assumed to be speaking literally.

Conversational Presumptions (ConPs)
Relevance: The speaker's remarks are relevant to the conversation.
Sincerity: The speaker is being sincere.
Truthfulness: The speaker is attempting to say something true.
Quantity: The speaker contributes the appropriate amount of information.
Quality: The speaker has adequate evidence for what he or she says.

If a speaker and hearer share the above presumptions on a given occasion, then the problem of successful communication is much easier to solve, since the hearer already has a fairly specific set of conversational expectations. Moreover, we will propose that the speaker and hearer also share a system of inference strategies, each of which handles one of the inadequacies in the Message Model. Thus, there will be strategies not only for direct and literal communication, but also for indirect and nonliteral communication. We can "flowchart" these strategies as shown in figure 9.2.

Strategies for Literal and Direct Communication

We have been advocating the idea that even the "simplest" forms of linguistic communication are complicated affairs, and that once we drop the idealizations that the Message Model imposes, we can see that we need more than just rules of language. Rather, we need notions like *intended inference, shared contextual beliefs,* and various *presumptions* to explicate the connection between sounds and communicative intents.

We now want to put these ingredients together into inferential *strategies* for literal and direct communication. That is, we want to represent the patterns of inference, presumption, and shared beliefs that go into this form of communication.

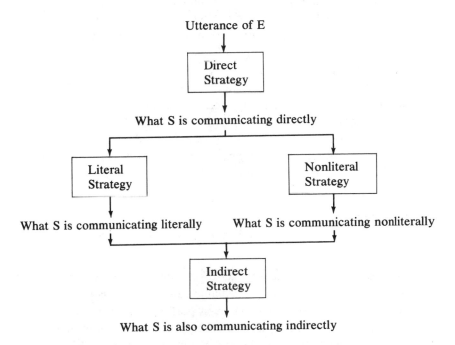

Figure 9.2
The system of inferential strategies

Our first strategy, the *Direct Strategy,* will enable the hearer H to infer from what H hears the speaker S utter to what S is directly communicating.

Any alternative to the Message Model of linguistic communication must represent any information the hearer is intended to make use of in order to understand the speaker, in spite of ambiguity. It may seem trivial, but clearly one of the most basic pieces of information the hearer needs for communication to be successful is to know what expression the speaker uttered. If the hearer mistakes the words, it is unlikely the message will be understood. So the first step in successful communication is for the hearer to recognize the speaker's utterance:

(Step 1)
Utterance Act
The hearer H recognizes what expression, E, the speaker S has uttered.

Recall that the first failure of the Message Model involves ambiguity. The Message Model makes no allowance for the fact that the expression uttered may be ambiguous and that the hearer will usually be expected (by the speaker) to realize which meaning was intended to be operative on that occasion. Often, one meaning is contextually inappropriate, and the speaker will be assumed to mean only the appropriate one. For instance, the sentence *Give me a cheap gas can* has the potential for meaning either *Give me a can for cheap gas* or *Give me a gas can which is cheap.* We normally take it to mean only the latter because we use the same cans for cheap and expensive gas. However, it is possible that cheap gas could require a different kind of can. Thus, once the expression is heard, the hearer must decide which meaning of the expression is the relevant intended one. This process is still not well understood, so we will simply represent the hearer's success as step 2:

(Step 2)
Operative Meaning
H recognizes which meaning of E is intended to be operative on this occasion.

However, even after the hearer has disambiguated the expression in the context, another task usually remains before it is possible to determine what communicative act has been performed. As noted before, this involves determining what, if anything, the speaker is referring to. This is a problem because reference is rarely determined solely by the meaning of the utterance. This is clearer if we remember that a message is often about particular objects in the world, but the *meaning* of an expression in the language rarely, if ever, determines *which* objects. Even "singular" referring expressions like *the book I left at your house, John,* and *he* can be used to refer to endless different objects without changing their meaning. In normal communication we presume that the hearer can use the operative meaning of the expression as well as the context to determine our references. Thus, the next step of H's inference will be to identify what it is that S is referring to:

(Step 3)
Speaker's Reference
H recognizes what S is referring to.

The third problem for the Message Model involves the "message." Just because a speaker produces some sounds (an *utterance*) does not guarantee that something is being communicated, since it is possible to utter words without communicating anything: we can talk in our sleep, give examples of grammatical sentences, practice our pronunciation, or just recite a pleasant-sounding phrase. Moreover, we do not expect hearers to figure out that we are intending to communicate each time we say something; rather, we rely on the Communicative Presumption to alert hearers to the presence of a communicative intent.

One of the most interesting facts about communicative intentions is that they are intended to be recognized. When speakers try to communicate something, they intend to be understood as trying to communicate, and they are successful in communicating when the hearer recognizes that intention. Thus, for a speaker to request hearers to do something and be successful in that communication, hearers must understand not only *what* is being requested, but also *that* they are being requested. To take our earlier example, if a speaker utters the sentence *I'll be there tonight,* then if it is a promise, the hearer must recognize the utterance *as* a promise in order for communication to be successful. If the speaker instead intends the utterance to be a threat, then the hearer must take it *as* a threat for communication to be successful. Communication breaks down if the speaker intends the utterance one way and the hearer takes it another way.

Given this, it is easy to see that in successful communication the hearer can use the Communicative Presumption as well as contextual information and the Operative Meaning to infer what it is that the speaker might be *doing* — what *communicative act* the speaker might be performing. If the inference is correct, the speaker's communicative intention will be recognized and communication will be successful:

(Step 4)
Direct
H recognizes what S is intending to communicate directly.

The *Direct Strategy* is therefore simply this: from step 1, infer steps 2, 3, and 4. We diagram this strategy in figure 9.3.

The next strategy, the *Literal Strategy,* will enable the hearer to infer from what the speaker would be directly communicating, if speaking literally, to what the speaker is literally (and directly) communicating. Recall that the fourth failure of the Message Model involves the nature of the connection between the message and the meaning of the expression uttered. The fact is that we do not always mean (to communicate) just what our words mean. The Message Model of communication has no way of handling cases requiring the message to be distinct from the meaning of the expression uttered. To accommodate nonliteral utterances, we must elaborate the above communicative step, since the hearer really has a choice to make upon hearing an utterance: is the speaker speaking literally (and if not, what *is* he or she trying to communicate)? Thus, the next step in the hearer's communicative inference would be to recognize the fact that it would be contextually appropriate for the speaker to be speaking literally:

(Step 5)
Contextual Appropriateness
H recognizes that it would be contextually appropriate for S to be speaking literally.

However, we do not seem to always be in a quandary about how to take people's words. According to the Presumption of Literalness, lit-

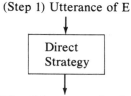

(Step 1) Utterance of E

Direct
Strategy

(Step 4) What S is communicating directly

Figure 9.3
The Direct Strategy

eral utterances seem to have a certain communicative priority in that we presume a person to be speaking literally unless there is some reason to suppose the contrary (for some psychological evidence, see chapter 10). Given this presumption, the hearer can infer what the speaker is communicating literally:

(Step 6)
Literal
H recognizes what S is intending to communicate literally (and directly).

The hearer who reasons to step 6 will take the speaker to be speaking literally simply on the basis that there is nothing contextually inappropriate in doing so. But what is it to be contextually appropriate? Many things can contribute to this, but among the most important are certain shared beliefs about the nature, stage, and direction of the talk-exchange. We can call these kinds of beliefs *Conversational Presumptions* (see Grice 1975). For example, there is a presumption of *Relevance* to the effect that the speaker's contribution to the talk-exchange is relevant at that point. There is a presumption of *Sincerity* to the effect that speakers believe what they say, want what they ask for, intend to do what they commit themselves to, etc. Moreover, there is a presumption of *Truthfulness* to the effect that speakers attempt to say what is true, and presumptions concerning the *Quantity* (speakers say not too much, not too little) and *Quality* (speakers have adequate evidence for what they say) of information that is offered. There are also Conversational Presumptions that speakers will speak clearly, politely, and ethically (see the Appendix). The violation of any of these presumptions, when they are thought to be in effect, can constitute a case of contextual inappropriateness.

In conclusion, the *Literal Strategy* is simply this: from step 4 of the Direct Strategy, infer steps 5 and 6, given the Presumption of Literalness and the Conversational Presumptions. We diagram this strategy in figure 9.4, adding it to the previously illustrated Direct Strategy. A hearer H who follows these strategies can infer what S is literally and directly communicating, from what H hears S utter. If H is correct in this inference, communication will have been successful; but if H fails, so will communication.

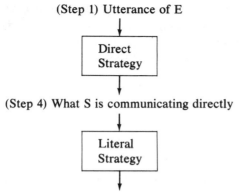

(Step 1) Utterance of E

Direct
Strategy

(Step 4) What S is communicating directly

Literal
Strategy

(Step 6) What S is communicating literally (and directly)

Figure 9.4
The Direct and Literal Strategies

Nonliteral Communication

Sometimes when we speak, we do mean something other than what our words mean. When what we mean to communicate is not compatible with what our expression literally means, then we are speaking nonliterally. Here are some typical examples of utterances that are sometimes uttered nonliterally.

Overstatement

(8)
a. No one understands me. (Not enough people understand me.)
b. A pig wouldn't eat this food. (A person, given a choice, wouldn't eat it.)
c. Her eyes opened as wide as saucers. (Her eyes opened very wide.)
d. I can't make a shot today. (I'm making very few.)

(9)
That was the worst food I've ever had. (It was very bad.)

(10)
a. Paul Newman *is* Jesse James. (Paul Newman plays the part convincingly, or with conviction.)
b. We do it all for you. (We look after your interests.)
c. When you say "Bud," you've said it all. (All that needs to be said about beer.)

d. If it's not Schlitz, it's not beer. (Not the way beer should be.)

e. The future is now. (You should prepare now for the future.)

Irony, Sarcasm

(11)

a. Boy, this food is terrific! (terrible)

b. That argument is a real winner. (loser)

Figures of Speech

(12)

a. I've got three *hands* (workers) here to help.

b. Look at the *TV Guide* and see what's on the *tube* (TV)!

c. Down in Texas, cattle are only $200 a *head* (animal).

If one thing bears a very close association to another, the utterance is sometimes classified as a case of *metonymy:*

(13)

a. The White House (the president or staff) said so.

b. The Crown (the monarch or staff) said so.

c. I have read all of Chomsky (Chomsky's works).

If the connection is some kind of similarity or comparison, then the utterance is sometimes classified as a *metaphor:*

(14)

a. He punted the idea away. (He totally rejected the idea.)

b. Kim is a block of ice. (Kim is cold and unresponsive.)

c. She's a ball of fire. (She's got a lot of energy.)

d. Time is money. (Time is valuable.)

Note that these examples differ in one crucial respect: some are rare or novel or in some way have to be figured out (for example, (14a)), whereas others are often heard and verge on being cliches (for example, (14b)–(14d)). The crucial difference is that in the novel cases we must not only reason from various cues and context that the utterance is in fact nonliteral, but also use these cues and contextual information to figure out *what the speaker means.* We will say that these forms of communication are *nonstandardized.* Owing to prior exposure, precedence, or training, however, the other forms are *standardized* for a particular nonliteral interpretation (or a narrow range of such interpretations). With standardized forms, such as (11a–b) uttered with that distinctive bratty and sarcastic intonation, or (14c), it is only necessary to know from context *that* the speaker is speaking nonliterally—the hearer then automatically knows what the speaker is communicating because that form of words is *standardized* for that alternative message. In general, standardized forms are often on their way to becoming *new meanings,* but they have not yet lost all vestiges of their origins and still require some rudimentary reasoning (see Bach and Harnish 1979 (chaps. 9, 10), Morgan 1978).

In the case of (mainly nonstandardized) nonliteral communication, the hearer must figure out what the speaker is trying to communicate, given that S is speaking nonliterally. Why should H suppose that S is not speaking literally—that is, meaning what the expression means? A glance back at examples (8)–(14) will reveal that utterances of these (and similar) expressions would, if taken literally, violate Conversational Presumptions that are supposed to be in effect. For instance, if S were being sincere and truthful, and generally had beliefs similar to ours, then S could not *literally* mean

(10a)
Paul Newman is Jesse James.

(10e)
The future is now.

(14a)
He punted the idea away.

In these cases there is conflict between the literal meaning of the expression and the Conversational Presumptions, *if* S is speaking literally. Since H has no reason to suppose that S is not still abiding by the presumptions, H will infer that S is speaking *nonliterally.* In short, contextual inappropriateness can lead H to take S nonliterally. So instead of step 5, which records contextual appropriateness, we have alternative step 5', which records contextual *in*appropriateness:

(Step 5')
Contextual Inappropriateness
H recognizes that it would be contextually inappropriate for S to be speaking literally.

Once H realizes that S cannot plausibly mean what he or she says, there is the problem of figuring out what *was* meant. At this point H must make an intelligent guess as to what S's communicative intent might be, based on shared background information as well as the literal meaning of the expression uttered.

The literal meaning of the expression helps H in a number of different ways. From examples (8)–(14) we can infer some very general shared principles that can help H make this inference:

(P1) Sarcasm, Irony
The opposite of what is said

(P2) Metaphor
Some relation of salient similarity

(P3) Exaggeration
The next evaluation toward the midpoint of the relevant scale

Notice how a normal hearer might use (P1)–(P3) to interpret the examples of nonliteral communication given earlier. Suppose that S and H have just seen a movie and they share the belief that it was terrible. Under these circumstances it would be contextually inappropriate for one to say *That was a real winner* and mean it literally. So H will conclude that it is nonliteral, and that (P1) is the appropriate principle connecting what S said literally with what S meant nonliterally. If H does this correctly, H will conclude that S was intending to communicate *That was a real loser,* which is just the message we wanted to account for.

Thus, the information a hearer must recognize in order to make nonliteral communication possible is that the speaker does not mean what he or she has said, but rather means something related to it:

(Step 6′)
Nonliteral
H recognizes what S is communicating nonliterally (and directly).

When a hearer reaches step 6′ correctly, nonliteral communication is successful.

Strategies for Nonliteral Communication

As with literal and direct communication, in order to account for a common type of talk-exchange we have had to supplement considerably the resources of the Message Model. We will now add to our previous strategies the *Nonliteral Strategy:* from step 4 of the Direct Strategy, infer Steps 5′ and 6′. Our system of strategies is summarized in figure 9.5.

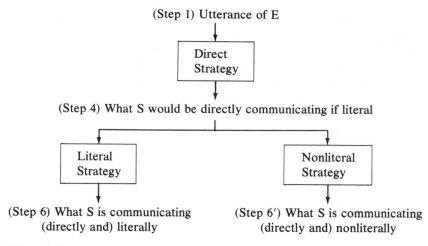

Figure 9.5
Literal and Nonliteral Direct Strategies

Indirect Communication

Sometimes when we speak we are not only performing some direct form of communication, but also speaking indirectly—we mean something *more* than what we mean directly. For instance:

(15)
a. The door is over there. (used to request someone to leave)
b. I want 10 gallons of regular. (used to request 10 gallons of regular)
c. I'm sure the cat likes having its tail pulled. (used to request H to stop pulling the cat's tail)
d. You're the boss. (used to agree to do what H says)
e. I should never have done that. (used to apologize)
f. Did you bring any tennis balls? (used to inform H that S did not bring any)
g. It's getting late. (used to request H to hurry)

Notice that indirect acts can be performed by means of either literal or nonliteral direct acts. Examples (15a) and (15b) are cases of indirect acts being performed by means of literal direct acts—S really does mean what is said, but also means *more*. In case (15c) this is not so; S does not, presumably, really mean that the cat likes having its tail pulled. Instead, S is being sarcastic—meaning directly, but nonliterally, that the cat does *not* like having its tail pulled, and wants H to conclude that H should stop it.

How does H know that S is not speaking merely directly? How does H know to seek an indirect use of language as well as a direct one? Mainly, again, by virtue of contextual inappropriateness. For instance, it would be strange if, on driving into a gas station, the speaker of (15b) had only been reporting his or her wants and was not also making a polite request for some gas. A mere report of what one now wants is relevant to the taking of a poll, perhaps, but is not contextually appropriate at a gas station. Thus, the same sorts of contextual information and presumptions used in recognizing previous communicative intentions and acts are also used with indirect acts.

The hearer is also able to use context and the Conversational Presumptions to *find* the speaker's indirect illocutionary intent. Once H identifies why S cannot merely be speaking directly, H is able to use this information to aid in recognizing S's indirect intent. Thus, reporting a desire for a tank of gas at a service station would be contextually inappropriate if that were all S was doing. Since requesting expresses the desire that H do something, it would be natural in the circumstances for H to conclude that in reporting this desire S was also requesting the gas, since requesting would be the contextually appropriate thing to do.

Once we are aware of such forms of communication, it becomes obvious how often we talk indirectly. (In fact, we do it so often that certain forms have become standardized for their *indirect* use. Such forms as "Could you lend me five dollars?", "Why don't you try the other key?", etc., are rarely used literally and directly in normal circumstances.) To account for the possibility of indirect communication, we must supplement our (literal and nonliteral) direct strategies with *indirect* strategies. To see how (nonstandardized) indirect communication works on an inferential model, we will examine one of the examples given earlier.

Suppose that S utters (15a) *The door is over there* to H, thereby indirectly requesting H to leave. How might H reason? The first thing H must notice is that it would be contextually inappropriate for S to be merely reporting the location of the door, assuming that S and H both already know the location of the door, and this is not relevant to the conversation. Thus, step 7 of the Inferential Model will be relevant to initiating a search for the indirect message; H will note the following information:

(Step 7)
Contextual Inappropriateness
H recognizes that it would be contextually inappropriate for S to be speaking merely directly.

As with nonliteral communication, H now faces a problem-solving situation; if S means something *more* than what is directly communicated, what is it? In the above example we might suppose that S and H were having a dispute, and in that case it would be clear that S was requesting H to leave. Unfortunately, little is known at present about the actual reasoning processes that take place during indirect communication, so we will represent only the result of an indirect inference:

(Step 8)
Indirect
H recognizes what S is also communicating indirectly.

In example (15a) the communication has both a direct and an indirect component. Moreover, the direct component is literal—S does really mean that the door is over there, though this is not all that is meant.

Strategies for Indirect Communication
We can now supplement the existing direct strategies with strategies for indirect communication. The *Indirect Strategy* says: from step 6 or 6', infer steps 7 and 8. The augmented system of strategies is shown in figure 9.6.

Looking back at (15c), we see an example of communication that has both a direct and an indirect component. The direct component in this case is *non*literal, however, in that S does not really mean that the cat likes having its tail pulled. In this case communication is successful only if H first applies the Direct Strategy and the Nonliteral Strategy, then the Indirect Strategy. That is, H must first reach step 6':

(Step 6')
Nonliteral
H recognizes what S is communicating nonliterally and directly; in particular, that S is nonliterally and directly claiming that the cat does not like having its tail pulled.

However, since the direct act would be conversationally inappropriate if it was the only communicative act being performed, H infers step 7:

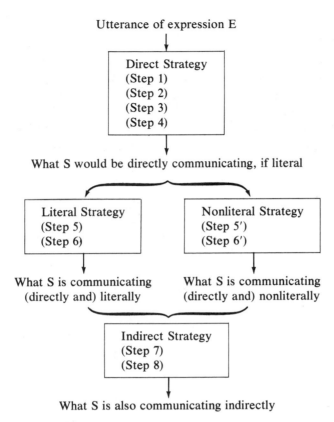

Figure 9.6
Strategies for direct and indirect communication

(Step 7)
Contextual Inappropriateness
H recognizes that it would be contextually inappropriate for S to be
merely speaking directly; in particular, merely claiming that the cat
does not like having its tail pulled.

H must recognize the indirect communicative intent as well, and will
therefore go on to step 8:

(Step 8)
Indirect
H recognizes what S is also communicating indirectly; in particular,
that S is requesting H to quit pulling the cat's tail.

When H reaches step 8, communication is complete and successful.

9.3 CONCLUSION: INFERENTIAL THEORIES VERSUS THE MESSAGE MODEL

The crucial defect of the Message Model of linguistic communication is that it equates the message a speaker intends to communicate with the meaning of some expression in the language. As we have seen, this leads to six specific defects: the Message Model cannot account for (1) the use of ambiguous expressions, (2) real world reference, (3) communicative intentions, (4) nonliteral communication, (5) indirect communication, and (6) noncommunicative uses of language.

To account for these sorts of facts, an Inferential Model is called for—that is, a model that connects the message with the meaning of the uttered expression by a sequence of inferences. This model involves a series of inference strategies that, if followed, take the hearer from hearing the expression uttered to the speaker's communicative intent. Moreover, each major step in the inference accounts for some failure of the Message Model. For instance, to infer step 2 is to infer the operative meaning, which is to contextually disambiguate the utterance and so avoid the first objection to the Message Model. The Inferential Model also includes referential, nonliteral, and indirect strategies, thereby avoiding the second, fourth, and fifth objections; and it provides an account of communicative intentions and noncommunicative uses of language, thereby avoiding problems three and six.

If the Inferential Model is correct, communicative competence is comprised, in part, by the mastery of certain pragmatic strategies, including the ones given above. Each strategy contains a pattern of inference and an appeal to various presumptions or shared contextual beliefs. These are the real building blocks of a theory of language use and communication.

9.4 DISCOURSE AND CONVERSATION

Even a casual survey of normal linguistic communication will reveal an important fact: the unit of communication is rarely a single complete sentence. Often we speak in single words, phrases, and fragments of sentences:

(16)
A: Want to see a movie tonight?
B: Uh, well, uh . . .
A: You don't want to, do you?

At other times we speak in units of two or more connected sentences:

(17)

A: Let me tell you about my ski accident. You see, I was . . .

Broadly speaking, the study of *discourse* is the study of units of language and language use consisting of more than a single sentence, but connected by some system of related topics. The study of discourse is sometimes more narrowly construed as the study of connected sequences of sentences (or sentence fragments) produced by a single speaker. In what follows we will construe the term *discourse* narrowly, and when more than one person is involved, we will speak of a *talk-exchange*. There are many forms of discourse and many forms of talk-exchange. Letters, jokes, stories, lectures, sermons, speeches, etc., are all categories of discourse; arguments, interviews, business dealings, instruction, and conversations are categories of talk-exchanges.

Conversations (and talk-exchanges in general) are usually structured sequences of expressions by more than a single speaker. This structure is rarely consciously apparent to speakers. However, we need only recall a conversation that has "gone wrong" in some sense, in order to become aware of the conversational principles we have mastered. Although the structure of conversations (and other talk-exchanges) has not been exhaustively described, being presently under intense investigation, we can summarize some of their major properties here. First, any reasonable number of people can participate, and there are principles that govern how and when people can take a turn. Second, there are principles that make certain aspects of the conversation socially obligatory, such as saying hello and goodbye. Third, as we have already seen, there are principles making contributions to conversations relevant to each other, such as answering questions or justifying refusals.

We will first illustrate some cases where English provides devices that are sensitive to communicative contexts and therefore useful in the study of both discourse in general and conversation in particular. We will then look at some of the salient features of conversational openings, turn-taking, and closings.

Language and Context

Our contributions to conversations both *reflect* and *affect* the linguistic and nonlinguistic context of utterance.

Our comments can *reflect* features of the context of utterance in that we often "watch our language" by avoiding certain words or phrases. More subtly, our language also has structural devices that allow us to merge more easily into the flow of conversation. Compare the following simple conversations:

(18)
Conversation 1
A: Who shot the bear?
B: John. John shot him. John shot the bear.
B': *It* was a bear *that* John shot.
B": *What* John shot *was* a bear.

(19)
Conversation 2
A: I don't see how the country is going to pull out of this economic slump.
B: *Speaking of* economics, . . .
B': *Speaking of* Reagan's economic advisors, . . .
B": *Speaking of North America,* . . .

The italicized devices are all sensitive to the speaker's beliefs and intentions concerning the communication situation; that is, to utter expressions containing these devices and be contextually appropriate requires certain beliefs and intentions on the part of the speaker. Thus, a speaker who does not believe that Reagan's economic advisors were spoken of in conversation 2 should not say "Speaking of Reagan's . . .". Likewise, in conversation 1, speaker A is focusing on John, but answers B' and B" focus on the bear; this disruption in continuity of topic makes these contributions subtly inappropriate.

Our comments also can *affect* the context by making it appropriate for the same speaker to go on and say one sort of thing rather than another. For instance, it would be appropriate for the speaker to follow (20a) with a joke and (20b) with a story, but not vice versa.

(20)
a. I heard a good joke yesterday. How many . . .
b. Here is the story, . . .

Or one speaker's remark might make it appropriate for another speaker to say one thing rather than another:

(21)

a. Tell me what you did in Paris!

b. Who remembers the plot of *King Lear?*

So language structure can both reflect and affect the course of a talk-exchange. In the sections that follow we will focus on a different kind of structure—the structure of conversations over time.

Openings

There are many ways of beginning a conversation or other talk-exchange. One is to start out with no preliminaries whatsoever: "Something's wrong with the Xerox machine." Another is to preface our remarks with an *opening*. For instance, there are a number of attention-getters (called *vocatives*) used at the beginning of a conversation, such as "Hey," "Hey, John," "Excuse me," "Say, . . ." Once we have the hearer's attention, we might then use a conversational parenthetical such as "You know," "Listen," "Know what?" But probably the most common opening in casual conversations is the *greeting*. Basically, a greeting is an expression of pleasure at meeting someone. But these expressions can vary enormously in complexity and formality. Consider, for instance, the following sample:

(22)

Casual

Hello! Good morning! Ahoy!

How are you? How have you been?

Look who just walked in! What a pleasant surprise!

(23)

Informal

Howdy! Hi! Greetings!

How y'doing? What's up?

Go ahead, don't say hello! (ironic) Long time no see!

(24)

Formal

Good day, Mrs.Smith.

To what do I owe this lucky meeting?

Greetings tend to be highly ritualized in form, in that we generally use a small number of them over and over again. They serve mostly to give everyone in the conversation a turn at saying something (notice that it would be odd if, halfway through the introductions, someone were to launch into a long narration on some topic). However, after a round of greetings it is normally quite proper for someone to take the floor and either begin the substance of the talk-exchange or initiate closings.

Turn-Taking

The person who starts speaking after the greetings are over in fact initiates the substance of the conversation by taking the next turn. How did that person get the conversational baton, and how is it passed on? One influential analysis (Sacks, Schegloff, and Jefferson 1974) has proposed that turn-taking is controlled by three principles:

(P1)
The speaker "selects" the next speaker.

(P2)
The first to talk becomes the speaker.

(P3)
The speaker continues his or her own remarks.

Current speakers "select" the next speaker in various ways, one of which, of course, is to ask someone a question. Generally the person being asked has the next turn, though someone else could, in accordance with principle 2, simply break in and start talking. Clearly, unless these remarks were urgent in some way, we would consider such an act rude. The same is true if the speaker asks someone a question and then keeps on talking, in accordance with principle 3. These observations suggest that principle 1 overrides principles 2 and 3 in the sense that principle 1 has conversational priority. A speaker who wants to violate that principle needs to have a good reason, on pain of being considered rude, ignorant, insensitive, etc. This in itself suggests that we have the sort of expectations about conversations that these principles describe.

Why do we have such principles governing conversations? One reason is that for information to get through, everyone cannot be talking at once, and sequencing principles help minimize the chances of disruptive overlap. When disruptive overlap does happen for any length of time, the result is usually embarrassing to other members of the conversation.

Even when turn-taking seems to be proceeding properly, a conversation might still go wrong. For instance, the participants may violate other conversational expectations by not accepting the conversational "roles" they should play in a given context. Certain styles of humor are based on conversations that have somehow gone wrong, a comic art brought to perfection by the Marx Brothers, as in the following "conversation" between Groucho and Chico in the film *Duck Soup* (quoted in Adamson 1973, 232):

Groucho: Now listen here. I've got a swell job for you, but first I'll have to ask you a couple of important questions. Now, what is it that has four pair of pants, lives in Philadelphia, and it never rains but it pours?
Chico: Atsa good one. I give you three guesses.
Groucho: Now, let me see. Has four pair of pants, lives in Philadelphia . . . Is it male or female?
Chico: No, I no think so.
Groucho: Is he dead?
Chico: Who?
Groucho: I don't know. I give up.
Chico: I give up too. Now I ask you another one. What is it got big black-a moustache, smokes a big black cigar, and is a big pain in the neck?
Groucho: Now, don't tell me. Has a big black moustache, smokes a big black cigar and is a big pain in the—
Chico: Uh—
Groucho: Does he wear glasses?
Chico: Atsa right. You guess it quick.
Groucho: Just for that, you don't get the job I was going to give you.
Chico: What job?
Groucho: Secretary of War.
Chico: All right, I take it.
Groucho: Sold!

The marvelous absurdity of this example shows, if nothing else, that "sensible" conversations involve much more than two people talking at each other.

Closings

Just as conversations rarely begin with their central topic, so they rarely come to an abrupt end. Participants don't simply quit talking—as with beginning conversations, they have a highly ritualized way of bringing normal conversations to an end. Schegloff and Sacks (1973) propose that the end of normal conversations consists of a *pre-*

closing sequence, where the participants more or less agree to close, followed by a *closing section,* where they actually do close. These two stages have some characteristic ways of being communicated. Consider the following samples:

(25)
Pre-closing
We-ell, it's been nice talking to you . . .
Say hello to Joan for me . . .

Closing
See you.
Goodbye. Bye bye. Bye. Cheerio. Ciao.

Except for special circumstances, such as forgetting something important, once the closing phase has been reached, the conversation should be brought to a conclusion. A speaker can do this either collectively with one remark or a glance at everybody, or separately with appropriate closings to each person or group of persons.

Conclusion

Normal conversations have a discernible structure. They tend to begin and end in certain ritualistic ways. The change of speakers tends to be orderly and based on principles of turn-taking. There tend to be recognizable levels of formality, informality, and familiarity in such interchanges. Moreover, the language seems to make available devices for smoothly integrating one's remarks into the flow of words. It should not be surprising that conversations reflect both social and linguistic principles; they are, after all, both social and linguistic events.

APPENDIX: SUMMARY OF PRESUMPTIONS AND INFERENCES

To overcome the major inadequacies of the Message Model of communication, we have appealed to various pragmatic presumptions as well as certain patterns of inference that are shared in a linguistic community. Here we will state these principles in a precise and convenient form.

Pragmatic Presumptions

Linguistic Presumption (LP)
The shared belief among members of the linguistic community C_L (i) that the members of C_L share the language L, and (ii) that whenever any member S utters an expression, E, in L to any other member H, then H can understand E and S's references, provided that H knows the meaning(s) of E and is aware of the appropriate background and contextual information.

Communicative Presumption (CP)
The shared belief among members of the linguistic community C_L that whenever a member S says something to another member H, S is doing so with some recognizable communicative intent.

Presumption of Literalness (PL)
The shared belief among members of the linguistic community C_L that if in uttering E, S could (under the circumstances) be taken appropriately as speaking literally, then S is speaking literally.

Conversational Presumptions (ConPs)
In the course of a talk-exchange, the speaker S and hearer H presume that at any point in the talk-exchange:
Relevance: S's contribution is relevant to the talk-exchange at that point.
Sequencing: S's contribution is of a communicative type appropriate to that stage of the talk-exchange.
Sincerity: S's contribution to the talk-exchange is sincere in that S has the attitudes expressed.
Quantity: S's utterance provides just the requisite amount of information, not too much, not too little.
Quality: S has adequate evidence for what is stated or presupposed in stating.
Truthfulness: S attempts to make the utterance true.
Manner: S speaks clearly; that is, S (i) avoids ambiguity, (ii) avoids obscurity of expression, (iii) avoids unnecessary wordiness, etc.
Politeness: S (in speaking) behaves politely; that is, S is not offensive, abusive, rude, vulgar, etc.
Morality: S (in speaking) behaves ethically; that is, S (i) does not reveal information that S ought not reveal, (ii) does not ask for information that S ought not have, (iii) does not direct H to do something H ought not do, (iv) is not committed to do something for H that H does not wish done, etc.

Pragmatic Inferences

In order for communication to be successful, the hearer must make certain inferences correctly, and the number of inferences required depends on the kind of communication the speaker intends to engage in; more inferences are required for nonliteral communication than for literal communication, and more inferences are required for indirect communication than for direct communication. Below we state the inferential steps for each major communicative strategy (Direct, Literal, Nonliteral, Indirect) and include as well the sort of evidential basis required for each step. After all, in order to make the correct inference, the hearer must have some reason to conclude one thing rather than another.

Direct Strategy
(Step 1)
Utterance Act: The hearer H recognizes what expression, E, the speaker S has uttered.
Basis: H has heard S utter this expression.

(Step 2)
Operative Meaning: H recognizes which meaning of E is intended to be operative.
Basis: Step 1, LP, contextual beliefs.

(Step 3)
Speaker's Reference: H recognizes what S is referring to.
Basis: Step 2, LP, contextual beliefs.

(Step 4)
Direct: H recognizes what S is intending to communicate directly, if speaking literally.
Basis: Step 2, step 3, CP, contextual beliefs.

Literal Strategy
(Step 5)
Contextual Appropriateness: H recognizes that it would be contextually appropriate for S to be speaking literally.
Basis: Step 4, ConPs, contextual beliefs.

(Step 6)
Literal: H recognizes what S is intending to communicate literally (and directly).
Basis: Step 5, PL.

Nonliteral Strategy
(Step 5′)
Contextual Inappropriateness: H recognizes that it would be contextually inappropriate for S to be speaking literally.
Basis: Step 4, ConPs, contextual beliefs.

(Step 6′)
Nonliteral: H recognizes what S is communicating nonliterally (and directly).
Basis: Step 5′, ConPs, contextual beliefs, and some connection between what E means and the nonliteral message.

Indirect Strategy
(Step 7)
Contextual Inappropriateness: H recognizes that it would be contextually inappropriate for S to be speaking merely directly.
Basis: Step 5 or step 6′, ConPs, contextual beliefs.

(Step 8)
Indirect: H recognizes what S is also intending to communicate indirectly.
Basis: Step 7, ConPs, contextual beliefs, and some connection between what S communicated directly and the indirect message.

Key Words

pragmatics
communication
speaking directly
speaking literally
speaking nonliterally
speaking indirectly
strategies
discourse
conversations

Study Questions

1. What is the problem of linguistic communication as formulated in the text?

2. What is the Message Model of linguistic communication?

3. What six problems does the Message Model have?

4. Does a speaker need to be intending to linguistically communicate anything to a hearer in firing, sentencing, or awakening that person? Discuss.

5. What are the four major types of communication outlined so far?

6. How has each type so far been characterized?

7. State the strategy for direct and literal communication.

8. State the strategy for nonliteral communication.

9. State the strategy for indirect communication.

10. What is the broad notion of discourse? What is the narrow notion of discourse?

11. What is a greeting?

12. State three principles of turn-taking.

13. What are the two major steps in closing a conversation?

Exercises

1. Find some example of humor that turns on one of the inadequacies of the Message Model.

2. The text gives no specific principles for inferring a direct and literal message from an utterance. In part this is because context can influence which inferences the hearer is intended to make (recall problem three of the Message Model). To see this, consider the following sentences and state what some of the most common literal and direct communicative acts performed in uttering them might be:

a. It's getting late.
b. Who won the battle of Waterloo?
c. Leave by the back door!

3. What are some literal and direct communicative acts commonly performed in the utterance of (a) declarative, (b) imperative, (c) interrogative sentences? What sorts of linguistic devices are used to mark sentences in these three categories? Discuss. (Look again at section 6.3.)

4. If a speaker were to utter the following sentences, what might that speaker commonly be taken as intending to communicate? Discuss.

a. Move and I'll shoot!
b. Move or I'll shoot!
c. You've been drinking again, have you!
d. You've been drinking again, haven't you?
e. Marry my daughter, will you!

f. Marry my daughter, will you?

g. What, me worry?

5. Consider the following sentences, then state what you take the speaker's intended meaning to be.

a. I'm all thumbs today!

b. He's plowing his profits back into the business.

c. Cat got your tongue today?

d. That movie was a real turkey!

e. You took the words right out of my mouth.

f. She's got something on her mind.

6. Which, if any, of the above sentences involve lexical or syntactic ambiguity? Identify the nonliteral word or phrase. Defend your answer.

7. Can the sentence *I promise I will call the police if you don't quiet down* be literally and directly used to promise, or only to warn? Or both? Defend your answer.

8. Sometimes the absurdity of taking a nonliteral remark literally can best be brought out by a drawing. Try your hand at drawing an absurd literal interpretation for one of the above sentences, or for an example of your own.

9. Find five everyday, commonplace examples of nonliteral language use. Try to include an imperative and an interrogative example in your list. Paraphrase the intended nonliteral interpretation as best you can.

10. Consider the following proverbs:

a. A rolling stone gathers no moss.

b. Look before you leap.

c. A stitch in time saves nine.

How would you paraphrase the intended message behind each of them? What kinds of communicative uses of language do proverbs exemplify?

11. In what sense, if any, are proverbs *nonliteral?* Defend your answer.

12. Think of ten more common proverbs and then paraphrase their intended message.

13. Using the results of the previous exercise, try to state how proverbs work; for instance, do they differ from *metaphors?* Discuss. (Note that we do not normally call proverbs metaphors, nor do we call metaphors proverbs.)

14. Find five typical, commonplace cases of speaking *indirectly* that are not given in the text. Say what the direct communicative message is (is it literal or nonliteral?) and also say what the indirect message is. Try to include an example from each major mood of English: declarative, imperative, and interrogative.

15. Is *I promise to be there* literally and directly a promise, or is it literally and directly a statement that you will be there, and only indirectly a promise? Defend your answer.

16. Show how the Inferential Model tries to overcome each of the inadequacies of the Message Model. Discuss.

17. Some forms of words do not receive their proper interpretation in any regular way; they are in effect *idiomatic* and must be learned case by case. Here are some typical examples; try to think of more:

Declarative Form
a. That just goes to show (you).

Imperative Form
a. Take it easy! (meaning: Calm down!)
b. Buzz off! (meaning: Leave!)
c. (Go) Fly a kite! Take a hike! Get lost! (meaning: Leave!)
d. Never mind! Forget it! (meaning: Don't bother doing it!)

Interrogative Form
a. Where does he get off saying that?
b. What do you say we leave?
c. How's things?
d. What's up?
e. What's the matter?
f. How about lunch?
g. How about that!

18. Try to paraphrase the declarative and interrogative examples above. Why might these cases be so difficult?

19. When is it normal not to open a talk-exchange with a greeting? Discuss.

20. Can you think of any modifications or additions that might be made to the three principles of turn-taking discussed in the text? Elaborate.

Bibliography

Adamson, J. (1973). *Groucho, Harpo, Chico, and Sometimes Zeppo: A Celebration of the Marx Brothers*, Touchstone Books, Simon and Schuster, New York.

Akmajian, A., R. Demers, and R. Harnish (1980). "Overcoming inadequacies in the 'Message-Model' of linguistic communication," *Communication and Cognition* 13, 317–336.

Austin, J. (1961). *How to Do Things with Words*, Oxford University Press, Oxford.

Bach, K., and R. Harnish (1979). *Linguistic Communication and Speech Acts*, MIT Press, Cambridge, Mass.

Carnap, R. (1939). *Foundations of Logic and Mathematics*, University of Chicago Press, Chicago.

Cole, P., ed. (1978). *Syntax and Semantics*, vol. 9, Academic Press, New York.

Cole, P., ed. (1981). *Radical Pragmatics*, Academic Press, New York.

Cole, P., and J. Morgan, eds. (1975). *Syntax and Semantics*, vol. 3, Academic Press, New York.

Coulthard, M. (1977). *An Introduction to Discourse Analysis,* Longman, London.

Gazdar, G. (1979). *Pragmatics,* Academic Press, New York.

Grice, P. (1975). "Logic and conversation," in P. Cole and J. Morgan, eds. (1975).

Harnish, R. (1983). "Pragmatic derivations," *Synthese* 54, 325–373.

Holdcroft, D. (1978). *Words and Deeds,* Oxford University Press, Oxford.

Katz, J. (1966). *The Philosophy of Language,* Harper and Row, New York.

Katz, J. (1980). *Propositional Structure and Illocutionary Force,* reprinted by Harvard University Press, Cambridge, Mass.

Locke, J. (1691). *An Essay Concerning Human Understanding,* reissued by Dover Publications, New York (1959).

Morgan, J. (1978). "Two types of convention in indirect speech acts," in P. Cole, ed. (1978).

Morris, C. (1938). *Foundations of the Theory of Signs,* University of Chicago Press, Chicago.

Mulholland, J. (1977). *The Abbott and Costello Book,* Popular Library Film Series, Popular Library, New York.

Ortoney, A., ed. (1979). *Metaphor and Thought,* Cambridge University Press, New York.

Reddy, M. (1979). "The conduit metaphor: A case of frame conflict in our language about language," in A. Ortoney, ed. (1979).

Sacks, H., E. Schegloff, and G. Jefferson (1974). "A simplest systematics for the organization of turn-taking for conversation," reprinted in J. Schenkein, ed. (1978).

Sadock, J. (1974). *Toward a Linguistic Theory of Speech Acts,* Academic Press, New York.

Schegloff, E., and H. Sacks (1973). "Opening up closing," *Semiotica* 8, 289–327.

Schenkein, J., ed. (1978). *Studies in the Organization of Conversational Interaction,* Academic Press, New York.

Searle, J. (1969). *Speech Acts,* Cambridge University Press, Cambridge.

Searle, J. (1975). "Indirect speech acts," reprinted in J. Searle (1979b).

Searle, J. (1979a). "Metaphor," reprinted in J. Searle (1979b).

Searle, J. (1979b). *Expression and Meaning,* Cambridge University Press, Cambridge.

Smith, N., ed. (1982). *Mutual Knowledge,* Academic Press, New York.

Chapter Ten

PSYCHOLOGY OF LANGUAGE: SPEECH PRODUCTION AND COMPREHENSION

10.1 COMPETENCE AND PERFORMANCE

We have seen that it is possible to analyze a natural language at a number of different levels: sounds (phonology), words (morphology), sentence structure (syntax), meaning (semantics), and communication (pragmatics). The task of linguistics is in part to discover the appropriate units of analysis at each level and to state generalizations in terms of these units that capture the regularities inherent in the language itself.

But languages are not just abstract structured systems. They are also used in thought and communication, and it is the task of *psycholinguistics* (or *psychology of language*) to discover how knowledge of language is represented in the mind/brain of a fluent speaker, how this information is utilized in the production and understanding of expressions in the normal way, and how speakers acquire these abilities.

Following Chomsky 1972, we will construct three models. The first Chomsky calls a *competence model* (see chapter 5). A competence model reflects what a fluent speaker knows (what information is stored) about the sound-meaning relations in the language—the speaker's linguistic competence (figure 10.1). This is to be distinguished from a *performance model*, which reflects the actual processes that go into producing and understanding speech (and language) (figure 10.2). Finally, a language *acquisition model* (or device) reflects the changes in the competence and performance of a child during the acquisition period, and thus provides a model of the child's language learning achievements (figure 10.3). In the remainder of this chapter we will explore some of the central issues surrounding current attempts to build a performance model. In the next chapter we will investigate language acquisition.

Sounds ← | COMPETENCE MODEL (Grammar) | → Linguistic Meaning

Figure 10.1
A competence model

Communicative Message ↔ | PERFORMANCE MODEL | ↔ Sounds

Figure 10.2
A performance model

Language Experience → | ACQUISITION MODEL | → | PERFORMANCE MODEL |

Figure 10.3
An acquisition model

10.2 SPEECH PRODUCTION

The easiest way of thinking about theories of speech production is to imagine building a device that will simulate the flow of information from message to sounds—in other words, a model of the phenomenon of a speaker expressing a message to a hearer. Thus, the speaker thinks of a message, plans how to express it, and finally articulates the expression with the vocal tract.

Conceiving the Message

A speaker brings to the communication situation a wide variety of general beliefs about the world, about the past, present, and future course of the conversation, and about the hearer's beliefs about these things. Accompanying these beliefs are the speaker's desires, hopes, intentions, and so forth. In the course of the conversation many of these beliefs, desires, and intentions can change as a result of what is said; thus, the background for speaking will be a cognitively complicated affair. We will organize our discussion of speech production around the idea that these mental states form the *cognitive background* for normal conversation:

(1)
Cognitive Background
The speaker S has a variety of beliefs and desires concerning such factors as
a. the nature and direction of the conversation,
b. the social and physical context of the utterance,
c. the hearer H's beliefs in general, H's beliefs pertinent to S's impending remark in particular, and whatever contextual beliefs H shares with S.

Given these cognitive states, the speaker next must formulate the beginnings of the message to be communicated, as well as the manner in which it is to be communicated. These we will refer to as *pragmatic intentions:*

(2)
Pragmatic Intentions
On the basis of the cognitive background, S begins to form pragmatic intentions (which may include the beginnings of intentions) to
a. refer to something (referential intent),
b. perform some communicative act(s) (communicative intent),
c. perform these acts literally, nonliterally, directly, or indirectly,
d. have various effects on H (perlocutionary intent).

We know very little at present about the psychological mechanisms underlying the storage of background information and the formation of pragmatic intentions, in part because there are serious methodological problems with studying speech production.

The standard methodology in psycholinguistics is to test for regular relationships between what subjects perceive and how they respond to it. Studying comprehension, the experimenter can manipulate characteristics of the input (such as the rate of the speech coming in) and look for regularities in the subjects' responses (such as the kinds of errors they make), but with speech production there is no good way of controlling the input, since the input is the subjects' *thoughts*. Unfortunately, psychologists know of no effective and ethically permissible way of controlling thoughts for experimental purposes, and so researchers in speech production must rely on very different kinds of procedures, such as the analysis of speech errors.

Planning the Expression: Speech Errors

Having begun to formulate at least some of the above pragmatic intentions, how does the speaker put them into words? What sort of process
is this?

The Message Model suggests one possibility: that expression is basically a word-by-word encoding of the message from beginning to end.
Thus, as the concept THE PLUMBER . . . comes into the message,
the words of an English speaker "The plumber . . ." might begin to
come out. Furthermore, when a word itself requires planning, the procedure is the same: build it up from left to right out of phonemes and
syllables.

There is considerable interesting evidence against this picture of
speech planning, some of which comes from the study of speech errors.
Speech errors have been the subject of both casual and scientific interest for centuries. Probably the most famous speech error maker of all
time was the Reverend William A. Spooner (1844–1930) of Oxford
University who lent his name (spoonerisms) to such classics as:

(3)

a. "Work is the curse of the drinking class" for "Drink is the curse of
the working class"

b. "Noble tons of soil" for "Noble sons of toil"

c. "You have hissed all my mystery lectures. I saw you fight a liar in
the back quad; in fact, you have tasted the whole worm" (the reader
may translate this one)

From a casual inspection of these errors, one might conclude that they
are unsystematic, that errors are virtually a random phenomenon. But
students of the subject agree that only certain types of errors predominate; in fact, the kinds of errors that predominate are those that involve
linguistic constituents in some way. Although there is a wide variety of
subtle types of error, a small number of types predominate. These
include:

(4)

a. Interchange errors: hissed all my mystery lectures

b. Anticipation errors: a leading list (for "reading list")

c. Perseveration errors: a phonological fool (for "phonological rule")

d. Blends: moinly (mostly, mainly), impostinator (imposter, imper-
sonator)

We have illustrated some of the main types of error with phonological segments, but they happen with all sorts of linguistic units, though rarely with nonunits. Consider, for instance, the following samples:

(5)
a. Phonetic features (voicing)
   glear plue sky (clear blue sky)
   pig and vat (big and fat)
b. Stress
   Stop beating your bríck against a head wall
c. Syntactic features
   (Indefinite) a meeting _arathon (an eating marathon)
   (Past tense) Rosa always date shranks (dated shrinks)
d. Stem and affix
   He favors pushing busters (busting pushers)
e. Negation
   I disregard this as precise (I regard this as imprecise)

These examples illustrate some important features of speech errors as evidence for the speech planning process. First, errors must always involve the alteration of some linguistic unit. Rarely are the speech error data completely random, and this suggests that *the speech planning process uses linguistic units in its planning operations*. Second, the errors reveal that the planning system must be looking ahead. A system that did not could hardly make the errors shown in (5a), for instance, where the voicing feature appears to have moved backward in the first example and forward in the second. The problem this example poses for the Message Model is clear, and it is one we will encounter again and again.

Consider next example (5b). The words *brick* and *head* were interchanged, but notice that the stress (indicated with ´) did not move with the originally intended stressed word (*head*). Instead, it stayed in its original location, suggesting that there must be a level of representation for stress that is abstract and detached from the words themselves.

The syntactic features examples are particularly interesting from the point of view of the Message Model. In the case of the definite article the speaker had intended to say *an eating marathon,* but when the /m/ moved forward and was attached to *eating,* the indefinite article changed to accommodate the error; the subject did not say *an meeting arathon.* This means that during the planning process there was a stage where the /m/ could move forward and a later stage where the indefinite article could be adjusted to the next vowel by the addition of /n/. Again, the error indicates that the processor has planned ahead. The Message Model cannot account for this, since it encodes messages strictly from left to right.

The examples involving negation and the past tense emphasize the point that the processor works in stages and is able to anticipate, using information about what is coming three or four words ahead. Consider (5e), *I disregard this as precise:* not only was negation anticipated by three words, but the form of the negation was adjusted to conform to morphological constraints as well; the subject did not say *I imregard this as precise*. Finally, the past tense example is interesting in that the tense feature moved onto a word that is homophonic with a verb (*to shrink*) but is in this occurrence a noun (*a shrink* "psychiatrist"). However, the speech planning system apparently could not use this information at this stage; it treated the word as a verb in the past tense, producing *shrank*.

Articulation

In considering articulation, many people have been misled by the representation of speech as a linear sequence of discrete symbols (such as in the alphabet). It is frequently assumed that such a sequence of symbols mirrors the sequence of signals sent by the brain to the vocal tract. It has been determined, however, that the brain does not send discrete and linearly ordered sets of nerve impulses to articulate each segment. Rather, the control of speech is a complex system, probably hierarchically organized at the level of the phrase or sentence.

Lenneberg (1967) has proposed that for some phonetic sequences *XY*, part of the signal to articulate the *Y* must leave the brain *before* the signal to articulate the *X*. An illustration of this type of phenomenon can be found in normal speech. Consider the fact that each speech sound can be analyzed as a set of features of articulation. For example, in articulating the vowel /u/ (as in *you*), the lips must be rounded, the nasal passages must be blocked off (by closing the velum), the vocal cords must be allowed to vibrate, and so forth. These features of articulation are independently controllable and are not always activated simultaneously. For example, in the word *construe,* the final vowel is produced with accompanying lip rounding. The rounding, however, is *anticipated* in the production of this word and is already present on the *-str-* sequence that begins the syllable (to see this, try pronouncing the word). In contrast, the final -*str*- sequence in the word *constrict* does not exhibit the extreme lip rounding found in *construe*. In other words, in *construe* the lip rounding associated with the final vowel has been sent three phonemes earlier.

The overlap of features with adjacent sounds can be even more extreme than the case of the single feature of lip rounding found in *construe*. In the production (and subsequent transmission) of some "adjacent" speech sounds the overlap may be complete, creating the phenomenon of *parallel transmission*. In figure 10.4, a schematic representation of the acoustic properties of the English word *bag* is displayed. The primary acoustic information for the sequence *bag* is carried by concentrations of energy at certain narrow frequency ranges (called *formants*), which are represented by the curving bars containing the dark circles. These energy concentrations are produced by resonant properties of the vocal tract, in much the same way that an organ pipe produces a tone. Although the physics of generating sound in organ pipes and in the human vocal tract are comparable, the vocal tract has soft (not rigid) walls, is flexible, and can be rapidly altered in shape, and thus the acoustic result is quite different. In figure 10.4, the vowel in *bag* is represented by the relative spacing and positions of the two bars (different vowels have different positions and relative spacings). The fact that the formants are both rising at the beginning of the signal is the primary acoustic cue that a sound involving the lips (in this case *b*) has been produced. Similarly, at the other end of the word, the respective falling and rising of the first and second formants carries the information that a *g* has been produced. There is no part in section 1 of figure 10.4, then, that is not simultaneously transmitting both the initial consonant *b* and the vowel *a,* and no part of section 3 that is not transmitting both the vowel *a* and the final consonant *g*. The overlap of features of articulation, then, is characteristic of speech, and poses a serious problem for the Message Model.

10.3 COMPREHENSION

The study of comprehension does not suffer from the problems of identifying and manipulating the input. If anything it is the output, understanding, that is the problem. On reflection it is not so clear what we really mean when we say that a hearer understood what a speaker said, or what a speaker meant (to communicate). For the time being we will leave the issue of the nature of understanding open and begin our re-

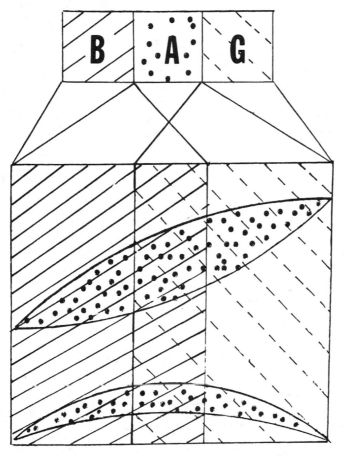

Figure 10.4
Schematic representation of some acoustic properties of the word *bag*. The figure depicts the parallel transmission of the segments *b* and *a* (section 1), *b, a,* and *g* (section 2), and *a* and *g* (section 3). (Adapted from Liberman 1970. Used by permission.)

view with the input to speech comprehension, the speech signal itself. The entire process of comprehension is summarized in figure 10.5.

It is generally assumed that the Speech Recognition Capacity identifies as much about the speech sounds as it can from the sound wave. Next, the Syntactic Parsing Capacity identifies the words by their sounds and analyzes the structure of the sentence, and the Semantic Interpretation Capacity puts the meaning of the words together in accordance with these syntactic relations. Finally, the Pragmatic In-

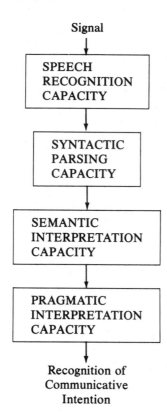

Signal

SPEECH
RECOGNITION
CAPACITY

SYNTACTIC
PARSING
CAPACITY

SEMANTIC
INTERPRETATION
CAPACITY

PRAGMATIC
INTERPRETATION
CAPACITY

Recognition of
Communicative
Intention

Figure 10.5
Functional analysis of comprehension into subcapacities

terpretation Capacity selects a particular speech act as the most likely
one the speaker is performing. If the hearer is right, communication is
successful; if not, there has been a breakdown.

It should not be assumed that these different capacities are carried
out either by different "areas of the brain" or necessarily one after the
other. Many of these processes can overlap both in time and in brain
activity. The question of the neurological realization of these linguistic
capacities is the province of the field of neurolinguistics, which is the
subject of chapter 12.

Speech Perception

The hearer, having heard an expression uttered by the speaker, must
now decode its meaning(s). For a fluent speaker of a given language this

might seem like a trivial task. After all, what is there to understanding sentences of our native language aside from knowing the individual words of the language plus a few simple word order rules for forming word sequences that "make sense"?

A serious problem with this view is that in actual speech, sentences are physically continuous streams of sound, not broken down into the convenient discrete units that we call words. A good illustration of this is the experience of a traveler in a foreign land who does not know the local native language. The traveler does not hear neatly arranged sequences of individual words—the sentences and phrases of the language all sound like streams of unintelligible noise. The idea that we *do* hear such sequences of discrete, linearly ordered units is only an illusion that results from the fact that in knowing a language we perceptually analyze a physical continuum into individual sounds (as well as words and phrases). A striking aspect of this perceptual analysis of sounds was demonstrated in a set of experiments by C. Schatz (1954). Tape recordings of various consonant-vowel combinations were made, then cut and respliced to create new consonant-vowel combinations. In one case, the word *ski* was cut between the *k* and the *i*, and the initial *sk* was then recombined with the new vowel-consonant sequences. When the *sk* from *ski* was combined with a new sequence *ar* and played to English speakers, the subjects did not hear the word *scar*, as we might expect. Instead, the subjects reported hearing the word *star* 96% of the time. Further, when the *sk* from *ski* was combined with the sequence *ool*, the word *spool* was heard 87% of the time, rather than the expected *school*. Thus, the acoustic signal corresponding to the *k* in the word *ski* can be perceived as a *k* (as in *ski*), *t* (as in *star*), or *p* (as in *spool*), depending on the following vowel. These cases show that a single acoustic signal can be perceived as different consonants, which cannot be identified until the following vowel is known.

Another illustration of the nonlinearity of speech processing comes from an experiment by Pollack and Pickett (1963). Sequences of speech were created by excising portions of conversations via an electronic gate of controllable width. Individual words that were excised from the tape were rarely intelligible when the gate was so narrow that the preceding and following words were not included. However, as the gate was widened after the original word to allow more and more of the original utterance, the entire sequence eventually became intelligible. As reported by Lieberman (1966), the excised portion does not become gradually more intelligible as the gate width increases; rather, the signal remains unintelligible until a particular gate width is reached. At this point, the entire sequence suddenly becomes intelligible.

The preceding two experiments indicate the significant role of contextual dependency in perceptual analysis. This contextual dependency is not at all reflected in the traditional Message Model, indicating that the model must be altered to take this phenomenon into account.

Syntactic Parsing

The output of the Speech Recognition Capacity is a representation of as much information as it can obtain about the speech sounds of the utterance, based on the sound wave alone. In most cases information about some of the segments will be missing, as will information concerning aspects of intonation and word or phrase boundaries. It is the job of the Syntactic Parsing Capacity to identify the relevant words and relate them syntactically. It is the job of the Semantic Interpretation Capacity to produce a representation of the meaning of the sentence (or other expressions). We will follow this process from words to sentence to meaning as best we can, though current research shows that we know very little about many of these operations.

Lexical Access

Given the speed at which comprehension is possible (over 4 words per second), it is clear that the time it takes to identify words need not be very long at all, perhaps an average of about 1/5th of a second (Rohrman and Gough 1967). Thus, it would be implausible to suppose that a hearer looks randomly through a mental dictionary (lexicon) to find which word (with its syntactic and semantic properties) is associated with what sounds. In fact, it appears that there is some system for *accessing* the *mental lexicon*.

First, the mental lexicon appears to some extent to be ordered by sounds—much as a normal dictionary is ordered by the alphabet (Fay and Cutler 1977). But lexical access also seems sensitive to how *recently* one has heard the incoming word, or one that is semantically related to it (Scarborough, Cortese, and Scarborough 1977, Meyer and Schvaneveldt 1971). If recent words are more easily accessed, then the more likely a word is to occur in one's experience, the more likely it is to be accessed easily. This so-called frequency effect says that the higher the frequency of a word, the easier it is to recognize. This has proved to be true. Foss (1969) presented sentences containing a frequent and an infrequent synonym and asked subjects to identify a particular target phoneme, say, /b/. It was found that subjects systematically took longer to announce that they had heard the target phoneme when it was in an infrequent word than when it was in a frequent one.

Ambiguity and Disambiguation

Not only are most of the words in English ambiguous; probably most of the words in each speaker's idiolect are ambiguous as well. This poses an interesting problem for the speech understander—should it note all of the meanings of each word, or only some (normally one), and if so which one? Since this process is so fast, we should not expect introspection to answer this question, though it does seem that we normally hit on the right or appropriate meaning most of the time.

Recent work suggests that more processing is going on than introspection may reveal. One sequence of studies (Bever, Garrett, and Hurtig 1973) found evidence that hearers typically access *all* of the meanings of the words they hear; by the end of a clause, the most plausible meaning is selected and the processing continues. If this should turn out to be the wrong choice, as in so-called garden-path sentences such as (6), then the processor must go back and try again.

(6)
The blind student felt the material in the art class [would be too difficult to understand].

It is still not clear exactly what causes a meaning to be selected: is it memory limitations, or time limitations, or the arrival of some structural unit (such as the end of the clause)? One study (Tanenhaus, Leiman, and Seidenberg 1979) found that up to about ¼ second, both meanings of ambiguous noun-verb words (such as *watch*) were activated, but after that period of time one reading was selected. A related study (Swinney 1979) found that by three syllables after an ambiguous word, a decision had been made on the appropriate meaning. All of this suggests that when we process sentences, all known meanings of the word are first automatically activated, then some as yet poorly understood process selects the most appropriate one based on various syntactic and semantic cues. In some cases the speaker can help the hearer out. In one study (Lehiste 1973) subjects were asked to listen to ambiguous sentences such as (7) where the speaker had a particular meaning in mind.

(7)
The steward (*greeted* [*the girl*) with a smile].

It was found that when hearers disambiguated the sentence correctly and got the intended smiling-girl meaning, the speakers had taken a longer time (by as much as $1/6$ second) in pronouncing the crucial words (italicized above), thus giving the hearers a cue as to what was meant.

Syntactic Strategies
Imagine that the speech comprehension capacity has determined which words it is presently hearing and has looked up their idiosyncratic syntactic and semantic characteristics. What does it do now? Recall that the goal is to figure out the meaning(s) of the whole sentence on the basis of the meaning(s) of its words and their syntactic relations. So it must begin to determine those relations.

One very influential proposal about how this is done was made by T. Bever (1970). He proposed that part of this system consists of perceptual *strategies*. These principles tell the system how to make decisions about syntactic structures in the face of uncertainty and incomplete information. For instance, given the speed of speech comprehension it is unlikely that *all* possibilities are investigated at every level of analysis; rather, hearers use strategies as rules of thumb to make intelligent guesses. Of course, if these principles are only strategies, and not exhaustive searches, then it should be possible for the speech comprehension capacity to err—we should be able to trick it. And trick it we can. Consider one of Bever's strategies:

(8)
Main Clause Strategy (MCS)
The first NP + V + (NP) sequence is the main clause of the sentence, unless the verb is marked as subordinate.

Such a strategy works well for sentences such as (9a), but it is tricked by sentences such as (9b), which should be read as (9c):

(9)
a. The horse raced the car, and won.
b. The horse raced past the barn fell.
c. The horse which (was) raced past the barn fell.

Thus, it would seem that something like the MCS is operating in understanding. But might the MCS be simply a special case of some more general processes? In fact, it has been proposed (Frazier and Fodor 1978) that parsing capacity involves two stages. The first stage, because of (short term) memory limitations, looks at about six words of the sentence at a time, attempting to categorize the words as nouns, verbs, etc., and to group as many of them together in a phrase as its limited capacity allows. The second stage takes these structured phrasal "packages" and attempts to build a coherent syntactic structure for the whole sentence. On this view, many errors can be accounted for by the operating characteristics of the two stages. In particular, these errors can, in many cases, be attributed to the "short-sightedness" of stage one; it will try to group the latest words it receives together under existing category nodes. When it cannot, it will instead start a new category.

This theory explains many intuitive and experimental results. For instance, consider sentences (10a) and (10b).

(10)
a. Sam hit [the girl with a book].
b. Sam [hit the girl] with a book.

The model predicts that speakers should prefer interpretation (10a) over (10b), and this seems intuitively right. In fact, Frazier (1979) reports a sequence of experiments in which such sentences were presented to subjects visually one word at a time (at the rate of about 3 words per second) and the subjects were asked to judge their grammaticality. If comprehension tends to follow the principles of the two-stage model, then sentences like (11b) will take longer to process than sentences like (11a) because subjects will have to go back and undo the error made during the first attempt.

(11)
a. We gave the man the grant proposal we wrote because he had written a similar proposal last year.
b. We gave the man the grant proposal was written by last year a copy of this year's proposal.

Intuitively, we would expect (11b) to be more difficult to process. The experiment confirmed this; it took on the average over twice as long to process sentences like (11b) than sentences like (11a).

Constituent structure of sentences is not merely an artifact of syntactic theory; there is reason to think that gross constituent structure in fact has reality in the minds of speakers. In various experiments that have come to be known as the *Click Experiments,* Fodor, Bever, and Garrett (1974) tried to show that test subjects utilize major constituent boundaries in their perception of sentences. Subjects wearing headphones heard a tape-recorded sentence in one ear, while in the other ear they heard a "click" noise simultaneously superimposed on some part of the sentence. They were asked to write down each sentence they had heard and to indicate where in the sentence they had heard the click sound. A typical sentence in this experiment was (12), where the dots underneath words indicate the various locations of the superimposed click noises:

(12)
That the girl was happy | was evident from the way she laughed.
      . . . .

The major constituent break in this sentence occurs between *happy* and *was,* and clicks were superimposed both before this major break and after it. The subjects in the experiment showed a definite tendency to "mis-hear" the location of the click: when the click actually occurred *before* the major break, subjects reported hearing it *later* (closer to the major break); when the click actually occurred *after* the major break, subjects reported hearing it *earlier* (again closer to the major break). When the click was located in the major break itself, the tendency to "mis-hear" its location was much lower.

This experiment has been interpreted as showing that hearers process sentences in terms of major *clauses* of a sentence, and that these major constituents *resist interruption.* Hence, when a click was placed within a major clause (say, at the word *was* in (12)), hearers tended to report it as occurring in the break, and not in the clause itself, suggesting that on a perceptual level major clauses are integrated units that resist being broken up. If this is true, then it appears that major constituent structure is both a theoretical device used by linguists to explain syntactic phenomena and a psychologically real basic unit of perception on the part of hearers.

The results of the Click Experiments are by no means uncontroversial, but the one described here illustrates the general sort of experimental work being done in the area of perception of syntax. We recommend Fodor, Bever, and Garrett 1974 and Clark and Clark 1977 for a review of much of this work, and of the problems and controversy that surround it.

In sum, the picture of parsing emerging from these and other studies is that as words are heard and identified, their meanings are activated and the comprehension device begins to try to put them together into phrases. As comprehension proceeds, the device runs out of immediate memory and must group the words together as best it can—possibly making a guess based on the most plausible meaning to emerge so far. As words come in, this process continues, but the comprehension device also tries to connect these phrases into a total coherent sentential structure. The details of this process are the topic of much current research.

Semantic Interpretation: Mental Representation of Meaning

How does the mind represent the meaning of words or morphemes, and how does it combine these to represent the meaning of phrases and sentences? These are the central questions of this area of research and although much interesting work has been done, we are only beginning to glimpse what the answers might look like.

Concepts: The Traditional View

So far we have left open the question of the nature of the mental representation of meaning. We saw in chapter 6 that images are not the answer, at least not the whole answer. The most popular and influential theory in psychology at present is that the mental representation of meaning involves *concepts*. But how are we to think of *concepts*? One way to think of them is in terms of their *role* in thought; another is in terms of their *internal structure*.

Probably the most pervasive role for concepts to play in thought is *categorization*. Concepts allow us to group different things that are similar in some respect into classes. We are then able to abstract from irrelevant details the properties that are important for the thought or action that follows conceptualization. As an example, consider the ways that tennis matches are all similar versus the ways that all giant slalom competitions are similar; clearly, the way we would train for one versus the other is the result of the similar characteristics of the members of each respective group. Without the concept of a tennis match it would make no sense to think of training for the *next one*. The stability of our everyday mental life, then, depends to a great extent on our capacity to categorize and conceptualize particular objects and events.

Concepts also combine to form *complex concepts* and *complete thoughts*. Thus, we might have the concepts MISCHIEVOUS and BOYS, and form the complex concept MISCHIEVOUS BOYS. Or we might form the thought that BOYS ARE MISCHIEVOUS, the wish that BOYS NOT BE MISCHIEVOUS, etc. From the point of view of semantics, some concepts are taken to be the mental representation of the meaning of *words* (following Fodor 1981, we call these *lexical concepts*), some concepts are taken to be the mental representation of the meaning of *phrases* (*phrasal concepts*), and thoughts are taken to be the mental representation of the meaning of *sentences*.

How may we describe the internal structure of concepts, especially the internal structure of lexical concepts? The traditional view, dating from the seventeenth-century British Empiricists, holds that there are two sorts of concepts: simple and complex. Simple concepts, such as RED, are thought to be the result of innate sensory and perceptual processes. Complex concepts, on the other hand, are generally learned and are the result of combining simple concepts in accordance with various principles (such as *conjunction*). Thus, the concept TRIANGLE might be constructed, using conjunction, out of the concepts PLANE, CLOSED, FIGURE, WITH, THREE, STRAIGHT, SIDES. Moreover, the traditional view supposes that these constituent simple concepts *define* the complex one. If a complex concept is the meaning of a word, then its constituent concepts *define* that word. In summary, the traditional picture of the mental representation of the meaning of words is as follows:

(13)
a. The meaning of words involves simple or complex lexical concepts.
b. Simple concepts are innate and derived from sensation or perception.
c. Complex concepts are learned and composed ultimately out of simple concepts, using such devices as conjunction and negation.
d. Understanding a word consists in activating the associated lexical concept.
e. Such lexical concepts are associated in memory with the word as its definition; and the defining concepts are each necessary and jointly sufficient.
f. Understanding a phrase or sentence involves activating or combining the associated lexical concepts in the right way.

Problems with the Traditional View: Decomposition and Typicality Effects

This traditional view has been under serious attack for the last decade. First, it is very implausible that *all* complex concepts can be analyzed eventually into innately determined perceptual properties. Consider the concept of a CHAIR or a HAT. Clearly, chairs and hats have certain structural characteristics that can be represented perceptually. However, they also have certain important *functions* or *uses,* and these are not perceptual properties, since we do not see "sitability" or "wearability." Even worse, think of BACHELOR: what is the *perceptual* property of being UNMARRIED?

Second, there is experimental evidence against the idea that understanding words, phrases, and sentences involves activating the kinds of complex defining concepts that the traditional view requires. For instance, Fodor, Fodor, and Garrett (1975) asked subjects to evaluate the validity of arguments such as the following:

(14)
a. If practically all of the men in the room are *not married,* then few of the men in the room have wives.
b. If practically all of the men in the room are *bachelors,* then few of the men in the room have wives.

Notice that (14b) contains *bachelors,* which is commonly thought to be definable in terms of NOT MARRIED. Since experiments have shown that negations add significantly to comprehension time, we would expect that if *bachelor* is in fact decomposed into the concepts including NOT MARRIED, (14b) should take at least as much time on the average to process as (14a). However, subjects processed sentences like (14b) significantly *faster* than sentences like (14a), suggesting that the definitional decomposition posited by the traditional view was not taking place.

A more recent and more elaborate study (Fodor, Garrett, Walker, and Parkes 1980) has provided further evidence against definitional decomposition. First it was established that subjects are experimentally sensitive to differences or "shifts" between surface grammatical relations and deeper grammatical relations. For example, consider (15a) and (15b).

(15)
a. John expected Mary to write a poem.
b. John persuaded Mary to write a poem.

These sentences have the same surface structure, but they differ in their underlying grammatical relations in that *Mary* is both the object of *persuade* and the subject of *write* in (15b), but only the subject of *write* in (15a). To see this, contrast the meaning of the following passives:

(16)
a. John expected a poem to be written by Mary.
b. ?John persuaded a poem to be written by Mary.

Given that these differences are experimentally detectable, Fodor et al. gave subjects sentences like (17a) and (17b):

(17)
a. John saw the glass.
b. John broke the glass.

On the traditional view, these should have very different conceptual structures. In (17a) *the glass* is only the subject of *saw,* but according to the traditional view, (17b) is *really* stored as something like (18).

(18)
John caused the glass to break.

Thus, *the glass* is really the subject of *break.* This "shift" should be detectable with the tests just described, but it was not, thereby providing further evidence against the traditional view.

Third, there is experimental evidence that the internal structure of many lexical concepts does not resemble that of definitions (that is, of equally necessary and sufficient conditions). In an influential series of papers E. Rosch and her associates (1973, 1975) provide evidence that the categorization process exhibits "typicality effects," demonstrating that concepts possess an internal structure favoring typical members over less typical ones. Let us look at two of these effects.

First, people are quite consistent in rating certain kinds of objects as more or less typical of a kind. For instance, in one experiment Rosch (1973, experiment 3) asked over 100 subjects to rank members of eight assorted categories with regard to typicality or exemplariness. Table 10.1 gives these categories, their members, and their ranking.

On the basis of these results and similar ones from other experiments, it is possible to see whether "typical" members of a category

Table 10.1
Judgments of "goodness of category membership." (From Rosch 1973.)

Category	Member	B & M[a] Frequency	"Exemplariness" Rank	Category	Member	B & M[a] Frequency	"Exemplariness" Rank
Fruit	Apple	429	1.3	Vehicle	Car	407	1.0
	Plum	167	2.3		Boat	145	2.7
	Pineapple	98	2.3		Scooter	99	2.5
	Strawberry	58	2.3		Tricycle	43	3.5
	Fig	16	4.7		Horse	14	5.9
	Olive	3	6.2		Skis	3	5.7
Science	Chemistry	367	1.0	Crime	Murder	387	1.0
	Botany	242	1.7		Assault	132	1.4
	Geology	76	2.6		Stealing	95	1.3
	Sociology	46	4.6		Embezzling	40	1.8
	Anatomy	19	1.7		Blackmail	16	1.7
	History	3	5.9		Vagrancy	3	5.3
Sport	Football	396	1.2	Disease	Cancer	316	1.2
	Hockey	130	1.8		Measles	168	2.8
	Wrestling	87	3.0		Cold	90	4.7
	Archery	49	3.9		Malaria	54	1.4
	Gymnastics	16	2.6		Muscular dystrophy	15	1.9
	Weight lifting	3	4.7		Rheumatism	3	3.5
Bird	Robin	377	1.1	Vegetable	Carrot	316	1.1
	Eagle	161	1.2		Asparagus	138	1.3
	Wren	83	1.4		Celery	96	1.7
	Chicken	40	3.8		Onion	47	2.7
	Ostrich	17	3.3		Parsley	15	3.8
	Bat	3	5.8		Pickle	2	4.4

[a] Frequency with which the member was listed in response to the category name from Battig and Montague 1969.

behave differently in thought from "atypical" members. For instance, Rosch (1973, experiment 4) constructed sentences such as (19a) and (19b) from the list in table 10.2:

(19)
a. A *doll* is a *toy*. (typical)
b. A *skate* is a *toy*. (atypical)

Subjects took significantly less time to judge a "typical" sentence true than an "atypical" sentence—they could decide that a doll is a toy faster than that a skate is a toy. This was found to be true not only for adults, but also for children. Moreover, these results have proved quite reliable in over 25 such experiments using a wide variety of materials.

Typical versus atypical members of a class also tend to be (1) more likely categorized correctly, (2) learned first by children, (3) recalled first from memory, (4) more likely to serve as cognitive reference

Table 10.2
Categories and members used in reaction time experiment. (From Rosch 1973.)

Category	Member	
	Central	Peripheral
Toy	Doll	Skates
	Ball	Swing
Bird	Robin	Chicken
	Sparrow	Duck
Fruit	Pear	Strawberry
	Banana	Prune
Sickness	Cancer	Rheumatism
	Measles	Rickets
Relative	Aunt	Wife
	Uncle	Daughter
Metal	Copper	Magnesium
	Aluminum	Platinum
Crime	Rape	Treason
	Robbery	Fraud
Sport	Baseball	Fishing
	Basketball	Diving
Vehicle	Car	Tank
	Bus	Carriage
Science	Chemistry	Medicine
	Physics	Engineering
Vegetable	Carrot	Onion
	Spinach	Mushroom
Part of the body	Arm	Lips
	Leg	Skin

points (for instance, an ellipse is judged "almost" a circle, rather than a circle being judged "almost an ellipse"), and (5) likely to share more characteristics and so have a high "family resemblance." These results (see Smith and Medin 1981 for a good survey) are generally thought to imply that concepts are structured in ways incompatible with the traditional view. In particular, on the traditional view component concepts are *equally* and *exhaustively defining*. Thus, the component concepts that define BIRD are all necessary for something to be correctly categorized BIRD. And if something is correctly represented as falling under all of the defining concepts, then it is correctly categorized BIRD. Yet when features of concepts for various birds are actually evoked from subjects (see table 10.3), it is clear that a trivial feature such as "says 'who' " can be sufficient to pick out one bird (an owl), and that no feature is necessary for all birds.

New Theories: Prototypes and Fuzzy Concepts

There has been a variety of responses to these experimental findings. Some theorists (see Miller and Johnson-Laird 1976) have attempted to revise the traditional view by distinguishing a conceptual *core* of defining concepts from an *identification procedure* sensitive to typicality characteristics.

Other theorists (Smith, Shoben, and Rips 1974) have moved to a *probabilistic* model of concepts. On this view, component concepts are given a certain probability of applying correctly, as shown in table 10.4. On this view, an object is categorized as (for instance) a robin rather than a chicken if it reaches some critical sum of probabilities.

Still others (Rosch and Mervis 1975) have proposed a *prototype* or *exemplar* model of concepts. On this view, concepts are structured around descriptions or images of typical/focal instances of the concept. As Rosch and Mervis (1975, 112) put it, "Categories are composed of a 'core meaning' which consists of the 'clearest cases' (best examples) of the category, 'surrounded' by other category members of decreasing similarity to that core meaning."

None of these more recent theories has been worked out to the point where it can be evaluated in detail, though all can handle the typicality effects. Unfortunately, each new theory has difficulties at present. Of particular interest and concern is the apparent failure of probabilistic and exemplar models to provide a general account of *phrasal* concepts. What, for instance, is the exemplar for the concept GRANDMOTHER LIVING IN A LARGE AMERICAN CITY or PET FISH? Without

Table 10.3
Feature listings for 12 concepts. (Adapted from Smith and Medin 1981.)

Features	Bird				
	Bluebird	Chicken	Falcon	Flamingo	Owl
Eats fish	0	0	0	0	0
Flies	12	0	7	0	0
Ugly	0	0	0	0	0
Eats insects	9	0	0	0	0
Eats dead	0	0	0	0	0
Is food	0	17	0	0	0
Pink	0	0	0	23	0
Stands on one leg	0	0	0	13	0
Says "who"	0	0	0	0	24
Tuxedo	0	0	0	0	0

such an exemplar we do not have a concept and without a concept, no meaning. But surely the associated phrases do have meaning, and we do have such concepts (see Fodor 1981).

Versions of the prototype theory have encountered both experimental and theoretical problems. Armstrong, Gleitman, and Gleitman (1983) ran a series of "typicality" experiments that seem to show that subjects respond to such well-defined concepts as "even number," "odd number," and "plane geometry figure" with the same graded responses that Rosch found for notions like "sport" and "bird." A sample of their results is shown in table 10.5. Clearly, it makes no sense to structure the concept of an *even number* around the number 2 rather than 6, because there is no numerical difference in their "evenness." If some numbers were "more even than others," then balancing a checkbook would be a lot harder than it already is. (How would you add,

Table 10.4
The probabilistic view: Featural approach. (See Smith and Medin 1981.)

Robin	Chicken	Bird	Animal
1.0 moves	1.0 moves	1.0 moves	1.0 moves
1.0 winged	1.0 winged	1.0 winged	.7 walks
1.0 feathered	1.0 feathered	1.0 feathered	.5 large size
1.0 flies	1.0 walks	.8 flies	
.9 sings	.7 medium size	.6 sings	
.7 small size		.5 small size	

Bird						
Penguin	Robin	Sandpiper	Seagull	Starling	Swallow	Vulture
11	0	0	18	0	0	0
0	9	5	9	6	7	2
0	0	0	0	0	0	15
0	20	8	0	4	5	0
0	0	0	0	0	0	22
0	0	0	0	0	0	0
0	0	0	0	0	0	0
0	0	0	0	0	0	0
0	0	0	0	0	0	0
11	0	0	0	0	0	0

subtract, and divide by both very even numbers and not-so-even numbers?) As Armstrong, Gleitman, and Gleitman comment, "What they [these results] do suggest is that we are back at square one in discovering the structure of everyday categories *experimentally* . . . the study of conceptual structure has not been put on an experimental footing, and the structure of those concepts studied by current techniques remains unknown."

Furthermore, Osherson and Smith (1981) have shown that prototype models yield counterintuitive conceptual and semantic results when combined with *fuzzy set* theories. In fuzzy set theory (Zadeh 1965), objects belong to a set *to a certain extent,* and the notion of set membership is a *graded* notion. Thus, Rover's membership in the class of dogs might be .85, and his membership in the class of females might be .10 (he might have some female characteristics).

The problem for conceptual combination arises when we look at the principles for combining fuzzy sets. For instance, the rule for conjunction (intersection) says that the membership of the resulting conjoined set is equal to *lower* membership rating of the components:

(20)
Rule for &
Membership of $(C_1 \& C_2)$ = lower of C_1, C_2.

Thus, Rover's membership rating in the combined class of FEMALE DOGS is .10, since his membership in FEMALE is .10, and that is the lower of the two.

Table 10.5
Categories, category exemplars, and exemplariness ratings for prototype and well-defined categories. Under each category label, category exemplars and mean exemplariness ratings are displayed (N = 32). (Adapted from Armstrong, Gleitman, and Gleitman 1983.)

Category	Exemplar	Exemplariness Rating	Category	Exemplar	Exemplariness Rating
Even number			Female		
Group A	4	1.1	Group A	Mother	1.7
	8	1.5		Housewife	2.4
	10	1.7		Princess	3.0
	18	2.6		Waitress	3.2
	34	3.4		Policewoman	3.9
	106	3.9		Comedienne	4.5
Group B	2	1.0	Group B	Sister	1.8
	6	1.7		Ballerina	2.0
	42	2.6		Actress	2.1
	1000	2.8		Hostess	2.7
	34	3.1		Chairwoman	3.4
	806	3.9		Cowgirl	4.5
Odd number			Plane geometry figure		
Group A	3	1.6	Group A	Square	1.3
	7	1.9		Triangle	1.5
	23	2.4		Rectangle	1.9
	57	2.6		Circle	2.1
	501	3.5		Trapezoid	3.1
	447	3.7		Ellipse	3.4
Group B	7	1.4	Group B	Square	1.5
	11	1.7		Triangle	1.4
	13	1.8		Rectangle	1.6
	9	1.9		Circle	1.3
	57	3.4		Trapezoid	2.9
	91	3.7		Ellipse	3.5

But this rule for conjunction is problematic with any concept whose intuitive prototype rating is *greater* for the conjoined concepts than for the minimal one. Thus, a guppy is low on typicality for fish and low on typicality for pets, but it is relatively high on typicality for the conjoined concept PET FISH, thus contradicting the rule for conjoining fuzzy sets. Similar examples can be found for other rules of fuzzy set theory as well. In the words of Osherson and Smith (1981, 55):

Amalgamation of any of a number of current versions of prototype theory with Zadeh's . . . fuzzy set theory will not handle strong intuitions about the way concepts combine to form complex concepts and propositions. This is an important failing because the ability to construct thoughts and complex concepts out of some basic stock of concepts seems to lie near the heart of human mentation.

To conclude, we have concentrated on the representation of lexical meaning because in general that is currently an area of intense study. But as can be seen from our brief discussion, much work needs to be done before we have a theory of concepts that is adequate as an account of word meaning. In particular, such an account must (1) relate to categorization, typicality effects, etc., (2) relate to how words apply to objects and events in the world, and (3) relate to how words and concepts can combine to form more complex expressions, concepts, and thoughts.

Communication and Speech Acts

It is clear from our discussion of language use in chapter 9 that understanding what *speakers* are trying to communicate is rarely if ever the same thing as understanding just the sentences (or other expressions) they utter. We have seen the need for a whole system of shared beliefs and inference strategies. What evidence is there from psychological experimentation that such principles do in fact function in speaker comprehension?

Very little is known about the exact nature of the inference principles underlying successful communication, but recent studies in three areas suggest that some general pragmatic principles are operative.

Given-New Information
We noted in chapter 9 that it may be helpful for a speaker to distinguish information that is unfocused or *given,* from information that is focused or *new*. Languages make available a number of different devices that

can be used to mark this distinction. English speakers often use the definite article (*the*), passive voice, repeating adverbs (*again*), cleft constructions, and various topicalization constructions to make the focus of their thoughts clear.

(21)
a. *The* boy came for the money.
b. A boy came for the money.

(22)
a. Sam *was* met at the airport *by* a friend of ours.
b. A friend of ours met Sam at the airport.

(23)
a. This Christmas Eugene got drunk *again*.
b. This Christmas Eugene got drunk.

(24)
a. *It was* Eugene *who* got drunk at Christmas.
b. *What* Eugene *did was to* get drunk at Christmas.
c. *As for* Eugene, *he* got drunk at Christmas.
d. Eugene got drunk at Christmas.

Thus, in (21a) the speaker may take the identity of the boy as known. In (22a) Sam is already the focus or a topic of conversation. In (23a) it is assumed that Eugene has been drunk at Christmas before. In (24a) it is assumed that someone got drunk at Christmas. In (24b) it is assumed that Eugene did something. And in (24c) Eugene is the focus or a topic of conversation.

On the basis of such examples, Haviland and Clark (1974) have proposed that speakers and hearers share the *Given-New Strategy:*

(GN1)
Divide the sentence into given and new information.

(GN2)
Match the given information in memory.

(GN3)
Integrate new information into memory.

Experimental evidence in fact exists for something like the Given-New Strategy. For instance, Haviland and Clark (1974) report a sequence of experiments designed to test GN2. Subjects were given sentences such as (25)–(27):

(25)
a. Last Christmas Eugene became absolutely smashed.
b. This Christmas he got very drunk again. (984 msecs)

(26)
a. Last Christmas Eugene went to a lot of parties.
b. This Christmas he got very drunk again. (1040 msecs)

(27)
a. Last Christmas Eugene couldn't stay sober.
b. This Christmas he got very drunk again. (1063 msecs)

In the first example, the context sentence (25a) provides an appropriate antecedent for *again* in sentence (25b), and the match at step GN2 should be quite direct. In the second example, the context sentence (26a) provides only the basis for an inference to an appropriate match, so step GN2 should be less directly or immediately carried out. In example (27), the context sentence specifies the appropriate condition negatively; an inference involving negation is required and thus (27) is also less direct than (25). The average amount of time that elapsed between the subjects' beginning to read the second sentence and their understanding it is given in parentheses for each case. These figures confirm the plausibility of step GN2 of the strategy.

Nonliteral Communication
Research on the development of linguistic abilities suggests that children up to the age of about 10 have considerable difficulty giving the figurative meaning of even the most common proverbs (Richardson and Church 1959). Since these children obviously have their literal linguistic abilities, we might suppose that understanding novel nonliterality is an additional layer of processing and as such takes additional time, even in adults.

Brewer, Harris, and Brewer (ms.) have found experimental evidence that this is so. Subjects were given pairs of sentences from such proverb sets as those in (28). They studied the first sentence, then were given the second sentence and were asked to judge whether the two sentences had a meaning in common. Their reactions were then timed.

(28)
a. Original Proverb
   It's a silly fish that's caught twice with the same bait.
b. Literal-Same Paraphrase
   Only a foolish fish is captured more than once on the same hook.
c. Figurative-Same Paraphrase
   Only a fool does not learn from experience.
d. Literal-Different Paraphrase
   A wise fish and a foolish fish, both caught, are equally dead.
e. Figurative-Different Paraphrase
   Wise men as much as fools do not learn from experience.

The central idea behind the experiment was this: if, when understanding proverbs, we represent both the literal and the figurative meanings, then there should be no significant difference in the amount of time it takes to judge a literal paraphrase plus proverb, as in (29), versus the reverse sequence.

(29)
a. Only a foolish fish is captured more than once on the same hook.
b. It's a silly fish that's caught twice with the same bait.

But when the subject is given a figurative paraphrase plus proverb, as in (30), there should be a significant difference in the amount of time it takes to judge them, versus the reverse sequence.

(30)
a. Only a fool does not learn from experience.
b. It's a silly fish that's caught twice with the same bait.

This is because after hearing (30a), when subjects judge whether (30b) has a meaning in common, they must represent both the literal and the figurative meaning to find a match. But for the reverse order, they are given the proverb first, and then have only one meaning to represent in order to find a common meaning.

The results were as predicted; as shown in table 10.6, when the proverb followed the figurative paraphrase, subjects took significantly longer to judge correctly. This experiment provides evidence, then, that when subjects hear and process proverbs, they form representations of both the literal and the figurative meanings.

Table 10.6
Time required to judge synonymy of proverb and paraphrase (Brewer, Harris, and Brewer (ms.))

	Literal Paraphrase	Figurative Paraphrase
Proverb first	4.32 secs	3.72 secs
Proverb second	3.87 secs	4.55 secs

Indirectness and Politeness

When we speak indirectly, we say less than we mean, and we expect our audience to infer what we mean on the basis of what we have said plus contextual information. Is there any experimental evidence for such principles?

In an influential study Clark and Lucy (1975) found evidence that with some literally based indirect communication, hearers first represent the literal meaning of the sentence, then infer the indirect communicative intent. Clark and Lucy's technique was to use a result familiar from picture verification experiments:

(31)
Three-Feature Pattern
a. Positive sentences are judged true of a picture faster than negative sentences.
b. Negative sentences are judged false of a picture faster than positive sentences.
c. Positive sentences are easier to process, overall, than negative sentences.

Using these results, Clark and Lucy presented subjects with visual displays consisting of a sentence like (32a) or (32b) followed by a circle colored either pink or blue.

(32)
a. Please color the circle blue. (positive indirect force)
b. Please don't color the circle blue. (negative indirect force)

Subjects were to respond "yes" (true) or "no" (false) by pushing an appropriate button, on condition that the displayed circle i. filled the directive conveyed by the sentence. Since each pair of sentences contained a negative element, it was possible to see whether the three-feature pattern emerged with respect to the indirect force of the sentence. Clark and Lucy found that it did: subjects judged positive requests true an average of 346 msecs faster than negative requests, negative requests false an average of 308 msecs faster than positive requests, and positive requests an average of 222 msecs faster than negative requests overall. These results, as well as the analysis of the individual pairs of sentences, indicate that subjects did represent the indirect force of the sentence in the course of comprehension.

But what evidence is there that the literal meaning of the sentence is also represented during comprehension? Among the sentences given to subjects were those shown in table 10.7. On the assumption that *unless* is inherently negative (= "if not"), it should take longer to encode *unless* than to encode *if*, and in fact it did take over ½ sec longer to verify pair B than pair A. This suggests that literal meaning was computed in the course of carrying out the verification task, which of course took longer. Moreover, this time difference in verification cannot be attributed to a difference in indirect force, since it is plausible to assume that verification of corresponding members of pairs A and B is roughly equivalent:

(33)
a. I'll be very *happy if* . . . = I'll be very *sad unless*. . .
b. I'll be very *sad if* . . . = I'll be very *happy unless*. . .

In a later study Munro (1979) asked approximately 30 subjects questions of three types:

(34)
a. Direct: What time is it?
b. Indirect$_1$: Could you tell me what time it is?
c. Indirect$_2$: Could you tell me the time?

Table 10.7
Results of verification task (Clark and Lucy 1975)

Sentence to Be Verified	Response Time (in msecs)		
	True	False	Mean
A. I'll be very happy if you make the circle blue.	1779	2103	1941
I'll be very sad if you make the circle blue.	2362	1880	2122
B. I'll be very sad unless you make the circle blue.	2367	2798	2577
I'll be very happy unless you make the circle blue.	2692	2322	2507

There are two main possible types of answers connected with these questions:

(35)

a. Direct: (One answer) "5:00."

b. Indirect$_2$: (One answer–cheeky) "Yes."

                (Two answers) "Yes, 5:00."

                (One answer) "5:00."

No subject gave the cheeky one answer, and the responses that were obtained are represented in table 10.8. Why was there a significant difference in the way subjects responded to direct and indirect questions?

One suggestion, favored by Munro, is that in the indirect case the hearer takes the speaker to be doing two things; the first part of the two-answer response is appropriate to the direct question, and the second part of the two-answer response is appropriate to the indirect request. Munro offers no account, though, of why approximately half of the subjects responded only to the indirect act. What determines when this will and will not happen?

Further evidence for inferential strategies in comprehension comes from work on politeness. After all, one of the main reasons for indirection is either to be polite, to avoid being rude, or to show deference and respect. Unfortunately, the notion of politeness is not all that clear, and to use it as an experimental tool requires that it be made precise. Clark and Schunk (1980) proposed to treat requests as polite to the extent that the *cost* to the hearer of complying with the request goes *down* and/or the *benefits* to the hearer go *up*. On the hearer's side, Clark and Schunk suggest the *Attentiveness Hypothesis:* the more attentive the hearer is to all aspects of the speaker's remark, within limits, the more polite it is.

Subjects were asked in a pair of experiments to rate various indirect requests, such as (36a–c), and various possible replies, such as (37a–c), for politeness:

Table 10.8
Two-answer responses to direct and indirect questions (Munro 1979)

Form of Question		
Direct	Indirect$_1$	Indirect$_2$
0%	45%	57%

(36)

a. May I ask you where Jordan Hall is?

b. Do you know where Jordan Hall is?

c. Do you want to tell me where Jordan Hall is?

(37)

a. Certainly, it's around the corner.

b. It's around the corner.

c. No.

It was found that the Attentiveness Hypothesis could account for a significant amount of the correlation in these rankings, and to that extent these experiments support the view that the literal meaning is being processed in such cases.

Of course, a hearer need not always wait until the end of a sentence to figure out that it is being used indirectly. Prior context can bias the hearer in favor of *expecting* indirect communication. In a pair of experiments, Gibbs (1979) gave subjects sentences such as *Must you open the window?* embedded in two different contexts—one that biased the interpretation toward the literal meaning, and one that biased the interpretation toward the indirect message:

(38)

Literal Context: Mrs. Smith was watering her garden one afternoon. She saw that the housepainter was pushing a window open. She didn't understand why he needed to have it open. A bit worried, she went over and politely asked, "Must you open the window?"

Paraphrase: "Need you open the window?"

(39)

Indirect Context: One morning John felt too sick to go to school. The night before he and his friends had gotten very drunk. Then they had gone surfing without their wetsuits. Because of this he caught a bad cold. He was lying in bed when his mother stormed in. When she started to open the window, John groaned, "Must you open the window?"

Paraphrase: "Do not open the window."

Subjects were to judge whether the paraphrase was true or false. It was found that subjects took less or equal time to judge the indirect interpretations in context as they took to judge the literal ones.

Conclusion

This completes our brief survey of some of the main areas of current experimental work on the comprehension of sentences and speakers. We have followed the flow of information from sounds through words, phrases, and sentences and on to the communicative intents of speakers. Along the way we have not only encountered alternative conceptions of the right answer to crucial questions, but also found that there are at present huge gaps in our understanding of them. In short, psychology of comprehension currently has all the signs of being a vital and active area of scientific research.

Key Words

competence
performance
speech production
speech perception
lexical access
parsing
concepts
prototypes

Study Questions

1. What is the competence vs. performance distinction? Discuss.

2. What methodological problems arise in the study of speech production?

3. How do speech error data shed light on aspects of the speech production process?

4. What evidence is there that a hearer normally processes (subconsciously) all of the meanings of an expression that he or she knows? Discuss.

5. What is the traditional doctrine of concepts?

6. What problems does the traditional doctrine have? Discuss.

7. What new theory has developed concerning the structure of concepts? How does it deal with the problems of the traditional theory? Discuss.

8. What are some problems with this new view of concepts? Discuss.

9. What are the major conclusions concerning the psychological mechanisms underlying successful nonliteral and indirect communication? Discuss.

Bibliography

Armstrong, S., L. Gleitman, and H. Gleitman (1983). "On what some concepts might not be," *Cognition* 13, 263–308.

Battig, W., and W. Montague (1969). "Category norms for verbal items in 56 categories: A replication and extension of the Connecticut category norms," *Journal of Experimental Psychology* 80 (Monograph Supplement 3, Part 2).

Bever, T. (1970). "The cognitive basis for linguistic structures," in J. Hayes, ed., *Cognition and the Development of Language,* Wiley, New York.

Bever, T., M. Garrett, and R. Hurtig (1973). "The interaction of perceptual processes and ambiguous sentences," *Memory and Cognition* 1, 277–286.

Brewer, W., R. Harris, and E. Brewer (Ms.) "Comprehension of literal and figurative meaning," unpublished manuscript, University of Illinois, Chicago.

Brown, F., and S. Levinson (1978). "Universals in language usage: Politeness phenomena," in E. Goody, ed., *Questions and Politeness,* Cambridge University Press, Cambridge.

Chomsky, N. (1965). *Aspects of the Theory of Syntax,* MIT Press, Cambridge, Mass.

Chomsky, N. (1972). *Language and Mind,* enlarged edition, Harcourt Brace Jovanovich, New York.

Clark, H., and E. Clark (1977). *Psychology and Language,* Harcourt Brace Jovanovich, New York.

Clark, H., and P. Lucy (1975). "Inferring what was meant from what was said," *Journal of Verbal Learning and Verbal Behavior* 14, 56–72.

Clark, H., and D. Schunk (1980). "Polite responses to polite requests," *Cognition* 8, 111–143.

Fay, D., and A. Cutler (1977). "Malapropisms and the structure of the mental lexicon," *Linguistic Inquiry* 8, 505–520.

Fodor, J. A. (1981). "Current status of the innateness controversy," in *Representations,* Bradford Books/MIT Press, Cambridge, Mass.

Fodor, J. A., T. Bever, and M. Garrett (1974). *The Psychology of Language,* McGraw-Hill, New York.

Fodor, J. A., M. Garrett, E. Walker, and C. Parkes (1980). "Against Definitions," *Cognition* 8, 263–367.

Fodor, J. D., J. A. Fodor, and M. Garrett (1975). "The psychological unreality of semantic representation," *Linguistic Inquiry* 6, 515–531.

Foss, D. (1969). "Decision processes during sentence comprehension: Effects of lexical item difficulty and position upon decision times," *Journal of Verbal Learning and Verbal Behavior* 8, 457–462.

Foss, D., and D. Hakes (1978). *Psycholinguistics,* Prentice-Hall, Englewood Cliffs, N.J.

Frazier, L. (1979). *On Comprehending Sentences,* distributed by the Indiana University Linguistics Club, Bloomington.

Frazier, L., and J. D. Fodor (1978). "The sausage machine: A new two-stage parsing model," *Cognition* 6, 291–325.

Fromkin, V. (1973a). "Slips of the tongue," *Scientific American,* 110–116.

Fromkin, V., ed. (1973b). *Speech Errors as Linguistic Evidence,* Mouton, The Hague.

Garrett, M. (1975). "The analysis of sentence production," in G. Bower, ed., *The Psychology of Learning and Motivation,* Academic Press, New York.

Garrett, M. (1980). "Levels of processing in sentence production," in B. Butterworth, ed., *Language Production,* Academic Press, New York.

Gibbs, R. (1979). "Contextual effects in understanding indirect requests," *Discourse Processes* 2, 1–10.

Haviland, S., and H. Clark (1974). "What's new? Acquiring new information as a process in comprehension," *Journal of Verbal Learning and Verbal Behavior* 13, 512–521.

Lehiste, I. (1973). "Phonetic disambiguation of syntactic ambiguity," *Glossa* 7, 107–122.

Lenneberg, E. (1967). *The Biological Foundations of Language,* Wiley, New York.

Liberman, A. M. (1970). "The grammars of speech and language," *Cognitive Psychology* 1, 301–323.

Lieberman, P. (1966). *Intonation, Perception and Language,* MIT Press, Cambridge, Mass.

Meyer, D., and R. Schvaneveldt (1971). "Facilitation in recognizing pairs of words: Evidence of a dependence between retrieval operations," *Journal of Experimental Psychology* 90, 227–234.

Miller, G., and P. Johnson-Laird (1976). *Language and Perception,* Harvard University Press, Cambridge, Mass.

Munro, A. (1979). "Indirect speech acts are not strictly conventional," *Linguistic Inquiry* 10, 353–356.

Osherson, D., and E. Smith (1981). "On the adequacy of prototype theory as a theory of concepts," *Cognition* 9, 35–58.

Pollack, I., and J. Pickett (1963). "The intelligibility of excerpts from conversation," *Language and Speech* 6, 165–171.

Richardson, C., and J. Church (1959). "A developmental analysis of proverb interpretations," *Journal of Genetic Psychology* 94, 169–179.

Rohrman, N., and P. Gough (1967). "Forewarning, meaning and semantic decision latency," *Psychonomic Science* 9, 217–218.

Rosch, E. (1973). "On the internal structure of perceptual and semantic categories," in T. Moore, ed., *Cognitive Development and the Acquisition of Language,* Academic Press, New York.

Rosch, E., and C. Mervis (1975). "Family resemblance studies in the internal structure of categories," *Cognitive Psychology* 7, 573–605.

Scarborough, D. L., C. Cortese, and H. S. Scarborough (1977). "Frequency and repetition effects in lexical memory," *Journal of Experimental Psychology: Human Perception and Performance* 3, 1–17.

Schatz, C. (1954). "The role of context in the perception of stops," *Language* 30, 47–56.

Shattuck-Hufnagel, S. (1979). "Speech errors as evidence for a serial-ordering mechanism in sentence production," in W. Cooper and E. Walker, eds., *Sentence Processing,* Lawrence Erlbaum Associates, Hillsdale, N.J.

Smith, E., and D. Medin (1981). *Categories and Concepts,* Harvard University Press, Cambridge, Mass.

Smith, E., E. Shoben, and L. Rips (1974). "Structure and process in semantic memory: A featural model for semantic decisions," *Psychological Review* 81, 214–241.

Swinney, D. (1979). "Lexical access during sentence comprehension: (Re)consideration of context effects," *Journal of Verbal Learning and Verbal Behavior* 18, 645–659.

Tanenhaus, M., J. Leiman, and M. Seidenberg (1979). "Evidence for multiple stages in the processing of ambiguous words in syntactic contexts," *Journal of Verbal Learning and Verbal Behavior* 18, 427–440.

Wanner, E., and M. Maratsos (1978). "An ATN approach to comprehension," in M. Halle, J. Bresnan, and G. Miller, eds., *Linguistic Theory and Psychological Reality,* MIT Press, Cambridge, Mass.

Zadeh, L. (1965). "Fuzzy sets," *Information and Control* 8, 338–353.

Chapter Eleven

LANGUAGE ACQUISITION IN CHILD AND CHIMP

Anyone concerned with the study of human nature and human capacities must somehow come to grips with the fact that all normal humans acquire language, whereas acquisition of even its barest rudiments is quite beyond the capacities of an otherwise intelligent ape.
—N. Chomsky, *Language and Mind*

The view expressed by Noam Chomsky in this quotation reflects a traditional idea about human beings, namely, that they are distinct from all other animal species in possessing language. Indeed, if we examine the natural communication systems of animals and humans—natural in the sense that these systems develop spontaneously in a normal linguistic environment—we see a wide gulf between the relatively simple animal communication systems (chapter 2) and human language. For example, if we compare monkey calls used in the wild with the elaborately structured sentences of human languages, it is evident that the two systems are strikingly different in complexity. Given the available evidence, it is reasonable to hypothesize that humans have a species-specific capacity to develop a set of complex linguistic structures typical of human language. In this sense humans can be said to have a biological (genetic) endowment that predisposes them to acquire and use human language. Thus, humans can be said to have a unique cognitive basis for language.

In recent years, however, in a fascinating set of experiments, the traditional idea about the uniqueness of language to the human species has been challenged. Psychologists, working in teams, have attempted to teach chimpanzees various communication systems (for example, sign language) that are thought to reflect certain essential properties of human language. Such projects have raised an intriguing possibility: even if a primate species (such as the chimpanzee) has a very rudimen-

tary natural communication system in the wild, perhaps a member of
this species could be taught a communication system not natural to the
species, with complex properties on a par with certain properties of
human spoken language.

Are chimpanzees in fact able to acquire and use language in a way
similar to the way humans do? Chimpanzees have often been compared
with children with respect to the acquisition of language, yet the contrast between the two is striking. As we shall see, young children
acquire complicated linguistic systems rapidly and apparently effortlessly, whereas chimpanzees have required massive training efforts to
master quite rudimentary communication systems. From one point of
view—the traditional one referred to above—this would hardly be
surprising. Humans, after all, are predisposed to learn language,
whereas chimpanzees are not. From this perspective, comparing children and chimpanzees with respect to language development is quite
instructive, and the contrast between the two serves to clarify the nature of the task that all ordinary children carry out in mastering their
native language. To illustrate this, we begin by examining language development in children.

11.1 LANGUAGE ACQUISITION IN CHILDREN

Biological Innateness of the Linguistic Capacity and the Role of Instruction and Imitation in Child Language Development

One of the most remarkable feats in human development is the mastery
of language by children. However, one need only study a foreign language, or take a course in linguistics, to begin to appreciate the enormous complexity of human language. At every level—phonological,
morphological, syntactic, semantic, and pragmatic—human language
is an intricate system of abstract units, structures, and rules, used in an
equally intricate system of communication. Once we appreciate the
nature of language and the true depth of its complexity, we can then
appreciate the surprising, and in many ways fascinating, feat that children accomplish in mastering it.

First of all, language development occurs in all children with normal
brain function, regardless of race, culture, or general intelligence. In
other words, the capacity to develop language is a capacity of the
human species as a whole. Even though different groups of people
speak different languages, all human languages have a similar level of

detail and complexity, and all languages share general abstract properties; for example, all human languages can be analyzed as systems consisting of discrete structural units, with rules for combining those units in various ways. Even though languages differ superficially, they all reflect general properties of a common linguistic system typical of the human species.

Second, language development in children occurs spontaneously and does not require conscious instruction or reinforcement on the part of adults. In a very short period of time (a span of 4 to 5 years) children are able to develop very complex linguistic systems, moving from a one-word stage to multiword stages, on the basis of limited and often fragmentary data. Although adults often imagine that they are "teaching" their children how to speak, there is no convincing evidence that children need such instruction. Indeed, as many a parent has discovered, the attempt to instruct children in language can produce frustrating results:

(1)
Child: I taked a cookie.
Parent: Oh, you mean you *took* a cookie.
Child: Yes, that's right, I taked it.

It may be that a certain amount of conscious instruction on the part of parents and peers has some effect on the language of the child, but the available evidence indicates that such tutoring plays a minor role at best. The child, simply by exposure to a language, is able to spontaneously master the overwhelming majority of its linguistic features.

Another mechanism that seems to play little or no role in the child's mastery of language is the process of imitation. Indeed, children show enormous creativity in their use of language. They utter words, phrases, and sentences they have never heard before; they also understand utterances they have never heard before. Anyone who has studied child language, or has observed children, can recount examples such as the following:

(2)
Parent: Did you like the doctor?
Child: No, he took a needle and shotted my arm.

The child (a six-year-old girl) has spontaneously created a new verb in this context, one that makes perfect sense, and one that she could not have learned by imitating adult speakers. This is not to say that imitation plays no role whatsoever in learning one's native language—for example, it may be a factor in learning some vocabulary—but the point, again, is that imitation, like overt teaching, plays at best a very minor role in the child's mastery of language.

Finally, language development takes place during a very specific maturational stage of human development. Sometime during the second year of life (at roughly anywhere from 12 to 18 months), children begin uttering their first words. During the following 4 to 5 years, linguistic development occurs quite rapidly. By the time children enter school, they have mastered the major structural features of their language. Refinements of the major features continue to appear, and the ability to learn language (one's native language or foreign languages) continues to be strong until the onset of puberty. At this point, for reasons that we do not fully understand, the "knack for languages" begins to decline, to a greater or lesser extent depending on the individual.

The properties of language development that we have cited—a spontaneous maturational development typical of the human species as a whole—strongly suggest that the linguistic capacity is part of the genetic endowment of human beings. The hypothesis of biological innateness of the language faculty has been most vigorously advanced by Noam Chomsky, who has put it this way:

We can think of every normal human's internalized grammar as, in effect, a theory of his language. This theory provides a sound-meaning correlation for an infinite number of sentences. . . . In formal terms, then, we can describe the child's acquisition of language as a kind of theory-construction. The child discovers the theory of his language with only small amounts of data from that language. Not only does his "theory of the language" have an enormous predictive scope, but it also enables the child to reject a great deal of the very data on which the theory has been constructed. Normal speech consists, in large part, of fragments, false starts, blends and other distortions of the underlying idealized forms. Nevertheless, as is evident from a study of the mature use of language, what the child learns is the underlying ideal theory. This is a remarkable fact. We must also bear in mind that the child constructs this ideal theory without explicit instruction, that he acquires this knowledge at a time when he is not capable of complex intellectual achievements in many other domains, and that this achievement is relatively independent of intelligence or the particular course of experience. These are facts that a theory of learning must face.

A scientist who approaches phenomena of this sort without prejudice or dogma would conclude that the acquired knowledge must be determined in a rather specific way by intrinsic properties of mental organization. He would then set himself the task of discovering the innate ideas and principles that make such acquisition of knowledge possible. (Chomsky 1969, reprinted in Bar-Adon and Leopold 1971, 429)

From this point of view, then, the development of language in children is guided by a set of "innate ideas and principles," that is, a genetically determined linguistic capacity that all humans are endowed with at birth. From this point of view, all children are biologically programmed with the capacity to develop language—namely, the language(s) they are significantly exposed to during the appropriate maturational stage. Language development can thus be regarded as analogous to other biological developments in human growth and maturation. In this way, the traditional view that language is unique to human beings may in fact have a sound biological basis. Just as other biological characteristics can be unique to a certain species (such as the shape of the body or the structure of internal organs), so too the capacity for language and other properties of human mental functioning may well be a unique part of the genetic endowment of human beings.

The Rule-governed Nature of Child Language and Language Development

Given that children have an innate capacity to develop language, and given that conscious instruction or imitation is not required for this development, exactly how do children go about learning a particular language? Unfortunately, we are still at a very rudimentary stage of understanding the psychological and neurological mechanisms that provide a basis for the child's actual mastery of his or her native language. However, one thing is quite clear. There is very good evidence that children do not merely internalize individual expressions of a language, but in fact learn *rules* for forming these expressions.

Consider the fact that all native speakers of English have learned how to interpret expressions such as the following:

(3)
a. the house
b. the house in the woods
c. the house in the woods near the river
d. the house in the woods near the river by the mountain

As noted in the discussion of recursion in chapter 5, phrases such as these can be iterated indefinitely—there is no upper bound on the length they can attain. The syntactic rules of English allow us to add modifiers to nouns as shown in (3), and no matter how long such phrases were to become, at no point could we say that the rules of English syntax had been violated (even if such phrases were stylistically awkward or difficult to comprehend due to performance factors). Such examples show that it is impossible *in principle* to memorize all the expressions of a language. Clearly, we have mastered *rules or principles*—not simply individual expressions—that allow us to associate sound and meaning for a potentially infinite set of expressions.

Not all areas of human language are infinite in scope. For example, we might consider the words of a language as forming a finite (though large) set, and one could imagine that children simply memorize all the words they are exposed to. Nevertheless, even in this realm there is evidence that children develop creative principles—in this case for word formation. A commonly cited piece of evidence for this is the phenomenon of *overgeneralization,* in which the child extends a rule-governed pattern to forms that do not follow the rule. For example, the regular past tense in English is formed by adding the suffix *-ed* to the verb stem: *talk–talked.* However, there are numerous verbs in English with irregular past tenses, such as *take–took.* A child who says *taked* is overgeneralizing the rule for the regular past tense by using the regular past ending with an irregular verb. Thus, the "error" reveals that the child has mastered the rule for forming the regular past tense.

In this regard, the form *shotted,* cited in (2b), provides a particularly interesting example. Here, the child has created a new verb (presumably the verb *to shot;* the verb *to shoot* already existed in the child's vocabulary and was used exclusively in situations involving toy guns and playing dead). However, having created a new verb stem, the child nevertheless assimilated it into the regular morphology of English and provided it with the regular *-ed* past tense ending.

In a well-known experiment involving English morphology, Berko (1958) provided nonsense words to children of ages 4 to 7 and asked them to give a variation of the nonsense word reflecting certain morphological properties, such as the plural morpheme. For example, children were presented with test frames like the following:

(4)

This is a wug. (accompanied by picture of imaginary bird-like animal)
Now there is another one.
There are two of them. (accompanied by picture of two of the imaginary animals)
There are two ____ .

The idea is to provide the plural form of the nonsense word *wug. If children have mastered a rule for forming plurals, they should be able to answer *wugs*. As Berko put it,

If knowledge of English consisted of no more than the storing up of many memorized words, the child might be expected to refuse to answer our questions on the grounds that he had never before heard of a *wug, for instance, and could not possibly give us the plural form since no one had ever told him what it was. This was decidedly not the case. The children answered the questions; in some instances they pronounced the inflectional endings they had added with exaggerated care, so that it was obvious they understood the problem and wanted no mistake made about their solution. (1958, 164)

Stages in the Development of Language

Studies of linguistic development have revealed that children pass through a series of recognizable stages as they master their native language. Although the age at which children will pass through a given stage can vary significantly from child to child, the particular sequence of stages seems to be the same for all children acquiring a given language. Here we will review some of the better-known stages of language development for children learning English (see References for more detailed summaries).

Babbling

Prior to the development of language, all children, regardless of the language they will ultimately learn, pass through a stage referred to as *babbling*. In this stage, which begins at around 5 to 6 months, the child utters sounds and sound sequences (syllables such as *ba, ma, ga*) that are as yet meaningless but nevertheless recognizable as being more language-like than earlier infant cries. Indeed, a number of sounds and syllables of the babbling stage will occur later as the child develops language. It has also been noted that certain sounds that occur in babbling are lost when the child begins to use language, but appear again at a later stage. As Clark and Clark (1977, 390) note:

. . . when children start to use their first words, they no longer seem able to produce some of the very sounds they used when babbling. One striking example can be found in their use of *l* and *r:* although these are very frequent in babbling, they rarely appear in children's first words and are among the latest sounds that children master.

It seems, then, that in the babbling stage children produce language-like sounds quite freely, but as they develop their native language they must master a systematic set of rules and patterns and they must, in effect, learn how to fit given sounds into those patterns.

The fact that *all* children (including the congenitally deaf) go through a babbling stage, regardless of language and culture, and make very similar kinds of sounds at this time suggests that humans are biologically predisposed to go through this phase.

The One-Word Stage
The babbling phase, which lasts for some 6 to 8 months, gradually gives way to the earliest recognizable stage of language, often referred to as the *one-word stage*. At some point in the late part of the first year of life or the early part of the second year, the child will begin using recognizable words of the native language. These words are usually the names of familiar people, animals, and objects in the child's environment (*mama, dada, kitty, doggie, ball, bottle, cup*) and words indicating certain actions and demands (*More!, No!*). Viewed from the perspective of adult grammar, the kinds of words that occur at this stage include simple nouns and verbs; there are as yet very few so-called function words (prepositions, articles, auxiliary verbs, interrogative words) in the child's language.

In evaluating children's language at the one-word stage, one must be extremely cautious about comparisons between the child's language and the adult language. For example, it is not clear that a given word used by a child at this stage has the same use that it would have in the adult language. Children's use of words sometimes shows an *overextension* or *underextension* of reference. For example, a certain child might use the word *doggie* to refer not just to dogs but to all common animals in the environment (an example of overextension). In contrast, a child might use the word *doggie* to refer not to all dogs (that is, all animals that could properly be referred to by the word *doggie*), but only to certain specific dogs (an example of underextension). Thus, it is not clear exactly what children's early words mean to them, and for obvious reasons we cannot interview young children to find out. The fact that adults (especially parents) claim to understand these early utterances should not be taken as evidence that children's utterances mean what adult utterances mean. Adults have a strong ability to interpret utterances in terms of the nonlinguistic context of the utterance (the time, place, situation, and participants involved), and based on this nonlinguistic context a child's utterances can be assigned an appropriate meaning by the adult. This method of *rich interpretation,* as it has sometimes been called, allows the adult to arrive at a certain understanding of the child's utterances, but this, in and of itself, does not reveal what the child might actually have in mind, nor does it reveal what the expression means to the child. For such reasons, it is difficult to determine whether an individual word uttered by the child is to be understood as *holophrastic* (as standing for an entire sentence or proposition), or whether it is to be taken as simply expressing a concept that is somehow relevant to the particular nonlinguistic context of the utterance.

Multiword Stages

At some point during the second year of life, the child's utterances gradually become longer, and the one-word stage gives way to multiword stages. As noted earlier, the exact age at which children will pass through a given stage varies significantly from child to child. For example, one child might enter the two-word stage at 20 months of age, and another might enter the same stage at 27 months. In general, the multiword stages we will describe here begin roughly in the second half of the child's second year and extend roughly to the child's fifth year. Although age varies, the particular sequence of stages described below is quite similar for all children.

As shown in table 11.1, during the early multiword stage—at roughly the two-word stage—children begin to express a variety of grammatical and conceptual relations. It is during this stage that children learning English begin to use word order to indicate certain relations—for example, Possessor followed by Possessed, or Subject followed by Predicate (again see table 11.1). In addition, the child's language begins to reflect the distinction between sentence-types, such as negative sentences, imperatives, and questions. In this stage of linguistic development, we see the beginnings of a structured language (for example, subject + predicate structure), and it is clear that the child is beginning to master the broader grammatical features of the language.

Table 11.1
Common types of utterances found in the early multiword stage. (Donald Foss and David Hakes, *Psycholinguistics: An Introduction to the Psychology of Language*, © 1978, pp. 248–249. Reprinted by permission of Prentice-Hall, Inc., Englewood Cliffs, N.J.)

Semantic Characterization	Syntactic Characterization	Forms	Examples
1. Nomination (naming, noticing)	Existential	$\left.\begin{array}{l}\text{here it}\\\text{there 's}\\\text{this see}\\\text{that hi}\end{array}\right\}$ + Noun	there book that car see doggie hi spoon
2. Possession	Noun Phrase	$\left\{\begin{array}{l}\text{Noun}\\\text{Pronoun}\end{array}\right\}$ + Noun	my stool baby book Mommy sock
3. Attribution	Noun Phrase or Predicate Adjective	Adjective + Noun $\left\{\begin{array}{l}\text{Noun}\\\text{Pronoun}\end{array}\right\}$ + Adjective	pretty boat party hat big step carriage broken that dirty Mommy tired
4. Plurality	Noun Phrase	Quantifier + Noun	two cup all cars
5. Actor-Action	a. Subject + Predicate	Noun + Verb	Bambi go Mommy push (Kathryn) airplane by
	b. Subject + Predicate	Noun + Noun	Mommy (wash) jacket Lois (play) baby record
	c. Predicate	Verb + Noun	pick glove pull hat helping Mommy

Category	Structure	Examples
6. Location		
a. object location	Subject + Prepositional Phrase	sweater chair
		lady home
		baby room
b. action toward location	Verb + Prepositional Phrase	sat wall
		walk street
7. Requests and Imperatives	a. Verb + Object	want milk
		gimme ball
	b. Quantifier + Object — $\{$more / 'nother$\}$ + Noun	more nut
		'nother milk
8. Negation		
a. nonexistence	Neg + Sentence — Neg + $\{$Noun / Verb / Adjective$\}$	allgone milk
		no hot
		nomore light
		any more play
b. rejection	Neg + Sentence — Neg + $\{$Verb / Noun$\}$	no dirty soap
		no meat
		no go outside
c. denial	Neg + Sentence — Neg + $\{$Noun / Verb / Adjective$\}$	no morning (it was afternoon)
		no Daddy hungry
		no truck
9. Questions		
a. requests and imperatives	Yes/No Question	Same word order as statements and imperatives; signaled only by rising intonation
b. information requests	Wh- Question	Fixed forms with wh-
		What dat?
		What (NP) do?
		Where (NP) go?

As the length of the child's utterances increases beyond the two-word stage, the major grammatical constructions of the native language begin to develop in more detail. Two constructions of English that have been studied from the point of view of their development in child language are negative sentences and questions. This development is summarized in table 11.2. Beginning first with negative sentences, we see that at the one-word stage negation is simply expressed by single words with negative meaning, such as *no* or *allgone*. In the early multiword stage, these negative words occur at the beginning (or, more rarely, at the end) of expressions—for example, *no eat, allgone milk* (see also table 11.1, section 8). At this stage the negative word does not intervene between other words; that is, it does not occur "internally" within an expression. However, in later multiword stages, the negative word begins to occur within expressions, between subject and predicate (*Mommy no play*).

Recall from the discussion of questions in chapter 5 that English makes a distinction between auxiliary verbs and main verbs. For example, in the adult grammar, the negative *not* (or the contracted *n't*) occurs with auxiliary verbs such as *do, does, did, is, am, are, have, has, can, could, may, might, shall, should, will, would, must,* and a few others. Thus, Modern English has no sentences of the form **I drink not,* but instead has sentences of the form *I don't drink, I won't drink, I mustn't drink,* and so on. In mastering English, then, children must become aware that a special class of auxiliary verbs functions both to "carry" the negative and to invert with the subject to form questions. At the stage where the negative word begins to appear internally in expressions (as in *Mommy no play*) we find the first negative auxiliary verbs in the child's language, usually the auxiliaries *can't* and *don't* (as in *I can't do that, I don't know him*). At this stage auxiliaries do not yet occur in the positive form. That is, although we find *can't* and *don't*, we do not yet find *can, do, does,* or *did.*

In the following stages, a wider range of negative auxiliaries begins to appear, and auxiliaries finally begin to appear in positive sentences as well as negative sentences. Thus, it seems that mastery of the system of negation in English is dependent upon, or at least tightly connected with, the mastery of auxiliary verbs.

The same connection is found in the development of questions, for auxiliary verbs play an important role here as well. Beginning with the one-word stage (see table 11.2), questioning is indicated solely by intonation and/or nonlinguistic cues in the context of utterance. As the child proceeds to an early multiword stage, auxiliary verbs have not yet developed, and yes/no questions (questions that can be answered "yes" or "no") are indicated by rising intonation at the end of the expression. So-called *wh*-questions (questions that begin with one of the "*wh*-words," such as *who, what, when, where, why,* and *how*) are quite limited at this early multiword stage, and it has been noted that *where* and *what* are predominant at this stage (*Where doggie? What dat?*).

As children enter later multiword stages, additional *wh*-words (such as *why, who*) begin to enter their language. Yes/no questions continue to be indicated by intonation until the stage is reached where auxiliary verbs develop in positive sentences as well as negative sentences. With the development of auxiliary verbs, inversion of subject and auxiliary begins to appear in children's yes/no questions (*Can't you get it?, Will you help me?*). However, even at this stage the inversion of word order has not yet begun to occur in *wh*-questions, which continue to be marked by *wh*-words at the beginning of expressions (as in *What she did?, What he can do?,* and so on). The inversion of auxiliaries in *wh*-questions (*What did she do?, What can he do?*) develops at a stage later than the stage where inversion of auxiliaries occurs in yes/no questions.

These examples, though brief, illustrate the fact that children develop their native language in a sequence of identifiable stages. Further, we see that specific constructions of a language develop in an interrelated way: the development of negative sentences and questions in English is intimately connected with the development of the auxiliary verb system.

Conclusion

Our discussion of language development in children has focused on two important and intimately interconnected properties of human language use: it is *rule-governed* (that is, humans master and follow rules for forming and using expressions of their native language); and it is *creative* (that is, humans spontaneously produce and understand expressions they have never encountered before in their linguistic experience). These are both properties that have been stressed in putting forth the claim that the human linguistic capacity is unique.

Table 11.2
Development of negative sentences and questions in child language. (Adapted from Foss and Hakes 1978 and Clark and Clark 1977.)

Stage	Negative Sentences	Questions	
		Yes/No Questions	Wh-Questions
One-word stage	Negation expressed by single negative word: no allgone	Questioning indicated by intonation and/or context	
Early multiword stage	Negative word occurs at beginning of expression; does not occur between other words: No eat No sit down Allgone milk No hot No mommy go	Auxiliaries have not developed; no inversion of word order; only intonation is used: That mine? See baby? Drink baba?	Very limited; where and what are predominant forms, used at beginning of expressions: Where doggie? Where Daddy go? What dat?
Later multiword stage	Negative word occurs inside expression, between subject and predicate; negative auxiliaries can't and don't appear: There no milk He not big Mommy no play I can't do that I don't know him	Continued use of intonation; no inversion of word order; auxiliaries do not yet occur in positive sentences: You can't fix it? She no play? See doggie? Dolly go boom?	Additional wh-words develop to include why; no inversion of word order: Why mommy go? What dolly do? Why kitty sleep?

Wider range of negative auxiliaries appears; auxiliaries begin to appear in positive as well as negative sentences:

I didn't do it
He doesn't like it
I'm not a baby
I won't read the book
Mommy can't find dolly

Auxiliaries begin to appear in positive sentences; inversion of auxiliary appears:

Can't you get it?
Will you help me?
Did you see him?

Additional *wh*-words develop to include *how*; still no inversion of word order:

What she did?
Why doggy run?
What he can do?
How she can do that?

11.2 IS THE HUMAN LINGUISTIC CAPACITY UNIQUE:
CHILDREN AND CHIMPANZEES COMPARED

Returning now to a question raised earlier in this chapter, we might ask whether any other species can be shown to use a communicative system in a way similar to the way humans use language. In posing this question, we will need to pay particular attention to the two just-mentioned properties of human language use that supposedly set it apart from other animal communication systems. Can these properties be shown to exist in the communication systems that have been taught to chimpanzees? To put it another way, are chimpanzees and children comparable in their acquisition and use of language? To answer this, we will now turn our attention to some of the chimpanzee projects that have attracted notice in recent years.

Washoe

In June 1966, Alan and Beatrice Gardner began a project that was to have immediate popular appeal, if not immediate academic acceptance. Their project was to teach a young (approximately one-year-old) female chimpanzee to communicate in American Sign Language (ASL). Although their avowed purpose was to probe "the extent to which another species might be able to use human language" (Gardner and Gardner 1969, 664), it is evident that they were challenging claims such as the one that opened this chapter. As might well be expected, the success of the project quickly became a hotly debated issue. The popular press concluded almost immediately that Washoe was able to converse in ASL, and articles began appearing with titles such as "First Message from the Planet of the Apes." This kind of reaction put the skeptic in a position comparable, in the public mind, with that of seventeenth-century defenders of the uniqueness of man, who argued that "brutes" (animals), unlike man, have no souls. It is unfortunate that the skeptic was placed in this position, because the Gardners' project is interesting and important enough to deserve serious intellectual consideration, and such consideration requires that we carefully scrutinize all claims about the linguistic proficiency of chimps. We will review Washoe's basic accomplishments, inviting readers to consider for themselves some of the central questions raised by these studies (see exercises).

The problem of teaching a member of another species a human language presents the investigator with two fundamental preliminary decisions: what species to pick, and what language to use. The Gardners' choice in these matters was inspired. First and foremost, chimpanzees are among the most intelligent creatures of the animal world. Combining this with the fact that they are notoriously imitative and quite sociable with their human cousins, one gets a promising picture of a prospective language learner. Chimps have other important characteristics as well. They are manually adept, are sociable with members of their own species, and grow to a convenient size through a sequence of phases that are comparable to those in human development. These latter characteristics are important in that they allow the possibility of investigating communication among members of the species as well as allowing comparison of the chimp's acquisition of language with that of a normal human child.

Why did the Gardners choose to teach Washoe ASL? Attempts to teach chimps *spoken* English have not been at all encouraging. For instance, Keith and Catherine Hayes attempted to teach spoken English to a chimp named Vicki (Hayes 1951). They raised Vicki like a human child, in an optimal home environment. Yet after six years of training, Vicki's speaking vocabulary was barely four words: *mama, papa, cup,* and *up.* The main problem seemed to be that a chimp's vocal apparatus is not suited to the production of many human speech sounds. Recalling the dexterous and imitative nature of chimps (who will occasionally gesture spontaneously to humans), the Gardners hit upon the idea of using a gestural language as the test system. A number of gestural systems of communication are available, but ASL was a natural choice for a number of reasons. Most important, it is a system used naturally by many people; it therefore affords a good basis of comparison for such things as acquisition rate, proficiency, and comprehension. It is also a system with structure comparable in many ways to spoken human language. Finally, there is an iconic aspect to many signs that may be of some value at early stages of instruction. We will see examples of this iconicity in Washoe's acquisition of the signs for *bib.*

Unlike Vicki (the Hayes's chimp), Washoe was not raised in the home like a child. She was not raised in a conventional laboratory, either. Most of her time with the Gardners was spent in a two-and-a-half room house trailer supplied with the usual trappings of human life and surrounded by a pleasant yard, 5000 square feet in area. Washoe spent her nights alone, but during the day she was provided with an

environment that was as stimulating as possible for learning ASL. She
never lacked an ASL communicant, and there was opportunity for
plenty of conversation, much play, and many outings. It will be easier
to follow Washoe's progress with the chronology of events provided in
table 11.3.

How Washoe Learned
Since the goal of the Gardners' experiment with Washoe was to assess
the extent of her ability to learn ASL, and not to test any particular
theory of learning, virtually any teaching method thought to work was
tried on occasion. In spite of this variation, the Gardners were able to
keep track of how Washoe learned at least some of her signs.

Just as human children do a great deal of verbal babbling, so chimps
do a certain amount of manual babbling, that is, natural and spontaneous gesturing. The Gardners thought that some of these natural gestures might form the basis of meaningful signs. But this hope was
thwarted: probably only one of Washoe's signs was based on her natural gestures (the sign for *funny*), and this sign proved to be unstable.
Babbling shades easily into invention, and it is possible to describe
Washoe's acquisition of signs for *come/gimme* and *hurry* either as
modified babbling or as invention. However, the Gardners describe a
less controversial example of an invented sign when they write,

Sometimes we could not find an ASL equivalent for an English word in
any of our manuals of ASL and no informant was available to supplement the manuals. In these cases we would adapt a sign of ASL for the
purpose. The sign for *bib* was one of these cases and we chose to use
the ASL sign for *napkin* or *wiper* to refer to bibs as well. This sign is

Table 11.3
Washoe chronology

Date	Event
1965 (c. June)	Washoe is born in the wild
1966 (June)	Is brought to Nevada and begins training
1966 (December)	Has acquired her first 4 signs
1967 (April) ˋ	Signs her first combinations
1967 (July)	Has acquired her first 13 signs
1968 (April)	Has acquired her first 34 signs
1969 (c. June)	Has acquired 85 signs; end of first three years of training
1970	Is sent to the Institute for Primate Studies in Norman, Oklahoma
1975	Is reported to have 160 signs

made by touching the mouth region with an open hand and a wiping movement. During Month 18 Washoe had begun to use this sign appropriately for bibs, but it was still unreliable. One evening at dinner time, a human companion was holding up a bib and asking her to name it. Washoe tried *come-gimme* and *please,* but did not seem to be able to remember the *bib* sign that we had taught her. Then, she did something very interesting. With the index fingers of both hands she drew an outline of a bib on her chest—starting from behind her neck where a bib should be tied, moving her index fingers down along the outer edge of her chest, and bringing them together again just above her navel.

We could see that Washoe's invented sign for *bib* was at least as good as ours, and both were inventions. At the next meeting of the human participants in the project, we discussed the possibility of adopting Washoe's invention as an alternative to ours, but decided against it. The purpose of the project was, after all, to see if Washoe could learn a human system of two-way communication, and not to see if human beings could learn a system devised by an infant chimpanzee. We continued to insist on the *napkin-wiper* sign for bibs, until this became a reliable item in Washoe's repertoire. Five months later, when we were presenting films on Washoe's signing to fluent signers at the California School for the Deaf in Berkeley, we learned that drawing an outline of a bib on the chest with both index fingers is the correct sign for *bib.* (Gardner and Gardner 1971, 39)

As a further possible case of innovation, Washoe was later reported (in Oklahoma) to have signed *water bird* for swans, though her attendant used the sign for *duck.*

Some signs—for instance, *sweet, flower, toothbrush,* and *smoke*— were acquired by imitation. On the other hand, *more* and *open* were selectively shaped from gestures that were similar in some respect to these signs.

Finally, *tickle* and many other signs were the result of guidance (also called *molding*). In these cases, Washoe's hand was formed or molded into the proper shape and then brought through the motion required for the sign.

There is some evidence that Washoe was able to generalize the use of a sign from its original referent to new cases, and thus an important feature of human language acquisition may have been present in her case. The sign for *key* is a relevant example:

A great many cupboards and doors in Washoe's quarters have been kept secure by small padlocks that can all be opened by the same simple key. Because she was immature and awkward, Washoe had great difficulty in learning to use these keys and locks. Because we wanted her to improve her manual dexterity, we let her practice with these keys until she could open the locks quite easily (then we had to hide the keys). Washoe soon transferred this skill to all manner of locks and keys, including ignition keys. At about the same time, we taught her the sign for "key," using the original padlock key as a referent. Washoe came to use this sign both to name keys that were presented to her and to ask for the keys to various locks when no key was in sight. She readily transferred the sign to all varieties of keys and locks. (Gardner and Gardner 1971, 162)

Recall that children will sometimes undergeneralize a word and will, for example, use *dog* to refer only to one particular dog. Similar observations have been made with other signing chimps.

Lucy was presented with twenty-four different fruits and vegetables. Over a period of four days she was asked what the fruits and vegetables were in order to gather baseline data for the responses to these items. The signs she had in her vocabulary that were food-related signs were: *food, fruit, drink, candy,* and *banana.* She used *food, fruit,* and *drink* in a generic manner, whereas *banana* was specific to bananas. After the four days of baseline data the sign *berry* was taught to her using a cherry as an exemplar. She was presented with the fruits and vegetables for eight more days in order to determine whether the *berry* sign would generalize to the other berry-like items, or whether it would remain highly specific to cherries as the *banana* sign is specific to bananas. The *berry* sign remained specific to the cherries. After day eight she was taught the *berry* sign using a blackberry as an exemplar. She called the blackberry *berry* for two days and then returned to using *fruit* or *food* to describe it; *berry* was not only specific to cherry but there seemed to be a resistance to using the sign for other items. (Fouts 1975, 381)

What Washoe Learned

Although it has been reported that by 1975 Washoe had a vocabulary of at least 160 signs (Fouts 1975), the most detailed report of her vocabulary is by Gardner and Gardner (1975), who describe Washoe's first 85 signs in the order of acquisition. These signs passed the test of being used spontaneously and appropriately on 15 consecutive days.

As Washoe's chronology indicates, her first combinations (such as *gimme sweet* and *come open*) were observed after about 10 months of training. Over the next 26 months she was observed to make 294 different two-sign combinations. By the spring of 1968, after about two years of training, Washoe was appropriately using four- and five-sign combinations such as *you me go out* and *you me go out hurry.* Does this mean that Washoe was spontaneously creating new combinations, the way children spontaneously create new multiword sentences? The Gardners' evidence does not establish this, and studies of other chimpanzees strongly suggest that multisign combinations used by chimpanzees are quite different in character from sentences used by children (see remarks by Herbert Terrace (1979), quoted below).

The Gardners have attempted to establish that in Washoe's idiolect the signs are grouped into such categories as proper names, common nouns, pronouns, modifiers, verbs, and locatives (Gardner and Gardner 1975). However, the evidence for this categorization comes mainly from comparing Washoe's question-and-answer sequences with those of young children; such comparison leaves open a number of issues that might call the conclusions into question. In particular, this procedure assumes that one can really motivate these syntactic categories in the analysis of child language, which, as we have already noted, is not obviously the case, because many of these tests are semantic and pragmatic, not syntactic.

Washoe Compared with Children
Part of the attractiveness of ASL as a language to teach Washoe was that it is a human language and thus it might be possible to compare Washoe's progress against that made by children. We know of no detailed comparison of Washoe's development and that of deaf children acquiring ASL, but the Gardners (1971) have compared her two-sign combinations with the earliest two-word utterances of hearing children, as shown in table 11.4.

As can be seen, the two schemes resemble each other closely. Curiously, though, there are no reports of Washoe spontaneously asking questions, and this distinguishes her in one important respect from the normal child.

What is one to conclude about Washoe's linguistic ability? Does she use ASL? Has she learned to communicate in a human language? These are extremely difficult questions to answer. It is important to keep in mind that chimps are quite clever, and care should be taken not to be too impressed by their ability to figure out complicated ways of getting what they want. Further, it should be noted that the Nim Chimpsky project (see below), carried out after the Washoe project, raised serious questions about the interpretation of data in chimpanzee projects, and at present there is little convincing evidence from the Washoe project (or others) for a linguistic ability among chimpanzees comparable to that of human children.

Table 11.4
Parallel descriptive schemes for the earliest combinations by children and Washoe (Thorpe 1974, from Gardner and Gardner 1971)

Brown's (1970) scheme for children

Types	Examples
Attributive: Adj + N	big train, red book
Possessive: N + N	Adam checker, mommy lunch
N + V	walk street, go store
Locative: N + N	sweater chair, book table
Agent-Action: N + V	Adam put, Eve read
Action-Object: V + N	put book, hit ball
Agent-Object: N + N	mommy sock, mommy lunch

Nim Chimpsky

The Washoe project presented the intriguing possibility that chimpanzees could master a sign language in such a way as to combine signs into structured sequences. If such projects raised hopes that chimpanzees could be shown to use a signing system in the way humans use structured sentences, these hopes have been dimmed by the results of a more recent project involving a chimpanzee named Nim Chimpsky. Under the direction of the psychologist Herbert Terrace and his associates at Columbia University, in a project involving over one hundred staff members, Nim was taught American Sign Language during a span of some four years (between 1974 and 1977). In one of the most systematic and well-documented projects to date (see Terrace 1979), Nim was taught by more than sixty teachers during the span of the project, and learned to express 125 signs during his first forty-four months. Even though the initial analysis of Nim's signs and sign combinations seemed

Scheme for Washoe	
Types	Examples
⎰ Object-Attribute	drink red, comb black
⎱ Agent-Attribute	Washoe sorry, Naomi good
⎰ Agent-Object	clothes Mrs. G., you hat
⎱ Object-Attribute	baby mine, clothes yours
⎧ Action-Location	go in, look out
⎨ Action-Object	go flower, pants tickle
⎩ Object-Location	baby down, in hat
Agent-Action	Roger tickle, you drink
Action-Object	tickle Washoe, open blanket
Appeal-Action	please tickle, hug hurry
Appeal-Object	gimme flower, more fruit

promising, on closer examination of the data Terrace began to have doubts that Nim's combinations were legitimate sentences:

One of the first facts that troubled me was the absence of any increase in the length of Nim's utterances. During the last two years in which Nim lived in New York, the average length of his utterances fluctuated between 1.1 and 1.6 signs. That state of affairs characterizes the *beginning* of a child's development in combining words. As a child gets older, the average length of its utterances increases steadily. This is true both of children with normal hearing and of deaf children who sign. . . . Despite the steady increase in the size of Nim's vocabulary, the mean length of his utterances did not increase. Apparently, utterances whose average length was 1.5 signs were long enough to express the meanings that Nim wanted to communicate. (1979, 210)

Another striking fact about Nim's sign combinations was the considerable overlap between two-sign combinations and three-sign combinations. For example, some typical frequent combinations produced by Nim are as follows (1979, 212):

(5)

a. Two-Sign Combinations	b. Three-Sign Combinations
play me	play me Nim
tickle me	tickle me Nim
eat Nim	grape eat Nim
me eat	banana Nim eat

As Terrace noted:

From a lexical point of view, a comparison of these combinations reveals that the topics of Nim's three-sign combinations overlapped considerably with the topics of his two-sign combinations. His three-sign combinations do not, however, provide new information. Consider, for example, Nim's most frequent two- and three-sign combinations: *play me* and *play me Nim*. Adding *Nim* to *play me* is simply redundant. (1979, 210–211)

Noting that the relationship between two-sign and three-sign combinations was marked by a high degree of repetition and redundancy, Terrace observed, "In producing a three-sign combination, it appears that Nim was simply adding emphasis. Nim's four-sign combinations reveal a similar picture" (1979, 213).

Perhaps the most interesting observation concerning Nim's signing, and one that has significant consequences for other studies of chimp signing, concerned the relationship between Nim's signing and the signing of his teachers. For it turned out that Nim's signing was very much influenced by the prior signing of his teachers. As Terrace put it:

It was while looking at playbacks of videotapes that I realized I had missed an important aspect of the context of Nim's signs. When the other teachers and I were working with Nim and recording what he signed, our attention had always been riveted on his signing. We had paid too little attention to what *we* signed to Nim. (1979, 214)

After systematic investigation of videotaped sessions between Nim and his teachers, Terrace concluded:

During Nim's last year in New York only 10 percent of his videotaped utterances were spontaneous. Approximately 40 percent were imitations or reductions. If the conversations we videotaped and transcribed were representative of the thousands of conversations from which our corpus was derived—and I have no reason to believe that they were not—I must conclude that Nim's utterances were less spontaneous and less original than those of a child. To a much larger extent than a child's, Nim's utterances were variations of the signs contained in his teacher's prior utterance. He was much less likely than a child to add new information to a conversation in his replies. (1979, 218)

Reviewing the overall performance of Nim, and the evidence of his communicative behavior during the project, Terrace summarized the situation as follows:

I must therefore conclude—though reluctantly—that until it is possible to defeat *all* plausible explanations short of the intellectual capacity to arrange words according to a grammatical rule, it would be premature to conclude that a chimpanzee's combinations show the same structure evident in the sentences of a child. The fact that Nim's utterances were less spontaneous and less original than those of a child and that his utterances did not become longer, both as he learned new signs and as he acquired more experience in using sign language, suggests that much of the structure and meaning of his combinations was determined, or at least suggested by, the utterances of his teachers. (1979, 221)

On the basis of the results of the Nim project, we have reason to be quite cautious about making any definitive conclusions regarding a chimpanzee's linguistic abilities. It cannot be said, at this time, that there is clear and uncontroversial evidence demonstrating that chimpanzees can create structured sentences in a spontaneous manner. Nevertheless, this lack of clear evidence may be a result of certain flaws in the particular experimental methods that have been utilized so far, and we must remain alert to the possibility that less problematic methods may be discovered in the future.

Is Language a Uniquely Human Cognitive Ability?

The chimpanzee projects we have discussed in this chapter, as well as other primate projects we have not reviewed (such as the Sarah project (Premack and Premack 1972), the Lana project (Rumbaugh 1977), and the Koko project (Patterson 1981)), represent a fascinating new direction in research on interspecies communication. In less than a span of two decades, the idea of systematic communication between humans and nonhuman species has become more than just a fanciful speculation. Whether or not the primate projects can ever show that apes are able to use a linguistic system in the way humans do, such research has indeed shown that apes can manipulate symbols and that they can learn simple communication systems that are not natural to their species. Building on these results, future research may well be able to give us an overall picture of how primate intelligence is structured, and this information in turn may provide interesting points of comparison and contrast with human intelligence.

To sum up, convincing evidence has not yet been presented that would indicate that a nonhuman species has the capacity to use a communication system in the way that humans use language. It seems that language use is indeed a uniquely human cognitive ability, and the development of language in children continues to be a cognitive development that is unparalleled in any other species.

Key Words

biological innateness
overgeneralization
babbling
overextension
underextension
Washoe
American Sign Language

Study Questions

1. What is the evidence that children acquiring language do not simply memorize words and sentences?

2. Discuss the experiment that demonstrated that children have not memorized the plural forms of all nouns.

3. In what ways is infant babbling different from the earliest forms of "real" language that the child begins to speak?

4. What is a *holophrastic expression* in child language?

5. What evidence is there that Washoe produces and understands ASL (American Sign Language)?

6. Recall, from chapter 5, four important aspects of syntactic structure. What evidence is there that Washoe's dialect has syntactic structure?

Exercises

1. Compare and contrast the sentence types found in table 11.2 (children's language) with the sentences in table 11.4 (children's language and Washoe's language).

2. Why might Washoe have called miniatures, but not pictures, *baby?* (Could *baby* also mean to Washoe "small example of"?)

3. Design an experiment (a thought experiment) that could show, to your satisfaction, whether Washoe can use ASL as a human does.

4. What semantic similarities and differences are there between Washoe's sign language and natural spoken languages? Can we attribute *meaning* to Washoe's code?

5. What are some similarities and some differences between the way Washoe was instructed in sign language and the way normal children learn their first language?

6. Suppose Washoe were to successfully pass a suitable language use test. What would this tell us about the answers to such questions as:
a. Is the capacity for language acquisition innate?
b. Is the capacity for language acquisition specific to the human species?
c. Is the capacity for language acquisition innate in the human species?

Bibliography

Bar-Adon, A., and W. F. Leopold (1971). *Child Language: A Book of Readings,* Prentice-Hall, Englewood Cliffs, N.J.

Berko, J. (1958). "The child's learning of English morphology," *Word* 14, 150–177.

Bloom, L. (1970). *Language Development: Form and Function in Emerging Grammar,* MIT Press, Cambridge, Mass.

Brown, R. (1970). "The first sentences of child and chimpanzee," in *Selected Psycholinguistics Papers,* Free Press, New York.

Brown, R. (1973). *A First Language,* Harvard University Press, Cambridge, Mass.

Chomsky, C. S. (1969). *The Acquisition of Syntax in Children from 5 to 10,* MIT Press, Cambridge, Mass.

Chomsky, N. (1969). "Language and the Mind," *Psychology Today,* February 1969.

Clark, H., and E. Clark (1977). *Psychology and Language,* Harcourt Brace Jovanovich, New York.

Dale, P. S. (1976). *Language Development,* second edition, Holt, Rinehart and Winston, New York.

Ferguson, C. A., and D. I. Slobin (1973). *Studies of Child Language Development,* Holt, Rinehart and Winston, New York.

Foss, D., and D. Hakes (1978). *Psycholinguistics,* Prentice-Hall, Englewood Cliffs, N.J.

Fouts, R. (1972). "The use of guidance in teaching sign language to a chimpanzee," *Journal of Comparative and Physiological Psychology* 80, 515–522.

Fouts, R. (1973). "Acquisition and testing of gestural signs in four young chimpanzees," *Science* 180, 978–980.

Fouts, R. (1974). "Language: Origins, definition and chimpanzees," *Journal of Human Evolution* 3, 475–482.

Fouts, R. (1975). "Capacity for language in great apes," in R. Tuttle, ed., *Socioecology and Psychology of Primates,* Mouton, The Hague.

Gardner, B., and R. Gardner (1971). "Two way communication with an infant chimpanzee," in Schreier and Stollnitz, eds., *Behavior of Non-Human Primates,* Academic Press, New York.

Gardner, R., and B. Gardner (1969). "Teaching sign language to a chimpanzee," *Science* 165, 664–672.

Gardner, R., and B. Gardner (1975). "Evidence for sentence constituents in early utterances of child and chimpanzee," *Journal of Experimental Psychology* 104, 244–267.

Hayes, C. (1951). *The Ape in Our House,* Harper & Row, New York.

Klima, E., and U. Bellugi (1978). *The Signs of Language,* Harvard University Press, Cambridge, Mass.

Linden, E. (1976). *Apes, Men and Language,* Pelican Books, Baltimore, Md.

Patterson, F. (1981). *The Education of Koko,* Holt, Rinehart and Winston, New York.

Premack, A., and D. Premack (1972). "Teaching language to an ape," *Scientific American* 227, 92–99.

Rambaugh, D. (1977). *Language Learning by a Chimpanzee: The Lana Project,* Academic Press, New York.

Terrace, H. S. (1979). *Nim,* Alfred A. Knopf, New York.

Thorpe, W. H. (1974). *Animal Nature and Human Nature,* Doubleday, Garden City, N.Y.

Chapter Twelve

LANGUAGE AND THE BRAIN

Speaking and understanding our native language is so spontaneous and apparently easy (for most normal individuals) that we are completely unaware of the remarkably complicated tasks carried out by the human brain to make it possible for us to use language so freely and effortlessly. It is interesting and somewhat ironic that until recently, advancement in our understanding of brain functions has come not from the study of normal individuals but largely from the study of individuals with injured brains. Whenever disease or injury affects the left side of the brain, some aspect of the ability to perceive, process, or produce language may be disturbed. Individuals with such brain disease or injury are said to be *aphasic,* and their brain disturbances can give us insight into how the human brain carries out its language-related tasks.

Aphasia is a broad term encompassing numerous syndromes of communicative impairment. Some aphasics labor to speak a single word, whereas others effortlessly produce long, but meaningless, utterances. By studying the effect of brain damage on speech and comprehension, researchers have obtained invaluable clues to the organization of speech and language in the human nervous system. *Neurolinguists* are interested in the correlation between brain damage and speech and language deficits. These language and brain specialists believe that the study of language form and use will reveal principles of brain function, and that the study of brain function may support or refute specific linguistic theories.

Of the many questions of interest to neurolinguists, three are fundamental: (1) Where in the brain are speech and language localized? (2)

This chapter was written by Kathryn Bayles, Department of Speech and Hearing Sciences, University of Arizona.

How does the nervous system function to encode and decode speech and language? and (3) Are the components of language—phonology, syntax, semantics—neuroanatomically distinct and therefore vulnerable to separate impairment?

12.1 WHERE IS LANGUAGE LOCALIZED IN THE BRAIN?

Language: A Left Hemisphere Phenomenon

For over a century scholars have debated the question of speech and language localization within the brain. In the 1860s, scientists known as localizationists speculated that the functioning of specific regions in the brain was responsible for language. Antilocalizationists argued that speech and language were the consequence of the brain functioning as a whole.

In 1861, Paul Broca, a French surgeon and anatomist, described to the Société d'Anthropologie in Paris a patient who in life had had extreme difficulty producing speech. Later, at autopsy, the patient was found to have damage in the posterior inferior part of the *frontal lobe* in the left cerebral hemisphere, now known as Broca's area (see figure 12.1). With the publication of this report Broca became the first individual to substantiate the claim that damage to a specific area of the brain results in a speech deficit. In 1865, Broca extended his claim about speech localization by reporting that damage to sites in the left cerebral hemisphere produced aphasia, whereas destruction of corresponding sites in the right hemisphere left linguistic capacities intact.

In 1874, Carl Wernicke, a young German physician, published a monograph describing patients with speech comprehension deficits who had damage (lesions) outside Broca's area, in the left posterior temporal lobe. Wernicke's work strengthened Broca's claim that left hemispheric structures are essential for speech and generated intense interest in the hypothesis that different areas within the left hemisphere fulfill different linguistic functions.

Today scientists agree that specific neuroanatomical structures, generally of the left hemisphere, are vital for speech and language, but debate continues as to which structures are committed to the various linguistic capacities. For most individuals the left cerebral hemisphere is dominant for language, regardless of handedness. Approximately 70 percent of all individuals with damage to the left hemisphere will ex-

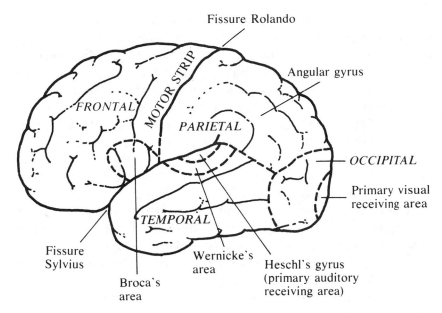

Figure 12.1
Landmarks of the left cerebral hemisphere

perience some type of aphasia, as compared with only 1 percent of those with right hemisphere lesions.

Confirmation of left cerebral language dominance has come from many research techniques, one of which was introduced by J. Wada in 1949. Wada reported that the injection of sodium amytal into the main (carotid) artery on the language-dominant side of the brain induces a temporary aphasia. Physicians have subsequently used this technique as a means of determining cerebral dominance in patients facing neurosurgery; in this way, they can avoid damaging the language centers during surgery.

Substantially adding to our knowledge of the neurology of language was a report published in 1959 by Wilder Penfield and LaMar Roberts, neurosurgeons at the Montreal Neurological Institute. Penfield and Roberts had been studying the brain as well as treating its infirmities. To provide relief from intractable seizures in patients with epilepsy, Penfield and Roberts surgically removed portions of the brain. Because of the threat of producing aphasia by removing regions subserving speech and language, they used electrical stimulation to map the functions of the exposed brains of their patients.

Electrical current applied to a spot on the brain can sometimes activate involuntary expression of the function associated with that brain
site. Stimulation may also interfere with a function being performed by
the conscious patient. For example, electrical stimulation applied to
areas on one side of the brain associated with motor function can produce limb twitching, numbness, and movement on the opposite side of
the body. Penfield and Roberts discovered that when electrical current
was applied to a brain area involved in speech, one of two things occurred: the patient either had trouble talking or uttered a vowel-like
cry. However, no patient ever produced an intelligible word as a result
of electrical stimulation.

Through the cooperation of hundreds of courageous patients, who
remained conscious during surgery, Penfield and Roberts were able to
conclude that three areas of the left hemisphere are vital to speech and
language: *Broca's area, Wernicke's area,* and *the supplemental motor
area* (see figure 12.2).

As evidence accumulated verifying left cerebral speech dominance,
researchers sought to discover whether the left hemisphere speech
areas were structurally unique. Geschwind and Levitsky (1968) were
the first to report that a region in the left temporal lobe was larger than
the same area on the right in 65 percent of the brains they studied. This
area, called the *planum temporal,* has also been found to be larger even
in fetal brains, a finding that suggests the readiness of the left hemisphere for language dominance at birth (Wada, Clarke, and Hamm
1975, Witelson and Pallie 1973).

In order to understand the details of localization theory, it is first
necessary to become familiar with some basic concepts about the
structure and function of the nervous system.

The Nervous System

The central and peripheral nervous system form an intricate communication network through which the behavior of the body is governed.
The brain and spinal cord constitute the central nervous system (CNS)
and are linked to the peripheral nervous system by bundles of nerve
fibers that extend to all parts of the body. Impulses received from
peripheral receptors are sorted, interpreted, and responded to by the
CNS.

The basic cellular unit of the nervous system is the *neuron,* of which
there are an estimated 12 billion. Each neuron is structurally distinct

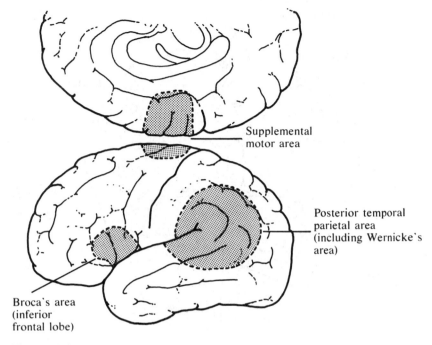

Supplemental
motor area

Posterior temporal
parietal area
(including Wernicke's
area)

Broca's area
(inferior
frontal lobe)

Figure 12.2
Primary cortical areas involved in speech and language function. After Penfield
and Roberts 1959.

and composed of (a) a cell body, (b) receptors known as dendrites, and
(c) a conductive mechanism, or axon. The dendrites receive input from
other neurons and transmit it *to* the cell body, whereas the axon trans-
mits impulses *away from* the cell body. Some nerve fibers transmit sensory information to the CNS, others carry information from the CNS to
the limbs and body parts, and still others form communicative links
between the different parts of the nervous system.

Levels of the Central Nervous System

The central nervous system is hierarchically organized, higher structures being more complex than lower ones (see figure 12.3). At the
lowest level is the spinal cord, which acts as a cable through which
streams of neuronal messages between the body and the brain are
transmitted. Above the spinal cord is the brain stem, the regulator of

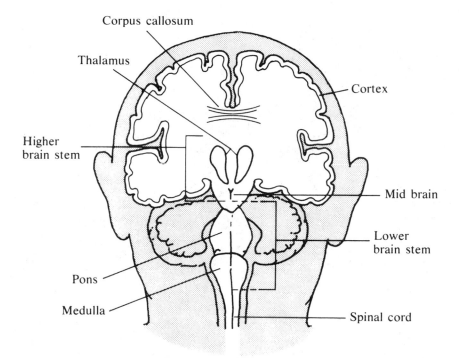

Figure 12.3
Hierarchical arrangement of the central nervous system

such things as breathing, muscle tone, posture, sleep, and body temperature. Lower nervous system structures, such as the spinal cord and lower brain stem, are primarily reflexive and controlled by higher centers. At the highest level of the nervous system are the cerebral hemispheres, responsible for voluntary activity.

The cerebral hemispheres emerge from the higher brain stem and are covered with a convoluted sheath of gray matter, called the *cortex,* which is approximately one-fourth of an inch thick. Within the cortex are approximately 10 billion neurons arranged in at least six layers. The degree of connectivity in this three-dimensional cellular network is almost beyond comprehension. Sholl (1956), a noted neuroanatomist, writes that the cortex contains fields of neurons where a single axon may influence up to 4,000 other neurons.

The Cerebral Cortex: General Characteristics

In outwaro appearance the two cerebral hemispheres are roughly similar, being composed of convolutions, called *gyri,* and depressions or fissures, known as *sulci.* Certain gyri and sulci serve as landmarks helping to differentiate the boundaries of the four lobes of each hemisphere. These structures are illustrated in figure 12.1.

The fissure of Sylvius separates the frontal lobe from the temporal; the fissure of Rolando separates the frontal from the parietal. No fissure separates the parietal and occipital lobes; these two lobes can be distinguished only by microscopic examination of cell structures. Located in the parietal lobe, at the upper end of the fissure of Sylvius, is the cortical area known as the *angular gyrus,* in which functions necessary to speech, reading, and writing are interrelated.

Within each hemisphere are areas known to serve specific functions. In front of, and running parallel to, the fissure of Rolando is a strip of cortex, known as the *motor strip,* which controls fine, highly skilled, voluntary motor movements. Sections of the motor strip are related to voluntary movements in particular parts of the body; for example, the facial and laryngeal muscles are represented at the lower end, in close proximity to Broca's area.

Next to Wernicke's area, in the temporal lobe, is *Heschl's gyrus,* known also as the primary auditory cortex. When auditory impulses arrive at Heschl's gyrus, a noise is perceived, but meaningful interpretation must be made by the adjacent auditory association area (Wernicke's area). This pattern of cortical organization, consisting of interpretive regions of the cortex lying adjacent to sensory receiving areas, is repeated in the visual cortical system as well as in the system receiving sensations from the body.

Cortical Conduction

The bulk of the cerebral hemispheres, beneath the outer layer of gray matter, is composed of three basic types of nerve fiber tracts that form a neural communication network of astonishing complexity. Association nerve fibers connect different portions of the same hemisphere. Projection fibers connect the cortex with lower portions of the brain and spinal cord, and transverse fibers interconnect the cerebral hemispheres.

Of particular importance to speech and language function is the massive transverse fiber tract called the *corpus callosum* (see figure 12.3). By means of the corpus callosum the two hemispheres are able to communicate with each other in the form of electrical impulses. Eccles (1972) estimated that if one assumes that each of the approximately 200 million nerve fibers constituting the corpus callosum has an average firing capacity of 20 impulses per second, then the corpus callosum can carry the astronomical number of 4 billion impulses per second.

You may wonder why, if speech is localized in the left hemisphere, it is necessary for the cerebral hemispheres to communicate with each other for speech to function normally. The reason is that sensations from right and left halves of the body go primarily to the *contralateral* (opposite) hemisphere. If, for example, an object is held in the *left* hand, impulses travel from the left side of the body to the *right* hemisphere, and although the right hemisphere would recognize the object, verbalizing the name of the object would require involvement of the speech center in the left hemisphere.

The importance of the corpus callosum has been made strikingly clear through split-brain research. Gazzaniga and associates studied the effect of disruption of communication between the hemispheres in patients who had had them disconnected surgically by severing the corpus callosum, an operation that is performed to reduce the frequency and severity of incapacitating seizures. Once the cerebral hemispheres are disconnected, there are techniques whereby stimuli can be visually presented to a single hemisphere. When Gazzaniga and Sperry (1967) presented stimuli in the form of written words, letters, and numbers to the left hemisphere alone, patients were able to describe them orally. But information perceived exclusively by the right hemisphere could not be verbalized, either orally or in writing. The right hemisphere was mute.

To investigate the possibility that even though split-brain subjects could not describe visual stimuli presented to their right hemispheres, they nevertheless comprehended them, Gazzaniga and Sperry gave the patients a nonverbal means of responding. For instance, subjects were asked to match a written word with its referent by pointing to the object when it was displayed as one item in a group of assorted items. Under these conditions the right hemisphere was found to be capable of reading letters, short words, and numbers.

To discover whether the right hemisphere could also comprehend spoken words, Gazzaniga and Sperry asked patients to identify words presented auditorily. Because auditory stimuli are received by both sides of the brain, Sperry and Gazzaniga limited the available answers to the right hemisphere. Subjects were instructed to push a button when they saw that one of a set of nouns projected serially to the left visual field (the right hemisphere) matched one previously spoken. Results with split-brain patients showed that the right hemisphere can understand oral (as well as written) language, although the limits of its comprehension have yet to be determined.

Recent research suggests that the right hemisphere may be limited in its linguistic competence. Split-brain subjects have been observed to have difficulty responding appropriately to verbal commands, simple active and passive subject-verb-object sentences, and word sequences when they were presented visually to the right hemisphere. Thus, although the right hemisphere is generally unimpaired in grasping the meaning of single words, it performs poorly with phrases. Perhaps only certain kinds of linguistic stimuli can be comprehended by the right hemisphere. More research is needed to explore its decoding capacities.

12.2 HOW DOES THE BRAIN ENCODE AND DECODE SPEECH AND LANGUAGE?

Speech and Language: A Cortical and Subcortical System

What the silence of the isolated right hemisphere has dramatized is that speech is not solely a cortical function. Subcortical fiber tracts as well as gray matter areas deep within the brain—particularly the *thalamus*—also participate in speech and language.

The thalamus can be conceived of as a great relay station, receiving nerve fiber projections from the cortex and lower nervous system structures and radiating fibers to all parts of the cortex (see figure 12.4).

Emerging as especially important to speech and language function is the left thalamus. Damage to portions of this structure produces involuntary repetition of words and disturbs the patient's ability to name objects. The thalamus is thought to be involved in the focusing of attention by temporarily heightening the receptivity of certain cortical sensory areas. Ojemann and Ward (1971) observed that information presented to patients during left thalamic stimulation was more easily retrieved, both during and after stimulation, than information that had been presented prior to stimulation. They speculated that the

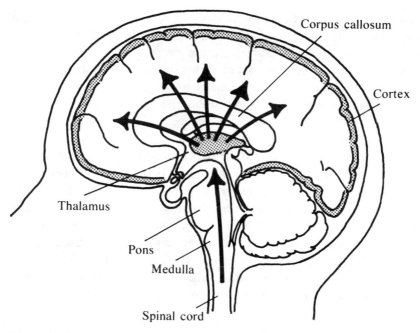

Figure 12.4
Fiber radiations from the thalamus to the cortex

thalamus may provide an interaction between language and memory mechanisms.

Neurolinguists are far from being certain which neuroanatomical structures are essential to the encoding and decoding of linguistic stimuli, but they agree that speech results from an integrated cortical and subcortical system. An awareness that the neural sensory, motor, and associative mechanisms are interconnected is basic to understanding how the brain functions to encode and decode language.

A simple model can represent our knowledge of the transmission of signals to the language mechanism. In figure 12.5, the dark band between the semicircles (which represent coronal sections of the cerebral hemispheres) represents the hemispheric connection. Notice that impulses coming from the right side of the body have direct access to the dominant speech center, whereas those from the left must touch base with the right hemisphere before passing over the corpus callosum for processing. The left hemisphere is not dominant, however, for the processing of *all* auditory signals. Nonspeech environmental sounds do not

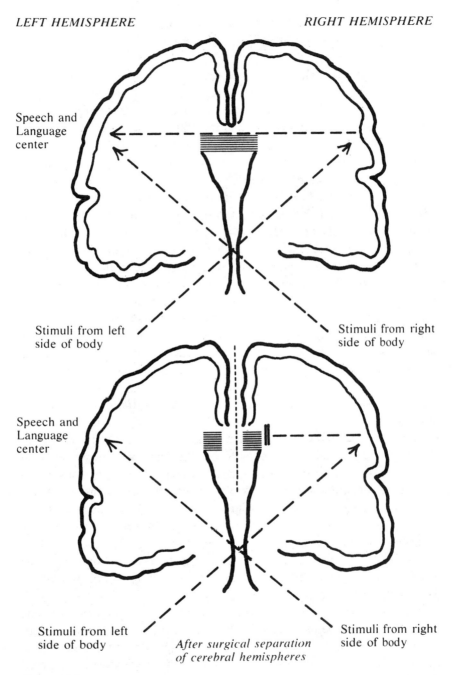

LEFT HEMISPHERE   RIGHT HEMISPHERE

Speech and
Language
center

Stimuli from left
side of body

Stimuli from right
side of body

Speech and
Language
center

Stimuli from left
side of body

*After surgical separation
of cerebral hemispheres*

Stimuli from right
side of body

Figure 12.5
Callosal connection

have to be passed on to the left hemisphere but are processed primarily in the right hemisphere. How do we know this?

Evidence from Dichotic Listening Research

By means of a research technique called *dichotic listening,* we can analyze the characteristics of incoming stimuli processed by the individual hemispheres. During a dichotic listening task two different stimuli are presented simultaneously, through earphones, to the left and right ears. For example, the right ear may be given the word *base* and the left ear *ball.* The listeners are instructed to say what they hear. Interestingly, certain types of stimuli delivered to a particular ear will be more accurately reported by the listener. This is because the nervous system is capable of scanning incoming stimuli and routing them to that area of the brain specialized for their interpretation. Kimura (1961) was the first to observe that when two digits were presented simultaneously, one to each ear, the listener more accurately identified those presented to the right ear. However, when the listener was known to have the less common right hemispheric dominance for speech, Kimura observed a left ear advantage. In other words, the ear having more direct access to the language center had an advantage. Although there is some auditory input to each cortex from the ear on the same side of the body, these uncrossed, or *ipsilateral,* inputs are thought to be suppressed.

The right ear advantage (REA) was originally thought to exist only for linguistically meaningful stimuli, but the same advantage has been found for nonsense syllables, speech played backward, consonant-vowel syllables, and even small units of speech such as fricatives. Intrigued by these findings, investigators have sought to discover those features of speech likely to trigger left hemisphere processing. One hypothesis was that an REA would be found for any sound produced by the vocal tract musculature. Research results have disconfirmed this explanation, for REAs have been found for synthetic speech and Morse code but not for laughing and coughing.

The REA associated with Morse code stimuli suggests that the left hemisphere may be dominant for more than the phonetic structure of language. In fact, the left hemisphere may be dominant for a number of nonlinguistic functions. For example, several investigators have noted that the ability to perform fine judgments of temporal order is a function of the left hemisphere: aphasics perform poorly, compared with controls and subjects with right hemisphere damage, on nonlinguistic tasks requiring temporal order judgments (Brookshire 1972, Swisher and Hirsh 1972). Lackner and Teuber (1973) have proposed that the left hemisphere has an advantage in temporal acuity and, as a consequence, language processing may have been drawn to the left hemisphere since speech is temporally ordered.

Much evidence implies that left hemisphere damage also impairs the ability to program complex motor sequences such as playing a violin. A disorder known as *oral nonverbal apraxia* is commonly associated with left hemisphere damage. DeRenzi, Pieczuro, and Vignolo (1966, 51) defined the disorder as "the inability to perform voluntary movements with the muscles of the larynx, pharynx, tongue, lips, and cheeks, although automatic movements of the same muscles are preserved." Patients have trouble voluntarily performing simple gestures such as whistling, blowing, clearing the throat, or sticking out the tongue. It has been argued that if the left hemisphere is dominant for programming motor sequences, it is logical that this special ability would be used to program the extremely complex motor sequences associated with speech, which, as pointed out in chapter 4, requires the simultaneous coordination of at least 100 muscles.

Besides having a superior capacity for processing temporally ordered stimuli and programming complex motor sequences, the left hemisphere is believed to be specialized for associative thought. Two notable studies support this hypothesis. DeRenzi, Scotti, and Spinnler (1969) observed that patients with left hemisphere damage performed more poorly than right-lesioned patients in an object matching task. Patients were handed an object and required to match it to one of ten on display in front of them; the held object differed in form and color from its displayed match. The left hemisphere was found to be superior at recognizing the same object in a different form. In the second study, by Faglioni, Spinnler, and Vignolo (1969), subjects with left hemisphere damage exhibited significantly greater difficulty than both right-damaged individuals and controls in matching a sound, such as a bell, with a picture of its source.

It may be the case, as some investigators theorize, that speech and language function is not cognitively unique but is imposed in the left hemisphere because speech and language functions require the special nonlinguistic capacities of this hemisphere.

Complementary Specialization of the Cerebral Hemispheres

For some time the view prevailed that the left hemisphere was superior, overall, to the right; but this misconception has recently been corrected. The research techniques providing insight into speech and language function have unveiled functions for which the right hemisphere is dominant, particularly those functions requiring spatial ability.

Injury to the right hemisphere can result in visuospatial impairment. An affected individual may have trouble getting from one place to another, drawing objects, assembling puzzles, or recognizing faces. Such an individual may disregard anything on the left side of the body, even to the extent that when asked to draw the face of a clock, the patient may squeeze all the numbers in on the right side of the face.

Psychological research suggests that the two hemispheres differ in the manner in which they treat incoming stimuli, the right hemisphere processing stimuli holistically (as wholes) and the left analytically (by parts). For example, Kimura (1966) exposed three to ten dots to each visual half-field for 80 msec. Subjects exhibited a left visual field superiority in guessing the number of dots. The brevity of the exposure time prevented subjects from counting the dots, lending support to the notion that the right hemisphere (associated with the left visual field) is superior at grasping the whole without a complete analysis of its parts.

Some musical skills are thought to be right hemisphere dependent. Although musical deficits are likely to exist after damage to the language-dominant (left) hemisphere, people with right hemisphere damage show deficits in discriminating complex sounds, timbres, and melodies. In a dichotic listening task, Kimura (1973) played a different melody to each ear simultaneously. Subjects were then asked to pick out these two melodies from among four melodies, each of which was played, individually, to both ears. Normal subjects were able to pick out the melody that had been presented to the left ear (right hemisphere) better than the one presented to the right ear.

Bever (1975) discussed Kimura's findings and suggested that to musically naive subjects the perception of melody is a holistic phenomenon, thereby generating a left ear advantage for those subjects. In his own experiments, however, Bever discovered that musically sophisticated subjects experienced a musical sequence better in the right ear (left hemisphere), because, he argued, they approached the task analytically.

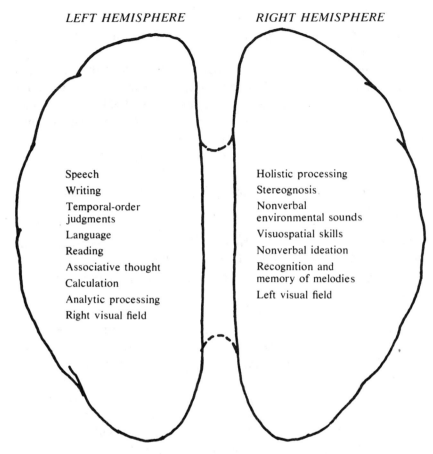

LEFT HEMISPHERE   RIGHT HEMISPHERE

Speech
Writing
Temporal-order
  judgments
Language
Reading
Associative thought
Calculation
Analytic processing
Right visual field

Holistic processing
Stereognosis
Nonverbal
environmental sounds
Visuospatial skills
Nonverbal ideation
Recognition and
memory of melodies
Left visual field

Figure 12.6
Complementary specialization of cerebral hemispheres

Inasmuch as each cerebral hemisphere has unique functional superi-orities (summarized in figure 12.6), it seems inappropriate to refer to the language-dominant left hemisphere as the major one. It is more accurate to conceive of the hemispheres as complementarily special-ized. The degree of hemispheric specialization, however, varies among individuals. Right-handed individuals who have a family history of right-handedness will show the greatest hemispheric specialization. Least likely to show hemispheric specialization are left-handed indi-viduals with a family history of left-handedness. Some of these indi-viduals are thought to have bilateral representation of basic skills. The possibility of bilateral representation is not surprising when we remember that each hemisphere has the capacity to replicate functions of the other; indeed, one hemisphere may take over for the other when it is injured or removed.

Right-hemisphere language dominance is not uncommon in adults who sustained injury to the left hemisphere early in life. The literature is replete with documented cases of the development of language by the right hemisphere after injury to the left. Nonetheless, the adaptability of the nervous system decreases with age and when left hemisphere injury occurs after puberty, the danger of permanent aphasia is great.

Do the Hemispheres Equally Support the Development of Speech and Language?

Although speech and language function can be taken over by the right hemisphere if necessary, there is evidence that the right hemisphere does not have the same potential for speech and language specialization as the left has.

Dennis and Whitaker (1976) monitored the development of three children in whom one hemisphere of the brain was surgically removed during infancy (hemispherectomy) to arrest seizures associated with Sturge-Weber-Dimitri syndrome. Of the three children, two (SM and CA) had only the right hemisphere and one (MW) only the left. At the age of ten these children were given psychological and psycholinguistic tests. Intelligence was found to be comparable among the three, as shown in table 12.1. However, other differences emerged. When given a variety of complex verbal commands varying in information and syntactic complexity, only MW, the child with the left hemisphere, was able to maintain proficient performance. Syntactic rather than semantic complexity appeared to impair the performance of SM and CA. By contrast, as might be expected, the isolated left hemisphere (MW) performed more poorly on visuospatial tasks.

Table 12.1
IQ scores of children in the Dennis and Whitaker study (1976)

IQ Test	MW	SM	CA
Verbal	96	94	91
Performance	92	87	108
Full Scale	93	90	99

Functional asymmetry of the cerebral hemispheres is economical, enabling brain tissue to perform a wider variety of functions than would be possible if each hemisphere were a replica of the other. On the other hand, the potential of each hemisphere to replicate the functions of the other, in a developing nervous system, provides a prudent backup system. As we conclude the discussion of how the brain functions to encode and decode speech and language, it seems appropriate to pose the question of whether the areas within the left-hemisphere speech and language system are functionally divisible into phonological, semantic, and syntactic subsystems. It is to this question we now turn.

12.3 ARE COMPONENTS OF LANGUAGE NEUROANATOMICALLY DISTINCT?

Within the left hemisphere there is neither uniform nor equal representation of linguistic functions. Damage to a small area in the hemisphere does not result in the impairment of *all* linguistic capabilities. On the contrary, lesions in different areas of the hemisphere lead to qualitatively distinct aphasia syndromes. A review of the language and speech behaviors associated with the different aphasia syndromes will suggest a crude definition of the boundaries of the various linguistic domains.

Aphasiologists have no uniform criteria for classifying types of aphasia, the consequence of which is considerable terminological diversity. Widely accepted, however, as distinct aphasia syndromes are the following: Broca's aphasia, Wernicke's aphasia, conduction aphasia, and anomia.

Broca's Aphasia

Broca's aphasia, named for Paul Broca, who first described its symptoms, is known also as expressive or motor aphasia. It follows from a lesion in the posterior part of the inferior frontal gyrus, or Broca's area (see figure 12.1). However, according to Mohr (1976) the cluster of symptoms traditionally associated with Broca's aphasia results from a more extensive lesion than the one described by Broca. Ironically, even Broca's own patient had a more diffuse lesion, but Broca focused on the more circumscribed area in the inferior frontal region because of the view of his contemporaries that large strokes always begin as a smaller focus.

The symptoms of Broca's aphasia will seem logical if we note the proximity of Broca's area to the cortical region of the brain controlling the muscles of speech (see figure 12.1). The foremost symptom is the inability of the affected individual to speak fluently. Great effort is required to utter short halting phrases, described as telegraphic because of the absence of function words (words like *the, by, but*). Literal *paraphasias*—substitutions, omissions, or distortions of sounds—are both frequent and inconsistent, and when the aphasic is permitted several repetitions of misarticulated phrases, articulation usually improves.

Bound morphemes such as tense, plural, and comparative markers are frequently missing. Surface word order is usually appropriate, however, and the verbal output makes sense. The characteristics of the spoken speech are mirrored in patients' reading and writing. Although comprehension of language may not be normal, it is usually good enough for these individuals to grasp the meaning of what they hear. In fact, most Broca's aphasics are painfully aware of their own mistakes. As you read the following samples of utterances produced by Broca's aphasics, remember that there is no way to reproduce on paper the intense effort these persons must make to produce even a few words.

Examiner: Tell me, what did you do before you retired?
Aphasic: Uh, uh, uh, puh, par, partender, no.
Examiner: Carpenter?
Aphasic: (shaking head yes) Carpenter, tuh, tuh, tenty [20] year.
Examiner: Tell me about this picture!
Aphasic: Boy . . . cook . . . cookie . . . took . . . cookie.

Neurolinguists agree that Broca's aphasics have suffered impairment to the phonological system but debate whether the syntactic component of language is impaired. Linguistic observations of aphasic language have a rather recent history compared with clinical studies. More research will be required to settle the issue of whether phonological theory can account for all of the linguistic aberrations displayed by Broca's aphasics when the lesion is confined to the frontal lobe.

Wernicke's Aphasia

Wernicke's aphasia, known also as sensory or receptive aphasia, is the consequence of a lesion in the auditory association cortex of the temporal lobe (see figure 12.1). This area is adjacent to the region that receives auditory stimuli. Predictably, the primary characteristic of this type of aphasia is impairment in the ability to understand spoken and written language. Wernicke's aphasics may suffer a severe loss of understanding even though their hearing is normal. Great variation in symptoms occurs in Wernicke's aphasia.

Fluency is usually not a problem, although interruptions in the flow of speech occur when the patient cannot retrieve a specific word. Often patients speak very rapidly, the content of what they say ranging from mildly inappropriate to complete nonsense, as in the following examples:

Examiner: Do you like it here in Kansas City?
Aphasic: Yes, I am.
Examiner: I'd like to have you tell me something about your problem.
Aphasic: Yes, I ugh can't hill all of my way. I can't talk all of the things I do, and part of the part I can go alright, but I can't tell from the other people. I usually most of my things. I know what can I talk and know what they are but I can't always come back even though I know they should be in, and I know should something eely I should know what I'm doing . . .

Circumlocutions are numerous: the aphasic talks in circles about an object he is unable to name, as when a patient says *what you drink* for *water*. Patients with word retrieval deficits overuse empty words like *thing* and *one*. Language alterations in the form of word substitutions may be numerous. At times the substitution bears a relation to the intended word, as when someone says *slipper* for *shoe* or *corn flakes* for *cereal*. At other times there is no apparent connection between the intended and substituted words. In extreme cases, patients use unrecognizable words called neologisms.

For patients with severe comprehension deficits the prognosis for recovery is poorer than for Broca's aphasics, who have better comprehension. Aphasiologists speculate that Wernicke's aphasics have damaged feedback systems, limiting their ability to monitor what they say and thus limiting their ability to correct themselves.

Whereas Broca's aphasia is primarily a deficit in the phonological component of language, Wernicke's aphasia affects the semantic and syntactic components. The Sylvian fissure separating Broca's and Wernicke's areas may represent a neuroanatomical boundary separating the phonological from the syntactic and semantic components at the cortical level. It must be pointed out, however, that Broca's and Wernicke's areas are connected subcortically by a bundle of nerve fibers called the *arcuate fasciculus*. This may serve as a transmission line carrying signals received in the auditory reception cortex to the auditory association cortex for interpretation and, subsequently, to the speech production cortex for verbalization. Should the arcuate fasciculus be damaged, the affected individual would be expected to have difficulty repeating auditory information. And that is exactly what does happen in conduction aphasia.

Conduction Aphasia

Conduction aphasia follows from localized lesions in the temporo-parietal regions that serve to synthesize meaning and form. All avenues of expression are affected. Spontaneous speech is fluent but circumlocutory and inadequately structured. Similar defects are found in spontaneous writing. Reading aloud is difficult, and repeating is severely disturbed. Comprehension of oral and written material is normal or only mildly affected.

Conduction aphasics can be differentiated from Broca's aphasics by their fluent spontaneous speech; Broca's aphasics find spontaneous speech harder than repetition. Conduction aphasics are like Wernicke's aphasics in that they are fluent, but unlike Wernicke's they have good speech comprehension. Conduction aphasia is not a problem of receptive or expressive mechanisms as much as it is a problem of the transmission between the two.

Anomia

In classic anomia the patient has difficulty finding words, both during the flow of speech and in naming on confrontation. That is, when presented with a stimulus object, the individual is unable to retrieve its name. Yet when these individuals are offered the correct name of the stimulus item, they instantly recognize it. Further, they can usually select the correct name from a group of names.

Comprehension and repetition of speech are normal, and speech is fluent although filled with circumlocutions. The following selected responses made by anomic aphasics aptly illustrate word-finding difficulties.

Examiner: Who is the president of the United States?
Aphasic: I can't say his name. I know the man, but I can't come out and say . . . I'm very sorry, I just can't come out and say. I just can't write it to me now.

Examiner: Can you tell me a girl's name?

Aphasic: Of a girl's name, by mean, by which weight, I mean how old or young?

Examiner: On what do we sleep?

Aphasic: Of the week, er, of the night, oh from about 10:00, about 11:00 o'clock at night until about uh 7:00 in the morning.

The brain lesions associated with classical anomia involve the dominant angular gyrus (see figure 12.1), that area of the brain thought to be necessary for the formation of association between the sensory modalities.

To sum up, the different forms of aphasia show that representation of linguistic functions in the left hemisphere is by no means uniform or equal. We have seen that lesions in different areas of the left hemisphere lead to distinct aphasia syndromes. Future research on these distinctions is certain to be both interesting and important.

Key Words

aphasia
neurolinguistics
Broca's area
Wernicke's area
dichotic listening

Study Questions

1. Many technical terms appeared in this chapter. Compose a definition for each of the following:

a. aphasia	g. Wernicke's area
b. neurolinguistics	h. dichotic listening
c. corpus callosum	i. ipsilateral
d. temporal lobe	j. arcuate fasciculus
e. neuron	k. anomia
f. Broca's area	l. cortex

2. In what cortical regions are speech and language thought to be localized?

3. What is the corpus callosum, and how is it relevant to speech and language function?

4. Describe one research technique that has provided neurolinguists with information about where speech and language are localized in the brain.

5. Suppose you were holding a pencil in your left hand and you wished to describe it. Discuss the chain of events occurring in the nervous system that would enable you to describe the pencil.

6. Discuss the complementary specialization of the cerebral hemispheres.

7. Why is it thought that speech and language function may not be cognitively unique?

Bibliography

Bever, T. (1975). "Cerebral asymmetries in humans due to differentiation of two incompatible processes: Holistic and analytic," in D. Aaronson and R. Rieber, eds., *Developmental Psycholinguistics and Communication Disorders*, New York Academy of Sciences, vol. 263, p. 251.

Brookshire, R. (1972). "Visual and auditory sequencing by aphasic subjects," *Journal of Communication Disorders* 5, 259–269.

Dennis, M., and H. Whitaker (1976). "Hemispheric equipotentiality and language acquisition," in *Language Development and Neurological Theory*, Brock University Conference, May 1975, Academic Press, New York.

DeRenzi, E., A. Pieczuro, and L. Vignolo (1966). "Oral apraxia and aphasia," *Cortex* 2, 50–73.

DeRenzi, E., G. Scotti, and H. Spinnler (1969). "Perceptual and associative disorders and visual recognition," *Neurology* 19, 634–642.

Eccles, J. (1972). *The Understanding of the Brain*, McGraw-Hill, New York.

Faglioni, P., H. Spinnler, and L. Vignolo (1969). "Contrasting behavior of right and left hemisphere-damaged patients on a discriminative and a semantic task of auditory recognition," *Cortex* 5, 366–389.

Gazzaniga, M., J. Bogen, and R. Sperry (1963). "Laterality effects in somesthesis following cerebral commissurotomy in man," *Neuropsychologia* 1, 209–215.

Gazzaniga, M., and R. Sperry (1967). "Language after section of the cerebral commissures," *Brain* 90, 131–148.

Geschwind, N. (1972). "Language and the brain," *Scientific American* 226, 76–83.

Geschwind, N., and W. Levitsky (1968). "Human brain: Left-right asymmetries in temporal speech region," *Science* 161, 186–187.

Kimura, D. (1961). "Cerebral dominance and the perception of verbal stimuli," *Canadian Journal of Psychology* 15, 166–171.

Kimura, D. (1966). "Dual functional asymmetry of the brain in visual perception," *Neuropsychologia* 4, 275–285.

Kimura, D. (1973). "The asymmetry of the human brain," *Scientific American*, March, 70–78.

Lackner, J., and H. Teuber (1973). "Alterations in auditory fusion thresholds after cerebral injury in man," *Neuropsychologia* 11, 409–415.

Levy, R. (1977). "The question of electrophysiological asymmetries preceding speech," in Haiganoosh Whitaker and Harry Whitaker, eds., *Studies in Neurolinguistics and Psycholinguistics,* Academic Press, New York.

McAdam, D., and H. Whitaker (1971a). "Language production: Electro-encephalographic localization in the normal human brain," *Science* 172, 499–502.

McAdam, D., and L. H. Whitaker (1971b). "Electrocortical localization of language production," *Science* 174, 1359–1360.

Mohr, J. (1976). "Broca's area and Broca's aphasia," in Haiganoosh Whitaker and Harry Whitaker, eds., *Studies in Neurolinguistics and Psycholinguistics,* Academic Press, New York.

Ojemann, G., and A. Ward, Jr. (1971). "Speech representation in ventrolateral thalamus," *Brain* 94, 669–680.

Penfield, W., and L. Roberts (1959). *Speech and Brain Mechanisms,* Princeton University Press, Princeton, N.J.

Sholl, D. (1956). *The Organization of the Cerebral Cortex,* Wiley, New York.

Swisher, L., and I. Hirsh (1972). "Brain damage and the ordering of two temporally successive stimuli," *Neuropsychologia* 10, 137–152.

Wada, J., R. Clarke, and A. Hamm (1975). "Cerebral hemispheric asymmetry in humans," *Archives of Neurology* 32, 239–246.

Wada, J. (1949). "A new method for the determination of the side of cerebral speech dominance: A preliminary report on the intracarotid injection of sodium amytal in man," *Medical Biology* (Tokyo) 14, 221–222.

Witelson, S., and W. Pallie (1973). "Left hemisphere specialization for language in the newborn: Neuroanatomical evidence of asymmetry," *Brain* 96, 641–646.

GLOSSARY

acoustic phonetics
The study of the physical properties of the sound waves generated by the larnyx and the vocal tract.

affix
A bound morpheme that is attached to a stem and modifies its meaning in some way. Prefixes and suffixes are two common kinds of affixes.

affricate
1. A single consonant sound that consists of a stop followed by a secondary fricative release. The English words *chip* and *jump* begin with affricates. 2. A distinctive feature assigned to single phonemes that consist of a stop followed by a secondary fricative release.

allophone
A positional or free variant of a phoneme.

alternation
The existence of two or more variant pronunciations for a given morpheme, each of which occurs under different conditions.

alveolar
A point of articulation formed by means of a constriction or blockage between the tongue tip or blade and the ridge just behind the upper teeth. The English words *too, see, now,* and *lie* begin with alveolar consonants.

alveolar ridge
The bony projection located just behind the upper teeth.

alveopalatal
A point of articulation formed by means of a constriction or blockage between the tongue tip or blade and the area just behind the alveolar ridge. The English words *ship* and *chip* begin with alveopalatal consonants.

ambiguity
The property of having more than one linguistic meaning.

ambisyllabic
A term used to describe consonants that occur at the border between two syllables and that can be thought of as both the coda of the first and the onset of the second. The /m/ in the middle of the English word *Emma* is ambisyllabic.

American Sign Language (ASL)
A system of manually produced visual signals, analogous to words, taught to the deaf in the United States. ASL is not the same as signed English; that is, it is not a representation of the letters, sounds, words, or syntax of English, but is rather a completely separate language. The signs of ASL have been analyzed into about fifty-five constituents, some involving the

configuration of the hand(s), some the position of the hand(s) with respect to the rest of the body, and some the action of the hand(s).

anaphora
The referential linking found between pairs of constituents in sentences such as *All people think they have a hidden talent.*

Anglo-Saxon
Another name for Old English.

anterior
A distinctive feature that character-izes speech sounds that are formed at the alveolar ridge or anywhere in front of it.

anticipatory
A term describing a coarticulation effect in which some motion of the vocal tract needed for one sound begins during an earlier sound. Antonym: perseverative.

aphasia
A cover term for various kinds of communicative impairment that occur as a result of brain damage.

aphasic
Suffering from a brain disease or injury that impairs communicative ability.

apical
An articulation formed with the tip of the tongue.

argot
A variety of jargon, especially the jargon used by criminals.

articulation
The formation of a speech sound by positioning some part of the vocal tract.

articulatory phonetics
The study of how speech sounds are produced by the speech organs, in particular the vocal tract and larynx.

aspiration
The puff of air that sometimes follows the pronunciation of a stop consonant. The *p* in English *pill* is aspirated.

assimilation
A process by which the phonetic features of one sound are transferred to a neighboring sound.

back
An articulation (or distinctive feature) that characterizes the speech sounds formed with the body of the tongue behind the resting position. The English word *go* has both a back consonant and a back vowel. Antonym: front.

backformation
The process of creating new stems by removing some part of a word that is incorrectly analyzed as a morpheme, especially an affix.

base
1. In syntax, the part of a grammar that contains only phrase structure rules, before any transformational rules apply. 2. In morphology, another name for stem.

bilabial
Formed by means of a constriction between the two lips. The English words *pay, bay,* and *may* begin with bilabial consonants.

Black English
An informal variety of English typically used by low-income urban Blacks in the United States.

blade
The part of the tongue just behind the tip.

borrowing
The incorporation of words (or some other characteristic) from one language into another language.

bound morpheme
A morpheme that does not constitute an independent word, but must be combined with some other morpheme. All affixes and some stems are bound morphemes.

Broca's area
Part of the frontal lobe of the left cerebral hemisphere of the brain. Damage to this area results in a kind of aphasia characterized by lack of fluency in producing speech.

central
An articulation that describes a speech sound in which the body of the tongue is neither forward nor back in the mouth. In American English, the vowel of *but* is central.

chance overlap
Accidental similarities between languages that are not genetically related.

cleft sentence
A kind of English sentence that consists of *it*, some form of the verb *to be*, a noun phrase, *that*, and a clause that modifies the noun. *It was Mary that I saw.*

closed class
A group of morphemes whose membership is small and that does not readily accept new members. Function words (such as articles and conjunctions) and affixes are examples of closed classes. Antonym: open class.

coarticulation
The process by which some of the motions of the vocal tract needed for one sound take place during neighboring sounds.

coda
Within a syllable, the consonant or sequence of consonants that follows the nucleus.

code-switching
A situation in which a speaker uses a mixture of different languages or different varieties of a single language in the same sentence or discourse.

coined word
A new word that is made up and added to the lexicon of a language.

communicative act
An act whereby a speaker succeeds in conveying a message by having his or her communicative intention recognized.

communicative intention
An intention that a speaker intends to be recognized as trying to communicate something specific, which is fulfilled when the intention is so recognized.

comparative linguistics
The subfield of linguistics that studies related languages in order to learn about their historical development.

comparative method
A collection of analytical techniques used by linguists to reconstruct the history of two or more related languages.

competence (linguistic)
Knowledge of language; the linguistic capacity of a fluent speaker of a language. Antonym: performance.

complementary distribution
A relation between two speech sounds such that each occurs in one or more positions where the other one never does. Two sounds that are phonetically similar and that are in complementary distribution are usually allophones of the same phoneme.

complex word
A word that can be broken down into two or more meaningful parts.

compositionality
The property by which the meaning of a complex expression is determined by the meaning of its constituents plus their grammatical relations.

compound
A word that is formed by combining two or more words or stems.

concept
A way of categorizing things, events, etc., into sets.

consonant
1. A speech sound produced with the vocal tract relatively constricted. Antonym: vowel. 2. A feature assigned to phonemes that are formed with a considerable degree of obstruction in the vocal tract.

constituent
A word or an intuitively natural grouping of words that behaves as a unit with respect to some grammatical rules.

constituent structure
The way in which the words of a sentence group together into phrases of various types.

constriction
The narrowing or closing off of some part of the vocal tract to produce a speech sound.

content word
A member of a large class of words to which new items can easily be added, for example, nouns and verbs. Antonym: function word.

continuant
A distinctive feature that characterizes speech sounds produced without a blockage of the airflow in the oral cavity. Noncontinuants are stops.

contrast
A relation between two speech sounds such that replacing one by the other sometimes makes a

difference in the meaning of a word. Two sounds that are in *contrast* are allophones of *different* phonemes.

conversation
Any set of connected utterances by more than one speaker that has the structure characterized by greetings, turn-takings, and closings.

coronal
A distinctive feature that characterizes speech sounds that are formed by a constriction between the tongue blade and the teeth, the alveolar ridge, or the area just behind the alveolar ridge.

correspondence set
A regular pattern of relationship among similar sounds in a group of related languages; such patterns are arrived at by comparing sets of related words.

creole
A language that developed from a pidgin by expanding its vocabulary and acquiring a more complex grammatical structure. Unlike pidgins, creoles have native speakers.

decoding
The process of converting a signal in some communication system back into the original message. Antonym: encoding.

denotation
Another name for semantic reference.

dental
1. A point of articulation formed by means of a constriction between the tongue tip or blade and the upper teeth. 2. A term that can also be used to describe interdental sounds.

derivation
1. In morphology, the process by which affixes combine with words or

stems to create new words or stems, for example, the *-able* suffix of English, which changes a verb into an adjective. Antonym: inflection. 2. In syntax, the successive stages in the generation of a sentence that result from applying the rules of the grammar.

diachronic
Concerned with changes taking place across a period of time. Antonym: synchronic.

diachronic linguistics
Another name for historical linguistics.

dialect
A distinct form of a language (or other communication system) that differs from other forms of that language in specific linguistic features (pronunciation, vocabulary, and/or grammar), possibly associated with some regional, social, or ethnic group, but that is nevertheless mutually intelligible with them.

dichotic listening
A research technique in which two different stimuli are presented simultaneously (through earphones) to the left and right ears. This technique is used to investigate the roles of the two hemispheres of the brain.

digraph
A sequence of two letters used to spell a single sound. Two common digraphs in English are *sh* and *ng* for the final sounds of *hash* and *hang*.

diphthong
A vowel that consists of two parts, a louder vowel and either an on-glide or an off-glide, which together serve as the nucleus of a single syllable. The English words *buy, boy,* and *cow* end in diphthongs.

discontinuous dependency
The situation in which a single constituent is broken into two parts that are separated by material from outside that constituent.

discourse
Narrowly construed, any set of connected utterances by a single speaker.

distinctive
(See *contrast*.)

distinctive feature
A feature that distinguishes phonemes from one another and plays a crucial role in the statement of phonological rules.

distributed
A distinctive feature that characterizes speech sounds that are formed with a relatively long area of contact or approximation between the tongue and the roof of the mouth.

domination
The relationship between a node and the material that branches down from it in a tree diagram.

embedding
The occurrence of one sentence (or other grammatical construction) within another one.

encoding
The process of converting a message into a signal by means of which it can be communicated to other individuals. Antonym: decoding.

entailment
A relation between sentences S and S' such that if S is true, then S' must also be true.

euphemism
A polite expression used as a substitute for taboo language or to refer to some topic regarded as delicate, such as death, sex, or certain body functions.

extraposition
The process of separating a modifying clause from the noun it belongs with by moving it to the end of the sentence.

feature
Any of several articulatory characteristics into which speech sounds can be analyzed.

flap
A consonant sound formed by making a quick tap with the tip of the tongue against the roof of the mouth. In American English, the word *better* is usually pronounced with a flap in the middle.

formal language style
A variety of a language that is used in official contexts, for example, making a speech in a courtroom. Antonym: informal language style.

free variation
A relation between two speech sounds such that either one can occur in a certain position, and the substitution of one for the other never makes any difference in the meaning of a word. Two sounds that are in free variation are allophones of the same phoneme.

fricative
A manner of articulation in which the airflow is channeled through a narrow opening in the vocal tract, producing turbulence. The English words *fill* and *soup* begin with fricatives.

front
An articulation that describes speech sounds in which the body of the tongue is forward from the resting position. The English words *beet* and *bet* have front vowels. Antonym: back.

function word
A member of a small class of words that does not easily permit new items to be added, for example, articles and conjunctions. Function words are usually hard to define because they indicate some grammatical relation, rather than referring to something outside of language. Antonym: content word.

generate
In syntax, to specify the grammatical sentences of a language by applying a set of rules.

genetically related
Descended from a common ancestor language.

glide
A vowel-like sound that precedes or follows a true vowel. The English words *you* and *we* begin with glides.

glottal
Formed by means of a constriction at the vocal cords. The English exclamation *oh-oh!* has a glottal stop between the two parts.

glottis
The space between the two vocal cords.

grammatical relation
The way a constituent of a sentence functions within that sentence. Two common grammatical relations for noun phrase constituents are subject and object.

Great Vowel Shift
A set of regular sound changes affecting the long (tense) vowels of English that took place around the fifteenth century. These changes account for many of the discrepancies between the pronunciation of English words and their spelling, which was established before they took place.

Grimm's Law
A set of regular sound changes that took place in Proto-Germanic, in which Proto-Indo-European voice-

less stops became voiceless fricatives, voiced stops became voiceless stops, and voiced aspirated stops became simple voiced stops.

hard palate
Another name for the palate.

high
An articulation (or distinctive feature) that characterizes speech sounds formed by placing the body of the tongue relatively close to the roof of the mouth.

historical linguistics
The subfield of linguistics that studies how languages change across time.

holophrastic speech
The utterance of a single word that expresses a thought usually expressed by an entire sentence.

hypercorrection
Overcorrection; the attempted rectification of a supposed error by introducing something that was never part of the original form, using as a model some other pattern in the language.

iconic
The relationship between an object and a representation of that object when the representation physically resembles the object in some way.

ideograph
A character in a writing system that represents some idea and is a picture of some object related to that idea.

idiolect
The variety of a language spoken by a single individual.

idiom
An expression whose meaning is noncompositional. (See *compositionality*.)

illocutionary act
1. Narrowly viewed, any utterance act that is also a communicative act.
2. Widely viewed, any utterance act that is either a communicative act or an institutional act.

indirect utterance
An utterance in which the speaker performs one illocutionary act by means of performing another.

Indo-European
A large group of historically related languages that includes many of the languages of northern India, Persian, and most of the languages of Europe.

inflection
The process by which affixes combine with words or stems to indicate such grammatical categories as tense or plurality, for example, the *-ed* and *-s* suffixes of English. Antonym: derivation.

informal language style
A variety of a language that is used in casual conversations with friends. Antonym: formal language style.

innate
Determined by the genetic makeup of an organism, rather than acquired by experience. Antonym: learned.

institutional act
An act that consists in affecting the institutional status (social relations) of some person or thing.

interdental
An articulation formed by placing the tongue tip between the teeth. For many English speakers, the words *thin* and *this* begin with interdental consonants.

jargon
A set of special vocabulary items used by members of some profession or specialized social group.

labeled bracketing
A linear representation of the information found in a tree diagram that uses nested brackets to show constituent groupings and subscript labels to show categories.

labial
A manner of articulation (or distinctive feature) that characterizes speech sounds that involve one or both lips.

labialized
Another name for rounded.

labiodental
An articulation formed by means of a constriction between the lower lip and the upper teeth. The English words *fee* and *vow* begin with labiodental consonants.

laminal
A manner of articulation formed with the blade of the tongue.

language universal
Any property that is shared by most, if not all, human languages.

larynx
The voice box, that is, the structure of muscle and cartilage at the upper end of the windpipe that contains the vocal cords.

lateral
A manner of articulation (or distinctive feature) that characterizes speech sounds made when the tongue tip or blade makes contact with the roof of the mouth and the airflow is permitted to pass on one or both sides of the tongue.

lax
1. A speech sound produced with relatively little muscular tension. Antonym: tense. 2. In describing English vowels, another name for short.

learned
Acquired by experience, rather than determined by genetic makeup. Antonym: innate.

lexical access
The process of identifying a word that has just been heard.

lexical ambiguity
The situation in which a word has two or more linguistic meanings. Contrasts with structural ambiguity.

lexical category
Another name for part of speech.

lexicon
A listing of all the words in a given language, each with its form, its meaning, and its part-of-speech classification.

lingua franca
Trade language; a language that is used by general agreement as the means of communication among speakers of different languages.

linguistic meaning
The meaning(s) that an expression has simply as a part of the language it belongs to.

liquid
A consonant sound in which the vocal tract is neither closed off nor constricted to a degree that produces friction. The English words *run* and *low* begin with liquids.

logical form
The representation of those aspects of a sentence that determine its logical relations.

logograph
A character in a writing system that represents a complete word. The Arabic numerals are logographs, and the Chinese writing system is mostly logographic.

long
1. In English, vowels of stressed syllables that have a relatively

greater duration, have off-glides to a higher vowel position, and are pronounced with relatively great muscular tension. The vowels of *feed, made,* and *mode* are long. Antonym: short. 2. A feature assigned to phonemes that have a relatively greater duration than average.

low
An articulation (or distinctive feature) that characterizes a speech sound formed by placing the body of the tongue relatively far from the roof of the mouth.

manner of articulation
The way in which a sound is formed, usually the type of constriction in the mouth. Contrasts with place of articulation.

matrix sentence
A sentence that contains another sentence embedded within it.

Message Model
A theory of communication in which the sender sequentially encodes the information to be communicated into a signal that travels to a receiver, who then sequentially decodes it to recover the original message.

metaphorical extension
The process of describing objects, ideas, or events from one realm by using words from a different realm (usually one that is more familiar or concrete), on the basis of some perceived similarity.

mid
An articulation of a speech sound formed with the body of the tongue neither close to nor far from the roof of the mouth. The English words *bet* and *code* have mid vowels.

minimal pair
Two words that have different meanings but differ in form only in having a different phoneme in the same position in each word. The English words *sip* and *zip* are a minimal pair; they differ in meaning and have different phonemes in initial position.

morpheme
The minimal unit of word-building in a language; in other words, any part of a word that cannot be broken down further into meaningful parts.

morphology
The subfield of linguistics that studies the internal structure of words and the interrelationships among words.

morphophonemic
A kind of writing system in which all phonetic detail that can be predicted by general rules is not symbolized.

mutual intelligibility
The situation that holds between two varieties of a language when speakers of either one are able to understand the other.

nasal
A manner of articulation (or distinctive feature) that characterizes sounds made with a lowered velum, thus enabling the natural resonances of the nasal passages to be excited. The English word *man* begins and ends with nasal consonants.

native speaker
A person who speaks a language fluently, typically because that person has been brought up speaking that language as a child.

natural class
A grouping of phonemes uniquely defined by a small number of phonetic features such that that grouping plays a significant role in expressing the phonological regularities found in natural languages.

neurolinguistics
The subfield of linguistics that studies the relation between language and the brain, especially the correlation between brain damage and speech and language deficits.

node
A point in a tree diagram at which lines connecting different constituents are connected.

nonliteral utterance
An utterance in which the speaker does not mean at least some of what the words uttered mean.

nonstandard language
Any variety of a language that lacks social prestige and is not considered acceptable in official contexts. Antonym: standard language.

nucleus
The loudest part of a syllable, usually consisting of a vowel or a diphthong.

obstruent
(See *sonorant*.)

Old English
The Germanic language spoken in Britain from the sixth to the eleventh centuries A.D. that is the ancestor of Modern English.

onset
Within a syllable, the consonant or sequence of consonants that precedes the nucleus.

open class
A group of morphemes whose membership is large and that readily accepts new members, for example, nouns, verbs, and adjectives. Antonym: closed class.

operative meaning
The linguistic meaning of an utterance that the speaker expects to lead the hearer to his or her communicative intent.

orthography
Any writing system that is widely used by the members of a given society to write their language. Most orthographies do not represent the speech sounds of the language in a systematic way. For example, this sentence is written in English orthography.

overextension
The use of a word to refer to more than what that word properly refers to.

palatal
A point of articulation that characterizes speech sounds formed by means of a constriction between the body of the tongue and the (hard) palate. The English word *you* begins with a palatal sound.

palate
The front part of the roof of the mouth, which has bone under the surface.

particle
1. In English, a word that combines with a verb to create an expression with an idiomatic meaning, for example, *up* in *call up*. 2. In other language, various kinds of affixes or function words; the class of particles must be defined separately for each language.

parts of speech
Groups of words that share certain grammatical properties, such as the kinds of affixes they take and the kinds of syntactic constructions they occur in.

performance
1. What a speaker actually does in speaking or comprehending an expression. 2. The speech that is actually produced by native speakers, in which some of their linguistic capacity may be obscured by such factors as coughing, memory limitations, or inebriation. Antonym: competence.

perlocutionary act
An act of intentionally affecting the thought or action of the hearer by performing an utterance act.

perseverative
The kind of coarticulation effect in which some motion of the vocal tract needed for one sound continues into a later sound. Antonym: anticipatory.

phone
A speech sound. (This term is generally used to avoid making any claim about the phonemic or allophonic status of the sound.)

phoneme
A speech sound that is psychologically a single unit, in contrast with other such units, but is often realized by two or more allophones that are either in complementary distribution or free variation with each other.

phonemic transcription
A writing system for representing speech sounds that omits some phonetic details that can be predicted by general rules.

phonetic transcription
A writing system for representing speech sounds that includes much detail.

phonetics
The study of speech sounds.

phonology
The subfield of linguistics that studies the structure and systematic patterning of sounds in human language.

phonotactics
The patterns into which phonemes and features can be arranged to form syllables and words in a given language.

phrasal category
A constituent of a tree diagram that is potentially larger than a single word. Phrasal categories are usually named according to the lexical categories that serve as their heads.

phrase marker
Another name for tree diagram.

phrase structure grammar
A description of the syntax of a language that contains only phrase structure rules.

phrase structure rule
A statement of an operation that expands a single symbol into two or more parts.

pictograph
A character in a writing system that represents some object by a schematic, physical representation of that object.

pidgin
A simplified version of some language, often augmented by features from other languages. A pidgin typically arises in colonial situations and is used solely as a trade language.

place of articulation
The part of the mouth, throat, or larynx where the airflow meets the greatest degree of constriction in the production of speech sounds. Contrasts with manner of articulation.

pragmatics
The study of language use and its relation to language structure and social context.

preglottalized
Preceded by a glottal stop or glottal constriction.

presumption
A special sort of shared belief in which speaker and hearer share the expectation that something is the

case, but in which that expectation can be overridden at any time by new evidence.

progressive
An assimilation process in which one sound affects a following sound. Antonym: regressive.

proto-form
A reconstructed word or stem that is hypothesized to be the ancestor of a set of related words or stems in daughter languages.

proto-language
A reconstructed language that is hypothesized to be the ancestor of some group of related languages.

prototype
A typical or representative instance of a concept.

prototype theory
Any theory that claims that concepts have an internal structure that reflects which members are prototypes of that concept.

psycholinguistics
A subfield of linguistics whose goal is to discover the psychological principles that underlie the human's ability to comprehend, produce, and acquire language.

reconstruction
The process of determining the probable forms of some earlier stage of a language by comparing related forms in two or more present-day languages.

recursivity
A property of grammars in which a finite set of rules can generate an infinite set of structures.

reduced
Weakened to the point where it loses its distinctive quality (usually said of vowels in unstressed syllables). The English word *sofa* ends in a reduced vowel.

reduplication
The repetition of all or part of a word in order to modify its meaning in some way.

regressive
An assimilation process in which one sound affects a preceding sound. Antonym: progressive.

retroflexed
A manner of articulation that characterizes speech sounds that are formed by curling the tip of the tongue upward and backward. For some speakers, the English word *red* begins with a retroflexed consonant.

rewriting rule
Another name for phrase structure rule.

round
A manner of articulation (or distinctive feature) that characterizes speech sounds whose formation is accompanied by a pursing of the lips.

round dance
A repeated circular motion with alternating direction performed by the European honeybee for its hivemates to indicate the presence of a food source near the hive.

rounded
Formed by pursing the lips in addition to a primary constriction elsewhere in the vocal tract.

schwa
1. A nondistinct (mid central) vowel often found in unstressed syllables in English. The final sound of *sofa* is a schwa. 2. The symbol /ə/ used to represent the final sound in *sofa*.

secret language
A variety of language that only some members of a society are permitted to learn.

semantic decomposition
The analysis of a single word or
morpheme into a set of semantic
primitives that define it.

semantic field
A group of words with related
meanings, for example, kinship and
color terms.

semantic presupposition
A relation between sentences S and
S' such that S would not be true *or*
false unless S' were true.

semantic reference/referent
The object, event, etc., that an
expression applies to by virtue of the
meaning of the expression. Antonym: speaker's referent.

semantics
The study of meaning, reference,
truth, and related notions.

semivowel
Another name for glide.

shared beliefs
A speaker and a hearer share a
belief when: they both have the
belief, each believes the other has
the belief, and each believes the
other believes they each have the
belief.

short
In English, vowels of stressed
syllables that have a brief duration,
lack off-glides, and are pronounced
with relatively little muscular
tension. The vowels of *bit, bet,* and
bat are short. Antonym: long.

sibilant
A fricative with a "hissing" or
"hushing" sound, made by forcing
the airflow through a small opening
between the tip or blade of the
tongue and the teeth, the alveolar
ridge, or the area just behind the alveolar ridge. The English words
soap and *ship* begin with sibilants.

simple word
A word that cannot be broken down
into smaller meaningful parts.

slang
A set of expressions that is
characteristic of informal language
style, tends to change rapidly, and
often serves to indicate solidarity
within a given social group.

sonorant
A distinctive feature that characterizes speech sounds whose articulation is not so narrow that the
airflow across the glottis is
appreciably inhibited; thus,
sonorants are typically voiced.
Nonsonorants are frequently
referred to as obstruents.

speaker's meaning
What the speaker means or intends
to communicate in uttering an
expression.

speaker reference
The speaker's act of referring to
some object, event, etc.

speaker's referent
The object, event, etc., a speaker is
referring to. Antonym: semantic
reference/referent.

specialized alarm calls
Specific vocal noises made by
animals to communicate the presence and location of some potential
predator.

speech comprehension model
An explicit representation of the
processes leading from the hearing
of speech sounds to the recognition
of the speaker's communicative
intent.

speech production model
An explicit representation of the
processes leading from a pragmatic
intent to the sounds that a speaker
produces.

standard language
The variety of a language that has social prestige and is used in official contexts. Antonym: nonstandard language.

stem
A morpheme that serves as a base for forming new words by the addition of affixes.

stop
A manner of articulation that characterizes consonant sounds made by temporarily blocking the airflow completely. The English words *pin* and *dog* begin with stops.

strident
A distinctive feature that characterizes speech sounds whose production is accompanied by high frequency turbulent noise.

structural ambiguity
The situation in which a sentence has two or more different linguistic meanings even though none of the individual words is ambiguous. The ambiguity of such sentences resides in their different constituent structures.

structural change
The operation carried out by a transformational rule.

structure-function adaptation
In communication, a relationship in which the structure of a signal enhances the transmission of the message.

syllabic
A distinctive feature assigned to phonemes that occur as the nucleus of a syllable; such phonemes are usually vowels, but are occasionally consonants.

syllable
A unit of phonological structure that usually consists of a vowel preceded and/or followed by various consonants.

symbolic
The relationship between an object and a representation of that object when there is no resemblance between the two.

synchronic
Concerned only with a single stage or time period. Antonym: diachronic.

syntactic parsing
The process of assigning the correct syntactic structure to a string of words by scanning it from beginning to end.

syntax
The subfield of linguistics that studies the internal structure of sentences and the interrelationships among their component parts.

taboo language
A set of expressions that are considered inappropriate in certain contexts. For example, profanity and obscenity are considered inappropriate in formal language contexts.

tag
Structured material added at the end of a statement. A tag contains an auxiliary verb, a pronoun that agrees with the subject of the sentence, and sometimes the word *not* or its contracted form -*n't*.

tail-wagging dance
A complex pattern of movement performed by the European honeybee for its hivemates to indicate the direction, distance, and richness of a food source located at distances beyond 100 meters from the hive.

tense
1. In phonetics, a speech sound pronounced with relatively great muscular tension. Antonym: lax.
2. For English vowels, another name for long. 3. Verbal affix indicating time.

transcription
Any system of writing used by
linguists that represents the speech
sounds of a language in a systematic
way.

transformational grammar
A description of a language that
contains both phrase structure rules
and transformational rules.

transformational rule
An operation that converts an input
tree structure into a different
structure by adding, deleting, or
rearranging material. Transformational rules consist of a structural
description of the input and the
structural change that they effect.

tree diagram
A graphic representation of syntactic
constituent structure that uses
branching lines and nodes that have
category labels.

truth
A relation between a sentence and
the world such that the world is the
way the sentence represents it as
being.

underextension
The use of a word to refer to less
than what that word properly refers
to.

utterance act
The production of an expression
from a language.

uvular
A manner of articulation that
describes a speech sound that is produced when the body of the tongue
is retracted and raised to approach
or touch the uvula.

velar
A place of articulation that characterizes speech sounds formed by
means of a constriction between the
body of the tongue and the velum.
The English words *coo* and *go* begin
with velar consonants.

velum
The back part of the roof of the
mouth; there is no bone under the
surface.

vocal cords
The two muscular bands of tissue
that stretch from front to back
within the larynx. The vocal cords
vibrate periodically to produce
voiced sounds.

vocal folds
Another name for the vocal cords.

vocal tract
The region above the vocal cords
that produces speech sounds; it
consists of the throat, mouth cavity,
and nose cavity.

voiced
A manner of articulation (or
distinctive feature) that characterizes
speech sounds whose production is
accompanied by periodic vocal cord
vibration. Antonym: voiceless.

voiceless
A manner of articulation that
characterizes speech sounds that are
not accompanied by vocal cord
vibration. Antonym: voiced.

voicing
The sound made by the vibration
of the vocal cords. This sound is
heard during the production of
vowels and some consonants.

Wernicke's area
Part of the left posterior temporal
lobe of the brain. Damage to this
area results in a kind of aphasia
characterized by fluent, but
meaningless, speech and the
apparent inability to comprehend
language.

word formation rule
A process by which an affix is added
to a word or stem to create a new
word, and the meaning of the word
is modified in some way.

INDEX